Archives: Recordkeeping in Society

Topics in Australasian Library and Information Studies

Series editors: Professor Ross Harvey and Dr Stuart Ferguson

This series provides detailed, formally refereed works on a wide range of topics and issues relevant to professionals and para-professionals in the library and information industry and to students of library and information studies. All titles are written from an Australasian perspective, drawing on professional experience and research in Australia, New Zealand and the wider Pacific region. Proposals for publications should be addressed to the series editors (RossHarvey@csu.edu.au; sferguson@csu.edu.au).

Number 23
Organising knowledge in a global society: Principles and practice in libraries and information centres. 2nd ed.
Ross Harvey and Philip Hider

Number 22
Computers for librarians: An introduction to the electronic library. 3rd ed.
Stuart Ferguson, with Rodney Hebels

Number 21
Australian library supervision and management. 2nd ed.
Roy Sanders

Number 20
Research methods for students and professionals: Information management and systems. 2nd ed.
Kirsty Williamson et al.

Number 19
Collection management: A concise introduction
John Kennedy

Number 18
Information management: A consolidation of operations, analysis and strategy
Michael Middleton

Number 14
The other 51 weeks: A marketing handbook for librarians
Lee Welch

Number 12
Disaster recovery for archives, libraries and records management systems in Australia and New Zealand
Judith Doig

Forthcoming:
Number 25
The other 51 weeks: A marketing handbook for librarians. 2nded.
Lee Welch

Archives: Recordkeeping in Society

Edited by

Sue McKemmish, Michael Piggott, Barbara Reed and Frank Upward

Topics in Australasian Library and Information Studies, Number 24

Centre for Information Studies
Charles Sturt University
Wagga Wagga New South Wales

ISBN 1 876938 84 6
ISSN 1030-5009

National Library of Australia cataloguing-in-publication data

---

Archives : recordkeeping in society.

Bibliography.
Includes index.
ISBN 1 876938 84 6.

1. Archives - Textbooks. 2. Archival resources - Textbooks.
3. Records - Management - Textbooks. I. McKemmish, Susan
Marilyn. II. Charles Sturt University. Centre for
Information Studies. (Series : Topics in Australasian
library and information studies; no. 24).

025.1714

The editors wish to thank colleagues in the School of Information Management and Systems, Monash University, for their contributions in this endeavour, in particular Don Schauder.
Project coordinator: Fiona Ross
Illustrations research: Anna Davis and Fiona Ross
Series editor: Ross Harvey
Copy editor: Rachel Salmond
Cover design: Tony O Neill
Text Processor: Nicole Anderson
Printed by: Quick Print

Centre for Information Studies
Locked Bag 660
Wagga Wagga NSW 2678
Phone: + 61 (0)2 6933 2325
Fax: + 61 (0)2 6933 2733
Email: cis@csu.edu.au
http://www.csu.edu.au/cis

**Dedicated to
our friend and colleague
Robert Hartland
1950 – 2004**

Contents

Figures

About this book

The study of archives involves studying the way societies shape, hold and access information about their activities. There is no area of human activity not shaped in the most fundamental ways by the archival storage of information and no continuing form of culture or community is possible without it.

The purpose of this book is to provide a conceptual base for archival science which coherently incorporates both established and emerging concepts within the discipline. The challenges posed by changing technologies necessitate such new overviews. Although archivists face these challenges directly, their implications reach beyond the archival profession. Almost everybody, not just those paid to do the work that this entails, is an archivist and a records manager and all of us have a stake in the relationship between archives and human activity. Accordingly we hope this book will be a valuable resource *within* and *beyond* the archival profession by exposing leading archival thinking to scholars, thinkers and practitioners in many disciplines.

We have brought together leading archival scholars and have invited them to present the results of their research and reflections around a number of issues and perspectives. One such perspective is the metaphor of the web. Archives are a web of recorded information and always have been. For some years archivists have been battling with the dilemmas posed by changing methods for recording all forms of information. Internet and web-browser technologies are shaping technological development in ways which run against the isolated approaches of many individual archives in the past, pointing to the ever-present interconnectedness of archives. Current advances in the control of the production of archives in this environment may be modest, but the potential for better operation in this area is undeniable.

There are many areas of debate in the archival profession. Sometimes the tensions and apparent contradiction within these debates suggest irreconcilable differences of opinion. In relation to individual expressions of views this may be the case. We wanted authors to bear in mind that such debates are indicators of key points for mediation and change, requiring balancing, attention, and continuing adjustment. An example is the book's recurring emphasis upon the relationship between evidence and memory within our archives. Any exploration of memory automatically brings with it perspectives about meaning and interpretation, including consideration of what may be termed Freudian constructs, and the relationship between individual and collective memory. Evidence is more amenable to common interpretation across the profession, but for much of the twentieth century archivists have allowed their views of evidence to be dominated by legal concepts, not recordkeeping ones. Only in the 1990s have archivists begun to seriously explore the nature of recordkeeping evidence. Recordkeeping evidence is related to accounts of our actions. But within those accounts memory, with all its quirks, cannot be ignored.

Cultural conditions are examined. Archives are shaped by the nature of the threads that tie different communities together, whether the community is a small tightly-knit group or something as large as a nation state or as dispersed as global communities. Again, there are problems in archival discourse. Just as legal evidence has dominated views of evidence (at least in English language discourse), there has been a widespread notion that recordkeeping serves current purposes and that cultural goals of archives are a temporally separate area of interest requiring a considerable lapse of time before they kick into operation, and then only in relation to records as end products held by archival institutions. In studies of cultural history, there has been a greater emphasis in recent decades on cultural formation and evidence of that formation. In the archival profession's discourse there has been a belated but growing interest in the formation of archives and the relationships between that formation and culture. Recordkeeping processes and cultural issues are entwined and, as historians such as Michel Foucault have demonstrated, much can be learnt about culture from the way culturally-controlled recordkeeping processes operate within our discourse.

We also asked authors to bear in mind the formation of global cultures and the problems and opportunities that the internationalization of an archival culture will present to individual cultures. Global approaches to archives within webs can be expected to give greater coherence and unity to world practice. To what extent will cultural conditions influence globalization, and globalizing processes reshape cultural conditions? How can countless generations of diversity and difference in practice be ironed out? And, if they can be ironed out, is that a blessing or a curse on the profession?

We want the book to present archives over broad sweeps of time. The historical perspective may seem to pale into insignificance when measured against the technological changes we are undergoing, but there is an ever-present reinvention of the past going on within our new techniques for managing recorded information. This deserves acknowledgment and understanding.

The issue of the divisions in archival practice between personal, governmental and business archives is addressed. The divisions have made sense in the past, but within our era of interconnections (the networked age as it is sometimes called) they are becoming pernicious. Perhaps the divisions reflect a fundamental division in the modern psyche between who we are and where we work, a division that has often been overdrawn, and in many disciplinary forums is beginning to be challenged.

We hope these themes, issues, and perspectives give some coherence to the work of the many authors involved in the preparation of this book. On the other hand we want each chapter to stand alone, notwithstanding the recurring issues, and to restrict cross-referencing between chapters to a minimum. This means that separate chapters can be dismantled from their current context and used more easily within educational and training programs at the program director's discretion. They can also be read in any order.

There are, however, more cross-connections between chapters than we had originally intended, particularly in part two. All the editors are records continuum thinkers and operators and the division of these chapters automatically requires cross-connections if their continuum nature is to be maintained. Other authors vary in the degree to which they adopt a continuum framework and, had the book developed from a conference discussion across the chapters, they would have ensured the transcript made lively reading. Our audience should feel free to follow suggestions and inferences from each author as it too interacts with the book.

We wanted some consistency in terms of formats of chapters, but this has also only been implemented partially. All chapters have additional reading lists. A few chapters have case studies that can be used in teaching and training programs, not part of the original intention, but clearly a useful approach to take.

The structure of the book reflects many of the philosophical positions outlined above. The first part provides stand-alone introductions, raising much that is wrong with approaches to recordkeeping in democratic societies today, giving a view of archives across time, and introducing the communities of practice which make up the recordkeeping and archiving enterprise. Part two looks at archivists in operation and, as mentioned above, is organized around the records continuum, although to appreciate this, the chapters have to be read in non-linear fashion. The third part of the book is open slather for thinking. A number of experts in particular areas of thought are brought together to explore a range of concepts. These are chapters that we most definitely would hope are widely read and used outside the archival profession and/or used by archivists to develop better cross-connections with others.

The sociologist Anthony Giddens, whose work is drawn upon by a number of authors in this book, has persistently argued that in his discipline there is nothing as pernicious as an empirical study working out from a poor conceptual base. One can say the same thing for all human action including the things that archivists do. The problem, as always, is determining what a good conceptual base is. Archivists over the last fifteen years have been forced by their immediate contact with changes in technological conditions to reconsider their concepts. We hope this book will both contribute to further professional discussion about how archivists can think and operate, and open up that thinking and operating to criticism and support from others.

CHAPTER 1

Traces: Document, record, archive, archives

Sue McKemmish

All events have their witness, their memory: the trace.[1]

Writing is one of the representatives of the trace in general; it is not the trace itself. The trace itself does not exist.[2]

And when we write, when we archive, when we leave a trace behind us – and that's what we do each time we trace something, even each time we speak, that is we leave a trace which becomes independent of its origin, of the movement of its utterance – the trace is at the same time the memory, the archive, and the erasure, the repression, the forgetting of what it is supposed to keep safe.[3]

For novelist Graham Swift man is quintessentially 'the storytelling animal', leaving behind 'not a chaotic wake, not an empty space, but the comforting marker-buoys and trail-signs of stories'.[4] Sociologist Anthony Giddens talks about how our very identity is bound up with the capacity to sustain a 'narrative of self', integrating external events into the ongoing story of a life.[5]

A narrative of self or the stories people tell may never be written down or documented, but for some people a diary or a journal is an indispensable part of keeping their personal story going, and exchanging letters or emails can be critical to the 'process of mutual disclosure' that Giddens sees as a feature of intimate relationships in the modern age. Janet Malcolm describes love letters as 'fixatives of experience', 'fossils of feeling', proof that 'once we

---

[1] Matt Matsuda, *The Memory of the Modern*, Oxford, Oxford University Press, 1996, p. 139.
[2] Jacques Derrida, in *Of Grammatology*, quoted in chapter 4, 'Deconstruction and the Question of Literature/Derrida', in David Carroll, *Paraesthetics: Foucault, Lyotard, Derrida*, New York, Methuen, 1987, p. 81.
[3] Jacques Derrida, 'Archive Fever in South Africa', in Carolyn Hamilton et al, *Refiguring the Archive*, Kluwer, Dordrecht, 2002, p. 54.
[4] Graham Swift, *Waterland*, London, Picador, 1992, pp. 62f.
[5] Anthony Giddens, *Modernity and Self-identity*, Cambridge, Polity Press, 1991, p. 54 and p. 76.

cared'.[6] Richard Holmes, biographer of Robert Louis Stevenson, Shelley, Coleridge and others, gives a fascinating insight into the nature of such 'biographical evidence' when he discusses how the individual subject of the biography can only be captured – brought alive in the present – through placing them in relationship to other people. He describes how he went about exploring how Stevenson 'fitted into the enormously intricate emotional web of other people's lives':

> Stevenson existed very largely in, and through, his contact with other people; his books are written for his public; his letters for his friends, even his private journal is a way of giving social expression – externalizing – his otherwise inarticulated thoughts. It is in this sense that all real biographical evidence is witnessed ... [7]

Extending beyond the individual, Edmund White, in writing about the AIDS epidemic and its devastating effect on the gay community, not only on individual lives, but on an entire culture, highlighted the need to 'bear witness to the cultural moment'.[8]

Throughout time individuals and societies have communicated, captured and passed on many of their stories by selectively storing, structuring, and re-presenting them – graphically, textually, on some kind of media and using whatever technology is available to them – the chalk on the cave wall, the carving on the monolith, the paint on the clay pot or the mummy case, the handwriting on the scroll, the sound recording on the CD, the bits on the computer disk, the image on the film. Other stories are remembered by being told, sung, danced or performed, captured in rituals and ceremonies, recalled and retold or performed again.

The urge to witness, to memorialize, has its dark counterpart in 'killing the memory', the acts of 'memoricide' that have occurred throughout history, such as the targeting of museums, archives and cultural institutions which accompanied ethnic cleansing in Bosnia and elsewhere. Derrida has reflected extensively on the notion of the death drive in archiving in *Archive Fever*.[9] He has also explored how it is at work in two ways in the shaping of the archive of the Truth and Reconciliation Commission in South Africa – in the drive by the former apartheid regime on the one hand to destroy memory in a way that no archive, no trace of the murder and violence is left, and, on the other, in the Commission's desire to witness, to record the testimony, to accumulate the archive and keep it safe. For Derrida archiving in the sense of inscribing a trace in some location, external to living memory, is an act of forgetting that carries with it the possibility of deferred remembering. And it is because the radical drive to destroy memory without trace is always also in play that 'the desire for archive is a burning one':

> If there is a passion, it is because we know that not only the traces can be lost by accident or because the space is finite or the time is finite, but because we know

---

[6] Janet Malcolm, *The Silent Woman*, London, Picador, 1994, p. 110.
[7] Richard Holmes, *Footsteps: Adventures of a Romantic Biographer*, London, Flamingo, 1995, p. 27.
[8] Edmund White, *The Burning Library*, London, Picador, 1995, p. 215.
[9] Jacques Derrida, *Archive Fever*, Chicago, University of Chicago Press, 1996.

that something in us, so to speak, something in the psychic apparatus, is driven to destroy the trace without reminder. And that's where the archive fever comes from.[10]

In most groups and societies there are people whose special role it is to look after our memory stores, the places where what Derrida terms the archiving trace is inscribed, and to recall, retell or re-present our stories on behalf of the group. Archivists as society's recordkeeping professionals are part of this larger community. Linked to the different natures, purposes and functionalities of the various forms of recorded information, different professional communities of practice have evolved to manage record stores, archives, libraries, museums, galleries, and historic sites on our behalf.

In this book we are concerned with the nature, purposes and functionalities of a particular form of recorded information, documentary traces of social and organizational activity, that are accumulated and managed by recordkeeping and archiving processes as record, archive and archives. We explore recordkeeping and archiving as a form of witnessing and memory making, a particular way of evidencing and memorializing our individual and collective lives – 'our existence, our activities and experiences, our relationships with others, our identity, our 'place' in the world'.[11]

The meanings behind the use of the terms record, archive and archives are as many and varied as the discourses in which they appear – from the very broadest sense of the word *archive* encompassing oral and written records, literature, landscape, dance, art, the built environment, and artefacts to the more precise and applied meanings used by recordkeeping professional communities:

> If we look at what we can say differently from others, then as a professional group with a professional knowledge of recordkeeping objects, we should be able to make statements about the interplay between recordkeeping objects and their evidential qualities, the identity of those who created them, and the social and business processes that brought them into being.[12]

In the rest of this chapter, we explore the meanings of the terms documents, record, archive and archives from this perspective. Woven throughout our exploration is the elusive nature of the trace itself in its evocation of the past in the present.

****

---

[10] Derrida, 'Archive Fever in South Africa', op. cit. p. 44.
[11] Sue McKemmish, 'Evidence of Me …', *Archives and Manuscripts*, 24, no. 1, 1996, pp. 28-45; quote from p. 29.
[12] Frank Upward and Sue McKemmish, 'In Search of the Lost Tiger by Way of Saint-Beuve: Reconstructing the Possibilities in 'Evidence of Me …'', *Archives and Manuscripts*, 29, no. 1, 2001, pp. 22-43; quote from p. 26.

So, let us begin with a story.

In the two years leading up to the Australian federal election on 10 November 2001 the Australian government had been waging a campaign against boat people, refugees or asylum seekers mainly from Iraq, Afghanistan and Pakistan who tried to reach Australia by boat, and the people smugglers who ran the boat trade. From the early 1990s, the increasing numbers of boat people and their children were treated as illegal immigrants and detained in remote desert camps, in breach of a number of United Nations conventions, while their refugee claims were processed. This is in marked contrast to the treatment of the much larger numbers arriving by air, who are generally released into the community while their claims are heard:

> The problem for boat people was always the boat: the symbol of Australia's old fears of invasion. People worried far less – indeed, hardly at all – about asylum seekers arriving by air, even though they were jumping the same queue, there were far more of them and they were about half as likely as those who came by sea to be genuine refugees.[13]

In late August 2001, against a background of growing numbers of boat people arriving in Australia, increasing unrest and disturbances in the detention camps, and the emergence of a new anti-immigration right wing political party, a Norwegian container ship, the Tampa, rescued 438 people from a sinking Indonesian boat. Captain Arne Rinnan, later to receive a United Nations Refugee Award for his commitment to refugee protection, was threatened with heavy fines and jail for people smuggling by the Australian government if he did not turn back to Indonesia, but for the safety of his crew and the people he had rescued, he decided that the only option he had was to go on to the Australian territory of Christmas Island, the closest port. On arrival offshore, the Tampa was refused permission to enter the port. There followed days of stalemate, the occupation of the Tampa by Australian soldiers from an elite SAS unit, and the eventual transfer of the refugees on an Australian naval ship to a camp set up for them by the government of Nauru.

Figure 1.1. The Australian territory of Christmas Island lies about 380km south of Java and 1500km from the Australian mainland.

---

[13] David Marr and Marian Wilkinson, *Dark Victory*, Crows Nest NSW, Allen & Unwin, 2003, p. 38.

In response to the Tampa crisis, the Australian government put in place Operation Relex, a naval blockade of the Indian Ocean to turn back any more refugee boats heading towards Australian waters. Operation Relex was directed from Canberra by a People Smuggling Taskforce, and special arrangements were put in place to ensure information flowed between naval ships involved in the blockade, Taskforce personnel and government ministers and their staff, much of it by word of mouth, rather than more formal written communications. At the same time, strict controls on the release of any military information to the public were put in place – all communication with the media was to be cleared via the Defence Minister's office. As these plans were being finalized, the nature of the threat the boat people posed to Australia was about to be redefined by the September 11 attacks on the World Trade Center and the Pentagon.

Thus the scene was set for the interception on 6 October by HMAS Adelaide of an Indonesian boat, the Olong, also known as SIEV 4 (Suspected Illegal Entry Vessel). SIEV 4 was overloaded with 223 refugees, including many children, and it was about to sail 'into Australian political history'.[14]

The story of what happened on the following days has been meticulously reconstructed by investigative journalists Marr and Wilkinson from documents that resulted from the social and organizational activities associated with the events that unfolded on 6-8 October and their aftermath. Accumulated in the records of HMAS Adelaide are the ship's logs, operation reports, videotapes of events, the videotape operator's logbook, email communications back to headquarters, the chronology of events based on the Adelaide's signals, and still photographs. There is also the 'oral record' of telephone calls and other communications, remembered or diarized, and retold to later inquiries. There are documents accumulated in the records of the Defence Strategic Command, Maritime Headquarters and Northern Command released to the media under FOI, and the documentary evidence submitted to the later inquiries conducted by the military and the Parliament, together with their transcripts of testimony, and of course the media reports.

Commander of the Adelaide, Norman Banks, had orders to stop SIEV 4 reaching Christmas Island. On 7 October warning shots were fired, and, as a boarding party took control and turned the boat around, there was trouble with the engines, and another boatload of sailors was sent over from the Adelaide. In the ensuing chaos, some refugees jumped overboard, others threatened 'to destroy the boat and commit suicide or throw their children overboard if they could not reach Australia':

> Water was streaming over the decks … Suddenly, some of the officers spotted a
> small girl about five years old in a pink jumper being carried by her father to the top
> of the wheelhouse. He … held her over the side gesturing to the sailors in the [boat]
> below to take her. Watching from the bridge [of the Adelaide] Banks was stunned.
> He thought the father was about to drop the child.[15]

---

[14] Ibid, p. 182.
[15] Ibid, p. 185: indented quote and in-text quotes in this paragraph.

At this critical stage, Banks took a call from a superior officer in Darwin, Brigadier Silverstone. In testimony to subsequent inquiries into this incident, Banks recalled saying that some of the refugees were jumping and threatening to throw their children into the water, while Silverstone reported hurriedly writing notes in his diary, including: 'Men thrown over side. 5, 6 or 7', and, after the call ended, 'Silverstone added the word 'child' to the note believing, he would say later, that Commander Banks told him a child about 5, 6 or 7 years old had been thrown over the side.' The message relayed by telephone back to the People Smuggling Taskforce meeting in Canberra was that people were jumping overboard and throwing their children into the water:

> The image of children being thrown overboard grabbed the attention of the bureaucrats because it confirmed the warnings they had been given – determined boat people would go to any lengths to play on the Australian navy's obligations to rescue drowning people at sea.[16]

Although there was nothing in the written operation reports thus far received from the Adelaide to back up the children overboard claim, during the meeting on 7 October, a fourth-hand version of the story was conveyed by mobile phone by a member of the Taskforce to the Minister of Immigration, who was about to go into a media briefing. He repeated the story to the press, and then rang the Prime Minister and Defence Minister to brief them on his comments, and later that night the Chair of the Taskforce confirmed the story in a report faxed to both Ministers. 'The 'Children Overboard' story was off and running', and the demonization of the boat people had begun.

Later the next day, 8 October, the Olong was sinking, with men, women and children jumping into the sea as water rose over the bow:

> From the second deck of the Adelaide, Able Seaman Laura Whittle saw a mother struggling in the choppy water with her young child. Without even waiting to put on her life jacket, Whittle dived twelve metres into the sea to haul the frightened pair to a life raft. Nearby, her mate, Leading Cook Jason Barker, was swimming out to a terrified father and child. Scores of passengers, supported by life jackets, bobbed in the water surrounded by debris as the Adelaide's crew scrambled to get the 223 men, women and children clear of the sinking boat … It was a miraculous rescue …
> In the early hours of the [next] morning, the Adelaide's communications room sent out a series of photographs on its secret email system, recording an unforgettable day in the lives of the crew, 8 October 2001. Two of the photos, captioned 'Courage' and 'Courage and Determination', pictured Able Seaman Laura Whittle and her mate, Leading Cook Jason 'Dogs' Barker, in their brave rescue of two stricken asylum seekers and their children …[17]

---

[16] Ibid., p. 186: indented quote and quote at end of paragraph.
[17] Ibid., pp. 191-193.

Figure 1.2. The 'Children Overboard' story on page 1 of *The Age*, 11 October 2001. Questions about the context and detail of both the photo and the story were raised immediately, but were not answered until months later.

The photographs were accompanied by an emailed commentary by the photographer about the courage and determination of the sailors involved in rescuing the passengers from the Olong on 8 October, as typified by Whittle and Barker.

> The following photographs (which show children in the water) were taken during the sinking, but later came to be misrepresented as providing evidence in support of the reports of children being thrown overboard on 7 October.

> Photograph 1 was saved as "laura the hero" and was attached to the email under the words "Whittle "COURAGE""

Figure 1.3. Extracts from *Investigation into advice provided to Ministers on 'SIEV 4'* (Bryant Report), Department of the Prime Minister and Cabinet, January 2002.

Meanwhile the press was demanding evidence to support the Children Overboard story. Although one of the Minister for Defence's senior advisers had been advised by telephone by a senior naval officer that there was no evidence in written reports, eyewitness accounts or the ship's video to support the story, a few days later the Minister for Defence released the photographs of the rescue on 8 October during a radio interview, claiming that they depicted children who had been thrown into the water on 7 October, the day before the boat sank, and stating that he had been told that there was also video of the incident: 'I am told that someone has looked at it and it is an absolute fact, children were thrown into the water'.[18] At the request of the Minister for Defence's press secretary, the photographs in question had been sent to the Minister without their captions, dates and accompanying commentary. They were thereafter shown on television and published in the newspapers with commentary and headlines indicating that they had been taken on 7 October. Many military leaders and personnel, including the crew of HMAS Adelaide, senior bureaucrats, and ministerial advisers knew from the beginning that there was in fact no written evidence, eyewitness accounts or first-hand oral records to support the Children Overboard story, that the videotapes from the Adelaide did not show children being thrown overboard, and that the photographs released by the Minister were taken during the mass rescue on 8 October when the Olong was already sinking. Although they made notes in their diaries of telephone calls they had made and provided written advice to this effect, the fiction of the Children Overboard was maintained until after the 10 November election, and the Ministers involved still claim that they 'were not told',[19] and the media controls relating to military information put in place during the Tampa crisis prevented military personnel from speaking to the press.

The documents at the heart of the Children Overboard story are the photographs, the proto-records, archival traces of an act or event. Such archival traces become records, in the sense used in the recordkeeping professional community, when they are stored by recordkeeping and archiving processes in ways which preserve their content and structure, link them to related documents, and record information about related social and organizational activities. Through these processes records come into being, and acquire their quality as evidence, both recording and shaping related events. Whether achieved by rudimentary accumulation processes or by highly formalized and systematic ones, documentary traces are incorporated into the record of an individual or organization by 'placing' them in relation to other documents that already form part of the record, and establishing their relationships to their contexts of creation, ongoing management and use. Recordkeeping systems capture the content of documents, re-present their structure, and link related documents together. They retain the information content and structure of records in reconstructible relations, and make audit trails about their subsequent management, access and use. As more archival traces are incorporated into the record, more documentary and contextual links and relationships are captured and documented. Recordkeeping systems thereby enable records to be retrieved at a later date in a form that re-presents their original content and structure, exposes their documentary relationships, and reflects their multiple contexts of creation, ongoing management and use, thus preserving their evidentiary nature. The relationships amongst documents in a recordkeeping system or accumulation of records and between records and their contexts of creation, management and use are multiple and dynamic. From this perspective, records are 'always in a state of becoming'.[20]

---

[18] Ibid, p. 203.
[19] Patrick Weller, *Don't Tell the Prime Minister*, Carlton, Scribe Publications, 2002.
[20] Sue McKemmish, 'Are Records Ever Actual?', in Sue McKemmish and Michael Piggott, eds., *The Records Continuum,* Clayton, Ancora Press in association with Australian Archives, 1994, p. 200.

Applying these understandings to the Children Overboard records, we can see how, if stored in the recordkeeping system of HMAS Adelaide with other documents relating to the ship's role in Operation Relex, linked to contextual information about the events they document in the form of captions and dates, and attached to the sender's copy of the email message that accompanied them, the photographs would come to form part of the records of HMAS Adelaide, and in that context they would function as evidence of the activities of the ship's company during the rescue of the boat people. The transmitted copies of the photographs with their captions, dates and accompanying email, received and filed in the central Navy recordkeeping system in Canberra might come to form part of another record, the record of the Navy, evidence of the role of headquarters in monitoring the operation to intercept the Olong. Copies of the photographs kept by individual sailors with other photographs and personal documents in albums, diaries and scrapbooks, or sent in letters or via email to family and friends could become personal records, evidence in that context of individual lives.

Sir Hilary Jenkinson, Deputy Keeper of Public Records, UK, 1948
Archives are the documents accumulated by a natural process in the course of the Conduct of Affairs of any kind, Public or Private, at any date; and preserved thereafter for Reference, in their own Custody, by the persons responsible for the affairs in question or their successors.
(Hilary Jenkinson, 'The English Archivist: A New Profession', in *Selected Writings of Sir Hilary Jenkinson*, Gloucester, Alan Sutton, 1980, p. 237, originally published 1948)

Ian Maclean, Commonwealth Archives Office, Australia, 1962
We in Australia agree with Jenkinson when he states that 'records' and 'archives' are really the same thing ... For my part I take the view that documents achieve 'record' or 'archive' status when they are made part of the record, whether they are eventually preserved permanently or not.
(Ian Maclean, 'An Analysis of Jenkinson's *Manual of Archive Administration* in the Light of Australian Experience', reprinted in Peter Biskup et al., eds, *Debates and Discourses: Selected Australian Writings on Archival Theory 1951-1990*, Canberra, ASA Inc, 1995, p. 55)

David Bearman, 1993 – *Archives as Recorded Transactions*
Archives are recorded transactions created in the course of organizational activities that have continuing evidential value. The criteria which distinguish archives from all of the information ever created or received in an organization are that:
- archives are records of transactions
- archives document activities or functions reflected in the mission of the organization, not just incidental to it; and
- archives are retained for their continuing value as evidence.

The data of the record are the words, numbers, images, and sounds actually made by the creator of the record.

The structure of the record is the relationships among these data as employed by the record creator to convey meaning. One kind of structure is the stylistic formalisms which we use to recognize the 'address', 'salutation', or 'body' of written documents. Another kind of structure is the pointers between physically or logically distinct groupings of information ...

The context of the record is the testimony it provides about the nexus of activity out of which it arose and in which it was used and about how it appeared and behaved in that setting.

(David Bearman, 'Archival Principles and the Electronic Office', in Angelika Menne-Haritz, ed., *Information Handling in Offices and Archives*, New York, K.G. Saur, 1993, pp. 177-193)

But what of the copies of the photographs, stripped of their captions and dates, and without the accompanying email, released by the Minister for Defence during a radio interview and subsequently published by the media in newspapers and television coverage? In one sense, these copies of the photographs became an information artefact, presented as evidence that the refugees threw their children overboard, but ultimately proved to be fake. However, during a critical decision-making time, this false re-presentation of an archival trace shaped an event that never happened. That event still exists insofar as the re-presentation of the trace, stripped of its context, and links to related documents, i.e. of its evidentiary qualities as part of the recording of an event, engendered the powerfully emotive construct of the children overboard. This construct was subsequently used to demonize and dehumanize the refugees on the boat, and their countrymen in Australia's detention camps, and it lives on in our national psyche, helping to justify the treatment of the refugees and their children.[21]

In another sense, these copies of the photographs are archival traces of a different event altogether – that event being the manufacturing of evidence, the construction of an event that did not happen. If stored in the recordkeeping systems of the newspaper offices and television stations together with other documents relating to the gathering and dissemination of news stories about the refugees, and 'master copies' of related publications and broadcasts, these photographs would become records of the media companies, evidence of their broadcasting and publishing activities in relation to the Olong, Operation Relex and the election campaign. And if the copies of the photographs, stripped of captions and date, and without the accompanying email, were ever filed in the office of the Minister for Defence, there these archival traces would form part of the records of the Minister, evidence of his role in the affair.

Copies of the photographs from various recordkeeping systems, with and without their captions, dates and accompanying email message, were also submitted to the inquiries into the Children Overboard affair, including the Senate inquiry. If stored with the other records

---

[21] As explored in Michael Piggott and Sue McKemmish, 'Recordkeeping, Reconciliation and Political Reality', in *Past Caring: Proceedings of the Australian Society of Archivists Conference, Sydney 2002*, pp. 109-122.

of the inquiry, the reports, exhibits, other documentary evidence, the oral records recalled and retold to the inquiries, and the transcripts of proceedings which captured oral testimony, these copies of the photographs would become part of yet another record, that of the organizations responsible for the various inquiries, evidence of the inquiry processes themselves.

McKemmish and Upward – The Archival Document (1990)

For anyone not familiar with the term, the archival document can best be conceptualized as recorded information arising out of transactions – it is created naturally in the course of transacting business of any kind, whether by governments, businesses, community organizations or private individuals. The recording of transactions may be in any storage media and is increasingly becoming an electronic process. The concept of the archival document is a common-place within European thought, but in English-speaking countries it is often confused with documents that have been selected for retention within an archival institution. The lack of an adequate construct to explain the processes of creating and maintaining recorded information arising out of transactions within English-speaking countries creates a distracting division within the recordkeeping profession between records managers, who look after current archival documents, and archivists, who look after our archival heritage which includes archival documents which have been selected for permanent retention. An understanding of the archival document which encompasses both current and historical documents directs attention to the continuum of processes involved in managing the record of a transaction from systems design to destruction or select preservation … Within this approach, documentation of a transaction is archival from the time the record is created and the archival document retains evidential value for as long as it is in existence …

The archival document also re-presents the experience of the parties to the transaction which it records. It is more than recorded information. Those archival documents which are selected for permanent preservation become part of the archival heritage of a society, transmitting the accumulated experience of the transactions they document to future generations.

Effective creation and management of the archival document to ensure its integrity and validity is a precondition of an information-rich society and underpins public accountability on the part of both government and non-government organizations, FOI and privacy legislation, protection of people's rights and entitlements, and the quality of the archival heritage.

(Sue McKemmish and Frank Upward, 'The Archival Document: A Submission to the Inquiry into Australia as an Information Society', *Archives and Manuscripts,* 19, no. 1, 1991, pp. 17-32; quote from pp. 19-22. This paper was originally prepared as a submission to the Inquiry into Australia as an Information Society in October 1990. McKemmish and Upward met with the Committee on 15 January 1991.)

What we are seeing so far in these examples is the operation of recordkeeping and archiving processes involved in transforming archival traces of the acts and events in which they participate into records which can function as evidence of those acts and events – by linking documents-as-trace to the transactions, acts, decisions or communications they document, the people, and related documents, and placing them in their immediate business or social context, as well as maintaining an audit trail of their management and use.

Beyond their immediate business and social contexts, records are transformed into a corporate or personal archive by recordkeeping and archiving processes that 'place' records-as-evidence in the broader context of the social and business activities and functions of the organization, group or individual, and manage them in frameworks that enable them to function as individual, group, or corporate memory.

To return to the records relating to the story of the Children Overboard, the various copies of the photographs, with or without captions and accompanying email, which form part of the Adelaide's record of the interception of the Olong, or of Navy headquarters' management of the Operation, the media organizations' election coverage, the Minister's Office's handling of the affair, the individual sailor's involvement, or the conduct of the specific inquiries also exist in the much broader contexts. Such contexts include all the different types of activities that the naval ship, the Navy, the Office of the Minister, the newspaper or television company, the individual or family, the committees of inquiry, or the Senate engage in. Together with the records of all these other activities, the records relating to the story of the Children Overboard would form the corporate or personal archive of the organization or individual concerned. For example, in the archive of HMAS Adelaide, they would be linked to other records of the ship's involvement in Operation Relex and its other tours of duty – together with the ship's logs, signals, operational reports, email system, and videotapes and logs, they constitute part of the ship's corporate memory. Or, together with the other records of an individual sailor, they would become part of a personal archive, memorializing an individual life.

And beyond the boundaries of organizations, and individuals, recordkeeping and archiving processes are involved in the transformation of the individual or corporate archive by 'placing' them into a larger archival framework that enables them to function as accessible collective memory. Thus the archive of a ship, department of state, office of a minister, media company, and individual or family could become part of the collective archives of the government of Australia, the business archives of Australia, or a state or national collection of the personal archive(s) of Australians. They are thus transformed from 'evidence of me' – the corporate entity or individual – into 'evidence of us' – components of our collective memory.[22]

Upward and McKemmish – The Records Continuum (2001)
Records can be distinguished from other forms of recorded information by their ongoing participation in social, business and other processes, broadly defined, i.e. by their transactional and contextual nature. Their evidential qualities are seen as integral to their 'recordness', and to their intents, multiple purposes, and functionality in terms of

---

[22] McKemmish, 'Evidence of Me ...', op. cit. The term 'evidence of me' was drawn from the writing of novelist Graham Swift (in *Ever After*) and it is used in the article as a synonym for the personal archive in the broadest sense. The article itself coined the term 'evidence of us' to refer to collective archives.

governance and accountability, their role in the formation of individual, group, corporate, and collective memory and the shaping of identity, and their value as authoritative sources of information. The concepts of transactionality and contextuality, as further developed in the records continuum, are complex and multi-layered. Transactionality is defined in terms of the many forms of human interaction and relationships that are documented in records of all kinds at all levels of aggregation. The concept of contextuality is concerned with the record's rich, complex, and dynamic social, functional, provenancial, and documentary contexts of creation, management, and use through spacetime. In the records continuum model framework these concepts find expression in a range of continua:

- the evidential continuum: trace, evidence, corporate and individual [whole of person] memory, collective memory;
- the continuum of recordkeeping objects: [archival] documents, records, the corporate and individual archive, and the collective archives;
- the continuum of identity: actor, work group/unit, organization/corporate body, and institution; and
- the continuum of transactionality: act, activity, function, purpose.

(Frank Upward and Sue McKemmish, 'In Search of the Lost Tiger by way of Saint-Beuve: Reconstructing the Possibilities in 'Evidence of Me…'', *Archives and Manuscripts,* 29, no. 1, 2001, pp. 22-43)

In the story of the Children Overboard, we can see that records take many different forms and are recorded in many different media. And woven through the story are records in oral forms including the words spoken, heard, remembered, recalled and witnessed as the story unfolded, and the oral testimony at the inquiries. We can see how records are both fixed and mutable, 'always in a process of becoming'. This view of records contrasts with more traditional ideas about records that have tended to stress the fixed and static nature of individual records, and conceptualized the archive as relic, an historical artefact, fully formed and closed. But in the story of the Children Overboard we see records as dynamic objects, fixed insofar as their original content and structure can be re-presented, but 'constantly evolving, ever mutating', to use an evocative phrase coined by Terry Cook to refer to archival thinking,[23] as they are linked to other records and ever-broadening layers of contextual metadata that manage their meanings, and enable their accessibility and usability as they move through spacetime. We also see how the corporate or personal archive and collective archives are constantly evolving and changing shape. Richard Holmes has discussed biography as 'a kind of pursuit, a tracking of the physical trail of someone's path through the past, a following of footsteps'.[24] Referring to his 'pursuit' of Stevenson, he writes:

> The more closely and scrupulously you follow someone's footsteps through the past the more conscious do you become that they never existed wholly in any one place along the recorded path. You cannot freeze them, you cannot pinpoint them,

---

[23] Terry Cook, 'What Is Past Is Prologue: A History of Archival Ideas Since 1898, and the Future Paradigm Shift', *Archivaria*, 43, 1997, p. 20.

[24] Holmes, op. cit., p. 27.

at any particular turn in the road, bend of the river, view from the window. They are always in motion, carrying their past lives over into the future. It is like the sub-atomic particle in nuclear physics that can be defined only in terms of a wave motion.[25]

For Holmes, biography can only be captured – brought alive in the present – through placing its 'single subject' in relationship to other people. Recordkeeping witnesses to our lives by evidencing, accounting for, and memorializing our interactions and relationships, thus 'placing' us in the world. But, as with Holmes' biographical subjects, records too are like the sub-atomic particle, only definable in terms of a wave motion – never existing in all their complexity in any one place or time, and only definable in terms of their multiple and dynamic documentary and contextual relationships.

Records have multiple purposes in terms of their value to an individual, organization or society. They are vehicles of communication and interaction, facilitators of decision-making, enablers of continuity, consistency and effectiveness in human action, memory stores, repositories of experience, evidence of rights and obligations. On a darker note, they can also be instruments of repression and abuse of power. Whether they are functioning as instruments of power, governance and accountability, memory stores, shapers of identity, or providing value-added sources of information, their utility, their recordness, is bound up with their evidentiary qualities defined in terms of their transactional and contextual nature. Thus the photographs of the children in the water can be trusted as accurate, complete, reliable and authentic records when preserved in systems that maintain their integrity, ensure that they cannot be altered or tampered with, contain information and related documents that link them to the acts and events which they document, and provide information about their wider context of social and organizational activity, and the people and organizations involved. By contrast, the photographs released by the Minister's Office ultimately were shown to be untrustworthy – they are fakes, digitally altered, stripped of their contextual information in the form of captions and dates, and linked documents, and purporting to be evidence of an event that did not take place. The power of records insofar as they are both shaped by, and shape the events which they record is perhaps no more evident than in such cases as this.

In recordkeeping professional discourse and practice, the differences between records and archives on the one hand, and other forms of recorded information on the other, rest on their transactional and contextual nature, evidential qualities, intents, purposes, and functionality rather than physical characteristics. All documents can be defined as communications having content, structure, and context in much the same way as David Bearman once defined the content, structure, and context of records as communicated transactions. What distinguishes the record, archive and archives from other forms of recorded information is not that they have content, structure, and context, but that the evidence-related nature of their content (particular types of social and business transactions), the specific documentary forms (structures) which they take, and their particular contexts of creation, management and use have been preserved in ways which

---

[25] Ibid, pp. 68-69.

enable them to continue to function as evidence. The recordkeeping profession and archival institutions in our society are charged with the mission of building and managing frameworks and systems which assure the preservation and accessibility of accurate, complete, reliable, and authentic records and archives in this sense. The accountability of the recordkeeping profession and archival institutions is therefore a critical issue in democratic societies. In the aftermath of the Children Overboard story, for example, a parliamentary committee inquiring into the staff of members of parliament, and the role of ministerial advisers in particular, scrutinized the role of the Australian national archival authority in providing advice and training to ministerial advisers on the importance of recordkeeping, and monitoring the standard of recordkeeping in ministerial offices.[26] The recordkeeping frameworks provided by the national archival authority are also referenced in a new code of conduct for the Commonwealth public service. The recordkeeping issues raised by the Children Overboard affair form the backdrop for the section of the code that relates to recordkeeping:

> Although there has been an increase in the transparency of recordkeeping, a number of organizations have raised concern about its quality and quantity: the Australian National Audit Office (ANAO) in its report Recordkeeping (No. 45 of 2001–02), the Australian Law Reform Commission in its review of the Archives Act, parliamentary committees, including the 2002 Report of the Inquiry into a Certain Maritime Incident [i.e. the Senate Select Committee inquiry into the Children Overboard affair].
>
> While it is not necessary to record every meeting, prepare file notes of every conversation or retain all emails, it is important to record and to maintain in an accessible form:
> * significant decisions by Ministers, and the basis for them including advice on options and risks
> * program decisions, including decisions affecting individuals or individual businesses that may be subject to administrative review, together with the basis for the decisions and the authority for making the decision
> * significant events, including meetings and discussions with Ministers or stakeholders or members of the public which may be significant in terms of policy or program decision making.[27]

Upward - The Dimensions of the Records Continuum (1996-1997)

1D Create
The first dimension encompasses the actors who carry out the act (decisions, communications, acts), the acts themselves, the documents which record the acts, and the trace, the representation of the acts.

---

[26] Parliament of Australia, Senate Finance and Public Administration References Committee, Inquiry into Members of Parliament Staff, Transcript of Discussion 3 September 2003.
[27] Australian Public Service Commission, *Values and Code of Conduct in Practice,* 2003, pp. 32-33.

2D Capture
The second dimension encompasses the personal and corporate records systems which capture documents in context in ways which support their capacity to act as evidence of the social and business activities of the units responsible for the activities.

3D Organize
The third dimension encompasses the organization of recordkeeping processes. It is concerned with the manner in which a corporate body or individual defines its/his/her recordkeeping regime, and in so doing constitutes/forms the archive as memory of its/his/her business or social functions.

4D Pluralize
The fourth dimension concerns the manner in which the archives are brought into an encompassing (ambient) framework in order to provide a collective social, historical and cultural memory of the institutionalized social purposes and roles of individuals and corporate bodies.

(Frank Upward, 'Structuring the Records Continuum Part One: Post-custodial Principles and Properties', *Archives and Manuscripts*, 24, no. 2, 1996, pp. 268-285; Frank Upward, 'Structuring the Records Continuum Part Two: Structuration Theory and Recordkeeping', *Archives and Manuscripts*, 25, no. 1, 1997, pp. 10-35)

Bound up with the notions of transactionality and contextuality is the contingent nature of recordkeeping. The story of the Children Overboard is told here from a particular point of view using the evidence provided by records of the Australian naval ship, the Navy, Australian government officials and boards of inquiry, and the Australian media. The voices of the people on board the Olong, the people smugglers involved in the human trade, even the individual sailors involved, are largely silent. There is little, if any, trace in the official record of the events as they experienced and witnessed them. Depicted in positivist writings as objective and impartial, the record, the archive and the archives, as defined here, always result from deliberate and partial acts of selection, accumulation, classification and description, acts that contribute to building social and organizational structures of remembering and forgetting. They inevitably represent a particular view of the events of 6-8 October formed within a particular configuration of power relationships and set of social values. The recordkeeping processes of selection, classification and description as described above are based on the records creators' view of their mission and the nature of the activities they engage in – in this case Operation Relex as an activity associated with border protection and immigration control. Within this context, in protection of our shores and to prevent an influx of illegal immigrants, HMAS Adelaide fires warning shots across the bow of a stricken, overcrowded vessel, and is under orders not to attempt a rescue until the boat is actually sinking, as its dangerous human cargo might go to any lengths to land on Australian soil. Whereas this particular incident ended in a heroic rescue, with the Australian sailors involved proud of their efforts in rescuing all on board the Olong, just weeks later, the game of cat and mouse that the ships and aeroplanes involved in the naval blockade were playing ended in tragedy with the loss of 352 men, women and children on board the ill-fated SIEV X.

From a different perspective, the activities of Operation Relex and the current Australian immigration policy might be seen as linked to the violation of human rights and non-compliance with international law relating to the treatment of refugees and their children. Within the contingent and transactional recordkeeping systems of the UN agencies responsible for addressing such abuse and non-compliance, records of what happened when HMAS Adelaide intercepted the Olong, and the subsequent detention and treatment of the refugees, might be placed in a very different context. From that context they will derive their particular meanings as corporate and collective memory.

Moving even further beyond the boundaries of the particular time and place in which the Children Overboard story unfolded, we can also see how the meanings of the terms record, the archive and the archives as explored here, and the social, business and recordkeeping processes that form and transform them are influenced and shaped by the evidentiary and memory paradigms of particular societies as reflected in their professional and social discourses. [28] Orality as a form of archive has never really been seriously contemplated in modern western archival discourse. Thus oral forms of records tend to be excluded from the professional meanings assigned to terms like record, archive and archives in those discourses. Similarly literature, art, artefacts, the built environment, landscape, dance, ceremonies and rituals as archival forms have rarely been considered by professional recordkeeping communities and their potential evidentiary nature, if subject to recordkeeping and archiving processes, has not figured in our evidentiary paradigms. However postmodernist ideas are opening up exciting possibilities for 'refiguring the archive'. In societies like South Africa, archivists are exploring 'the archive outside the archival inheritance of colonialism, and later, apartheid' – the oral record, literature, landscape, songs, dance, ritual, art, artefacts and so on.[29]

The very form of the archive provides evidence of the power relationships and social values of the society that produced it, including the prevailing evidentiary paradigm. In this vein, Ann Laura Stoler has explored the insights into colonialism in Africa that can be gained through 'the ethnography of the archive', i.e. by studying the form of the archive, the processes that shape it, its systems of classification, and 'cultures of documentation', rather than its content. Challenging the view that colonial archives need to be read 'against the grain' because of their inherent bias, Stoler suggests a reading 'along the grain' of the inevitable bias of these 'paper empires', not only to understand them as 'documents of exclusion and monuments to particular configurations of power', but also as 'telling prototype[s] of a postmodern [state], predicated on global domination of information'.[30] One of her most powerful insights relates to the way archival notions of authenticity,

---

[28] Ann Laura Stoler discusses the concept of evidentiary paradigms, a term coined by Carlo Ginzburg, in 'Colonial Archives and the Arts of Governance: On the Content in the Form', in Carolyn Hamilton et al. (eds), *Refiguring the Archive*, Dordrecht, Kluwer, 2002, pp. 83-101.
[29] Hamilton, op. cit., Introduction.
[30] Stoler, op. cit., pp. 89, 91-92.

reliability and trustworthiness at any given time are shaped by the evidentiary paradigms of the day. In similar vein, archival writers in Australia have explored how the form of the archive of the administration of indigenous people is in itself powerful evidence of dispossession and denial of identity:

> The recordkeeping system in which the only evidence of a child's removal from her family is not an individual file, or personal dossier, but a passing reference in a Protector's journal or an entry in a ration book, referring to the child and her 'country' by a European name, tells a compelling story about how the records creators and the regime of which they were a part regarded that child.[31]

In yet another sense, the archive(s) is always being reshaped in the context in which it is used where it is always open to different readings, interpretations and contestations.[32]

Records and Archives as Mediation – Tom Nesmith (1999)
Records: an evolving mediation of understanding about some phenomenon – a mediation created by social and technical processes of inscription, transmission and contextualization.
Archives: an ongoing mediation of understanding of records (and thus phenomena) or that aspect of record making which shapes this understanding through such functions as records appraisal, processing, and description, and the implementation of processes for making records accessible.
(Tom Nesmith, 'Still Fuzzy, But More Accurate: Some Thoughts on the 'Ghosts' of Archival Theory', *Archivaria,* 47, 1999, pp. 136-150; quotes from pp. 145 and 146)

In the postmodern archival discourse, positivist ideas about the objective nature of the record, and the impartial and neutral roles played by archivists in their preservation, are giving way to explorations of processes of remembering and forgetting, inclusion and exclusion, and the power relationships they embody, depicting archives as political sites of contested memory and knowledge, following Derrida's 'there is no political power without control of the archive'. Throughout time, societies have used recordkeeping as an instrument of governance, power and authority, a way of regulating their networks of relationships, and extending their control over distances of time and space. Giddens' concept of recorded information as both an authoritative resource and an allocative resource informs our understanding of this role. He depicts:

> transactional recorded information as authoritative resource, fundamental to 'the coordination of numbers of people together in society and their reproduction over time', and essential to the 'engendering of power', as well as to the Janus-like 'knowledgeable management of a projected future and recall of an elapsed past'.[33]

---

[31] Piggott and McKemmish, 'Recordkeeping, Reconciliation and Political Reality', op. cit., quote p. 116.
[32] Hamilton, op. cit., Introduction, p. 7.
[33] Sue McKemmish, 'Recordkeeping, Accountability and Continuity: The Australian Reality', in S. McKemmish and F. Upward, eds, *Archival Documents*: *Providing Accountability Through*

From this perspective, the role of recordkeeping professionals becomes an active one of participation in record and archive making processes, inscribing their own traces on a record that is always in a state of becoming.

Readings

- Sue McKemmish, 'Placing Records Continuum Theory and Practice', *Archival Science*, 1, no. 4, 2001, pp. 333-359; available via http://www.kluweronline.com/issn/1389-0166/contents

  This article provides an overview of the evolution of records continuum theory and practice in Australia, including continuum understandings of the evidentiary, transactional and contextual nature of records.

- Sue McKemmish, 'Evidence of Me ...', *Archives and Manuscripts*, 24, no. 1, 1996, pp. 28-45; also available at http://www.sims.monash.edu.au/research/rcrg/publications/recordscontinuum/smckp1.html

  'Evidence of Me ...' broke new ground by exploring the nature of personal recordkeeping and broad social mandates for its role in witnessing to individual lives, and constituting part of society's collective memory and cultural identity.

- Sue McKemmish, 'Are Records Ever Actual?', in Sue McKemmish and Michael Piggott, eds, *The Records Continuum: Ian Maclean and Australian Archives First Fifty Years*, Clayton, Ancora Press in association with Australian Archives, 1994, pp. 187-203; available at: http://www.sims.monash.edu.au/research/rcrg/publications/smcktrc.html

  This chapter introduced the notion that 'the record is always in a process of becoming', focusing on the virtual and logical nature of records, regardless of medium, and their multiple contextual and documentary relationships.

- Sue McKemmish and Frank Upward, 'The Archival Document: A Submission to the Inquiry into Australia as an Information Society', *Archives and Manuscripts*, 19, no. 1, 1991, pp. 17-32

  Based on a submission to the 1990-1 Parliamentary Standing Committee for Long Term Strategies' Inquiry into Australia as an Information Society, this paper explored the nature and role of the archival document, arguing that the effective creation and management of the archival document is a precondition of an information-rich society and underpins the public accountability of government and non-government organizations, freedom of information and privacy legislation, protection of people's rights and entitlements, and the quality of the archival heritage.

Recordkeeping, Clayton, Ancora Press, 1993, p. 22, quoting Frank Upward in 'Institutionalizing the Archival Document: Some Theoretical Perspectives on Terry Eastwood's Challenge', in the same publication, pp. 41-54.

CHAPTER 2
Archival institutions

Adrian Cunningham

Nothing is less reliable, nothing is less clear today than the word 'archive'.[1]

There is no political power without control of the archive, if not of memory. Effective democratization can always be measured by this essential criterion: the participation in and the access to the archive, its constitution and its interpretation.[2]

Far from standing as enduring monuments to the past, archives instead appear somewhat fragile, eternally subject to the judgement of the society in which they exist. Neither atemporal nor absolute, the meaning they convey may be manipulated, misinterpreted or suppressed. ... the archives of the past are also the mutable creations of the present.[3]

One of the features that has characterized all human societies since time immemorial has been an instinct for collective cultural self-preservation. While culture is contestable and ever-evolving, human beings nevertheless like their cultures and cultural achievements and experiences to endure across generations. This cultural persistence is made possible through the preservation of stories, both orally and in writing and through dance, rituals, art, music and performance. The keeping of many of these valuable cultural 'records' is fostered and institutionalized in an 'archive(s)'. The forms, functions and mandates of archival programs and institutions have varied and continue to vary enormously depending on the nature of the society in which they exist and the objectives of those who own or have control of the archives.

This chapter provides an overview and comparative analysis of the varied manifestations and roles of archival institutions throughout the ages, across the world and, in particular, within Australia. One of the aims of the chapter is to illustrate by example just what mutable creations archival institutions really are and to argue for the recognition of this seemingly obvious fact in the face of any tendency that other authors may have to argue in favour of universal laws and immutable truths about the nature of the archival institution. While common themes, objectives and issues can be identified through such a comparative

---

[1] Jacques Derrida, *Archive Fever*, Chicago, University of Chicago Press, 1996, p. 90.
[2] Ibid., p. 4, n. 1.
[3] Judith M. Panitch, 'Liberty, Equality, Posterity?: Some Archival Lessons from the Case of the French Revolution', *American Archivist*, 59, Winter 1996, p. 47.

analysis, the main argument of this chapter is that there is no universal law governing the form and mission of archival institutions. All archival institutions fulfil their mission by, as a minimum, controlling and preserving the records that constitute the archive, but the nature of the mission served can and does vary from case to case. The ever-shifting, always-contested form and mission of the archive reflects the dynamic nature of human experience, aspiration and activity in all its infinitely rich variety.

The secondary aim of this chapter is to illustrate not only that all archival programs and institutions are the contingent products of their time and place, but also that they are active shapers of their time and place. In the words of Verne Harris, archives 'at once express and are instruments of prevailing relations of power'.[4] Indeed, as we shall see, it is the nature of the prevailing power relations and the particular roles archives play as contested sites of power struggle that determine the forms and functions of archival programs – forms and functions that can and do change as the dynamics of societal power relations evolve and/or transform around them.

Archives and human impulses: The institutionalization and pluralization of the record

Records are made as a means of conducting and/or remembering activity. They are created for pragmatic or symbolic purposes – as enablers and evidence of experience and activity, as aids to memory and/or as artefacts. Some of these records are consciously retained for future reference as archives in order to transmit the activity and experience through time. As authors such as James O'Toole and Sue McKemmish have argued, human beings throughout the ages have demonstrated impulses to save and to bear witness.[5] Human beings are the sum of their memories. The nature of their interaction with other humans, indeed their very identity, is determined by their memories. While all memory is cognitive, literate individuals learn to rely at least to some extent on the written word to document, express and supplement cognitive processes. In turn, these cognitive processes give meaning to the archives for, as Jacques Derrida says, the archive does not speak for itself – users inscribe their own interpretations into it.[6]

When these impulses move beyond the purely personal and take on a broader collective or societal purpose the archives so retained take on a more formal character. One manifestation of this phenomenon is that the records can become part of an archival program or institution. This institutionalization of the record, which Derrida calls

---

[4] Verne Harris, 'The Archival Sliver: Power, Memory, and Archives in South Africa', *Archival Science*, 2, 2002, p. 63.
[5] James M. O'Toole, *Understanding Archives and Manuscripts*, Chicago, Society of American Archivists, 1990, pp. 13-15; Sue McKemmish, 'Evidence of Me...', *Archives and Manuscripts*, 24, no. 1, 1996, pp. 28-45 .
[6] Derrida, op. cit., p. 68.

domiciliation or 'house arrest', marks the passage of information from the private to a collective domain.[7]

There are a wide variety of reasons why records may be institutionalized in this way:

- Organizations need to retain their archives in order to meet their legal obligations, to protect and advance their rights and entitlements, and to retain corporate memory of the decisions and activities of the collective over time to support future decision-making and organizational continuity;

- Communities, including entire nations, retain archives as a means of remembering and connecting with their pasts, their origins. There are many complex and subtle variations driving this kind of institutionalization of memory. Derrida labels the desire to possess the past as 'archive fever'. Somewhat less cynically, Eric Ketelaar describes archives in this sense as 'time machines' – 'a bridge to yesteryear'.[8] Others describe the need to capture and retain ancestral voices or to listen to the whispers of the souls of long ago.[9] In serving this role archival institutions have much in common with other cultural and memory institutions such as museums;

- Similarly, communities and nations often establish archives to inform, enlighten, educate and sometimes to entertain. Related to this is the collective need to support and control storytelling about the pasts and origins of the community. Often archives are retained as a means of expressing, asserting and preserving a unifying group consensus on the nature of its identity, as forged through a shared history – or alternatively to support competing articulations of group identity and plurality;

- Organizations and communities retain archives for their symbolic significance. Objects stored in the archives can themselves be invested with and convey enormous symbolic significance.[10] The creation of a national archives can be symbolically significant as a form of solidification and memorialization in the context of nation building.[11] The heavy symbolism of the archives and its contents can in turn cause the archives to be a site of mythmaking and myth perpetuation.[12] Powerful rulers or administrators often

---

[7] Ibid., p. 2.

[8] Eric Ketelaar, 'Is Everything Archive?', Seminar presentation at Monash University, Melbourne, 5 August 2002.

[9] Monica Wehner and Ewan Maidment, 'Ancestral Voices: Aspects of Archival Administration in Oceania', *Archives and Manuscripts*, 27, no. 1, 1999, pp. 22-31; Carolyn Steedman, *Dust*, Manchester, Manchester University Press, 2001, p. 70.

[10] James O'Toole, 'The Symbolic Significance of Archives', *American Archivist*, 56, Spring 1993, pp. 234-255; 'Cortes's Notary: The Symbolic Power of Records', *Archival Science*, 2, 2002, pp. 45-61.

[11] Jacques Le Goff, *History and Memory*, New York, Columbia University Press, 1992, pp. 87-88.

[12] Roberto Echevarria, *Myth and Archive: A Theory of Latin American Narrative*, Cambridge, Cambridge University Press, 1990.

establish archives as symbolic monuments to their own power and as a means of controlling and directing mythmaking activities concerning their achievements;[13]

- Powerful rulers create archives not only as symbolic monuments to their greatness, but also to legitimize, reinforce and perpetuate their power. The deeds, treaties and founding documents in such an archive can legitimize power in a legalistic and evidential sense, while the information on individual subjects and their relationships and activities in such an archive can provide the information such rulers need to control their dominions and perpetuate their power. Moreover, because archives exercise control over selective memory, they are a source of power that is of enormous utility to autocratic rulers. When endeavouring to control the past, deciding what should be forgotten is just as important as deciding what should be remembered. As Antoinette Burton says, 'the history of the archive is a history of loss';[14] and

- Conversely, in democratic societies archives are meant to provide a means of democratic accountability as a means of empowering citizens against potential maladministration, corruption and autocracy. In addition to, or perhaps instead of, protecting the rights and entitlements of rulers and governments, such archives are meant to protect the rights and entitlements of the governed. In the words of John Fleckner, such archives are bastions of a just society where 'individual rights are not time bound and past injustices are reversible', where 'the archival record serves all citizens as a check against a tyrannical government'.[15]

As will be seen, these reasons for the existence of archival institutions are not mutually exclusive. Most such institutions exist for a combination of these reasons. Indeed, many archival institutions struggle either consciously or subconsciously with the ambiguities, complementarities and contradictions associated with serving these multiple purposes, whether the purposes are served explicitly or implicitly. The ongoing crisis of identity of government archives in democratic countries is a major theme of this chapter. Are archives a part of government or a check on it? Do government archives exist to serve the legal and administrative needs of government and/or the people, or do they exist primarily as cultural and memory institutions? How do archival institutions balance the often-competing demands of public and private interests and the differing imperatives of public and private records and their uses? What is the interplay of symbolic roles with these other functions and mandates? Most importantly, what factors influence responses to these dilemmas in practice and what are the consequences of the different responses?

---

[13] See for instance Verne Harris on the role of the South African Archives Service as 'an important vehicle for Afrikaaner nationalist historiography, with the legitimation of white rule and the exclusion of oppositional voices being key objectives in the selection policy.' Harris, op. cit., 2002, p. 74.
[14] Antoinette Burton, 'Thinking Beyond the Boundaries: Empire, Feminism and the Domains of History', *Social History*, 26, no. 1, 2001, p. 66.
[15] John Fleckner, '"Dear Mary Jane": Some Reflections on Being an Archivist', *American Archivist*, 54, Winter 1991, p. 13.

Figure 2.1. For centuries, towers as archival repositories accorded security from attack and larceny as well as symbolic prominence. In the case of the Oxford University Archives, a tower has been in continuous use since the early seventeenth century.

Of course, being brought under the control of an archival institution is not the only form of institutionalization that can be experienced by records. Registrar-style arrangements in public administrations, identification by auditors, records commissions and/or documentation programs are all examples of alternative forms of institutionalization, some of which will be explored later in this chapter.

Institutional form and function since the dawn of time

Ernst Posner has argued that the first archives were created by the Sumerians in the middle of the fourth millennium B.C. These records took of the form of clay tablets with cuneiform characters. The archives were used to support commercial activity and property ownership. Later ancient societies, such as the Hittites, Assyrians and Mesopotamians, all kept archives, although one can only speculate today on just how institutionalized these archives were and what form, if any, such institutions took. In at least some of these societies archives were kept in temples and courts for religious, legal, administrative, commercial and genealogical purposes.

During the second and third millennium B.C. the Egyptians developed an extensive system of archives to support their empire, as did the later Persian Empire. These archives existed primarily to serve the legal, administrative and military purposes of the rulers. An early indication of the perceived role of archives as tools of political oppression occurred in Egypt around 2200 B.C. when, during a revolt, an angry mob destroyed a records office 'as the custodians of hated property rights'.[16] Persian archives often incorporated the captured archives of defeated governments to help establish control over the newly occupied territories. In an illustration of the importance of archives to Alexander the Great, it is interesting to note that when records were burnt in the tent of his chief of chancery, staff were ordered to reconstruct them by obtaining copies from provincial sources.[17]

Archives in China can be traced back almost as far as the Sumerians. These records were inscribed on bones and tortoise shells for religious, administrative and symbolic purposes. By 700 B.C. bamboo, silk and stone tablets were in use, with records of military value being stored in secure buildings. While the Egyptians used papyrus, the Chinese began using plant-fibre paper after 200 B.C. The Chinese also demonstrated an early interest in the use of archives to control the writing of history. In the first century A.D. the Han Dynasty established a Bureau of Historiography.

The Greek city-state of Athens began housing its archives in the Metroon, the temple of the mother of the gods next to the courthouse, by around 400 B.C. This archive contained laws, decrees, minutes, financial and diplomatic records, contracts, records of court proceedings, and manuscripts of plays by Sophocles, Euripides and others. In what was perhaps the first example of an archival institution fulfilling the function of public access to records and consistent with the democratic principles of Athenian government, private citizens could obtain copies of the records in the archives.

The power that resides in the archives is illustrated in the etymology of the word archives, which can be traced to this time. The Greek *archeion* referred to the office of the magistrate or *archon* and the records kept by that office. *Archons* wielded executive power, which in

---

[16] Ernst Posner, *Archives in the Ancient World*, Cambridge, Mass, Harvard University Press, 1972, pp. 71-85.

[17] J.G. Bradsher and M.F. Pacifico, 'History of Archives Administration', in J.G. Bradsher, ed., *Managing Archives and Archival Institutions*, London, Mansell, 1988, pp. 19-20.

large part was legitimized by the legal documents in the *archeion*. Similarly, the Greek *arkhe* meant to command or govern. The Latin *archivum* was likewise the residence of the magistrate and the place where records of official legal and administrative significance were kept.

Rome's first public archives was founded about 509 B.C. in the Aerarium, or treasury, of the temple of Saturn and housed laws, decrees, reports and financial records. Like the Metroon, the laws housed in this archives could be consulted by all citizens. When the Aerarium was destroyed by fire in 83 B.C. it was replaced by the Tabularium, a large stone building. In later imperial Rome the Tabularium adopted a narrower mission as the archives of the Senate. It was supplemented by imperial archives and a network of provincial, municipal, military and religious archives. Various emperors, most notably Justinian I, were keen advocates of archives. The Justinian Code of 529 A.D. was not only written with the assistance of archives, it also included a section on the role of archives and archivists. This code emphasized the importance of archives as a public place of deposit and as guarantors of the integrity and authenticity of the records housed therein.

Bureaucratically formalized recordkeeping systems and administrative archives were foundation characteristics of innovative Islamic military and economic empires during medieval times. State Chanceries or central 'register' offices called diwans were established in places such as Persia, Damascus, Baghdad and North Africa during the seventh and eighth centuries. Later, many mosques adopted archival functions in support of religious scholarship, particularly in cultural centres such as Damascus.[18]

Most medieval European archives were maintained in ecclesiastical settings, often in 'muniment rooms'. By the middle of the sixth century a papal archives had been established. In the eighth century the Venerable Bede was able to make use of archives to write his landmark history of the church in England. Following the collapse of the Roman Empire a number of municipal archives persisted in Italy and France until the ninth and tenth centuries. Venice and Florence established archives during the eleventh and thirteenth centuries respectively. It was common practice for royal archives in Europe to have no fixed location, but instead to travel with the King's household. Towards the end of the twelfth century, however, there were some moves towards the establishment of a central government archives in England. A century later Exchequer rolls began to be housed in the Tower of London.[19] In time, this archives was expanded to include all of Britain's Chancery records. In 1323 the first inventory of English archives was completed and served as a model for similar initiatives elsewhere in western Europe. In 1346 the archives of the kingdom of Aragon were created.[20] Around this time paper began to come into more common usage in Europe.

---

[18] Ernst Posner, 'Archives in Medieval Islam', *American Archivist*, 35, July/October 1972, pp. 291-315.

[19] M.T. Clanchy, *From Memory to Written Record, England 1066-1307*, 2nd ed., Oxford, Blackwell, 1993, p. 72.

[20] Michel Duchein, 'The History of European Archives and the Development of the Archival Profession in Europe", *American Archivist*, 55, Winter 1992, p. 15.

In 1524 the archives of the crown of Castille was established by Charles V at Simancas near Valladolid. The archive was greatly expanded by Philip II, who regarded archives as vital for controlling, administering and legitimizing an empire and who also viewed archives as symbols of power and prestige. The Simancas archive is now regarded as the classic prototype of a centralized 'national archives'. Two hundred years later the Archives of the Indies was established in Seville for the same reasons. When Cortes conquered the Americas, it was considered essential to not only burn the archives of the conquered Incas and Aztecs,[21] but also ensure legitimate documentation of the occupation by a legally appointed Notary, whose records were eventually deposited in archives back in Spain.[22] Between the sixteenth and early eighteenth centuries royal archives repositories were established in France, Sweden, Denmark, and China. The combined effect of the advent of the printing press and the emergence of the modern administrative state generated a significant growth in records creation and, as a consequence, archives holdings.

The creation, control and use of archives became increasingly important in the context of religious, legal and political power struggles such as the Reformation and parliamentary reform movements, when opposing factions used records to support their arguments. The Renaissance had created demand for access to information for the purpose of supporting scholarly enquiry as opposed to the more common political, financial, legal, administrative and symbolic purposes. Nevertheless, access to archives was strictly controlled by their owners, usually monarchs or churches, who very often kept them inaccessible to all except themselves and their functionaries.

The French Revolution and the nineteenth century

The French Revolution provides perhaps the clearest example of the mutable nature and purpose of archives and their tendency to inspire extremes in human emotion. Between 1789 and 1793, much of the archives of the *ancien régime* were attacked and destroyed by mobs or in state-sponsored bonfires and paper recycling campaigns, with the aim of obliterating what the revolutionaries regarded as symbols of their erstwhile oppression. While such actions might sometimes have had the practical benefit of destroying the evidence of feudal debts and obligations, by and large they were cathartic acts of retribution and ritual cleansing of the body politic.

In the midst of this destruction of old archives there co-existed a desire to create new archives, out of which emerged a new archival system for the new society. A legislative repository was provided for by the new Assembly just two weeks after the fall of the Bastille. In September 1790 a law was passed establishing a new National Archives that was to be open to the public and which was to report to the Assembly. By 1794 the desire

---

[21] Henri-Jean Martin, *The History and Power of Writing*, Chicago, University of Chicago Press, 1988, p. 26.
[22] James O'Toole, 'Cortes's Notary: The Symbolic Power of Records', *Archival Science*, 2, 2002, pp. 45-61.

to destroy the documentary evidence of the *Ancien Régime* had been replaced by a desire to preserve and manage those records as nationalized public property, reinvented for the purpose of symbolically highlighting the glory of the new Republic in contrast to the sinful decadence and oppression of the old regime. A decree issued in June 1794 granted the National Archives jurisdiction over the records of government agencies, provinces, communes, churches, universities and noble families, thus creating the world's first centrally controlled national archival system. The same decree also proclaimed the right of public access to these records, thus establishing the first modern instance of archives fulfilling a legal role as protectors of the rights and entitlements of the people and as instruments of accountability and transparency in government. The creation of national archives as both symbols of nation building in the midst of turbulent change and ideological – indeed almost mythological – assertions of legitimacy by new orders is a pattern that has been repeated often since. The fate of the archives of the *Ancien Régime* testify to the fact that no archives can assume an eternal mandate – in the words of Judith Panitch, they are forever 'subject to the judgement of the society in which they exist'.[23]

Another aspect of the impact of the French Revolution on archives is worth exploring at this point. Luciana Duranti has argued that the 1794 decree created for the first time a dichotomy between administrative and historical archives – the distinction between the archives of the Republic and the archives of the *Ancien Régime*. Duranti considers this an unfortunate development in that it represents a usurpation of the administrative and legal functions of archives by social and cultural functions – a usurpation that has echoes in various places and times since the Revolution.[24] Other commentators, however, beg to differ. Judith Panitch, for instance, argues that in the 1790s the notion of French archives as sites of 'historical or cultural scholarship had yet to take hold'. While they had acquired the new function of public access for the new purpose of accountability, their essential role as legal, administrative and symbolic institutions remained unaltered.[25]

Nevertheless, Duranti is correct in highlighting the distinction between the administrative/legal and cultural/historical roles of archives – a source of contestation that shall be explored in more detail later – even if the cultural role of French archives did not become apparent until some decades after the Revolution. Duranti's portrayal of one role as being innately superior to another is, however, a position that is far more difficult to sustain, as we shall see. Nor, as we have already seen, is it true that the world had to wait until the late eighteenth century to witness an example of an archives that was established for cultural and historical purposes. While such phenomena were indeed unusual, they were not unprecedented – see for example the case of the Han Dynasty Bureau of Historiography referred to above.

The creation of a centralized national archives in France provided a model for archival development in a number of other countries such as Finland, Norway, the Netherlands and

---

[23] Panitch, op. cit., pp. 101-122; Ernst Posner, 'Some Aspects of Archival Development Since the French Revolution', *American Archivist*, 3, July 1940, pp. 161-162.
[24] Luciana Duranti, 'Archives as a Place', *Archives and Manuscripts*, 24, no. 2, 1996, pp. 248-249.
[25] Panitch, op. cit., p. 118.

Belgium during the nineteenth century. Similarly, in Sweden, Denmark and Prussia central archives evolved out of pre-existing royal or administrative repositories. Forty-eight years after the creation of the French national archives, the English followed suit, but for very different reasons and in much less dramatic circumstances. Between 1800 and 1837 a variety of committees and commissions of inquiry had highlighted the scattered and poorly controlled and preserved state of public records in that country. These efforts culminated in the passage of the Public Records Act in 1838 and the eventual establishment of the Public Record Office during the 1850s by a government that was concerned to ensure the proper care and preservation of records that guaranteed the legal rights and entitlements of English people. Lawmakers in Westminster were no doubt aware of the fact that their counterparts in Scotland had beaten not only themselves but also the French in establishing a national archives, when their principal collection of public records had been assembled in Edinburgh's General Register House as early as 1784.

By the middle of the nineteenth century the growth in historical scholarship based on the use of written sources was becoming an important factor in the evolution of European archival institutions. Selected series of historical documents were published, such as the 'Roll Series' and the 'Calendars of State Papers' in England. In 1869 the Historical Manuscripts Commission was established in the United Kingdom to identify, describe and promote the preservation and use of significant historical records that were not otherwise catered for under the Public Records Act. The Commission, which existed until April 2003 when it was amalgamated with the Public Record Office to form a rebranded National Archives, is probably the best example of a state-sponsored documentation program for the nationally distributed holdings of historically significant private records.

Archival institutions in twentieth-century post-colonial societies

Globalization, the spread of modern bureaucracies and the worldwide interest in history and cultural/national identity together provided the impetus for the emergence of archival systems around the world during the twentieth century. Soon after the Bolshevik revolution the Soviet Union established a highly centralized archival system as both a reflection and enabler of centralized state power. In contrast to democratic states, access to archives in totalitarian states was not a guaranteed right of the citizen.

In Asia, Latin America, Africa and the South Pacific, European colonial powers were responsible for the creation of administrative archives that in turn formed the basis for national archives once independence was achieved.[26] For instance, the National Archives of Malaysia was established in 1957 and was based on the model of the Public Record Office

---

[26] Philip Alexander and Elizabeth Pessek, 'Archives in Emerging Nations: The Anglophone Experience', *American Archivist*, 51, Winter/Spring 1988, pp. 121-129; and Ann Laura Stoler, 'Colonial Archives and the Arts of Governance', *Archival Science*, 2, 2002, pp. 87-109.

in London.[27] In Vietnam the French colonial administrators established an Archives in 1917. This was eventually superseded by the State Archives Department in 1962, which in turn was consolidated by the 1982 Decree on the Protection of National Archives Documents. The scope of this decree is, however, limited to government records.[28] In many such territories archival development has also benefited from a strong pre-colonial archival tradition. Thailand, which was never colonized by a European power, inherited an impressive system of royal legal/administrative and cultural archives of palm leaf manuscripts and bark paper stretching back many hundreds of years. This system was overlaid with a more western approach, including the adoption of a registry system, during the late nineteenth century. In the early twentieth century records retention schedules were introduced and a National Archives was established in 1952 with responsibility for preserving the historical records of government administration.[29]

A common feature of archival institutions in the post-colonial developing world is that institutions established with the best of intentions on a European model have often struggled to fulfil expectations in the harsh economic and political reality of independent governance. Just as these emerging nations have struggled to consolidate inherited democratic institutions, so too have inherited archival institutions often failed to establish themselves as robust organic components of the culture and governance of post-colonial societies.[30] Not only have administrators often been inclined to view archives as at best luxuries and at worst irrelevant western white elephants, but also citizens living in predominantly oral cultures have often been slow to develop attachments with institutions primarily associated with preservation of the written word for use by western academics.[31] Indeed, an interesting variant on the traditional archival institutional model in non-Western territories has been the emergence of alternative forms of memory institutionalization such as so-called 'keeping places'[32] and memory institutions that deal primarily with orality in preference to or because of the cultural irrelevance of written records.

---

[27] Zakiah Hunum Nor, 'The National Archives of Malaysia – its Growth and Development', in *Archives in the Tropics: Proceedings of the Australian Society of Archivists Conference, Townsville, 9-11 May 1994*, Canberra, ASA, 1994, pp. 94-98.

[28] Pham thi Bich Hai, 'Professional Identity of the Archivist in Vietnam', in M. Piggott and C. McEwen, eds, *Archivists – The Image and Future of the Profession: 1995 Conference Proceedings*, Canberra, Australian Society of Archivists, 1996, pp. 142-148.

[29] Somsuang Prudtikul, 'Records and Archives Management in Thailand', Paper presented at the Annual Congress of the International Federation of Library Associations, Bangkok, 1999; available at: http://www.tiac.or.th/thailib/ifla/ifla99_20.htm

[30] See for instance the summary of current issues and developments from the Proceedings of the 9th Conference of the Pacific Regional Branch of the International Council on Archives, Palau, 2001, p.12; and Sophie Papadopoulis, 'The Image and Identity of Africa's Archivists', in M. Piggott and C. McEwen, op. cit., pp. 149-156.

[31] Monica Wehner and Ewan Maidment, 'Ancestral Voices: Aspects of Archives Administration in Oceania', *Archives and Manuscripts*, 27, no. 1, 1999, pp. 22-41.

[32] Glenys McIver, Ysola Best and Fabian Hutchinson, 'Friends or Enemies?: Collecting Archives and the Management of Archival Materials Relating to Aboriginal Australians', in *Archives in the Tropics*, op. cit., pp. 135-140.

Archival institutions in these territories are having to develop flexible new conceptions of indigenous knowledge ownership, control and access in response to a rejection of the inappropriate aspects of Eurocentric archival theory, which support the systematic marginalization and dispossession of the indigenous by dominant global discourses. The more successful of these have been able to demonstrate the potential of archives to support the rediscovery of suppressed cultural identities and the redressing of past injustices.[33] Indeed, the often-tenuous place of archival institutions in oral societies tells us much about the mutable and contingent nature of such institutions. While many have endeavoured to increase their relevance by instituting oral history programs, others argue that such activities fail to comprehend the difficulties involved in converting fluid orality into fixed material custody without destroying the very thing that the archives is trying to capture. In the words of Verne Harris there exists 'A reluctance to engage indigenous conceptualizations of orality not as memory waiting to be archived, but as archive already.'[34]

Archival institutions in North America

Contrary to the more usual pattern of legal/administrative archives gradually acquiring a cultural/historical role (or alternatively being supplemented by the establishment of separate cultural/historical records programs), in North America cultural/historical imperatives were the primary impetus for the creation of archival institutions. The Public Archives of Canada was established in 1872, only five years after confederation, following a petition to government by the Quebec Literary and Historical Society. Of particular concern to Canadian historians was the desire to have access to records of Canadian historical interest held in Britain and France. Driving the cultural/historical interest was a perceived need to build national unity and identity through the study of the origins of the Canadian people. Although the Public Archives of Canada lacked both proper facilities and a legislative mandate during its early decades, these shortcomings were rectified in 1906 with the construction of an archives building and in 1912 with the passage of archival legislation. This legislation was informed exclusively by the need to preserve records for historical rather than for legal/administrative purposes.

From its outset the Canadian archival endeavour encompassed both public and private records, a concept later articulated as 'total archives'.[35] The total archives concept reflects a long-standing social consensus that public funds should be used to preserve a wide range of Canadian documentary heritage, regardless of its origins and format, and that this

---

[33] See the 'Archives and Indigenous Peoples' theme issue of *Comma, International Journal on Archives*, 2003.

[34] Verne Harris, *Exploring Archives*, 2nd ed., Pretoria, National Archives of South Africa, 2000, pp. 92-93; Sello Hatang, 'Converting Orality to Material Custody: Is it a Noble Act of Liberation or is it and Act of Incarceration?', *ESARBICA Journal*, 19, 2000.

[35] Laura Millar, 'The Spirit of Total Archives: Seeking a Sustainable Archival System', *Archivaria*, 47, 1999, pp. 46-65; and 'Discharging Our Debt: The Evolution of the Total Archive Concept in English Canada', *Archivaria*, 46, 1998, pp. 103-146.

preservation effort should be pursued via a planned national system. As a result Canada has not experienced the emergence of separate (and sometimes warring) archival tribes or traditions for public records and historical manuscripts, as has been the case in the United States and Australia. With Canadian national identity constantly at risk of being swamped by the more dominant identity of its southern neighbour, recognition of the need to take coordinated action to preserve something distinctly Canadian has compelled generations of Canadians to take a holistic approach to the preservation and management of their archival heritage. The National Archives of Canada (since 2002 the Library and Archives of Canada) has, at least in theory, always given equal priority to the preservation of records originating in private sector and to the preservation of records originating in the public sector. Nevertheless, it was not until the 1950s that the then Public Archives of Canada began to exert authority over public records and perform the legal/administrative role that provided the original basis for its counterpart institutions in Europe.[36]

Like Canada, it was cultural/historical concerns that led to the creation of a national archives in the United States. Unlike Canada, which wasted little time in establishing a central archival program, the USA had to wait until 1934 – over 150 years after the Declaration of Independence – before its national archives was established. This represented the culmination of many decades of agitation by historians, most notably the American Historical Association. By that time the desire to rescue, preserve and provide access to historical records had manifested itself in the emergence of the so-called 'historical manuscripts tradition'. This tradition, which dated back to the earliest years of the nation, had been shaped by an antiquarian collecting instinct and had become institutionalized in organizations such as state historical societies and the Library of Congress, where the main focus was the collecting, researching and publishing of the private papers of prominent individuals.

Why did the United States take so long to establish a national archives? In 1939 Ernst Posner argued that a major contributing factor was American ambivalence, if not hostility, towards state bureaucratic power. So, while manuscript collecting endeavours pursued for scholarly purposes were considered laudable, proposals to create an archival institution as an integral part of the state bureaucracy was something that was regarded, at least subconsciously, with suspicion.[37] Americans had to wait until the latter part of the twentieth century before there was a clear articulation of the role of archives as guarantors of the democratic rights of citizens and as means of holding public officials to account – a role that, while recognized as an ideal, is yet to be fully realized both in practice and in public perception.

Just as the Public Archives of Canada was established for historical purposes and had to wait until the 1950s to acquire an administrative/legal role, so too the US National Archives

---

[36] Ian Wilson, 'A Noble Dream: The Origins of the Public Archives of Canada', *Archivaria*, 15, 1982/83, pp. 16-35; Jay Atherton, 'The Origins of the Public Archives Records Centre, 1897-1956', *Archivaria*, 8, 1979, p. 42.
[37] Ernst Posner, 'Archival Administration in the United States', in Ken Mundsen, ed., *Archives & the Public Interest*, Washington DC, Public Affairs Press, 1967, pp. 114-130.

had to wait until 1950, with the passage of the Federal Records Act, before it acquired a role as a supporter and enabler of public administration. Public records archivists such as Margaret Cross Norton from Illinois pursued a campaign to articulate and assert an administrative and legal accountability role for archives in the face of the primacy of the historical/cultural role.[38] While Norton had very good reasons for pursuing these efforts, they had the unfortunate effect of creating a polarization of the American archival community – a polarization that persists to this day in a profession which seems unable to attain a comfortable and balanced view of the dual role of archival institutions.[39]

The American experience highlights in sharp relief the tensions and contradictions that have emerged in the roles of archives worldwide since the nineteenth century and which represent contested ground everywhere. Arguably, the polarization is more pronounced in the United States because there is more at stake. Archives in Europe were initially established for legal and administrative purposes, thus conferring on them a valuable legitimacy in the eyes of government that has enabled them to acquire a cultural/historical role from a position of strength. In contrast, at the time of their establishment American archives had no such legal/administrative legitimacy and have had to struggle ever since to attain such a role and the government support and funding that it could attract. The addition of democratic accountability to the legal/administrative role by proponents such as Margaret Cross Norton merely helped the struggle to work against itself. So, while the general public may be suspicious of the legal/administrative role of archives and supportive of the accountability role, the reverse is very often the case from the perspective of those that control the corridors of power in government. Once again we see the mutable nature of archives and the fact that they are forever subject to the judgment of the societies in which they exist.

Public records institutions in Australia

The emergence of archival institutions in Australia mirrors in many respects the experience of the United States. As in the United States, the establishment of government archival authorities was the result of advocacy from historians, with a unique Australian contribution coming from leading librarians. In most jurisdictions the government archives programs started their lives as units within the government research libraries, which themselves inherited control of colonial-era records from heterogeneous administrative locations.[40]

---

[38] Margaret Cross Norton, *Norton on Archives*, Carbondale, Southern Illinois University Press, 1975.
[39] Richard C. Berner, *Archival Theory and Practice in the United States*, Seattle, University of Washington Press, 1983; and Luke J. Gilliland-Swetland, 'The Provenance of a Profession: The Permanence of the Public Archives and Historical Manuscripts Traditions in American Archival History', *American Archivist*, 54, Spring 1991, pp. 160-175.
[40] Russell Doust, 'The Administration of Official Archives in New South Wales 1870-1960', Master of Librarianship Thesis, University of New South Wales, 1969; Ross Harrison Snow, 'The Developments That Led to the Establishment of the Public Record Office of Victoria', in Peter Crush,

The decision to establish a Commonwealth Government archives was made during World War II, forty years after Federation, and was informed primarily by the desire to 'ensure the availability of material for the preparation of a history of the war'.[41] The Archives Division was initially located administratively within the Commonwealth Parliamentary Library, later the National Library. Despite these cultural/historical origins, early Commonwealth archivists were heavily influenced by the legal/administrative tradition as embodied in the writing of English archivist Sir Hilary Jenkinson. While this was partly a reflection of the British origins of the Australian bureaucracy, it also reflects the simple fact that Jenkinson provided the only archival handbook in the English language to which neophyte archivists could turn for guidance.[42]

Two North American visitors to Australia exerted a significant subsequent influence on archival development in Australia. T.R. Schellenberg from the US National Archives and W. Kaye Lamb from Canada were both firmly of the historical/cultural tradition. Schellenberg toured Australia in 1954 on a Fulbright Fellowship at the invitation of National Librarian Harold White.[43] Perhaps Schellenberg's most enduring legacy in the Australian profession was his philosophy regarding the appraisal of voluminous modern public records. While Schellenberg's cultural/historical message may have registered well with Harold White, the government archivists themselves were determined to stick to the Jenkinsonian path – a determination that manifested itself in a desire to break free from their cultural/historical roots and what they saw as the ill-informed control of librarians. Doubtless also by this time, the North American debates surrounding the campaign of Margaret Cross Norton were resonating in Australia. Despite their philosophical differences on the role of archival institutions, the local Jenkinsonians nevertheless also found in Schellenberg an ally in their arguments in favour of separation from the Library. A Committee of Inquiry recommended separation of the Archives Division from the Library, influenced partly by the differences between the two professional disciplines and partly by the view that the role of the Archives was to manage government records for the benefit of

---

ed., *Archives and Reform – Preparing for Tomorrow: Proceedings of the Australian Society of Archivists Conference, Adelaide, 25-26 July 1997*, Canberra, ASA, 1998, pp. 256-262.
[41] Michael Piggott, 'Beginnings', in Sue McKemmish and Michael Piggott, eds, *The Records Continuum*, Clayton, Ancora Press in association with Australian Archives, 1994, p. 8. For a description of an earlier failed attempt to establish a Commonwealth Government archives see Ted Ling, 'The Commonwealth's First Archives Bill 1927', *Archives and Manuscripts*, 29, no. 1, 2001, pp. 98-109.
[42] Ian Maclean, 'An Analysis of Jenkinson's "Manual of Archive Administration" in the Light of Australian Experience', in A.E.J. Hollaender, ed., *Essays in Memory of Sir Hilary Jenkinson*, London, Society of Archivists, 1962, pp. 1281-52; and Sir Paul Hasluck, 'A Narrow and Rigid View of Archives', *Archives and Manuscripts*, 9, no. 2, 1981, pp. 3-10.
[43] Michael Piggott, 'The Visit of Dr T.R. Schellenberg to Australia 1954: a Study of its Origins and Some Repercussions on Archival Development in Australia', Master of Archives Administration Thesis, University of New South Wales, 1989: available at:
http://ourhistory.naa.gov.au/library/visit_schellenberg.html

the government and its departments – a very different role than that asserted by Harold White of building a systematic record of national life and development.[44]

In 1961 the Commonwealth Archives Office separated from the National Library, much to the chagrin of Harold White. The newly independent Office then proceeded to bury itself deep into the Federal bureaucracy and largely turn away from any cultural/historical role – indeed from the rest of the profession in Australia, a situation that persisted into the 1990s and which in some ways still characterizes the work of the organization. The most positive aspect of this bureaucratic focus was, through the efforts of Ian Maclean and Peter Scott, the development of an innovative and enduring Australian school of thought on the management and intellectual control of current records.[45] Nevertheless, throughout the 1960s and 1970s the Australian Archives, as it became known in 1974, proved to be ambivalent about pursuing an active role in support of democratic accountability in the manner that opinion leaders such as Sir Paul Hasluck and Margaret Cross Norton had advocated. It appeared to define its role solely in terms of supporting the administrative and legal requirements of the Commonwealth Government.[46]

At this time the Government was contemplating the need for legislation to govern the work of the national archives. Canadian Dominion Archivist Kaye Lamb was invited to investigate and recommend a way forward. Lamb's 1973 report was critical of the lack of support and assistance provided to researchers by the Archives and recommended legislation that gave the organization a broad cultural and administrative mandate and a leadership role at the centre of a national archival system.[47] Lamb's recommendations were eventually enacted in legislation with the passage of the Archives Act in 1983 – itself part of a suite of administrative law reform bills including a Freedom of Information Act. This law created the Archives as a quasi-independent entity with an appointed Advisory Council.

The national leadership and cultural/historical provisions of the legislation were, by some accounts, retained in the legislation despite the objections of senior staff in the Archives. While the advent of legislation gave the Archives a mandate to pursue a range of activities, during the 1980s only those activities relating to a narrowly defined administrative/legal role were pursued with any vigour. Although lack of resources and institutional inertia help

---

[44] Michael Piggott, '"An Important and Delicate Assignment": The Paton Inquiry, 1956-57', *Australian Academic and Research Libraries*, 21, no. 4, 1990, pp. 213-223.

[45] Frank Upward, 'In Search of the Continuum: Ian Maclean's "Australian Experience" Essays on Recordkeeping', in Sue McKemmish and Michael Piggott, eds, *The Records Continuum*, Clayton, Ancora Press in association with Australian Archives, 1994, pp. 110-130; Peter J. Scott, 'The Record Group Concept: A Case for Abandonment', *American Archivist*, 29, no. 4, 1966; and Mark Wagland and Russell Kelly, 'The Series System - A Revolution in Archival Control', in Sue McKemmish and Michael Piggott, eds, *The Records Continuum*, Clayton, Ancora Press in association with Australian Archives, 1994, pp. 131-149.

[46] Hilary Golder, *Documenting a Nation*, Canberra, Australian Archives, 1994, p. 37; Colin Smith, 'A Hitchhikers Guide to Australian Archival History', in S. McKemmish and F. Upward, eds, *Archival Documents, Providing Accountability Through Recordkeeping*, Melbourne, Ancora Press, 1993, pp. 197-210.

[47] Australia. Parliament, *Development of the National Archives*, Canberra, AGPS, 1975.

explain this situation, the changes initiated by George Nichols as Director-General during the 1990s that resulted in the Archives pursuing a vibrant and proactive role as both a cultural institution[48] and an agent of democratic accountability merely highlight the poverty of vision of some of his predecessors.

In State Government jurisdictions archival institutions have suffered from a variety of malaises including under-funding, lack of public visibility and control by the sometimes stifling hand of librarians. More recently, however, new public records legislation in a number of jurisdictions has given State and Territory archives greatly enhanced powers as cultural institutions and as semi-independent agents of democratic accountability. In many cases these positive developments have been assisted by spectacular examples of failed public administration, assisted at least in part by a lack of regulation regarding public recordkeeping.[49] Time will tell if the State and Territory Archives are given the resources and the true independence both to reinvent themselves organizationally and pursue their new mandates with the vigour that they deserve.

The collecting tradition in Australia

An Australian equivalent of the Historical Manuscripts Tradition, in the form of a network of State and Commonwealth Government research libraries, was the first to apply serious endeavour to the business of identifying, preserving and making available valuable archival materials. These efforts grew out of the antiquarian work of private collectors and historical societies and, until the 1940s were characterized by a desire to preserve documents relating to the origins of European settlement in Australia. The Mitchell Library, opened in Sydney in 1910, was founded on the bequest of the prodigious collector David Scott Mitchell. Similar, though less extensive, collections of personal papers preserved alongside other categories of historical source material were subsequently established in State Libraries in each of the other jurisdictions.[50]

During the 1950s and 1960s there was an almost exponential expansion in the institutional collecting of private archives in Australia. At the forefront of this expansion was the National Library in Canberra,[51] but also significant was the emergence of new collecting

---

[48] Gabrielle Hyslop, 'For Many Audiences: Developing Public Programs at the National Archives of Australia', *Archives and Manuscripts*, 30, no. 1, 2002, pp. 48-59.

[49] Anne-Marie Schwirtlich, 'Overview of archival legislation in Australia', in *Archives at Risk: Proceedings of the Australian Society of Archivists Annual Conference, Brisbane, 1999*, Canberra, Australian Society of Archivists, 2001, pp. 95-99; Ted Ling, 'Acts of Atonement: recent developments in Australian archival legislation', *Journal of the Society of Archivists*, 23, no. 2, 2002, pp. 209-221; and Chris Hurley, 'From Dust Bins to Disk-drives and Now to Dispersal: the State Records Act 1998 (New South Wales)', *Archives and Manuscripts*, 26, no. 2, 1998, pp. 390-409.

[50] Graeme Powell, 'The Collecting of Personal and Private Papers in Australia', *Archives and Manuscripts*, 24, no. 1, 1996, pp. 62-64.

[51] John Thompson, '"Let Time and Chance Decide": Deliberation and Fate in the Collecting of Personal Papers', in Peter Cochrane, ed., *Remarkable Occurrences*, Canberra, National Library of Australia, 2001, pp. 105-122; and Graeme Powell, 'Modes of Acquisition: The Growth of the

programs such as the University of Melbourne Archives[52] and the Australian National University's Archives of Business and Labour, which have specialized in collecting the records of Australia's leading businesses and trade union organizations.[53] In large part this expansion reflected a similar expansion in the study and teaching of Australian history in Australia's rapidly expanding university system. According to Stuart Macintyre, the number of full time professors and lecturers in history in Australian tertiary institutions expanded from fewer than 20 in 1939 to more than 700 in 1973.[54]

The emergence of new collecting programs and the simultaneous expansion and shift in collecting emphasis by the existing programs stemmed from a desire to serve the needs of this expanding researcher clientele. Both phenomena reflected a more self-confident, nationalistic and prosperous Australia, a nation that was keen to apply the methods of scientific history to the task of understanding and articulating a national identity. There was also continuity between the old amateur collecting paradigm and the new professional, institution-building paradigm. Both types of collecting constituted, in the words of James Clifford, 'a form of western subjectivity' and a 'crucial process of Western identity formation'.[55] Human beings are storytelling creatures. Every society develops mechanisms for the formation and persistence of collective memory for storytelling purposes. Archives, when they pursue a cultural/historical role, provide one such mechanism that will very often secure and retain the support of the society in which they exist.

Just as the growth of social history, with its commitment to uncovering the lived experience of ordinary people, provided a major boost to the collection and preservation of textual archives, so too did it foster the growth of associated documentation and preservation programs such as oral history, film and sound archives and, more recently, computer data archives. The National Library commenced gathering and preserving sound recordings and transcripts of oral history interviews with prominent Australians during the 1950s as an adjunct to its manuscript collecting program. Initially based on the Columbia University model of an oral history program, the Library's efforts have since expanded to encompass thematic social history projects such as the history of the timber industry and documentation of the HIV/Aids epidemic. The Library's oral history holdings now include some 30,000 hours of original recordings. The program also incorporates a component of field recordings of folkloric tales and music, similar to that pioneered by the US Library of

Manuscript Collection of the National Library of Australia', in Peter Biskup and Margaret Henty, eds, 'Library for the Nation', *Australian Academic and Research Libraries special issue*, Canberra, 1991, pp. 74-80.

[52] Leigh Swancott, 'Origins and Development of the University of Melbourne Archives', *Archives and Manuscripts*, 27, no. 2, 1999, pp. 40-47.

[53] Peter Moore and Ewan Maidment, 'The Archives of Business and Labour, 1954-1982', *Labour History*, 44, 1983, pp. 107-112.

[54] Stuart Macintyre, 'The Writing of Australian History', in D.H. Borchardt and Victor Crittenden, eds, *Australians: A Guide to Sources*, Sydney, Fairfax, Syme & Weldon Associates, 1987, p. 22.

[55] James Clifford, *The Predicament of Culture,* Cambridge, Mass., Harvard University Press, 1988, quoted in Tom Griffith, *Hunters and Collectors,* Cambridge, Cambridge University Press, 1996, p. 25.

Congress.[56] Over 400 similar, though much smaller, oral history collections have been established in libraries and archives such as the Northern Territory Archives Service.[57]

The National Library also pioneered the collecting of another category of Australia's documentary heritage in the form of films and sound recordings. As early as 1935 the Library established (as a result of a Cabinet decision) a 'National Historical Film and Speaking Record Library'. After some years of lobbying by the film and sound industry and others, the National Film Archive and Sound Recording Section were eventually separated from the Library in 1984 as a new institution called the National Film and Sound Archive, with its headquarters in Canberra. Although it lacks a legislative mandate and the kind of bureaucratic independence that is enjoyed by both the National Library and the National Archives, ScreenSound Australia, as it is now branded, enjoys a solid international reputation for professional excellence in the field of film and sound preservation and is an active participant in international professional forums such as the International Association of Sound Archives (IASA) and the International Federation of Film Archives (FIAF). For the most part ScreenSound Australia restricts its collecting activity to the output of the Australian private sector media industries, with the various public records archives in each jurisdiction being responsible for the control and preservation of archival value audiovisual records produced in the public sector.[58] In the Commonwealth the picture is further complicated by the fact that custody of the audiovisual records of the Australian Broadcasting Corporation, which as Commonwealth records are all ultimately the responsibility of the National Archives, is shared between the ABC's own in-house archives and the various repositories of the National Archives.

Another strand in the collecting archives scene can be found in the area of data archives. The leading archive of this type in Australia, the Social Science Data Archives, was established at the Australian National University in 1981. Its brief is to collect, preserve and make available for use computer readable data and statistical sets emanating from social, political and economic research projects in the disciplines of the social sciences. The creators and depositors of these data sets include academics, government and private organizations and individuals. Such initiatives are consistent with an international tradition of data archiving in the sciences and social sciences, as represented by the activities of the International Federation of Data Organizations and institutions such as the UK Data Archive, based at the University of Essex. In recent years data archives have made great use

---

[56] Barry York, '"Impossible on Less Terms": The Oral History Collection', in Peter Cochrane, ed., *Remarkable Occurrences,* Canberra, National Library of Australia, 2001, pp. 183-197.

[57] National Library of Australia, *Australia's Oral History Collections,* available at: http://www.nla.gov.au/ohdir/about.html; and Francis Good, 'Technology and oral history at the Northern Territory Archives Service', in *Archives in the Tropics,* op. cit., pp. 60-66.

[58] Peter Cochrane, 'Rescuing "The Sentimental Bloke"', in Peter Cochrane, ed., *Remarkable Occurrences,* Canberra, National Library of Australia, 2001, pp. 78-80; Graham Shirley, 'Activism Towards a National Film Archive', *Cinema Papers,* July 1984; Ray Edmondson, 'Sacrilege or Synthesis? An Exploration of the Philosophy of Audiovisual Archiving', *Archives and Manuscripts,* 23, no. 1, 1995, pp. 18-29; and Ray Edmondson, 'A Case of Mistaken Identity: Governance, Guardianship and the ScreenSound Saga', *Archives and Manuscripts,* 30, no, 1, 2002, pp. 30-46.

of the World Wide Web to help identify and disseminate qualitative and quantitative statistical data sets for secondary use research and learning.

Unlike their public records counterparts, collecting archives programs have been little troubled by existential dilemmas caused by the need to either combine or choose between the often conflicting roles of supporting a bureaucracy, enabling democratic accountability and supporting cultural/historical endeavour. The collecting archives' sole *raison d'être* is a cultural/historical one. In this, they have much in common with museums, which are themselves significant players in the collecting and preserving of archival materials in Australia.[59] For instance, one of the country's best-known museums, the Australian War Memorial in Canberra, also acts as a collecting archive and as a repository of Commonwealth records relating to Australia's various military endeavours.[60] The expansion in funding for archival collecting activities during the 1950s and 1960s provides ample evidence of the value Australian society placed on the pursuit of this role by means of collecting.[61] Today the funding and relative fortunes of the collecting programs may not appear as impressive as they were during this earlier period of rapid growth. This is in part a reflection of declining support for academic history coupled with changes in historiographical philosophy, which nowadays places less emphasis on finding 'truth' in source documents. Certainly the quantity of holdings, in terms of items and shelf metres, in Australia's various collecting archives today is dwarfed by that of the public records institutions. Nevertheless, the collecting archives enterprise in Australia today remains impressively robust and continues to enjoy good public support and a reasonable, though sometimes uncertain, level of funding, including the provision of taxation incentives for donors in the form of the Commonwealth Government's Cultural Gifts Program. In the field of science and technology the work of collecting archives is also complemented by the long-standing contributions of the Australian Science and Technology Heritage Centre (first established as the Australian Science Archives Project in 1985), based at the University of Melbourne. This non-collecting archival documentation program locates, identifies, describes and publicizes significant archival material relating to scientific endeavour in Australia and, when necessary, arranges for the preservation of such records by a suitable collecting organization.[62]

The distributed national collection of private records in Australia is, however, not without problems. Graeme Powell has highlighted the lopsided nature of these holdings – the fact that certain areas of activity such as politics and literature are very well represented, while other significant areas of human endeavour in Australia are grossly under-represented.[63]

---

[59] Bruce Smith, 'Archives in Museums', *Archives and Manuscripts*, 23, no. 1, 1995, pp. 38-47.
[60] Anne-Marie Schwirtlich, 'The Australian War Memorial and Commonwealth Records, 1942-1952', in Sue McKemmish and Michael Piggott, eds, *The Records Continuum*, Clayton, Ancora Press in association with Australian Archives, 1994, pp. 18-34.
[61] Suzanne Fairbanks, 'Social Warrants for Collective Memory: Case Studies of Australian Collecting Archives', Master of Arts (Archives and Records) Thesis, Monash University, 1999.
[62] See the Centre's website at: http://www.austehc.unimelb.edu.au/
[63] Powell, op. cit.; and Marie-Louise Ayres, 'Evaluating the Archives: 20th Century Australian Literature', *Archives and Manuscripts*, 29, no. 2, 2001, pp. 32-47.

Doubtless a contributing factor to this is the ad hoc acquisitions policies of the various collecting programs, a problem accentuated by a lack of a centrally coordinated national archival system,[64] such as exists in many other countries. The fostering of such a system is in fact a legislatively mandated, but largely ignored, responsibility of the National Archives of Australia. This malaise has its roots in Australia's federal system of government and lingering colonial/states rights issues. Arguably, a contributing factor is the National Archives' apparent view that its core responsibilities begin and end with Commonwealth records, while lingering historical tension and competition between the National Archives and the National Library may also have been an important factor for many years.

Business archives in Australia

At the beginning of this chapter it was argued that many archives combine multiple roles. Good examples of this can be found in Australian business and university archives. Mention has already been made in our examination of collecting archives of the University of Melbourne Archives and the ANU's Archives of Business and Labour (now called the Noel Butlin Archives Centre). Both archives were established with the main aim of collecting the records of Australian businesses, primarily to serve the needs of economic historians. In ANU's case this occurred at the instigation of historian Noel Butlin, while in Melbourne the initiative came from one of the most interesting and significant groups ever to exert an influence on recordkeeping in Australia, the Business Archives Council of Australia (BACA).

BACA was established at the University of Sydney in 1954 and was modelled on the British Records Association. It brought together historians, archivists, librarians and businessmen with the aim of promoting awareness amongst the business community of the importance of and methods for preserving valuable business records in order to support the pursuit of business history. Initially the aim of BACA was to encourage good recordkeeping within companies, including the establishment of in-house archives. The collecting of business records by other organizations was very much an afterthought. A Victorian Branch of BACA was established in 1957 at the suggestion of the ubiquitous and indefatigable Harold White. White used his contacts with senior Melbourne librarians, history professors and captains of industry to assemble a formidable alliance of business archives advocates. Inevitably, White was attracted to this endeavour by the prospect of eventually enriching the National Library's collection with the records of some of Australia's leading businesses. This collecting aim was, however, a longer term objective. To achieve that objective White recognized that the collecting archives had to both establish a positive working relationship with the potential donors and also provide immediate assistance to businesses to ensure that the most valuable records were properly identified and managed by their creators in the short term. By emphasizing the business benefits of the latter to his corporate audience White hoped to also achieve the former – a

---

[64] Adrian Cunningham, 'From Here to Eternity: Collecting Archives and the Need for a National Documentation Strategy', *LASIE*, 29, no. 1, 1998, pp. 32-45.

positive working relationship that could lead to later donations of records from the corporate sector.[65]

The Victorian Branch of BACA was based at the University of Melbourne, where historians like John La Nauze and Geoffrey Serle decided that Melbourne should emulate the collecting efforts that Noel Butlin was energetically pursuing in Canberra. Before long, Harold White found himself in collecting competition with not one, but two university archives. Eventually White agreed that the National Library would leave the collecting of business archives to the universities, but the concession was not granted without a bitter struggle. In the meantime White, Frank Strahan (inaugural University of Melbourne Archivist) and others had pursued a campaign under the auspices of BACA to educate businessmen in the fundamentals of professional records management, using the argument that good recordkeeping is good for business. This was a rare and relatively successful example of archivists with overriding cultural/historical objectives adopting and pursuing objectives associated with supporting the business needs of organizations.[66]

The innovative adoption of a dual historical/administrative role by archivists operating in a private sector records environment proved to be quite successful, especially considering the relatively low level of total resources that constituted the combination of BACA and the two university archives. A survey of the state of Australian business archives conducted by Simon Ville and Grant Fleming in the late 1990s found a remarkably high retention rate of archives of Australia's top companies for the first sixty to seventy years of the twentieth century – preserved either by in-house archives such as the Archives of Westpac Bank or BHP Billiton or by collecting archives.[67] It is not unreasonable to attribute this success, at least in part, to the work of BACA and the major collecting archives. Sadly, they and others have noted an alarming decrease in the preservation of significant Australian business records dating from the early 1970s after BACA had effectively ceased to operate, a situation that may also reflect a decline in interest in economic history in the tertiary education sector.[68]

Educational and religious archives in Australia

The significance of the role of two university-based collecting archives, the Noel Butlin Archives Centre and the University of Melbourne Archives, has already been discussed in some detail. Similar collecting programs have also been established at university archives in Wollongong and Newcastle and at the University of New England in Armidale and

---

[65] Fairbanks, op. cit., pp. 61-67.

[66] Ibid., pp. 77-85.

[67] Simon Ville and Grant Fleming, 'Locating Australian Corporate Memory', *Business History Review*, 73, 1999, pp. 256-64; and D. Terwiel, S.P. Ville and G.A. Fleming, *Australian Business Records,* Canberra, Department of Economic History, Australian National University, 1998.

[68] Kathryn Dan and Bruce Smith, 'Where Have all the [Business] Archives Gone?', in *Archives at Risk*, op. cit.; and Colleen Pritchard, 'Survey of business records', *Archives and Manuscripts*, 15, no 2, 1987, pp. 139-148.

Charles Sturt University in Wagga Wagga, each of which adopt a regional emphasis in their collecting programs.[69] The University of Queensland's Fryer Library has for many years collected records associated with literary endeavour in Australia as, more recently, has the Australian Defence Force Academy's Library in Canberra. These university-based collecting archives are generally the product of the energies of enthusiastic and committed individuals responsible for the creation and continued existence of collections that relate to their research interests. In theory they exist primarily to support the research and teaching activities of the university concerned, although in practice their continued existence often relies on patronage and is, as a consequence, tenuous.

Equally precarious is the existence of in-house university archives responsible for the universities' own records. While most of Australia's thirty-eight publicly funded universities have records officers and/or records managers, they do not always have an in-house archives. Those in-house archives that do exist find themselves in a variety of structural reporting arrangements, with some reporting to the university librarian and others associated with the administrative/chancelry arm of the university. In many cases the in-house archives that do exist are severely under-resourced. As a result of recent legislative changes in some State jurisdictions, university recordkeeping requirements are now more formally mandated, with the relevant State Archives exercising overall responsibility for setting recordkeeping standards and authorizing the destruction of university records.

Some university archives combine a collecting and an in-house function. Don Boadle has argued that this marriage is not always a successful one, with university administrators and in some cases the archivists themselves being unable to articulate a clear and compelling mission for a unified archival program. Indeed, in some cases it could be argued that the combined function has resulted in an identity crisis that suggests the worst of both worlds rather than the best of both worlds.[70] As with many of their State and Commonwealth Archives colleagues, these archivists have struggled to achieve consensus on the value of simultaneously pursuing legal, administrative, cultural and accountability roles, much less consensus on how such an integrated vision might actually be pursued and achieved in an environment where support from senior university administrators is often ambivalent at best. Moves towards a national or even State-based strategy in this area will, if past experience is any guide, struggle in the face of the tendency by universities to guard their independence and autonomy with jealousy and vigour.

---

[69] Don Boadle, 'Origins and Development of the New South Wales Regional Repositories System', *Archives and Manuscripts*, 23, no. 2, 1995, pp. 274-288; and 'Documenting 20th Century Rural and Regional Australia: Archival Acquisition and Collection Development in Regional University Archives and Special Collections', *Archives and Manuscripts*, 29, no. 2, 2001, pp. 64-81.
[70] Don Boadle, 'Australian University Archives and Their Prospects', *Australian Academic and Research Libraries*, 30, no. 3, 1999, pp. 153-170; 'Australian University Archives and Their Management of the Records Continuum 1953-1997', in Peter Crush, ed., *Archives and Reform – Preparing for Tomorrow*, op. cit., pp. 247-255; and 'Archives at the Edge? Australian University Archives and the Challenge of the New Information Age', in *Place, Interface and Cyberspace: Archives at the Edge – Proceedings of the Australian Society of Archivists Conference, Fremantle, 6-8 August 1998*, Canberra, ASA, 1999, pp. 73-82.

Finally, to conclude this examination of the types of archival institutions in Australia, there exist a very large number of in-house archival programs in Australia's various independent (non-government) schools and religious organizations. These programs are often staffed by part-time and/or volunteer staff and struggle to attain resourcing commensurate with the scope of their operations.[71] Church archives house records of dioceses, parishes and/or religious orders. In recent years their work has been thrust into the spotlight because of the role churches played in the now controversial and emotive issues of child migration and the Aboriginal 'stolen generations'. Access policies of these archives have been greatly tested in the context of the churches coming to terms with their role in these unfortunate episodes of Australian history and their relationships with aggrieved individuals who were separated from their families and often badly mistreated in the hands of church officials.[72]

Archives as a place and virtual archives

Throughout the ages one of the regularly recurring functions of archival institutions is to provide a secure place for the safekeeping of valuable records to guarantee the ongoing legal authenticity of those records. This is especially common for archives that serve solely or primarily a legal/administrative role, where control and possession of the records is recognized as a source of power. Luciana Duranti has highlighted the importance of this function in archives stretching back to the days of the Justinian Code and the Tabularium in Ancient Rome, while Michel Duchein has identified the same issue as being important to archives in Flanders and Hungary. One of Sir Hilary Jenkinson's more influential contributions to the archival discourse is the related notion of the need to guarantee an uninterrupted transmission of custody from records creator to archival institution – the physical and moral defence of the record. Duranti has argued that when records 'cross the archival threshold' they are attested to be authentic and henceforth guaranteed to be preserved as such by an archives that is independent from the records creating office and for which the preservation of the authenticity of its holdings is its *raison d'être*.[73]

While this is a common theme in the history of archival institutions, it is not a universal one. Duchein has argued that there are many countries in which the notion has never existed, including France 'where the fact of its being preserved in a public archival repository does not give a document any guarantee of authenticity'.[74] Similarly, while the preservation of authenticity is undoubtedly an objective of most collecting/historical

---

[71] Jan Riley, 'Integrating Archival Programs into the Core Business of the Independent School', *Archives and Manuscripts*, 25, no. 1, 1997, pp. 50-61.

[72] Australia. Parliament. Senate Legal and Constitutional Committee, *Healing: A Legacy of Generations, The Report of the Inquiry into the Federal Government's Implementation of the Recommendations Made by the Human Rights and Equal Opportunity Commission*, Canberra, 2000; Kirsten Thorpe, 'Indigenous Records: How Far Have We Come in Bringing the History Back Home?', *Archives and Manuscripts*, 29, no. 2, 2001, p. 28.

[73] Duranti, 1996, op. cit.; Duchein, 1992, op. cit., p. 15; Hilary Jenkinson, *A Manual for Archive Administration*, Oxford, Clarendon Press, 1922.

[74] Duchein, 1992, op. cit., p. 15.

archives programs, it cannot be said to be their *raison d'être*. More recently, archivists who agree with Duranti and Jenkinson about the absolute importance of guaranteeing the authenticity of records, have disagreed with Duranti's argument that this can only be achieved by means of archival institutions taking physical custody of the records. To these critics adequate control of records to guarantee authenticity in the digital age can be achieved without the need for archives to provide a physical place of safekeeping. In the digital age the very physicality of records is superseded by a virtual concept or 'performance' where the idea of a record having a set physical location becomes meaningless. Records continuum theorists also object to the notion of records crossing an 'archival threshold' at some point in time after their creation. To these critics the 'archival bond' and subsequent guarantees of authenticity should commence at the point of records creation which, by definition, cannot be physically in the archives. If the archival bond is achieved and guaranteed at the point of records creation the decision when or whether to perform a physical act of custodial transfer to an archives becomes a minor administrative consideration, not a matter of central significance.[75]

Figure 2.2. 'This temple of our history will appropriately be one of the most beautiful buildings in America, an expression of the American soul.' (Herbert Hoover, 20 February 1933 at the laying of the foundation stone of the National Archives building, Washington D.C.)

---

[75] Terry Cook, 'Electronic Records, Paper Minds: The revolution in information management and archives in the post-custodial and post-modernist era', *Archives and Manuscripts*, 22, no. 2, 1994, pp. 300-328; Frank Upward and Sue McKemmish, 'Somewhere Beyond Custody', *Archives and Manuscripts*, 22, no. 1, 1994, pp. 136-149; F. Gerald Ham, 'Archival Strategies for the Post-Custodial Era', *American Archivist*, 44, Summer 1981, pp. 207-216; and Margaret Hedstrom, 'Archives as Repositories: A Commentary', in *Archival Management of Electronic Records, Archives and Museum Informatics Technical Report no. 13*, Pittsburgh, 1992.

Another strand to this topic is the architectural use of archival buildings to make symbolic statements about the role and significance of archives in society. Many archival buildings throughout the ages have architectural features suggestive of solidity, impenetrability, durability and authority. Indeed, such featurism is so common as to be almost a cliché – something which itself speaks volumes about perceptions of archival institutions. Recent, more imaginative architectural representations of the form and function of archives, such as the Gatineau Preservation Centre in Canada, have attempted to convey an image of archives as 'the epitome of liberal-humanist and objective-scientific activity', but perhaps unwittingly reflect instead the ultimately indeterminate and mutable nature of the archival pursuit.[76]

Figure 2.3. The National Archives of Canada's Gatineau Preservation Centre, Quebec, opened in 1997.

One feature of the 'archives as a place' debate has been the perhaps naïve assertion by the post-custodialists that technological change has made it possible, indeed essential, for digital records to be archivally captured, described and controlled in such a way as to

---

[76] Lilly Koltun, 'The Architecture of Archives: Whose Form, What Functions?', *Archival Science*, 2, no. 3/4, 2002, pp. 239-261.

guarantee the authenticity and integrity of the records from the instant of creation onwards. Perhaps the closest archivists have yet come to achieving this vision is with the 'VERS encapsulated objects' of the Victorian Electronic Records Strategy (VERS). The fact remains, however, that the assertion remains an unproven – though appealing – hypothesis.

Ultimately, different archives will make their own choices as to how important guarantees of authenticity are and, if they are considered vital, which strategies they feel will give them the best chance of achieving that objective. Certainly, the post-custodialists argue for a more proactive and virtual 'archives without walls' as an antidote to the traditional passive custodial view, although there is no reason why a custodial approach could not also be combined with a more proactive role. Jeannette Bastian has recently argued that (distributed) custody and authenticity should not be ends in themselves as argued by Duranti and Jenkinson, but rather the means to a more important end – that of facilitating use of the archives by those who stand to benefit from such activity.[77] As Frank Upward has argued, 'the externalities of place are becoming less significant day-by-day … the location of the resources and services will be of no concern to those using them'.[78] In the online world the development of virtual archives is not only desirable, but also essential for continued relevance and survival. Users will wish to be assured of authenticity, but will not care less about the existence of or necessity for places of custody. It may still be too early in the digital age to know which of the opposing sides in the post-custodial/archives-as-a-place debate is right, or if indeed the debate is even a relevant one. It will, however, be interesting to watch as archival institutions respond to new virtual access opportunities, learn from their experiences and confirm or modify their philosophies and strategies accordingly.

Conclusion

We have seen how archives in different times and in different places take different forms, pursue different strategies and different combinations of objectives. We have seen that these differences can be explained with reference to the political and cultural environment in which archives exist and the objectives of those who own, control or are responsible for the existence of the archives. We have seen that archives are not passive, objective and 'neutral repositories of facts', but rather active and subjective participants in and shapers of political and cultural power relations.[79] The power to decide which records constitute the archives and, conversely, which records do not, coupled with the power to determine who can have access to the archives are powers that can be used for good or for bad. Usually, they are used by those who control the archives to support and bolster their own political and economic position, views and mythologies. In democracies, however, there is at least

---

[77] Jeannette A. Bastian, 'Taking Custody, Giving Access: A Postcustodial Role for a New Century', *Archivaria*, 53, 2002, pp. 76-93.

[78] Frank Upward, 'Structuring the Records Continuum Part One: Post-custodial principles and properties', *Archives and Manuscripts*, 24, no. 2, 1996, p. 282.

[79] Joan M. Schwartz and Terry Cook, 'Archives, Records, and Power: The Making of Modern Memory', *Archival Science*, 2, 2002, pp. 1-19.

the potential for archives to act as enablers of citizen empowerment and democratic accountability and transparency – a potential that unfortunately remains more latent than actual in most cases. While public records archives in democratic nations should be substantially independent from the executive government of the day, so that they can play a proactive role in ensuring the accountability of that government, most such archives are in fact a part of executive government and enjoy only limited independence. This suggests that the main role of these archives is to serve the legal, administrative and culture constructing objectives of the government, rather than any truly democratic purpose. Even in democracies, governments do not surrender lightly the power of archival consignation.

We have also seen that the political and social purposes of archives are never eternal. These purposes are always being contested, reconsidered, reinvented and transformed, reflecting the judgments of and changing power relations in society. This was seen most dramatically as a result of the French Revolution, but there are other notable examples, such as the transformation of archives in post-Apartheid South Africa, in post-Communist Eastern Europe and in post-Colonial Asia and the Pacific. We have also seen that archives that were originally established to serve the narrow legal, economic and administrative purposes of a ruling elite can also be transformed and reinvented to serve broader cultural objectives of society – objectives that are themselves eternally subject to contestation and reinvention.[80]

The consequences of these lessons depend on your values and perspectives. From this author's perspective the best archives are those that serve broad social, cultural and democratic accountability purposes. In reality, we have seen that such archives often struggle to emerge from or succeed within a governance environment that does not place high value on such purposes. In more tightly controlled and less democratic environments archives that serve the narrow political, legal, economic and symbolic objectives of the ruling elite will generally enjoy greater funding, support and patronage. As we have seen, however, circumstances can change. Any archives are better than no archives and those which today serve a narrow set of power interests may tomorrow be reinvented to serve broader social and democratic interests. The key is for archivists to understand the roles that they play and to remain ever alert and sensitive to the political and social dynamics in which their archives operates. Archivists should always be ready to take advantage of changing circumstances that may permit their archives to serve more pluralistic, socially inclusive and democratically empowering roles.

Discussion of the role of archives as enablers of democratic transparency and accountability cannot ignore the issue of archival accountability and transparency. If the archives should

---

[80] Verne Harris, 'The Archival Sliver: Power, Memory, and Archives in South Africa', *Archival Science*, 2, 2002, pp. 63-86; Ann Laura Stoler, 'Colonial Archives and the Arts of Governance', *Archival Science*, 2, 2002, pp. 87-109; Friedrich P. Kahlenberg, 'Democracy and Federalism: Changes in the National Archival System in a United Germany', *American Archivist*, 55, Winter 1992, pp. 72-85; Imre Ress, 'The Effects of Democratization on Archival Administration and Use in Eastern Middle Europe', *American Archivist*, 55, Winter 1992, pp. 86-93; and Patricia Kennedy Grimstead, 'Beyond *Perestroika*: Soviet-Area Archives after the August Coup', *American Archivist*, 55, Winter 1992, pp. 94-124.

help to hold a government accountable, to whom is the archives accountable? The answer should be the wider community. Unfortunately, however, most archives have a long distance still to travel before they can claim to practise what they preach with regard to transparency and accountability for their own politically charged decisions and activities. Too often archives and archivists are guilty of making their decisions behind closed doors and justifying their actions with spurious claims of sacrosanct professionalism and scientific objectivity. The first steps for archives in a democracy to become truly effective enablers of transparency and accountability are for this role to be effectively communicated to and understood by the wider community and for the archives itself to become fully transparent and accountable for its own operations and decisions.

Depending on their social and political circumstances and on their own choices and actions, archives can pursue missions that can either hinder or assist society in being civil, pluralistic, open, just and democratic. To sum up the alternatives in the form of haikus, the question is should:

> *Archives bolster and*
> *perpetuate the power*
> *of ruling elites*

or should

> *Archivists help our*
> *society to tell stories*
> *about itself*

and

> *Archives nurture and*
> *sustain the soul and conscience*
> *of human beings?*

Readings

- Ernst Posner, *Archives in the Ancient World*, Cambridge, Mass., Harvard University Press, 1972.

  The definitive text on the development of archival institutions in the ancient world.

- Judith M. Panitch, 'Liberty, Equality, Posterity?: Some Archival Lessons from the Case of the French Revolution', *American Archivist*, 59, Winter 1996, pp. 30-47.

  Using the pivotal example of the French Revolution, this article illustrates how archival institutions are the mutable and contestable products of their time.

- Luke J. Gilliland-Swetland, 'The Provenance of a Profession: The Permanence of the Public Archives and Historical Manuscripts Traditions in American Archival History', *American Archivist*, 54, Spring 1991, pp. 160-175.

  Traces the origins and history of the split between public records institutions and those working in the so-called 'Historical Manuscripts Tradition' in the United States and considers the implications of the existence of these very different views of the role and functions of archival institutions.

- Michael Piggott, 'Beginnings', in Sue McKemmish and Michael Piggott, eds, *The Records Continuum: Ian Maclean and Australian Archives First Fifty Years*, Clayton, Ancora Press in association with Australian Archives, 1994, pp. 1-17.

  Surveys the activities that culminated in the establishment in the 1940s of the organization that is today called the National Archives of Australia.

- Suzanne Fairbanks, 'Social Warrants for Collective Memory: Case Studies of Australian Collecting Archives', Master of Arts (Archives and Records) Thesis, Monash University, 1999.

  Examines the activities that informed the development of key collecting archives institutions in Australia during the 1950s and 1960s, exploring the warrants and mandates that gave impetus to these archival programs.

CHAPTER 3

Professing archives: A very human enterprise[1]

Ann E. Pederson

Every person who has mastered a profession is a sceptic concerning it. (George Bernard Shaw)

Homo sapiens is the only species on earth that systematically documents its thoughts and activities by making and keeping records. Whilst some other species may also use language-like communication and tools, form complex social relationships and navigate over long distances, humans alone have devised a system of external 'memory' to multiply their intelligence and ingenuity. As human enterprise became larger and more complex, robust yet flexible and trustworthy means for recording, sharing and keeping important information across time and distance became vital.

Today, recordkeeping provides the intellectual infrastructure that underpins all human endeavours. Networks of records enable us to remember our past, organize our present, plan our future, and share our cultures across space and time. They underpin our presumptuous dominance of earth's resources and all other species sharing them. Records insulate our societies from dementia, ensure their continuity and balance and enable us to realise both the best and the worst in ourselves. The components of an ideal society, freedom, responsibility, accountability, integrity, industry and justice, cannot exist without effective recordkeeping support.

As recordkeeping is one of the most ubiquitous aspects of modern society, almost every process we undertake – working, studying, shopping, driving, dining, communicating by email or telephone – generates or involves some form of record. Furthermore, we all participate in this recordkeeping and so are de facto recordkeepers, though few of us are aware of this role. However, in this chapter, we are concentrating on those of us who

---

[1] The views presented are largely products of the author's own Australian-American experience and research, informed and tempered by the opinions of other educators and discipline leaders as expressed in English-language literature. Because recordkeeping specialists hold as many views about their profession as they have interests and contexts of practice, this chapter aims to summarize and comment upon the dominant Anglophone discourse on the topic and to evoke further discussion from colleagues around the world.

undertake the design and management of recordkeeping systems and service regimes as their paid work. Recordkeeping specialists oversee the infrastructure – the principles, standards, policies, plans, guidelines and technologies – and provide the advice and support that enables people in different contexts to produce and safeguard the documentation they require to meet their personal, business, regulatory and cultural needs in and through time and space.

As we begin the twenty-first century, recordkeeping specialists around the world are engaged in intensive self-examination – studying their professional origins and patterns of development, exploring their social and organizational roles, and defining their domain of knowledge and skills. Other authors have explored the nature of records and recordkeeping in society from a range of different perspectives. This chapter turns the spotlight on both those who 'profess' to provide recordkeeping services as their major work and on the nature of their communities of practice.

Understanding professions and professionalization

Professionalization of occupations has been widespread in English-speaking countries over the last hundred years. Essentially both of the modern concepts of professionalism and recordkeeping came into currency during the second half of the nineteenth century and embodied the nobler aspirations of that age. The heady mix of logical positivism, scientific methodology and progressivism underpinned society's belief in continuous improvement through self-regulation, thus enabling excellence in governance, commerce and culture.

Professionalization is the process by which a socially significant occupation organizes itself to ensure its practitioners perform their services well and thereby earn a larger share of societal respect and reward. Members of professions pledge themselves to ongoing performance monitoring and improvement regimes that set out standards regulating behaviour, expertise and standards of practice. For someone to be professional means they 'profess' that they are trustworthy, possess appropriate specialist knowledge and skills, and aspire to excellence in performing their work. Professions and professionalization promote distinctiveness and reliability amid the homogenizing complexity and interdependence of modern life.

A profession is

> a vocation whose practice is founded upon an understanding of the theoretical structure of some department of learning or science, and upon the abilities accompanying such understanding. This understanding and these abilities are applied to the vital practical affairs of man. The practices of a profession are modified by knowledge of a generalized nature and by the accumulated wisdom and experience of mankind, which serve to correct the errors of specialism. The

profession, serving the vital needs of man, considers its first ethical imperative to be altruistic service to the client.[2]

Occupations choose the professionalization path to attain societal kudos, but, in doing so, their members agree to subject their own attitudes, skills and conduct to the discipline of verifiable expertise, collective rules and constraints. This aspect of professional status, the voluntary tempering of individuality, is a prerequisite to forging a professional identity, mission and core knowledge base that society can recognise. If members of an occupation do not meet this challenge, their professional ambitions will not be realized. Achieving professional cohesion is an important issue for recordkeeping specialists and will be revisited later in the chapter.

Researchers who study social organization generally use two types of indicators or models of professionalism to distinguish between an occupation and a profession. The first model researches the presence or absence of key attributes or characteristics of professions. These comprise claiming and transmitting a specialist core of knowledge, community endorsement and sanction, organized cohesion, 'structural altruism', i.e. asserting a role for client benefit and society's good, and autonomy coupled with self-regulation.

The second model measures the process known as professionalization – key activities benchmarking the extent to which an occupation has transformed itself into a profession and realized commensurate societal status, privileges and rewards. In both models, professional status ranges across a continuum of possibilities to a full profession. In the final analysis, whether an occupation is a profession or not depends upon the extent of autonomy and privileges society in general gives to it. There is some self-fulfilling logic at work here: if most people in a society think an occupation is a profession, it is.

While the 'classic' professions – academe, medicine, law and religion – established themselves in antiquity, most fields claiming professional status have achieved recognition within the past hundred or so years, for example accountancy, architecture, education, engineering, pharmacy and veterinary science. In addition, there are a number of fields that are still undergoing professionalization, fighting to recover lost status or nurturing professional aspirations. These semi-, or *part*, professions, and proto-, or *aspiring*, professions such as IT, journalism, librarianship, nursing and social work, are of particular interest as most recordkeeping specializations in the newer Anglophone countries have this status.[3]

---

[2] Morris L. Cogan, 'Toward a Definition of Profession', *Harvard Educational Review,* 23, Winter 1953, pp. 33-50.

[3] Placement of disciplines into categories is based on the author's understanding of Howard M. Vollmer and Donald L. Mills, *Professionalization*, Englewood Cliffs, NJ, Prentice-Hall, 1966, pp. 2-33; Amitai Etzioni, ed., *The Semi-Professions and Their Organization,* New York, NY, The Free Press, 1969; Kenneth S. Lynn and the editors of *Daedalus, The Professions in America*, Boston, Mass, Beacon Press, 1965; U.S. Department of Labor, Bureau of Labor Statistics, *Occupational Outlook Handbook,* available at: http://stats.bls.gov/oco/oco1002.htm, accessed 16 December 2002.

Building a profession: The journey so far

While the necessity for recordkeeping in society has always been acknowledged, its role, importance and commensurate status in the workplace and in the wider community rises, falls and grows more complex over time. The very use of the words *recordkeeping* and *recordkeepers* to identify the enterprise of making and keeping records over time, and to distinguish those engaged in it, is new to the English language. In fact, these terms have come into being so recently, and are still so limited in use, that they do not yet appear in any authoritative dictionary. So why are we using such terms? Because they are the most accurate terms to describe an emerging profession that encompasses all the records, archives and manuscript management responsibilities performed by the constituent specialities of archivists, records managers and manuscripts curators.

In the early literate societies of the ancient world, recordkeeping was an elite function underpinning political, military, commercial and religious power. The making and keeping of records were conjoined activities, undertaken and managed at the highest levels of authority. Education was limited and men who combined superior administrative skills with literacy attained positions of pre-eminent trust, rank and wealth. However, population expansion and ever more complex societal relations led to improved access to education, which in turn raised the level of literacy and expanded the career opportunities in recordkeeping. By early modern times, recordkeeping documented most important relationships concerned with the distribution of wealth and privilege in western societies. Apprenticing oneself as a clerk (then a synonym for recordkeeper) in service to the church, a legal firm, a government office or a commercial establishment improved the prospects of many a working-class young man.

Part of the explanation for modern recordkeeping's mixed fortunes lies in the professional separation of record-*making* from record-*keeping* which occurred gradually as modernity transformed western societies, punctuated by the French Revolution as a 'watershed' event. In France, the Revolutionary Directorate effectively 'closed the files' of the Old Regime, designating them to be kept as inactive or 'historical' archives, and set up a new order of administrative record-making for the emerging Republic. The split in other contexts was more gradual and came about as the complexity of affairs, populations and literacy grew, increasing the need to formalize transactions via records. Infrequently consulted older records were unceremoniously removed from office recordkeeping systems into isolated vaults and mostly forgotten. This separation induced an occupational schizophrenia that was exacerbated by the rise of bureaucracies and of scientific management accompanied by shifts in workplace role, gender and status. The record*makers* gradually devolved into functionaries ruled by bureaucrats and bound by detailed procedures and regulations for organizing and retrieving files, whilst policy and program decision-making was commandeered by an emerging elite of professional managers. The record*keepers* evolved into a more scholarly class, increasingly absorbed with diplomatics, palaeography and historical research and located at a distance from the corridors of power.

This truncation also occurred in the United States of America following its successful war for independence from Britain and its effects were aggravated further by three factors: a rejection of things associated with the perceived tyranny and corruption of the Old World, i.e. English and European recordkeeping systems/practices, a fierce and localized individualism and a general view of recordkeeping as pedantic paper shuffling. The documentary heritage of this new federal republic was scattered and generally neglected for the first century, during which fragments of it were intermittently collected and occasionally published by a few historians and manuscript collector/librarians. Thus the emergence of recognized records/ archives management profession in the USA was delayed until the mid-twentieth century.[4]

In Britain there was also a division between administrative and scholarly domains, even though public records moved from office- to repository-based upon administrative judgment. The public service administrator was the 'records/archives manager' exercising intellectual authority over the policies and processes of record-making and keeping, while those who implemented the policies/procedures were registry functionaries. Older records of enduring value were transferred to public records office repositories, largely staffed by keepers, i.e. archivists, expert in their understanding of the form, content and context of historic texts. However, lack of official concern and inadequate funding for public records management was, and continues to be, endemic, as periodic special commission reports attest.[5]

In Australia, the local copies of older records from colonial times were often housed in the colonial, and later state, public libraries, which supplemented this official record by acquiring private papers, manuscripts and works of art from leading individuals and families. As a result, in Australia, historically oriented librarians performed the function of keepers until an archival specialty evolved to independence in the 1960s and 1970s. Although the sorting out of functions and spheres of authority among the older state and the newer commonwealth bodies, and between the collecting libraries and dedicated archival authorities will engage the Australian community for years to come, a hybrid recordkeeping enterprise and identity has accelerated its process of becoming over the past decade.[6]

---

[4] H.G. Jones, *Local Government Records,* Nashville, TN, American Association for State and Local History, 1980, chapters 1 and 2; Richard C. Berner, *Archival Theory and Practice in the United States,* Seattle, University of Washington Press, 1983; Richard J. Cox, *Closing an Era,* Westport, CT, Greenwood, 2000, pp. 1-44.
[5] Elizabeth M. Hallam and Michael Roper, 'The Capital and the Records of the Nation: Seven Centuries of Housing Public Records in London', *London Journal,* May 1978, pp. 73-94.
[6] Robert Sharman, 'Library Control of Archives', *Australian Library Journal,* 9, 1959, pp. 125-128; Michael Piggott, 'The History of Australian Recordkeeping: A Framework for Research', *Australian Library Journal,* 47, no. 4, 1998, pp. 343-354; Suzanne Fairbanks, 'Collecting Archives in the Electronic Age', in *Convergence 2001: Joint National Conference of the ASA and the RMAA, Hobart, September 2001,* available at:
https://www.rmaa.org.au/StaticContent/StaticPages/pubs/nat/natcon2001/section016.pdf

Recordkeeping heritage: Major strands of practice

In the first half of the twentieth century, the expansion of government regulation and services during the Great Depression and World Wars dramatically increased the volume and complexity of recordkeeping. An urgent need to develop effective management regimes, coinciding with improvements in mass education, communication and transport, provided a catalyst for those responsible for records to discuss common issues and problems more regularly. Concerned practitioners identified principles and responsibilities that distinguished records work from the 'parent' disciplines of librarianship, office administration and history, thus initiating the journey towards defining a recordkeeping identity.

By the 1960s, specialist recordkeepers in developed Anglophone countries had coalesced into proto-professional groups reflecting three strands of practice: special collections or manuscript librarianship, records management, and archives administration. Whilst all specializations 'kept records', their primary obligation to serve the needs and interests of individualistic employers meant that contextual pressures often made it difficult to reach consensus. Manuscript librarians serviced a growing 'knowledge industry', developing collections of records and other historical materials that reflected the interests of researchers and donors. The records managers operated regimes designed to meet the current business and regulatory requirements of their host organizations. Archives administrators protected and provided research access primarily to non-current records of long-term value. Those in the public sector had greater legal, social and cultural obligations than those in the private sector.

Manuscript librarianship strand: The collections legacy

The librarianship strand, through its manuscripts and rare book specialties, has been especially attentive to the intrinsic value of unique and rare materials, particularly with acquiring and making them known and available for use as research objects. Many records would not have survived had manuscripts librarians not collected or copied them for posterity. Furthermore, it has been the rare imprints such as the non-fiction books, gazetteers, broadsheets and newspapers down through the centuries that have partially filled the gaps after official records were lost or destroyed. Finally, all recordkeeping regimes utilize books and journals extensively in the conduct of their work and manage record sets of publications produced by their host organizations. In many cases, these published sources provide the core information of administrative histories. Similarly, all libraries make and manage records supporting their work and many collect holdings of manuscripts and archives.

Librarianship's society-wide mandate has given it a higher public profile, larger numbers and greater resources. Although far from wealthy or secure, public and academic libraries are seen as an integral part of the formal educational process and have the backing of powerful allies in the publishing, education and information technology industries. These attributes, plus librarianship's common interest in managing preservation, electronic information systems, local studies materials and oral history, make it a strong potential ally for records/archives managers.

Records management strand: The administrative legacy

The records management strand emerged during the 'management revolution' of the late nineteenth and early twentieth centuries which gradually divided the significant functions of office work into three segments: technical, operational and administrative. Within the third function, administration, lay the important infrastructure activity of records management which, influenced by management science and technological advances, gradually split into two, record-making and recordkeeping.

In the area of record-making, the substantive and highly valued aspects involved in creating the authoritative information or 'content' carried by the records were gradually subsumed by the emerging professional class of 'managers' across all three functions, technical, line and staff. The facilitative and essential, but increasingly routine, aspects were delegated downward to a growing army of menial, increasingly female workers who implemented established techniques to record, then distribute, store and retrieve the resulting records. However, as problems associated with the increasing volume and complexity of records systems and the proliferation of new office technologies developed, there emerged in the clerical stream, a quasi-professional class of office administrators who served as intermediaries between managers and the clerical rank-and-file. These super-clerks, empowered with extensive knowledge of the organization acquired through years of operating its information system and committed to facilitating the work of management, became the first de facto 'records managers'.

By the decade of the 1950s the importance of information to organizational effectiveness was gaining recognition as new record-making and recordkeeping technologies (electrostatic copiers, micrographics, and electric typewriters) began to penetrate the mainstream workplace. While owners and managers of organizations were keen to utilize these innovations to maintain growth and keep a competitive edge, they lacked the knowledge and experience to evaluate them. Thus the need to designate someone demonstrably capable and trustworthy to investigate them and ensure their orderly acceptance in the organization became urgent. Often the person selected would be the 'good and faithful' super-clerk described above. This role of two-way mediator between the management decision-makers and vendors of new technologies and between the management and the support staff who would use the new technologies, concentrated increasing power and influence into the hands of a stream of administrative officers operating under the job title records manager.

As controllers of the information infrastructure critical to the achievement of organizational objectives, this group continues to press for full acceptance into the professional management pantheon, an aspiration which has been hampered by a continuing perception of records managers as filing clerks, a reliance on short-term, or on-the-job, rather than tertiary training, and inter-industry and intra-industry rivalries that retard professional cohesion.

Traditionally, records managers have been most knowledgable about and involved with the creation, use and maintenance activities within their context of origin and focused on the primary use of records to support core business. They have also been foremost in disposal actions, implementing decisions and managing low-cost facilities for storing and servicing records prior to destruction or recycling. Their work is built upon knowledge of the host organization's goals, structure, workflow, information and other needs (security, economy, efficiency), and emphasizes, above all, service to advance and protect the interests of their employer. This focus demands attention to the requirements of regulatory authorities and promotes regular contact with in-house experts (accountants, legal officers) concerned with cost and risk management.

Archival administration strand: A double-edged inheritance

We have seen how, in the early nineteenth century, public recordkeeping activity was pragmatically separated into two operational domains: the office where records managers served the current needs of management; and the repository where archivists protected the evidence required for long-term organizational and cultural accountability and continuity and serviced the needs of the research community.

Through tertiary qualifications emphasizing culture and history, traditional archivists and, to some extent, manuscript librarians, have acquired the perspective, research methodology and values for understanding and exploiting archives as sources for wide-ranging research. Historical study also provides substantial background knowledge needed for mastery of the *content* of records and/or understanding those from a specific *context*.

The value of this historical legacy is threefold. First, good history demands rigorous research methodology, accuracy, objectivity and documentation of any opinions and interpretations drawn from a diversity of sources, especially reliable records. These skills are valuable in any context, not just those concerned with heritage or cultural concerns. Second, history enables and imposes the added dimensions of perspective over time and underscores the cultural importance of recordkeeping, i.e. recordkeeping professionals ensure evidence to promote responsibility, responsiveness, continuity and memory in society. The archivists interpreted this role as defending the cumulative human record against distortion by potential enemies in any single generation. Third, history commands a unique weapon – the emotional power inherent in cultural objects. As most cultural managers will attest, many a battle to purchase, restore or develop has been won by harnessing and focusing this energy succinctly.

Historical heritage also has its drawbacks. Undertaking historical research is often a solitary and guarded enterprise, seen by some as antithetical to approaches required by team-based management. Furthermore, the combined impact of this with the artificial separation of the intellectual and technical aspects of record-making and the further division of recordkeeping into separate repository and office domains had important consequences for archivists. The initial truncation of making from keeping removed the archives and archivists from regular contact with the ongoing managerial processes of creating offices, shifting their orientation from economy and efficiency in the present to caretakers of 'old stuff' – material no longer required for the conduct of mainstream business. The out-of-sight-out-of-mind isolation of repositories diminished managers' use of the archives and, correspondingly, their understanding of the value of them as essential corporate resources. This downward spiral has been termed the 'Cycle of Impoverishment', a vortex wherein marginalization results in fewer resources, undermines morale and degrades services. Often archival programs are lumped together with cash-strapped museums, historical societies, libraries and galleries as not-for-profit 'culture and heritage' bodies competing for decreasing public and philanthropic dollars. In worst-case scenarios, such archival operations may mirror the stereotype of an irrelevant 'boneyard of information' and be closed down.

Often feeling a bit isolated or devalued within their own organizations, archivists turned to each other for succour, celebrating together their wider cultural role as keepers of evidence of the past and reaching out to the academic and research communities for appreciation and support. As servants of scholarship, archivists nurtured relationships within the historical profession who dominated the search rooms of early archives and manuscript collections attached to great private or public libraries, historical societies and institutions of learning. Indeed, the traditional path to an archival career was completing tertiary study in some specialty of history, topped off with on-the-job or specialist training in a large, usually public, archival institution.

Cultivating academe did not always lead to more resources or to a better understood and satisfying professional status. The overarching archival 'mission' exposes archivists to a maelstrom of competing responsibilities, protecting the interests of records creators and depositors vs. safeguarding the evidence of organizational and cultural accountability vs. promoting the search for historical truths vs. keeping one's job. Archivists can be regarded with confusion and some apprehension by record creators, organization managers – particularly those responsible for allocating resources to the archives, researchers and colleagues in related professions such as records management. Being too academic, not team players and not having the welfare of the current organization foremost are common complaints made by internal critics. In short, lack of harmony among key groups whose cooperation and good will is vital for success can compromise archival interests.

Traditional roles and relationships

Historically, books have been associated with libraries, records with 'filing' in offices and archives with caring for cultural heritage objects held in repositories, making achieving recognition of a comprehensive recordkeeping professional identity protracted and difficult. Whilst most of us have used libraries and visited museums in the course of our lives and formal education, mostly we have only vague notions of how the work of professional recordkeepers and their workplaces compares with these more familiar institutions. Important differences in expertise, methods and materials are frequently overlooked by managers who perceive recordkeeping, librarianship and curatorial duties as more or less the same.

For recordkeeping specialists, whose functions have sometimes been combined with those of related but different information disciplines, understanding how the recordkeeping mission is both distinctive and complementary becomes vital to success. The ability to distinguish what is unique and what is shared with kindred institutions and professions both defines their own identity and defines those with whom they share a similar purpose.

The separate strands of recordkeeping practice have hampered professional cohesion in several ways. For example, records managers view disposal as cleansing the system of obsolete material and minimizing the legal and financial liabilities of their organizations. Archivists see it as the orderly process of building organizational memory and satisfying societal requirements for corporate and cultural accountability. Librarians are primarily interested in having cultural evidence accessible to a wide range of researchers, an aim that may not be supported by those who generated the records. Some records managers view archivists and librarians as out of touch with the realities of administrative and regulatory recordkeeping. Repository-based archivists feel that their holdings of 'old stuff' and physical isolation unfairly limit their participation in organizational management. Librarians express impatience with records managers and archivists because both are cautious and demanding critics of new technology applications involving recordkeeping.

Insightful writers from all specializations have long lamented the fragmentation as artificial and dangerous, but it was not until the 1990s that the electronic revolution with its metamorphic impact upon the workplace and upon recordkeeping provided a catalyst for reunification.

Electronic revolution: Catalyst for integration

The move towards integration began in the early 1970s when it became clear that no matter how diligently recordkeepers worked, modern documentation continually outstripped their best efforts to manage it. More and more complex records were produced; backlogs grew; money and resources became harder and harder to acquire.

Throughout the 1980s, the crisis mounted as modern offices became increasingly desperate for space and obsessed with technological solutions. Whatever the question, it seemed that technology, the newer the better, was the answer. Vast sums were spent on designing and implementing new information systems within an environment of volatile technological change. In the workplace, smart typewriters gave way to dedicated word-processors. These in turn gave way to multi-functional personal computer workstations that were subsequently networked to replace many transactions performed by centralized mainframe systems.

Managers, confusing possession of technology with the exercise of power, reclaimed the desktop workstation, abolished the typing pool and steadily trimmed the so-called clerical staff. This technology-driven flattening of the Weberian hierarchy created multi-skilling. Every manager became a secretary, data processor, records manager and archivist, as well as a decision-maker. Unsurprisingly, efforts to 'do everything' led to confusion and waste; and the problems of 'paperwork' did not disappear as advertised. Information stored on non-standard, unstable, easily manipulated media did not satisfy legal requirements for evidence; lack of standards for creating and identifying digital objects made management impossible; high-speed printers spewed forth new tidal waves of paper and microfiche to meet legal and financial recordkeeping requirements. The new frontier of the electronic office became wilder and wilder.

By the early 1990s the networked personal computer was seriously transforming work and workplaces. Alarm bells sounded across the management and recordkeeping literature as discipline leaders struggled to identify and resolve the crisis in organizational recordkeeping. The need to ensure effective management of electronic records and information within networked environments had become so urgent that archival researchers were able to obtain substantial public funding to address the problem.

Four striking realities quickly became clear. Firstly, the inadequacy of traditional strategies and methods employed to manage modern records, paper or electronic, was resoundingly confirmed. Appraisal was perhaps the most obvious in need of reinvention. Recordkeeping specialists would have to unite and redefine a professional enterprise and identity able to achieve recordkeeping effectiveness. Secondly, society was shifting its management infrastructure from dependency on 'hard copy' to fully electronic environments. Suddenly managing essential corporate knowledge in networked environments was a 'mission-critical' concern within government and large private organizations. What was needed was a regime for virtual recordkeeping that would be analogous to, that would succeed and that would be more effective than the traditional apparatus for managing records in the paper world. Management was seeking expertise to ensure a smooth and successful transition, presenting an unparalleled opportunity for recordkeepers to become involved in a meaningful way. Thirdly, the electronic revolution was a global phenomenon that required recordkeepers to undertake global approaches and cooperation. And finally, recordkeeping specialists had essential knowledge and skill, but it was misapplied and they were so professionally diffuse that no-one understood what they had to offer. The best minds in recordkeeping needed to work together systematically and thoroughly to:

- deconstruct and reinvent the recordkeeping enterprise, articulating its mission, terminology, theory and practice with a degree of accuracy and specificity never before attempted;
- apply the new knowledge and approaches to forge a cohesive professional identity and unity of purpose among practitioners;
- market the profession and its expertise to society's power elites; and

- work with other disciplines to provide recordkeeping functionality across the paper and virtual worlds.[7]

This exacting and complex challenge had very high stakes. The electronic revolution would thunder on regardless, totally ignorant of its potentially fatal flaw – the need to revolutionize the invisible functionality of recordkeeping. If professional recordkeepers failed to accomplish their transformative tasks, society's 'paper trail' would disappear and the infrastructure essential for responsible and responsive organizations and societies would slowly implode. Accountability mechanisms would be neutralized or dismantled, leaving society increasingly vulnerable. Whilst knowledge base destruction has happened in societies before – following the collapse of the Roman Empire and during excesses of religious persecutions – these were not global and some traces survived. In a global and virtual world, recovery will be considerably harder, if not impossible, unless failsafe mechanisms are designed in advance.

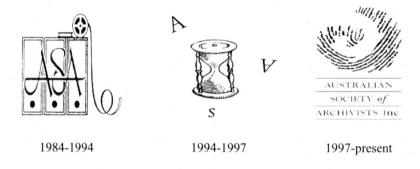

| 1984-1994 | 1994-1997 | 1997-present |

Figure 3.1 Images of a profession's changing self-awareness: logos of the Australian Society of Archivists.

Acting quickly to obtain funding and utilizing the Internet to facilitate deliberations, 'think-tanks' of elite researchers from across the globe worked virtually and actually, analyzing how records performed their work within organizations and interacted with other functions and systems in the workplace. They have questioned and reassessed the 'received wisdom' and exposed fallacious professional assumptions, reaffirmed or discarded values and concepts, arriving at a number of baseline conclusions. Over the last decade, thanks to the

---

[7] Sue McKemmish, 'Placing Records Continuum Theory and Practice', *Archival Science*, 1, no. 4, 2001, pp. 333-339. Those behind this move made a conscious choice to focus on improving organizational recordkeeping to the neglect of private recordkeeping because its impact extended to recordkeeping in all domains. If this strategy succeeded, business solutions would be adapted to meet the requirements of the private domain; if it failed, all recordkeeping would fail. It was always intended to develop a 'personal' world analogue to the business recordkeeping model, once the immediate crisis in organizational recordkeeping had been resolved.

long term commitment and hard thinking within the discipline of recordkeeping, important progress towards understanding recordkeeping effectiveness has been made.

Reinvented global professional mission

In the course of, and as a result of this work, institutional recordkeeping, in particular, has been transformed. Recordkeeping specialists now see their principal role as enabling society to achieve effectiveness by embedding and managing recordkeeping functionality within the conduct of affairs, not by doing all the recordkeeping themselves – steering not rowing. These new insights enable them to stand together in all their diversity under the banner of a common goal. The associated sweeping changes in what it takes and means to be a recordkeeping 'professional' are summarized below.

The Profession's Paradigm Shift from Traditional to Current Recordkeeping[8]

CHANGE	TRADITIONAL	CURRENT
Mission	Identifying, acquiring, organizing, maintaining and accessing 'stuff', i.e. records in offices and archives in repositories and libraries.	Managing regimes to ensure the capture of essential recorded evidence in the course of personal and work activity and its integrity and accessibility over time.
Role of records and record-keepers	Objective, organic, representative stores of records with recordkeepers as passive, objective, neutral conduits of meaning from creators to users.	Value-laden, selective, consciously constructed memory stores with recordkeepers as active, interpreters shaping the meaning of the record and its unfolding context.
Responsibility for record-keeping success	Lone responsibility for recordkeeping – doing it all ourselves.	Shared responsibility and partnership to enable those responsible for actions and decisions to make and maintain reliable records for as long as needed to satisfy their managerial, regulatory and cultural requirements.

[8]A complete matrix of changes including definitions of the record, concepts and functions and archival methods draws on the insights of, inter alia, Glenda Acland, 'Archivist – Keeper, Undertaker or Auditor?' *Archives and Manuscripts*, 19, no. 1, 1991, pp. 9-15; David Bearman, 'Archival Strategies', *American Archivist*, 58, no. 4, 1995, pp. 374-407, available at: http://www.archimuse.com/publishing/archival_strategies; Ann Pederson, 'Empowering Archival Effectiveness: Archival Strategies as Innovation', *American Archivist*, 58, no. 4, 1995, pp. 412-442; Terry Cook, 'Fashionable Nonsense or Professional Rebirth: Postmodernism and the Practice of Archives', *Archivaria*, 51, 2001, pp. 14-35; and 'Archival science and postmodernism: new formulations for old concepts', *Archival Science*, 1, no. 1, 2001, pp. 3-24.

Professional relationships	Affiliating our cause with heritage scholars and other information professionals, i.e. powerless 'outsiders' or equally marginalized 'insiders'.	Making common cause with 'records aware' in-house legal, fiscal and IT professionals, quality auditors and other regulators, i.e. powerful 'insiders' or influential 'outsiders'; tapping into interest in the 'truth' behind seminal experiences [war, disaster, discovery, scandal], personal identity and relationships.
Locus of work	Records managers and records in office and record centres; archivists and archives in repositories; manuscript and private materials in libraries.	Everyone making, keeping and accessing records and other information resources any time anywhere using the recordkeeping infrastructure managed by recordkeeping specialists.
Education	Archivists and manuscript librarians have interest and/or tertiary training in history; records managers from business disciplines; most learned recordkeeping on-the-job and via technical colleges, short courses; emphasis on how to carry out recordkeeping tasks.	Recruits from varying contexts; history still important interest; understanding recordkeeping technologies, functions and activities and developing knowledge, skills and attitudes that enable new entrants to think, research and work with others to manage recordkeeping regimes and solve problems.
Research	No research infrastructure or culture; outputs mainly finding aids – historical studies describing the lives of record creators and/or explaining the content and provenance of bodies of archives.	Communities of practice centred on university-led national and international team-based research employing a range of methodologies to examine and improve recordkeeping concepts, behaviours, processes, outcomes, entities and solutions.

Towards a reinvented professional

Recent research in Australia and North America provides an interesting insight into the type of people currently working as archivists in the recordkeeping profession and suggests that they might not be well-suited to the kind of steering roles envisaged above.[9] Whilst these

---

[9] Barbara L. Craig, 'Canadian Archivists: What Types of People Are They?', *Archivaria*, 50, 2000, pp. 79-92; Ann E. Pederson, 'Understanding Ourselves and Others', *Archives at Risk: Accountability, Vulnerability and Credibility Proceedings of the 1999 Conference and Annual General Meeting of the Australian Society of Archivists Inc., Brisbane, Queensland, 29-31 July 1999*, Canberra, ASA, 2002,

findings apply to archivists only, the researchers involved have hypothesized that comparable studies of record managers and manuscript curators would produce similar results. The research findings indicate that career recordkeepers are attracted to the field because they want to do something worthwhile in society and because they enjoy investigative research. In general they can be characterized as hard-working, respectful, modest, tenacious, decisive, problem-solvers who:

- are accurate, reliable, trustworthy;
- maintain stability, continuity, traditions;
- value sense of belonging, procedures, rules, detail;
- are logisticians, i.e. prefer work with things than with people; and
- have integrity and concern to 'do right' in the real world.

The research also indicates that, although employers and colleagues generally think archivists are nice people, they would like them to be more strategic and possess much better people management skills and to:

- exhibit positive, flexible 'can-do' attitudes;
- combine good strategic sensibilities with team playing and leading skills;
- work productively within organizational culture; and
- develop the negotiation, communication and conflict resolution skills necessary to optimize our superior analytical and problem-solving abilities.

A key element differentiating a profession from an occupation is its commitment to a common mission. Looking at the list of changes above, it is clear that most are better implemented in current organizational recordkeeping regimes than in programs managing a mix of legacy materials inherited from the past. Tensions emanating from this disparity have hampered efforts to improve professional cohesion. To overcome these, recordkeeping theorists have laboured to devise an inclusive, yet meaningful phrase to express the overarching professional goal. Probably the best phrase to capture their intent is: *Ensuring Evidence for Organizational and Societal Effectiveness.* It attempts to transcend differences of specialization and context by promoting the *outcome* sought by all professional recordkeepers, i.e. reliable documentation of human endeavour. This approach does not prescribe *what* constitutes evidence, *how* it must be ensured or whether the effectiveness achieved will lead to better or worse quality societies. It does, however, assert that those *who* will oversee the outcomes should be recordkeeping professionals managing professional recordkeeping regimes. Intentionally general, it promotes a common vision that practitioners and stakeholders in each context will realise using the mix of professional concepts, ethics and methods they believe will work for them.[10]

---

pp. 61-93, available at: http://www.archivists.org.au/publications.html; Charles R. Schultz, 'Archivists: What Types of People Are They?', *Provenance*, 14, 1996, pp. 15-36.

[10] Chris Hurley, 'Beating the French', *Archives and Manuscripts*, 24, no. 1, 1996, pp. 12-18; Sue McKemmish, 'Placing Records Continuum Theory and Practice', *Archival Science*, 1, no. 4, 2001, pp. 333-339; Elisabeth Kaplan, '"Many Paths to Partial Truths": Archives, Anthropology, and the Power of Representation', *Archival Science*, 2, no. 3/4, 2002, pp. 209-220.

A holistic view of the recordkeeping mission contends that the differences among recordkeeping specializations arise from undertaking dual responsibilities – documenting the present, and reconstructing the past – in a wide variety of settings or contexts. In short, the functions and most activities of recordkeeping are universal; the sense of difference comes when these are tailored and applied to fit the dynamics of the context.

Documenting the present

This responsibility supports and documents ongoing work functions and activities within organizational and personal environments. Recordkeeping takes place within and on behalf of a host entity, i.e. a household, enterprise or organization that is government or private, for profit or not-for-profit.

The current recordkeeping aspects of in-house or institution-based recordkeeping regimes usually provide centralized coordination and/or services within the organization's headquarters, as well as maintain a lower cost off-site repository to service older records and archives. Large recordkeeping establishments, such as those of a state, nation or multinational body have complex and comprehensive responsibilities and provide a range of centrally coordinated services suitable for local adaptation and implementation. Some organizational programs, particularly those that are small and not-for-profit, outsource their non-current recordkeeping. In such cases, a recordkeeping services vendor is contracted to provide a range of expertise, facilities and services. For example, a contract repository may give advice on recordkeeping system improvements, protect vital records, undertake confidential disposal of temporary records and managing records having longer term and/or archival value.

Private individuals, small businesses and members of professions also generate records in the course of their lives and work, but their efforts are less formal and rely on bundled software and publications designed for small business or home office needs. In some cases, families and small enterprises may employ a recordkeeping service consultant to assist them in addressing their recordkeeping requirements.

Recordkeeping professionals specializing in documenting the present may be designated records managers, information managers, documentation specialists or information resource managers or have a hybrid title attesting to the extent of their organizational responsibilities.

Reconstructing the past

Regimes having this focus construct and manage a collective memory comprising the culturally significant older materials, including records, generated by a number of individual and organizational 'creators'. Once acquired, these items and bodies of records are organized in a way that accurately represents their context of origin and are made available for research. These regimes vary widely in function, holdings, size and complexity. Examples include school, club and business archives, manuscripts and local studies collections, film, photo or sound archives. Often such programs are attached to learning or heritage institutions such as universities, public libraries, museums or galleries and pursue interests that are international, national, state or local in scope. Collecting archives primarily document the personal, creative and community-building aspects of life, leaving the care of official organizational records to institutional programs hosted by governments and businesses. Recordkeeping professionals working within such regimes may have the title of archivist, historian, research officer, manuscript librarian or curator, depending upon the custom of their host institution.

Comprehensive responsibilities

Most archives and records programs perform both of these roles, but seldom equally. Institutionally based professionals generally emphasize the documentary role over the reconstructing role, and collecting professionals, the reverse. Certainly, in-house recordkeepers solicit the personal papers of their organization's top employees, while collecting archivists safeguard the culturally significant records of local businesses and institutions, often including their own host.

The responsibility mix also reflects the fact that recordkeeping programs were founded for different reasons and are in different stages of professional development. The variety is particularly pronounced in collecting archives. Some were established to commemorate individuals (presidents, inventors, statesmen), past events (The Holocaust, World War II) or unfolding phenomena (life in a locality, space exploration, war). Some have highly qualified staff and state-of-the-art facilities; others have volunteers and a broom closet. Some have generations of material; others are just opening up. Their diversity naturally reflects the richness and complexity of human enterprise. But it is true that the number and extent of contextual differences sometimes obscure their common functions and goals. As one American archivist was heard to say 'Sometimes I feel my program has as much in common with the National Archives as Tibet has with the USA'.

Certainly, best practices for documenting the present or reconstructing the past can only stay 'best' if recordkeeping specialists work together to expand their competence and inclusiveness. There will always be gaps in the record of what happened, events and needs of groups beyond the scope of mainstream recordkeeping to be addressed. Recordkeeping specialists must also fight against their tendencies to assume that documentation-worthy events are only transacted in literate cultures with access to the latest recordkeeping technology. People across the planet are living and organizing their affairs in a diversity of concurrent contexts that are recognisably neolithic, medieval, pre-industrial, modern, postmodern and futuristic. The recordkeeping infrastructure suitable for western countries is unsuitable for cultures whose records resonate through ritual, story, dance, song and art.

In such cases where gaps are uncovered, recordkeeping specialists need to find ways of joining together to design new recordkeeping solutions.[11]

Professional associations

As noted earlier, one of the major indicators distinguishing a profession from an occupation is an infrastructure for self-regulation and promotion. Aspiring professionals pursue their ambitions by establishing a governing association – to set and monitor best practice and ethical standards regulating members' knowledge and skill requirements, values, education, research, employment and practice. Such bodies often accredit educational programs and curricula, examine or license new recruits, mandate ethical behaviour, evaluate quality of services, set conditions of employment and protect the reputations of the profession and its members in society.

Initially formed to make common cause and solve problems, successful professional bodies gradually expand in scope from local to regional to national levels, ultimately attaining international standing. In the case of recordkeeping, professional association growth has exhibited a classic pattern of formation, differentiation, and separation. Each of the three recordkeeping 'parent' disciplines – history, public administration and librarianship – had its own professional body, within which recordkeepers comprised specialist subgroups. As their distinctiveness and numbers reached a critical mass, they separated to form professional associations of their own. In the case of recordkeeping, two major associations were established in the mid-twentieth century, reflecting the two foci of practice: societies of archivists and manuscript curators involved in *reconstructing the past* and associations of records and corporate information managers engaged in *documenting the present.*

Within these coordinating frameworks, special interests cater to the diversity of types of records (photographs, sound recordings, electronic, scientific, medical) and contexts of practice (businesses, government, religious, cultural and educational institutions). At present, an estimated one-third of recordkeeping specialists are members of one professional association, while the leadership elite may be active in several at national and international levels.

One of the keys to professional cohesion is commitment to shared values and ethics as embodied in a formal declaration or code of ethical conduct. In their work, recordkeeping professionals strive to balance a number of competing responsibilities and obligations involving a range of entities and stakeholders, including the human record, the creators, donors and depositors of records, the people whose activities and lives are documented in the records, the users of records, employers of recordkeeping professionals, other

---

[11] Terry Cook, 'Beyond the Screen: The Records Continuum and Archival Cultural Heritage', in *Beyond the Screen: Proceedings of the Australian Society of Archivists Conference, Melbourne, 18-20 August 2000,* available at: http://www.archivists.org.au/sem/conf2000/terrycook.pdf; Evelyn Wareham, 'From Explorers to Evangelists: Archivists, Recordkeeping, and Remembering in the Pacific Islands', *Archival Science*, 2, no. 3/4, 2002, pp. 187-207.

professionals and recordkeeping institutions, and the profession itself. Achieving a balance in terms of competing responsibilities is an ongoing challenge to be faced with a mix of commitment, skill, good judgment and humour. There is some comfort in knowing that in ethical matters things are seldom clear-cut; mostly ethics involves compromises, some better, some worse. The important things are that 'best' is spelled out in a code and that recordkeeping professionals are pledged to uphold it.

Professional knowledge and education

Previously we also pointed to the crucial importance to professional status of an agreed body of knowledge. Recordkeeping practice is increasingly based upon an internationally developed and understood corpus of knowledge deemed necessary to manage recorded information effectively from the moment it is conceived. This evolving knowledge base reflects rigorous research and testing and comprises the general concepts, principles, attitudes, skills, analytical tools and processes that recordkeeping professionals apply to solve problems and manage regimes appropriate to their employer's needs and resources. In application, this body of recordkeeping knowledge is separate from, complementary to, interdependent with, and filtered through a research-based understanding of the cultural and administrative contexts generating the records. A practitioner effectively combines recordkeeping knowledge with contextual knowledge to achieve professional competence. Each culture will thus evolve its own variation of the internationally accepted professional knowledge base that suits the conditions and concerns of its own context of implementation.

Recordkeeping education: Then and now

In most Western cultures prior to its own professionalization, recordkeeping was an auxiliary skill serving disciplines that used records intensively in their work. Aspiring accountants, company secretaries, lawyers, public servants and auditors, among others, learned the rules and forms of records specific to their needs, as well as the benefits of good and risks of poor recordkeeping.

In the first half of the twentieth century, business colleges taught basic recordkeeping and office skills to the trainee clerks and secretaries servicing a burgeoning and increasingly feminized public and corporate bureaucracy. As the volume and complexity of documentation grew, governments in particular responded by setting standards and codifying principles for quality recordkeeping in the public sector. The national and state records and archival authorities responsible for recordkeeping developed publications and training programs focusing on the key functions of record classification and registration, disposal, long term-storage and guidelines for the application of new technologies such as micrographics.

After World War II, it was clear that the magnitude and difficulty of the work required managers to have a high level of education as well as specialist recordkeeping expertise. Initially, the managerial class of recordkeepers comprised public or Foreign Service administrators, ex-military experienced in supply/logistical recordkeeping and/or historians, many with European or British archival training and experience. Public record offices and archives provided internships for rising university graduates and encouraged the most promising of them to qualify for employment by scoring well on the public service examination.

In the 1960s further professionalization saw the publication of training manuals and the development of courses of study under the leadership of national archives. Definitions and practical know-how dominated the scant literature, and professional formation involved on-the-job training, capped off with a specialist national archives and membership in the professional association.

In the 1970s, university schools of librarianship and of history widened the prospects of their graduates by hiring leading practitioners to teach specialist recordkeeping electives such as archives administration, oral history, manuscripts librarianship and administrative history within their degree programs. Major employers encouraged professionalism amongst their employees by paying association memberships and university fees, sponsoring professional events and granting special leave for study. In turn, nascent professional associations issued educational guidelines, accredited degree programs, recognized the new graduate appointees as professionals and allied with leading public recordkeeping authorities, cultural institutions and universities to promote a fully professionalized infrastructure and culture amongst recordkeepers.

By the mid 1980s, the qualification most often requested in advertisements for entry level recordkeeping professionals was a tertiary degree with some recordkeeping content. The *preferred* credential for aspiring managerial professionals was a tertiary credential followed by a specialist postgraduate recordkeeping degree. As a long-term result of the professional association-employer-university alliance, recordkeeping education and research have achieved a degree of recognition within academe, as seen in postgraduate programs with full-time specialist staff offer a range of recordkeeping qualifications and undertake profession-critical research. There is no guarantee, of course, these positions will always be secure.

Throughout the 1990s, a small cadre of educators servicing the hybrid profession's knowledge and research requirements refocused and expanded their curriculum and research. However, the required metamorphosis has been made more complex in some Anglophone countries because the social equity infrastructure has been neglected.

In Australia, governments have privatized or curtailed a number of basic public service responsibilities and have withdrawn their subsidies for low-earning social equity and 'infrastructure' disciplines, such as education, social work, nursing, arts, librarianship and recordkeeping. Less government funding means many universities now only support disciplines that can 'pay their way' and attract sufficient students who are able to pay high fees to qualify in a field that pays well. As publicly funded universities have been forced to neglect goals of enabling learning and ensuring societal quality in pursuit of 'earning their own keep', educational standards inevitably fall. Critics assert that programs are shorter and curriculum is less rigorous. Particularly damaged are disciplines such as recordkeeping that require extra background, time and circumstances to ensure 'deep learning' takes place through reading, reflection, research experiments, discourse analysis and workplace projects.[12]

Reinventing recordkeeping education in other Anglophone countries has also encountered an unexpected degree of contextual inertia and passive resistance from within academic and practitioner communities. The persistence of a preference for the relative clarity of 'doing things to stuff' has slowed the process of change. Empirical evidence suggests that university programs in the USA are still enrolling a majority of students wishing to work with historical materials. It seems that working with research sources provides practitioners with something they may prize more than achieving recordkeeping effectiveness – being left alone to exercise their own judgment to manage their holdings and themselves as they see fit. Exploratory research certainly indicates that professionals who prefer strategic recordkeeping may be temperamentally different from the majority of those now working in many archives. If further professional success depends upon supporting a unified recordkeeping paradigm, then the profession needs to adopt inclusive continuum thinking and combat separatist tendencies that hamper professional cohesion.

Despite these difficulties, professional bodies in Australia and Canada have produced guidelines detailing the knowledge, skill and attitude competencies required of new recordkeeping paradigm specialists,[13] though the uptake of these new tools has been slow outside the vocational and technical education sectors and a few pioneering university programs. While educators and trainers agree they need to address competency standards as they develop new learning materials and programs, many believe competencies emphasize training, rather than education, and enshrine the *status quo*, rather than encourage

---

[12] Richard Cox, *Closing an Era*, Westport, CT, Greenwood, 2000, pp. 230-236; Terry Cook, '"The Imperative of Challenging Absolutes" in Graduate Archival Education Programs: Issues for Educators and the Profession', *American Archivist*, 63, Fall/Winter 2000, pp. 380-391.

[13] While it is not possible to discuss these important learning resources, readers may view them at the following websites: Australia. National Training Information Service, *Competency Standard 236: Records and Archives*, 1997, available at: http://www.ntis.gov.au/cgibin/waxhtml/~ntis2/std.wxh?page=80&inputRef=515; National Archives of Canada. Information Management Standards and Practices Division, *Preliminary Study on the Core Competencies of the Future Records Specialist*, Ottawa, June 1996. This report identifies distinct roles for recordkeepers as Recordkeeping Systems Analyst, Recordkeeping Educator/Consultant, Recordkeeping Strategist, Recordkeeping Policy Driver, Recordkeeping Logistician, Retrieval Expert; Canada. Alliance of Libraries, Archives and Records Management in partnership with the Cultural Human Resources Council, *Competency Profile: Information Resources Specialists in Archives, Libraries and Records Management,* April 1999. Jeannette Bastian of Simmons College and Beth Yakel of the University of Michigan are compiling data on US archival core curricula that will be reported in 2004. (Jeannette Bastian, 11 February 2003 mail to Forum for Archival Educators, archive-educate@forums.nyu.edu).

innovation. Employers also indicate that they find them valuable as criteria for recruitment and promotion, but have lacked the time to revise existing human resources mechanisms to effectively incorporate them.[14]

Looking to the future

Public outrage at growing corporate and government malfeasance has forced governments and organizations to strengthen accountability regimes and pay more attention to recordkeeping infrastructure. Will they do so in sufficient numbers to ensure a quality society? Will the rediscovered and new recordkeeping tools and intellectual constructs of continuum-based recordkeeping regimes serve or fail to meet the dynamic challenges ahead? Will the personal side of life ever be adequately documented? Can recordkeeping specialists thrive in environments, despite being buffeted by volatile technologies, scarce resources and exponential change? These are the questions recordkeeping professionals are asking themselves in the first years of this new century and millennium. Positive answers will require unprecedented professional unity and determination.

The cumulative human record is the most fragile and essential of all the world's cultural assets. A new strategic professional mission is required to ensure today's essential records are captured and survive as tomorrow's archives. Leaders within our discipline have articulated a new professional paradigm and nascent infrastructure – but to ensure success, however, recordkeeping communities of practice will need to influence those with the power, will and capacity to achieve recordkeeping effectiveness and provide professionals with the right mix of attitudes, knowledge and skills to take up the challenges of the work.

---

[14] Janet Knight, State Records of NSW, email message to author, 4 February 2003, discussing community feedback on the uses being made of the Australian Recordkeeping competencies.

Readings

- Richard E. Barry, *Report on the Society and Archives Survey*, January 29, 2003, available at: http://www.mybestdocs.com/barry-r-soc-arc-surv-report-030129toc.htm

  Analyzes anecdotes from archivists describing their interactions with employers and members the wider community. The perceptions of archives and attitudes expressed have relevance for recordkeeping as a whole.

- Karen Benedict, ed., *Ethics and the Archival Profession: Introduction and Case Studies*, Chicago, IL: Society of American Archivists, 2003.

  Forty case studies exploring the ethical issues raised in the course of archival work with advice for resolving conflicts.

- Terry Cook, 'Fashionable Nonsense or Professional Rebirth: Postmodernism and the Practice of Archives', *Archivaria*, 51, 2001, pp. 14-35.

  Highlights recent efforts of recordkeeping theorists to recast traditional ideas and practices to meet the challenges of the postmodern world.

- Terry Cook, 'What is Past is Prologue: A History of Archival Ideas Since 1898, and the Future Paradigm Shift', *Archivaria*, 43, 1997, pp. 17-63.

  Offers an excellent summary of the development of recordkeeping theory over the past century and provides a foundation for understanding the profession today.

- Richard J. Cox, *Closing An Era: Historical Perspectives on Modern Archives and Records Management*, Westport, CT, Greenwood, 2000.

  Thoughtfully analyzes key issues facing the major recordkeeping specializations. See in particular chapters 1-3 on the history of recordkeeping, chapter 6 on records and memory, chapter 7 on professional education and chapter 9 on the future.

- Luciana Duranti, 'The Odyssey of Records Managers', in Tom Nesmith, ed., *Canadian Archival Studies and the Re-Discovery of Provenance*, Metuchen, NJ, Association of Canadian Archivists and the Society of American Archivists in association with Scarecrow Press, 1993, pp. 28-60. Originally published in two parts in ARMA *Records Management Quarterly*, 23, no. 3, 1989, pp. 3-6, 8-11, and 23, no. 4, 1989, pp. 3-6, 8-11.

  Presents an overview of recordkeeping concepts, practices and societal standing from ancient to early modern times.

- Sue McKemmish, 'Placing Records Continuum Theory and Practice', *Archival Science*, 1, no. 4, 2001, pp. 333-339.

Explains the records continuum conceptual framework for the re-integrated recordkeeping enterprise.

- Ann E. Pederson, 'Understanding Ourselves and Others: Australian Archivists and Temperament', in *Archives at Risk: Accountability, Vulnerability and Credibility Proceedings of the 1999 Conference and Annual General Meeting of the Australian Society of Archivists Inc., Brisbane, Queensland, 29-31 July 1999*, Canberra, ASA, 2002, pp. 61-93, available at: http://www.archivists.org.au/publications.html

  Presents insights from an exploratory survey of temperaments among professional archivists in Australia and a discussion of implications for workplace and professional success.

- UNESCO *Archives Portal. Associations*, available at: http://www.unesco.org/webworld/portal_archives/pages/Associations

  Provides an extensive list of, and links to, professional archives/records management associations around the world.

CHAPTER 4

Documents

Robert Hartland, Sue McKemmish and Frank Upward

We live in a web of documents

Documents are everywhere. Whether we take a wide view and associate the word document with its Latin origins as a trace, or define it more precisely as a form of recorded information, then every day we are constantly engaged in creating and accessing documents. We use documents to inform, communicate, entertain, convey knowledge, conduct business, authorize actions, control or regulate relationships between people, establish our rights and obligations, represent an action or deed, and to provide evidence.

Documents might be everywhere, but there are certain places and media we have traditionally associated more strongly with documents than others. We expect to see paper documents inhabiting physical spaces like the office or workplace, the home, libraries, archives and other records repositories. In an electronic world we are beginning to view other places as the natural habitat of documents – or document-like objects. They live in our computers and the Internet and our intranets are places where they abound. We are all living witnesses to the new document architectures of our era which suggest that documents are only 'document-like', reconstructed from digital components, their documentary form made manifest on the screen or reproduced for us in more traditional formats via a printer or other output device. But there is also the continuing sense that the documents we see or hear on the web are not really new, just a new way of giving effect to the notion of the document, an instantiation or performance of an abstract work.

We *live* in a web of documents and have done so ever since civil societies first began to emerge regardless of the enabling technologies at any given point of time. Our personal documentary web includes many things that document our existence and life. Right at this moment we might have quick access to many strands of that web such as a driver's licence, a library card, a business card, bankcard, a receipt, tickets for a bus, train or aeroplane, a bank statement, a letter, an email or SMS message, a title deed, a marriage or birth certificate, a novel, an encyclopaedia, a music CD, a set of conference proceedings on floppy disk, a home video, a rented movie on DVD, a newspaper, or a web page accessible to us via a mobile device.

The notion of a document can be broader than a constructed information object. One can, for example, look at buildings and the built environment, examining how the processes of change over time, the functionality and use of the built objects, and the interaction of people with them are documented in the objects themselves as well as providing leads to associated documentation of the more conventional kind. Forensic evidence left at the scene of a crime is part of the documentation of that crime. Performance art can be documented in conventional ways through text, music, drawings, software programs and other forms of recorded information. There is, however, also something of the documentation process in the very performance and the way that performance can be passed down from performer to performer through experiencing and witnessing. Similarly orality creates its own documentary forms, for example in the stories and songs that are heard, remembered, told and sung. Ceremonies and rituals in society also play a large part in documenting important aspects of the lives of those involved in them, in recording and transmitting information about the human experience.

It might seem fanciful to imagine tree-rings as documents, but they are physical objects that document the age of a tree. Using the physical traces provided by the stunted growth of tree-rings, we know that some time around 540 A.D. there was an event that caused the world to be much colder and overcast for a period of about five years, leading to theories linked to documentation of a massive volcanic explosion in the Indonesian archipelago around that time. Fossils are documents in the same sense. The art, artefacts, machines and tools of a society, its burial places, shipwrecks, and rubbish tips provide further documentation, as do the remains of humans – consider the wealth of information recorded for posterity in the form of the glacier man, frozen in ice for generations.

Unless we allow ourselves to become fixated upon paper as the physical storage media for a document, the web of documents in which we live can be seen to encompass many different documentary relationships, both serendipitous and constructed. Documentary relationships may be formed by deliberate acts of remembrance, authorship, accumulation, selection, collection, appraisal, disposal, registration, classification, management, storage, publication, and dissemination by individuals and organizations, as well as by natural events, happenstance and accidental associations. Collections or accumulations of documents are found in registries, recordkeeping systems, document management systems, Internet web sites, video rental stores, libraries, museums, galleries, archives, sacred sites, in email folders on personal computers, personal collections of art, books or ephemera, and the personal or family archive, as well as in burial grounds, shipwrecks, archaeological digs, and fossil sites, and in places where stories are told, sung or performed, and rituals enacted.

Concept of genre

The concept of a *genre* as a communication type, recognizable by its stylistic elements, can be a useful starting point for the analysis of a particular document. A genre tag is a classification applied to (sometimes imposed upon) a communication in order that we might have a convenient starting point for identifying what it is that we are actually dealing with – a structural template and a set of assumptions that facilitate our search for 'meaning.'

It is a term most commonly encountered when applied to creative works of fiction and in the visual and performing arts where one expects to find labels such as 'romantic', 'realist', 'noir', 'satiric', 'adventure' and 'historical' applied to works as they are described in catalogues and publicity blurbs or as they are presented to us for retrieval purposes in libraries of all sorts, bookshops and galleries. A genre can contain, in some cases, an apparently infinite number of sub-sets of related genres of increasing specificity. Add to this the tendency among creators to hybridize genres in ways which suit their purposes, creating the 'western film noir', Truman Capote's 'faction' and the 'historical satire' and the convenience of genre-based classification starts to appear a little moot. Look too closely at some documents and the insanity of Hamlet's 'tragical-comical-historical-pastoral' classification is never too far away.

So why do we persist with genre labeling, and of what use can it be in our approach to a multiplicity of communication types beyond the creative or artistic? Well, we persist with labelling of all sorts because it is a basic way of imposing order upon what would otherwise remain a chaos of documents and, more importantly here, because the label – i.e. the identification of the genre – contains clues as to how a particular communication is to be 'read.' A genre template has embedded within it not simply some pointers to structure and style but also a whole range of assumptions about how the communication is to be understood or, at least, approached.

Take for example the 'knock knock joke.' It is a widely understood sub-set of a genre called 'the joke' with a rigid structure (which is in fact central to its humour) and which relies for its effectiveness upon the hearer's familiarity with its conventions *and* a level of linguistic skill sophisticated enough to enable them to recognize a pun when they hear one. That is, the genre here presumes that the recipient of the communication knows to reply 'Who's there?' in response to the opening gambit and that they will *expect* a punning reference in the punch line. These presumptions are widely understood now, but, just as many of Shakespeare's jokes have to be extensively annotated these days, so some future researcher into a putative 'joke archive' may require to have the conventions of this particular sub-genre explained for them.

The point we wish to make here is that, in this case as in many others, the genre's conventions not only dictate the structure of the document and, to a large extent, the content of the communication, they also take for granted a certain preparedness to receive on the part of the recipient. (In many cultures this form of joke is unknown and the hearer of the joke would be most unlikely to know what to reply to a 'knock knock' opening, let alone understand the usually execrable pun to which that response would lead!)

Looking at an example from the other end of the spectrum of communications 'types' – an Act of Parliament – we see similar factors in play. This genre also has its conventions of language, structure and form which are readily understood by those who develop and interpret them. Acts constitute a genre in that, in certain basic ways, one Act is very much like another in the way in which it represents content – a statement of purpose, jurisdictions, numbered sections and subsections, an explanation of terms, and appropriate legalisms make it impossible to mistake this genre for any other. The preparedness of the intended audience to receive the document is taken for granted. A specialist audience of judges and legal practitioners know the genre and, therefore, know where to go for particular information, which jurisdictions and authorities to look for and how to identify dimensions of it as fundamental as its currency.

Getting reasonably full access to the information value of these communications is largely dependent upon familiarity with the conventions of the particular genre. Sometimes that familiarity with a genre is cultivated through formal instruction – particularly when dealing with highly specialized documentary forms in the context of arcane knowledge and skills such as an accountant's spreadsheets, a doctor's X-rays or an archaeologist's pottery shard. More frequently we come to understand the conventions of a document genre through our cultural immersion in its form. That is, in much the same way that human infants acquire language with relatively little or no formal instruction as a result of simply being constantly exposed to it, we learn to identify and use most of the documentary forms with which we deal in our daily lives just because we see and use them more or less all the time. Acquire the knack of reading one sort of railway timetable and you can find your way around an aircraft schedule. Understand the structure of one catalogue by using it and you can apply that to another. See one family photograph from a particular era and, in a sense, you've seen them all.

New genres and their associated forms are so rare (or they evolve so gradually) that few of us are routinely confronted with a document which leaves us completely stumped. As Figure 4.3 demonstrates, even something as fundamental as a foreign language need not be a complete barrier to understanding. We can identify the genre and its associated form and, by so doing, we also have some sense of its 'meaning'. That is because a good deal of its meaning or intent is actually embedded in the form this particular genre takes.

It seems that audiences arrive at an understanding of the conventions of a particular genre with remarkable ease. The motion picture is often identified as a 'new' genre, even though it has been with us for nearly a century. Many elements of it were, in fact, familiar to the first audiences from earlier and related genres; fictional narratives involving settings and characters in some sort of dramatic conflict had been with us in the form of simple and complex stories, epic poems, dramas and novels etc for a very long time. Audiences took with them to the cinema their understandings and expectations of these genres and their forms to the new medium. (In fact, the earliest motion pictures were little more than 'filmed plays' – time bound and space bound within static locations and sets.)

The 'newness' of the movie emerged only when its creators began to exploit the potentialities of the medium and the technologies underpinning it by dismantling linear narratives in non-linear ways, manipulating time and space, applying lighting and camera angles and movements to create particular dramatic and visual effects, cutting and splicing film to give fresh perspectives on movement, responding to musical soundtracks and generally defying the logic of the unmediated human eye and ear. The fact that the motion picture is now the world's single most popular form of entertainment and the focus of a good deal of our species' creativity is a testament to our capacity to translate our expectations of one genre to a variant of it and to acquire a new language for 'reading' it.[1]

Movie audiences are now so thoroughly immersed in the genre that they now *expect* non-sequential time, disjunctions in space, emotions reinforced by music and a comprehensively edited reality. In fact, the conventions of the genre (or sub-genre?) are so well established and widely accepted that it is the revisiting of its earliest limitations that are hailed as 'new' – real time narratives and films stripped of soundtracks, lighting effects, artificial camera angles and other 'Hollywood' techniques, as in the Danish Dogme movement are examples.

In any discussion of genre, it is easy and tempting to be distracted by the potentialities of new media. For two or more decades we have been much preoccupied with the 'newness' of information communications technologies and, in many areas to do with the analysis and management of information, this is clearly warranted. But in terms of identifying and applying genre classifications, there appears to be less interest. An application form is an application form whether it exists on paper or in electronic form. A newspaper is a newspaper even if it is published on the Web. An encyclopaedia is an encyclopaedia in both bound volumes and on a CD-ROM. A digital movie is still recognizable as belonging to a genre called 'movies.' What one can or must *do* with these forms in this new medium is a different story and one which raises a whole raft of challenging and stimulating issues. Genre groupings always have room for further subsets. Entirely new genres come along only rarely. Junk email is an electronic version of familiar junk mail. An unsolicited popup advertisement on the Internet is not all that different from an unexpected billboard advertisement or a flyer shoved into one's hand. Cookies and other 'spyware' are Internet variations on well established ways of surreptitiously gathering data for marketing purposes.[2]

Genre and document analysis

A range of approaches might be adopted in documentary analysis. The method or methods employed will depend very much upon the purposes and contexts within which the analysis is taking place. Using a genre label as a starting point for this process is merely one of these options but it has the advantage of focusing the analyst's attention upon what a particular example of 'information-as-thing', another way of categorizing documents, actually *is*.[3] An

---

[1] For a summation of one writer's exploration of time and movement in the cinema see Claire Colebrook, *Gilles Deleuze*, London, Routledge, 2002, Chapter 2, 'Cinema, Perception, Time and Becoming'.

[2] What is changing, of course, is the ubiquity of many of these items, and consequently their impact. Advertising material in a letter-box still has impact and is seen as overly intrusive by a minority of recipients, whereas electronic junk mail is a much more widely detested phenomenon.

[3] Michael Buckland, 'Information as Thing', *Journal of the American Society for Information Science*, 42, no.5, 1991, pp. 351-360 sets up a form of analysis based on information as knowledge, thing and process.

item-by-item analysis is often, even usually, necessary. Knowing that an art gallery houses a collection of the following medium-based genres – paintings, works on paper, sculptures, decorative arts, digital works, photographs and installations – is useful if one is simply browsing, but not very helpful if one is interested in particular works, by a particular artist or craftsman, in a particular medium from a particular period in their career. To meet the latter need, each item within a genre must be individually described. Nevertheless, the genre-based starting point has its place here.

The advantages of a genre-based tag are that it enables one to approach an individual document in terms of the ways in which it is *like* other documents and, then, to identify the ways in which it is unique and, possibly, of particular value. Information content is the obvious area of potential differentiation here, but there is also the possibility that a particular document might be of interest because of the ways it defies or manipulates the conventions of the genre to which it is assigned. Either way, though, it is the genre label which makes this sort of identification possible.

THE DAVID DREW FAMILY - LATE 1880's
Left to Right: Standing are Lurie, Hattie, Helen Minette and Solon. Bottom Row, Seated, are Helen Mar Drew, David Ellis, Julia, Charles and David Drew. (Florence was not yet born.)

Figure 4.1. The David Drew family – late 1880s

Once a document's genre has been identified it is possible to move on in its analysis from a number of different perspectives such as its:

- **form**: the shape or contours of something which can be a template (an actual or a mental model) associated with that genre which to some extent determines its structure (see Figure 4.3)
- **format**: a recognizable shape given to the information such as a book, booklet or web page
- **medium**: the material (or immaterial) substance on or in which the information is created and stored (paper, spoken word, celluloid or bits)
- **context**: the social, political, business, personal, etc., settings and systems in which it was created and used and which affected its creation and assist in interpreting the information value it can provide.
- **authority**: what credibility, if any, should we give to it? What authentic links can be made to the person or agency which generated it, and has it been altered?
- **content**: what is it about? What does it contain? What is it *for?* What relationships does it convey?
- **purpose**: why was it created? Retained? Does it authorize actions? Serve as evidence? Memorialize an event or an action?
- **technologies**: what means were used to create and access it?
- **accessibility**: the extent to which an understanding of all the above has an impact upon how much information value can be drawn from it.

Figure 4.2. Family Christmas 1997

Figures 4.1 and 4.2 represent typical examples of a common documentary form – the family portrait. Once subject to the type of preliminary analysis outlined above, one might make observations on these documents like those listed in the table below:

	Figure 4.1	**Figure 4.2**
FORM	The family portrait. A subset of an ancient document genre called 'the portrait' featuring three or more realistic, satiric or idealized representations of recognizable human figures related to each other by law or birth.	As for Figure 4.1
FORMAT	The conventions of this form include: • subjects represented in full-face or profile to meet the requirement to be 'recognizable' • age and other hierarchies suggested through the physical arrangement of subjects • subjects are 'self-consciously' aware that a moment is being captured • groups of six or more are most frequently captured in 'landscape view' • objects and features which compete for the viewer's attention are minimized or eliminated • seated or stiffly erect poses.	As for Figure 4.1, BUT: • a whole range of different poses are 'acceptable' – kneeling, leaning, gesturing etc. • families must be captured as being 'happy' • family pets are welcome.
MEDIUM	• Monochrome photography • Chemically processed photosensitive 'paper' (Or is the negative/negative plate from which the image is printed the medium? There is a sense in which a photographic print is only a 'version' of this documentary form in *this* medium because it is subject to various forms of editing during the exposure and printing process.)	• Colour photography • Chemically processed photosensitive 'paper' • See note on the negative for Figure 4.1.
CONTEXT	• A common human desire to have relationships memorialized • A formal nineteenth-century studio portrait in which the subjects have	• A common human desire to have relationships memorialized • An informal snapshot requiring a minimal investment of time or

	invested time, thought and, compared with Figure 4.2, a not inconsiderable amount of money • This family wishes to be seen at its best, hence the attention to grooming and the formality of the representation. (See *Technologies* below) • Photography gave middle class families access to the types of memorialization that the aristocracy had previously enjoyed through other more expensive media such as painting and sculpture.	money due to advances in technology (see below) • Subject 'cheerfulness' is a convention of the twentieth-century snapshot reflecting the ways in which family relationships have become more informal • Colour photography technologies are inexpensive, fast and the norm for domestic consumers.
AUTHORITY	See commentary below.	
CONTENT	• A representation of physical appearances at a particular moment • Evidence of relationships.	• As for Figure 4.1.
PURPOSE	• Aide-memoire • Evidence of social status.	• Aide-memoire • Memorialization of a family occasion.
TECHNOLOGIES	• Nineteenth-century photography was essentially a specialist technology hence the preponderance of studio portraits • The constraints of the technology (expense, long exposure times required etc.) dictated the decorum of the format. For example, the requirement not to move for 60 seconds or more militates against the relaxed cheerfulness which is the norm for the twentieth-century snapshot. Perhaps Victorian families were not as grim as they appear • The expense entailed in the production of this document gave is a 'value' dimension largely missing from Figure 4.2 • Monochrome photographs, processed to certain standards and stored under appropriate conditions, are of archival quality.	• The technology for creating the document is widely and inexpensively available • Amateur snapshots are infinitely more common than formal studio portraits • Nineteenth-century constraints have been obviated by improved technology • The document is cheaply produced and regarded as, more or less, disposable or replaceable • There is no archival standard for colour photography. Chemical reactions continue after processing and fixing causing colour shifts. This document is *changing*.

ACCESSIBILITY	An understanding of all of the above has an impact upon the way we read and value this document. In addition there is another level of contextual detail, not present, but intrinsic to the document, on which our access to all of its information value is dependent, such as: • Who *are* these people? • When was the document created? • What is its provenance?	As for Figure 4.1.

The question of a photograph's authority, in the sense of its being an exact record of a particular moment in time and, as such, deserving of some level of special credence from its audience, is an interesting and complex one – too complex to explore at any length here. However, just as any intentional document can be analyzed as an information construct filtered through a raft of structural and other conventions, media constraints, creator intentions and user perceptions and needs, a photograph or film is the product of technological mediation and human *choice*. The images analyzed in the table above, for example, are, variously, the product of a photographer's selection of the moment, the conscious arrangement of content elements, the subjects' decisions about how they wish to be captured, chemical and other manipulation of the negative and print and technological compensations for (or 'ignorance' of) the quirks of human visual perception. (Have you ever wondered why the impressive mountain range you photograph appears as a series of inconsequential bumps on the horizon in the prints returned by the processor?) Both these images are as much the product of art and artifice as they are unmediated records of reality. The boundaries between snapshot and Art are quite indistinct. The most recent technological advance – the digital camera and the highly (and *seamlessly*) editable documents it produces – has created a whole raft of new issues for this form.

Fortunately, other document genres and sub-genres are less fraught with layers of complexity simply because they are less ambitious, like a shopping list, or because we are so immersed in their conventions, their structural and other templates, that we can negotiate with them with unalloyed confidence.

The traditional business letter, for example, is readily and unambiguously analyzable. Figure 4.3, written as it is in a language other than that of this text, is nevertheless quite easily identifiable as a letter and, upon a closer examination, almost certainly a business letter in particular. Even when we are denied access to the content, we can still recognize the form because we recognize the structure. The placement of the date/place of origin, salutation, signing off, and signature, the (cultural) expectation that the text runs left to right / top to bottom are hallmarks of the letter form. That it is probably a business letter is signalled in the use of letterhead and the presence of some text below the signature, which is probably an indicator of the author's official position within an agency. Moving onto a more speculative level, it would not be completely outrageous to infer that part of the content of this communication is to do with publications of some type since several terms are underlined – a still-current convention, in handwritten English at least, for identifying published materials.

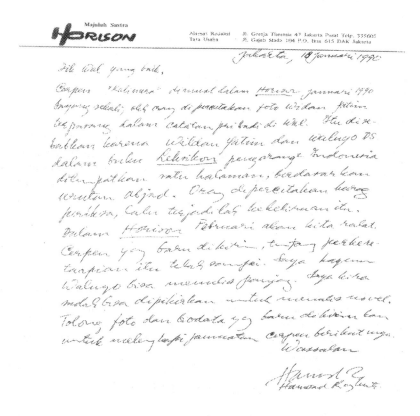

Figure 4.3. 'almost certainly a business letter'?

Because the template and protocols of the form are familiar to us we are able to make some inroads into the content and purpose of the document, even if we can't literally or narrowly *read* it. In a real sense, the form is part of the content – the part we read intuitively.

Inevitably, it is impossible to separate out analytical threads like structure and content, content and context, or medium and purpose, in ways which allow one to discuss one element in isolation from another. Available technologies have their impact upon a form's format and purpose. Is an email just an electronic letter? Does a business email have the standing of a business letter? The democratization of key technologies in the twentieth century has changed perceptions of the value of different forms. How can we tell that a digital image is not *all artifice* and not a record in any sense? Regardless of technology or medium, the content, context, purpose and format of a form are highly interdependent.

Nevertheless, documents need to be 'readable', classifiable, and usable. We can't exploit or value a document if we don't know what it is and identification of a genre, a sub-genre and a form are a starting point.

Document analysis: The near and far, the side by side

Different professional communities manage the different types of memory stores contained in documents on behalf of individuals, organizations and society. Their practices and theoretical frames of reference relate to the purpose and role played by documents, individually and collectively as art, knowledge, evidence and infotainment, and in constituting corporate and collective memory. Librarians, for example, manage collections of documents as knowledge repositories. They construct relationships between documents primarily on the basis of their subject content, and the people and organizations responsible for their authorship and publication. Museum curators manage artefacts, weaving into their management the stories they can tell about people and their sciences and technologies. Records managers and archivists manage accumulations of documents as evidence of social and organizational activity. The documentary relationships in the archive are formed with reference to the functions, activities, and transactions they document, and the people and organizations engaged in them.

By focusing on their own functions these professions have been able to establish separate identities but technological changes over the last half of the century have begun to challenge these identities. This has been made apparent, for example, in the growing emphasis in our era on knowledge management Many communities of practice can claim to be contributors to knowledge management for society, our organizations, our work groups, and for individuals. The quest has begun for 'a new discourse that integrates largely disconnected domains of knowledge management research and practice'.[4]

The integration ideal within the study of knowledge management can be said to raise what Michel Foucault saw as the quintessential form of analysis of our times, the juxtaposition of the near and far, the side by side.[5] Foucault practised what he preached. As an historian he took the analysis of documents contained within nearby archival non-discursive practices (what archivists do on a daily basis which was side by side with Foucault as a researcher using archival search rooms) applying it to literary documents within his histories of ideas.

---

[4] Cited from the call for papers, Knowledge Management Track, for the IRMA (Information Resources Management Assocation) conference, New Orleans, May 23-24, 2004.
[5] See Edward De Soja, 'Heterotopologies: A Remembrance of Other Spaces in the Citadel-LA', in *Postmodern Cities and Spaces*, ed. by Sophie Watson & Katherine Gibson, Cambridge, Blackwell, 1995, pp. 13-34 for an account of this style of Foucauldian analysis, including setting out Foucault's belief that we are in 'the epoch of the near and far, of the side by side, of the dispersed' (p. 17).

The result was a genre of historical writing that was capable of spanning vast periods of time and looked at ideas in the specificities of their occurrence rather than seeing their development as linear and progressive.

The three authors of this chapter can give a broadly situated example of what this 'near and far, side by side' analysis means. Less than a decade ago we worked together in a School of Information Management, bringing together 'side by side' professionals interested in document management (librarians, archivists and records managers). Our nearest familial relations were with the Faculty of Arts but within the decision-making apparatus of the University we seemed to be too 'practical' a form of study for that setting. With a number of other 'applied' discourses uncomfortably located within academic departments we were shifted into a ragbag Faculty of Professional Studies. At that time, the University's School of Information Systems with its emphasis on routine transactions within data-based computing seemed distant from us. Changing technologies were altering that proximity however, and we now are an element of a School of Information Management and Systems within the Information Technology faculty. Our School contains a number of cognate disciplinary formations including information systems analysis, information technology management, decision support systems, information management, librarianship, and records and archives management. Beyond the University there are sites of practice to which we must also relate and, in those sites, side by side meanings of the word management have to be considered. These include project management, time management, financial management, resource management, legal management, risk management, and the historical management of documents over time.

These immediate structural relationships can be said to provide our prime integration concerns in a practical survival sense, but within the University and beyond the Faculty of Information Technology there are many other academic sites at Monash University that are part of the 'disconnected' domain of knowledge management research and practice which at any time can be subject to 'near and far, side by side' analysis. These include all of the arts and language disciplines (part of our earlier nearness), but no discipline will be without a perspective on the relationship between documents and knowledge derived from their learning and experiences. The meanings of documents, their nature as signs of action, their significances and how we value (or do not value) them can and is able to be probed from many directions. And underlying all the probing of documents there is diplomatics, the first emergence of a study of documents codified by Jean Mabillon in the eighteenth century, interest in which is undergoing resurgence within the archival profession because of its possible relevancies when placed side by side with electronic recordkeeping issues.

In picking our ways through the relational challenges that changing technologies and structural change have imposed we have relied much on a recordkeeping approach because of its ability to connect with different discourses. In the next sections of this chapter we will look at some examples of changing relationships between archivists and a few other disciplines, working out from document analysis and illustrating recordkeeping approaches to such analysis.

Recordkeeping and sociology

The nearness of some aspects of sociology with recordkeeping resides in our common valuing of the storage of recorded information and in the concept of communicative transactions. One of the twentieth century's most influential sociologists, Anthony Giddens, for example, is interested in the way recorded information connects communities spatially (across the members of the community) and through the broader reaches of time, enabling the stability and continuity of those communities as recognizable groups. The very construction of the community is built out of the way it stores information, by which Giddens means the way information is represented, recalled and disseminated. Giddens argues that recorded information can be allocative (able to be shared by the community) or authoritative (a control upon what can be said and done in a society). Giddens sees this resource as one which operates within the memory traces of individual members of a society (the size of the community the word society represents is scaleable, and can be quite a small grouping of people through to national groupings).[6]

A thorough monograph about print communications at a distance by David S. Kaufer and Kathleen M. Carley draws a lot of sustenance from Giddens' work and puts forward an interactive explanation of how memory traces operate in a society. They present a dynamic model dealing with the communicative transactions which occur between agents. As agents communicate, the transactions *change* the positioning in which further communicative transactions take place:

> Through the communicative transaction, individuals interact, communicate, adapt and reposition themselves in the socio-cultural landscape. The communicative transaction is a cyclic process in which the full cycle is repeated each time period. Through each cycle of the transaction, social structure and culture co-evolve.[7]

Within their model communicative transactions are comprised of content (that which is communicated), code (the material structure of the communication) and meaning.

The section in their book on the ecology of a printed communication (see the reading list at the end of this chapter) provides useful explanations of the socio-cultural landscapes, technological conditions in that landscape, the fixity and durability of a communication, and the importance of signatures, handles on information for retrieval purposes, the fidelity of the communication, its reach, ways to view the agents, and its authority. From a recordkeeping viewpoint, Kaufer and Carley's explanation has many similarities with the form of document analysis presented earlier, but extends the analysis into a fuller treatment of the ecology of documents in ways that tease out many of the issues connected to the print communication as an authoritative resource which, by the very nature of its stable presence in the landscape, exerts some controls over what can be said and connects to the notion of documents as a structuring component of social processes. Within these sorts of theories in

---

[6] Anthony Giddens, *The Constitution of a Society,* Cambridge, Polity Press, 1984.
[7] David S. Kaufer and Kathleen M. Carley, *Communication at a Distance*, New Jersey, Lawrence Erlbaum and Associates, 1993.

sociology, recorded information becomes more than a stored object, a thing. The storage of that object sets up processes influenced by the nature of its storage. Documents can be seen as vehicles for action which initiate or control subsequent actions in ways that in turn shape communities.

There is a nearness to recordkeeping in such theories, but there is also an element of farness that needs to be conceptually juxtaposed. Recordkeeping is more concerned with the physical and logical representation of the resource itself, with the formation of the resource as it accretes within what Kaufer and Carley describe as communicative transaction cycles which take them back to the thing. They describe recorded information, appraise it for continued retention, and make it accessible. The purposes are the actual storage processes themselves, not their impact, and traditionally the archival purpose has been shared with librarians in relation to all forms of recorded information. To be able to access or retrieve something, first we must have stored it, and stored it in a way that will enable it to be accessible for as long as required. Storing authoritative transactional records so that they can be accessed are the essence of recordkeeping processes, storing them for as long as is required is the essence of archiving processes.

Documents and records as evidence

Within common English usage, documents as objects can be seen as functioning as information products that can inform, perpetuate knowledge, convey ideas, feelings and opinions, and entertain. Documents intended to serve these purposes are usually published or broadcast widely. That common usage, however, has been slow to find its way into English-language dictionaries, many of which have persisted in maintaining original Latin meanings of the word with the addition of a bias towards paper as a medium of storage. Within that approach the evidential value of documents is a matter related to its internal content. Documents in these modern paper-fixated meanings are likely to be defined as written or printed matter that furnishes conclusive information or evidence. The examples dictionaries give are usually original, legal or official papers or records. Indeed many documents are consciously created on paper to provide evidence or conclusive information. Diaries, journals, receipts and legal documents such as contracts all serve this purpose, but increasingly such supposedly conclusive information or evidence is being kept electronically. The way we keep such documents is part of our 'official' record, its originality is important, and there is often a legal or official aspect present in what we choose to document.

In Australia the Commonwealth and State evidence acts have defined documents more in accord with common usage and with no bias towards any medium of storage. A document is defined as any type of discrete object that has been recorded and can be retrieved. In a classic treatise R.A. Brown canvassed all Australian legislation in the 1980s and concluded that

documents are defined in legal terms as:
(1) some physical thing or medium
(2) on which data are
(3) more or less permanently recorded
(4) in such a manner that data can be subsequently retrieved.[8]

Such a definition sets up an approach where the evidential nature of the document can be tested in courts of law. As things under Australian law documents to be tested can comprise text (writing, numbers, and musical notation), image (pictures, paintings, photographs, diagrams, graphs, and maps), moving image (film, video), recorded sound (speech, music, noise) or products of a database, providing the output can be shown to have been a product of a system working continuously in accordance with its own rules of operation, including the recording of any alterations to the content.

Until the last decade English-language archival literature has tended to focus on legal concepts of evidence when discussing the issue of evidence itself, but in the 1990s archivists worldwide within what is being described here as a recordkeeping approach have moved back to exploring the Latinate approach to documents in which the proving process resides in the document. The high level of transactionality in modern societies is directing attention at the need for more immediate explorations of documents as proof of something than are available through courts of law. More readily applicable recordkeeping tests have been developed within research projects over the last decade in which the testing device is the way records have been made and managed.[9]

This shift might seem minor and technical but the difference between recordkeeping evidence and legal evidence has coincidentally become a major issue on the world stage. The rethinking has been timely, even if it can also be politically uncomfortable for government archivists. After the terrorist attacks on New York's 'twin towers' (September 11, 2001), the United State's government started to gather international support for an attack on the Taliban government of Afghanistan. The recordkeeping-based evidence which linked the Taliban with international terrorism was strong and many countries fell quickly into line with the United State's projected invasion of Afghanistan. The United States was not interested in using this evidence within legal forums, pleading the case for prompt action. In 2003, however, when the United States tried to draw similar widespread support for an attack on the government of Iraq it was not forthcoming. There was not enough evidence in the intelligence records before the attack was mounted to sustain the charge that

---

[8] R.A. Brown, *Documentary Evidence in Australia*, Sydney, The Law Book Company, 1996, p. 9.
[9] Major sites of research include InterPARES, based at the University of British Columbia (http://www.interpares.org/), Functional Requirements for Evidence in Recordkeeping at the University of Pittsburgh (http://web.archive.org/web/20001024112939/www.sis.pitt.edu/~nhprc/), and the Monash University Records Continuum Research Group (http://www.sims.monash.edu.au/research/rcrg). The Pittsburgh research influenced Australian records management standards and international ones which provide an application view of requirements. Applications of the Australian standard can be further explored on the records management related web pages of the National Archives of Australia (www.naa.gov.au) and State Records, NSW (www.records.nsw.gov.au).

the Baathist party dictatorship in Iraq represented a 'clear and present danger' far beyond its own borders.[10]

This movement back to non-legal tests of evidence raises the issue of the synonymous nature of the terms documents and records. In many Latin-influenced languages there is no word for record; the term document suffices since it incorporates the notion of evidence. The legal systems in such countries have always given more weight to the testimony in documents, subjecting them to less rigorous scrutiny than British and British-derived legal systems. In English, however, the synonym record has a very useful diffracted meaning. It is a memorial directed at the establishment of authentic evidence of a fact or event. Here a key issue is a preconceived intent to keep a document as a record, indicated by dictionary examples of records which specify as records such documents as rolls, registers and calendars. How this intent is working itself out in the recordkeeping at the beginning of this century will be discussed in the next chapter of this book when the focus will turn to forming documents as records, but one section of the recent International Records Management standard (which uses the term record in its English version but clearly relates to the notion of a legal document in Australian law) is worth citing here, the quality of integrity:

7.2.4 Integrity
The integrity of a record refers to its being complete and unaltered. It is necessary that a record be protected against unauthorized alteration. Records management policies and procedures should specify what additions or annotations may be made to a record after it is created, under what circumstances additions, or annotations may be authorized, and who is authorized to make them. Any authorized annotation, addition or deletion to a record should be explicitly indicated and traceable.[11]

Recordkeeping professionals, then, share with the legal profession an interest in the document as an object that contains evidence and have a special interest in managing it in ways that maintain its integrity. Documents that record personal and organizational activities function as evidence and such documents are increasingly being viewed in a recordkeeping sense. A relationship which was so near that archivist bowed to legal views when discussing records as evidence is now becoming a side by side relationship. Recordkeeping evidence may or may not stand up in court but within highly transactional societies built around electronic communications it will be the main testing ground of the way documents provide proof of personal, business and cultural activity; establish personal and cultural identity; and function as personal, corporate or collective memory. As instruments of power and authority, documents have always regulated and controlled business and social relationships between people and organizations, but the issue is

---

[10] After victory was claimed, enquiries into whether reliable and authentic evidence had been provided to the Government by intelligence agencies were set up in the USA and Great Britain.
[11] ISO 15489, *International Standard for Records Management, Part 1 – General*, 2001, is cited here because of the manner in which it corresponds with the type of object described by R.A. Brown in the quote used in this section.

resuming a centrality to social operations that it has not had in English-speaking countries since the days of Geoffrey Chaucer and *The Canterbury Tales*.

Documents, information objects and metadata

The renewed interest in the archival profession in evidence is knitting together a small community of archivists from many cultural backgrounds who can see the importance of developing more global approaches to recordkeeping systems, and within this group changes are occurring in their views of the juxtapositioning of the archivist with information management, information engineering and information systems professionals. Perhaps the area of activity where this is most apparent is metadata research and application.[12]

For thousands of years people have been using what we now call metadata – structured or semi-structured data about information objects – as a powerful tool in the identification, classification, and description of documents to serve multiple purposes. Such objects are often inscribed with metadata, e.g. by etching notches onto message sticks which serve as aide-memoires for the messengers and establish their credentials as transmitters of oral documents; by annotating a letter with its date of receipt; numbering the spines of a set of financial ledgers; by labelling a book with the name of the owner; by including a copyright date and cataloguing-in-publication data in the preliminary pages of a book; by putting a registration number on a file; by captioning a photograph; adding titles and credits to a film; or by including meta-tags in the headers of HTML documents. Metadata is also captured in specially constructed metadata repositories like registers, indexes, catalogues, classification schemes, and descriptive systems, which manage documents individually and collectively as records.

The process of developing metadata schemes and applying them is, then, a long-standing information management and recordkeeping activity, even if the word metadata itself has only recently been ascribed to the processes involved. Over time, the professional communities responsible for managing documents as knowledge, evidence and infotainment have developed standardized ways of identifying, classifying and describing them in order to manage their storage and preservation, assure their accuracy, reliability and authenticity, assist in their discovery, retrieval, dissemination and use, and manage the rights, and conditions of access and use associated with them. Examples of such schemes include the Dewey Classification Scheme, the Anglo American Cataloguing Rules, the International Standard for Archival Description (General), the taxonomies developed by the museum community, and the descriptive schemas used by archaeologists and palaeontologists.

The process is now becoming a major component of information engineering. In global contexts, interoperable frameworks are evolving for the development of standard sets of

---

[12] See footnote 9.

metadata that are common to all objects (general metadata), as well as the development of metadata schemas that are unique to the management of particular types of information objects for particular purposes (special metadata).

Resource discovery metadata standards like the Dublin Core and the closely related Australian Standard, Australian Government Locator System (AGLS), are examples of general schemas that aim to define standardized sets of common elements for the identification and description of document-like objects in Internet environments. The AGLS standard groups its metadata elements in three categories.[13]

Resource Ownership & Creator Metadata	Resource Intellectual Content Metadata	Resource Electronic or Physical Manifestation Metadata
Creator	Title	Date
Publisher	Subject	Type
Contributor	Description	Format
Rights	Source	Identifier
	Language	Availability
	Relation	
	Coverage	
	Function	
	Audience	
	Mandate	

For those archivists interested in evidence a general scheme for classifying metadata relating to documents or aggregations of documents is as follows:

- Identification
- Content
- Structure
- Context
- Rights management, and terms and conditions of use
- Document management events
- Metadata management events.

The approach is directed at the ongoing management of communicated transactions over time, making them as self-managing as possible. In terms of this classification, it may be

---

[13] The National Archives of Australia was given oversight responsibilities for the application of AGLS (www.naa.gov.au, accessible over time via www.archive.org – see for example the NAA's 2002 archived sites).

possible to use standardized common metadata elements to identify documents and to describe aspects of their content and structure, as well as to provide an audit trail of metadata management events. However to extend this approach into fully workable sets there will be a need to standardize across different documentary forms and purposes. Metadata will be needed that describes aspects of content and structure that are unique to those forms and purposes and which cater to their particular documentary contexts, rights management, terms and conditions of use, and management events. This requires specially engineered sets of metadata elements to uniquely identify, name, date and locate documents according to their form or purpose, and to describe their logical and physical structure and format, their documentary contexts (e.g. their source, control, and authority), the nature of their relationship with associated people and organizations, related activities and events, and the processes involved in managing them. These sets will be unique to particular professional communities of practice. This takes us on to what, borrowing from information systems analysis, could be called a use case approach where there is need to explore different cases leading reliably to a required output.

For a while this object-oriented process can be expected to cause confusion. The archival profession, for example, initially saw metadata schemes as a major solution, and like most professions that are involved in information management have witnessed with some alarm the proliferation of metadata standards into a confusing soup of approaches for different information objects including databases. As familiarity grows with the utility of particular cases, as interested groups engineer their own sets more effectively, and as more and more cross-walks (comparisons across schemes) develop the confusion can be expected to diminish.

One of the problems being addressed within archival research into metadata is its layering of data related to recordkeeping and archiving processes. Within what can be described as the document layer there is the issue of what data can be impressed upon the document (addresses, signatures, dates of creation, topics and the like) and what needs to be expressively added during initial creation and reception processes. In terms of developing metadata to carry information objects through time space, including documents, there is a need to consider the impact of other layers of management needs through:

- recordkeeping data (see chapter 5);
- data needed to manage the object within organizational or enterprise-wide systems and even for personal documents, within 'whole of person' approaches, fitting the document into all the documentation of an individual (see chapter 6); and
- data needed to manage the archives as a multiple resource containing the documentation of many organizations, enterprises and individuals (see chapter 7).

As indicated above, the next three chapters in this book will all present information relevant to understanding such research, but the problem can be expressed here working out from the earlier method of document analysis and the example of photographs. Imagine you are creating a document such as a photo for your photograph album. It might be purely for your own use, and that use might be short-term. You may not want to do much more than capture items in fixed form by printing out a copy and not place much importance on your electronic copy other than as a temporary production mechanism. You can then put an electronic copy on your computer with no surrounding information and no other control than placing it into a 'my pictures' directory. You may however want to remember what the document was all about some time in a more distant future and pass it on to friends, so you will enter it into a photograph album and include data associated with it (when it was taken, who is in the photograph, where it was taken and so on). Physically this might be an album for prints, an electronic file within a photograph album directory or both. This is venturing into records capture. You may, however, want to post it to a private web site, accessible by your parents and close friends. This could affect the data you capture about the photograph, and might involve organizing a different view of the album from your own personal album. You may not want your friends to see that ugly photograph of you taken at the beach. You may however have a personal web site with unrestricted access to all. The access paths to your photograph album might again be different from your personal album or your family and friends' album with access paths and forms of capture and organizing that are distinctly different. When you take a photograph, you may have all of these uses in mind, or only one, and that will affect how you manage the photograph. If you aim to do all or many things at once you will have a different approach to one where you have only one purpose in mind. At a later date, however, you might curse yourself for having only one purpose in mind. It is much harder to establish other purposes if they have not been included in your original systems design and within the information engineering you have undertaken to implement your intentions.

Returning to an earlier reference in this chapter to the importance of storage for access, complex decisions with far reaching implications will have to be made in relation to the format for storage of both the photograph and the metadata. One of the aims of metadata research within the archival profession is to set up the reliable use of data that can assist in the storage of information objects over time. In the paper world this may involve the use of appropriate papers which have a guaranteed lifetime, or making reference copies of fragile or much sought-after records on alternative media, such as microfilm or digital images, to protect the original. In the electronic world, the issue of storage and accessibility involves more complex strategic decisions which will affect accessibility over time, including decisions about both data and media formats. Concerns about the format of data in which to store the records are primarily related to trying to avoid known proprietary formats where the lifetime of the format is dependent on a specific manufacturer or product vendor.[14] In our current office automation environment most of the major records-creating mechanisms are proprietary. Media formats and locations also require decisions – will the records be online via a web site, in a local store on your computer, in a corporate store, on CD or on

---

[14] Preservation formats will pose fewer carriage-through-time problems as appropriate readers can be retained and used along with the material, but, by capturing a document in fixed form, there is currently a considerable loss of functionality relating to retrieval and ongoing management, and any applications must address this. A good web site for exploration of the use of one of the earliest preservation and metadata strategies in Australia is that of the Public Record Office Victoria. The US National Archives and Records Administration has at the time of writing begun to develop detailed systems approaches.

DVD? Many of these issues will need to be addressed by policy decisions applicable across systems and the decisions made will impact on how the processes of migration or management of software-dependent records over time are applied. Metadata tags can be used to assist in such migration and management.

Document computing

The previous section indicates the growing nearness of information systems and information engineering discourses and the management of documents. Yet there is also a farness that has shaped those discourses. It is only a decade ago that information systems analysts were regularly told via their textbooks that documents were unstructured data, a proposition that wipes out the very existence of Jean Mabillon and the science of diplomatics in which the main object of study is how documents are structured through the positioning of (linguistic) data. What the textbooks meant was that documents were not structured out of data in the same manner as the structuring processes set up within database paradigms. They were structured in linguistic forms beyond the routines that the data processing capacities of mainframe computers could recognise.

In this era at practical levels proprietary products like Lotus Notes began to come on the market setting up repositories for electronic documents which failed to consider satisfactorily the notion of the fixity of documents, their authenticity, or their authoritative nature. More recently in information technology texts there is a growing closeness in the views of technologists and archivists about the need for fixed documents, but it is a closeness that mirrors the concept of a document within paper-fixated views of the document. In these approaches there will be a very small section in the textbook on imaging systems and the capture of the document within formats that provide for the storage of a fixed object but there is still no consideration in basic texts about the authoritative nature of documents.[15] At practical levels electronic document management programs are now being implemented widely in our organizations that are derived from this patchy way of thinking about documents.

There is, however, another view developing in information systems and technology discourses which can be placed alongside the recordkeeping strand of archival theory and practice. The first analyst to present it was David Bearman, an information systems consultant who became involved in archival research projects for ten years or so from the late 1980s. Bearman produced one of the first descriptions of an electronic document phrased in terms that his fellow analysts (and archivists with an interest in recordkeeping systems or diplomatic science) would understand:

---

[15] See for example Patrick G. McKeown, *Information Technology and the Networked Economy*, 2nd ed., Boston, Mass., Course Technology, 2003, where document management systems are defined broadly in the glossary, but in the text are dealt with briefly in terms of the conversion of paper into a digital format (see pp. 471 and 163-164).

The data of the record are the words, numbers, images, and sounds actually made by the creator of the record. The structure of the record is the relationships among these data as employed by the record creator to convey meaning. One kind of structure is the stylistic formalisms which we use to recognize the 'address', 'salutation', or 'body' of written documents. Another kind of structure is the pointers between physically or logically distinct groupings of information ... The context of the record is the testimony it provides about the nexus of activity out of which it arose and in which it was used and about how it appeared and behaved in that setting.[16]

Although Bearman uses the synonymous term 'record' in this description, he is describing a document as the laws of evidence in the legal systems in English-speaking countries would understand it to be and is pointing to something which can loosely be called document computing, although over the last ten years or so there has been a reluctance to call an electronic document a document. It has been customary to talk of

- virtual documents (a document where the form seems the same but the structure is dramatically different from paper documents)
- compound documents (a document which can be built up from the bits when we need to do so, or interactively changes and alters as related data within the document is changed as in spreadsheet applications)
- fluid documents (documents which can be changed or reconstructed, which is usually set against the term 'fixed' documents) and
- document-like objects (a general term that implies that what we are looking at is like a paper equivalent, but we know its structural conditions are different).

Document computing can, despite the uneasiness with the very term document, be summarized briefly. The data in documents are the internal bits of the electronic document, its linguistic elements, photographs, sound and other media elements which can be manipulated and managed in computerized systems every bit as much as data can be within traditional database approaches. Surrounding the documents as discrete objects there are more bits of data, constructible within metadata schemes. Using the external data about the document one can retrieve the documents for reuse and manage it through various events that may take place. The object can be captured as a fixed object when it is communicated (including the system communication processes involved in saving a document).

When a document is communicated the parallels with paper models of a fixed document become relevant, but fixity restricts the continuing functionality of the document as a fluid object. Bearman proposed solving this dilemma by having recordkeeping systems sitting underneath our information systems. The information system would hold fully functional fluid entities and the recordkeeping system would hold fixed objects, capturing the changes and alterations and holding the objects in native formats which could be migrated forward drawing on the developing power of the Internet as a point of storage for migration

---

[16] David Bearman, *Electronic Evidence,* Pittsburgh, Archives and Museum Informatics, 1994, pp. 147-148.

programs. It was too futuristic an approach for its time even though it was not too advanced a conceptualization within then existing technologies.[17] To implement it one needs to address technical delivery issues such as gaining the commitment of software providers to making migration programs available on the Internet. One also needs to apply a host of business management techniques operating in side by side fashion including work flow analysis, functional analysis, risk management, and enterprise resource planning. Archivists and records managers also have to be committed to maintaining and extending metadata management through time.[18]

In another clear indicator that by the mid 1990s the document was beginning to find its way into information systems sites of discourse in ways that recordkeeping professionals can recognize, a US organization, Delphi Computing, produced a white paper on the document as process. In it the potential for businesses to incorporate documents into their business processes more fully within electronic environments was indicated clearly, a potential which these days is being realized within electronic commerce and many forms of business communications between organizations.[19]

It also, in a more hypothetical passage than anything David Bearman ever presented, set out a clear view of a projected form of knowledge management as process:

> You require additional documentation to formulate an opinion for today's meeting. You enter the corporate filing room and begin making enquiries regarding this matter. Like clockwork, you are directed to specific areas and documents. Certain documents pique your curiosity. You reach into the cabinets and turn them in such a way that the documents of similar or related content cluster together. Moments later, a condensed version of all financial related documents is sent to your desk; it includes predictions over future trends, using your premise statement as a springboard. You are about to leave for the meeting feeling very much more prepared; suddenly you are tapped on the shoulder. It is another document, just published, which is crucial to the argument you are going to make. Sound too good to be true? Then consider this – you have never left your desk.

You may not have left your desk, but you may well have left your chair a few inches from the shock of being touched on the shoulder by an electronic document. You would have also moved a fair way into the twenty-first century. It raises all the side by side business analysis issues mentioned above (and in the next chapter), but, unlike the Bearman proposition, it lacks any attention to the authoritative nature of the resource. How reliable would this shoulder-tapping document be? Was it constructed within good recordkeeping

---

[17] David Bearman, 'Item Level Control and Electronic Recordkeeping', a paper delivered to the 1996 conference of the Society of American Archivists, published in *Archives and Museum Informatics,* 20, no. 3, 1996, pp. 195-245.

[18] This business analysis and metadata approach has shaped the work of IT 21, the committee of Standards Australia that has been developing records management standards.

[19] The Delphi Group, 'The Document is the Process, *Delphi White Paper*, 1994, available at: http://dheise.andrews.edu/courses/MIS/KM/DocIsProcess.pdf

systems, how has it been arranged within corporate stores so that it knows when to present itself and is capable of doing so, and how well does it draw on recorded information external to the organization? When you finally escape from your desktop and get to the meeting, will you talk sense or nonsense? Not surprisingly Delphi Computing and similar companies have been led from their initial realizations that 'the document is the process' into deeper and deeper explorations of knowledge management.

Conclusion

In Australia the attempt to create a side by side relationship between systems design and recordkeeping is a serious one. For those who want to explore this issue further the web sites of the Commonwealth and State archives, particularly State Records NSW, provide a wealth of information and ideas, and standards for records management can be purchased from Standards Australia. If such comments seem outside the parameters of a chapter on documents, it must be borne in mind that many Australian initiatives in the area operate within a records continuum framework. As we said at the beginning of this chapter, we live in a web of documents, but the documentary web is a broad construct. Managing documents will never be achieved by focusing exclusively upon them. The web is spun out of data. Data provides both the internal constituent elements of documents (for example the words as text, the images, the tables and charts and other elements that make up the structure of the content of a document) and is an external mechanism for managing and controlling the objects we have created. The document itself can be compared with the joining points in the web, the nodes that hold it together. Its threads are like the records, and the web's sectional structuring is like the archive of organizations and individuals. The totality is the web itself, the archives as the sum total of data, documents, records and archives that envelop us. The next three chapters of this book will examine the structuring of the web of archives building out from the document and its analysis.[20]

---

[20] In looking at documents from a recordkeeping viewpoint, one can just as easily work back from the archives or from the record or archive. The linearity is imposed by chapter structuring but the editors have tried to make sure the chapters in this book are sufficiently stand-alone to be read in any order.

Readings

- Michael Buckland, 'Information as Thing', *Journal of the American Society for Information Science*, 42, no. 5, 1991, pp. 351-360.

  This article sets out in rigorously argued fashion the concepts of information as knowledge, process and thing.

- Luciana Duranti, *Diplomatics: New Uses for an Old Science*, Lanham, Scarecrow Press, 1998.

  A major treatise providing an archivist's perspective on diplomatics based on articles which were first published in the Canadian journal, Archivaria.

- David S. Kaufer and Kathleen M. Carley, *Communication at a Distance: The Influence of Print on Sociocultural Organization and Change*, New Jersey, Lawrence Erlbaum and Associates, 1993, pp. 87-162 (chapter 4: Communicative Transactions and their Ecology).

  Although this deals specifically with print, its constructivist approach is of general application and in chapter 4 there is an extensive and finely honed discussion of the ecology of communications that is pertinent to document analysis.

- Heather MacNeil, 'Proving Grounds for Trust II; the Findings of the Authenticity Taskforce of InterPARES', *Archivaria*, 54, 2002, pp. 24-58.

  Perhaps more relevant as reading for the next chapter, but contains comments on the relevance of diplomatics and the document aspects of the InterPARES project (see www.interpares.org).

- James M. O'Toole, 'The Symbolic Significance of Archives', *American Archivist*, 56, no. 2, 1993, pp. 234-255.

  This article looks at the symbolic aspects of documents and records, (both the 'loved and the hated') as part of the context of their occurrence.

- Linda Schamber, 'What is a Document? Rethinking the Concept in Uneasy Times', *Journal of the American Society for Information Science,* 47, no. 9, 1996, pp. 669-671.

  An introduction to the changing nature of documents as discrete units of information.

CHAPTER 5

Records

Barbara Reed

Introduction

Records are part of our mass culture. They can be observed in the forensic scientist on
television speaking quietly into a tape recorder making observations on a corpse, in the
making of incident reports in every television crime show, in the recording and storing of
'precog's visions' in the Hollywood film *Minority Report*, or in paper-chase films, such as
Erin Brockovich or *Disclosure*. We see records in historical contexts in novels and films
such as *Schindler's List* or *Possession*. Recordkeeping appears frequently in novels,
particularly crime-related novels. Every day on the front pages of our papers, stories
referring to records appear,[1] especially at times of crisis, presenting phrases like 'missing
records', 'review of Anderson's records management policy' (in the light of the Enron
scandal) and headlines relating to the standards of evidence used to justify the United
States-led attack against Iraq, by which some governments claimed to have wiser
intelligence about the situation in Iraq than that in the reports made by the Chief United
Nations Weapons Inspector, Dr Hans Blix, to the United Nations Security Council.

These randomly compiled examples show two things: firstly that, as members of society at
the beginning of the twenty-first century, we are enmeshed in the world of records to the
point where they become almost invisible as just a part of the background to the conduct of
our lives. Every day, both in our business and personal lives, we interact with the records of
others, build our own and rely on records in many ways. The second point is that, at times
of crisis, however they are defined – personally, locally, nationally or internationally – we
turn to or seek authoritative records to support or deny actions and provide us with accounts
of what happened, when and who knew about it.

Every one of us carries around cards with barcodes or identification numbers that enable us
to transact business with banks, video stores, libraries, and so on. The routine nature of
these transactions often provides uncomplimentary representations of the professionals that
are responsible for records (boring, staid, obsessive people linked to metaphors of the
constraining nature of bureaucracy). But the systems sitting behind individual transactions

---

[1] See for example Charlie Farrugia, 'Print Media Perspectives on Recordkeeping', in Sue
McKemmish and Frank Upward, eds. *Archival Documents*, Melbourne, Ancora Press, 1993.

enable us to do things, and they hold societies and their members together in their day-to-day interaction.

Records are everywhere. But was not exactly the same assertion made in the previous chapter about documents? One could just as easily say in the two chapters following that the archive is everywhere and that all is archives. Documents and records have a particularly close relationship. The preceding chapter discusses oral documents, for example, yet this overlaps with oral traditions of recordkeeping, where the record is not committed to writing, but rather deliberately committed to memory by a 'remembrancer', a specifically entrusted person who was the keeper of the record. This chapter continues the exploration of the shades of meaning begun in the previous chapter, but is directed more at the question of what makes a record a record.

In the examples discussed above we can begin to extract some of the characteristics of a record. The critical characteristic is that a record has to be linked to doing something – it is inherently transactional in its nature. Doing something is a very broad notion – broad enough to cover actions that we take in our personal lives as well as those that are taken in work contexts. In our professional definitions, the notion of doing something is often expressed using the term 'business', as 'in the transaction of business', which points to a hallmark of a recordkeeping approach, the documentation of business activities. The use of this term has led some to a narrower view of business activities than the view described above. In this narrower view, the interpretation is restricted to the organizational context. But as individuals we also do things, whether it be participating in community organizations, ensuring that our children are immunized, or participating in family events. Documentation arising from these types of social transactions has equal potential to be records as documentation that arises in organizational contexts.

Records are different from other information resources because of this transactional aspect, which makes it important to identify the characteristics that must be present to ensure that records are reliable and authentic. The transactional aspect also makes it necessary to develop techniques for ensuring that records are created and managed in ways that assist in maintaining these characteristics. These characteristics make records quite different to data, documents and information. And yet, records consist of data/documents/information. They may consist of all of these things simultaneously. Thus a record may be a collection of data. It may be one document or a sequence of documents. It will definitely consist of information in some form. The distinguishing factor which makes records records is that they are managed in a particular way to ensure the characteristics identified throughout this chapter are present.

This way of conceptualizing what a record is removes it from the realm of the physical. We can manage anything as a record. The physicality of the object – electronic bytes, paper folios, pieces of furniture, photographs etc – is important as the starting point, but the critical nature of managing it as a record commences with the placement of that object in the context of doing something, into a relationship with other objects and ensures that all management processes to do with the object are documented according to recordkeeping standards. For example, in one of the most bizarre extremes, the entire cabin of the

Unabomber, Ted Kaczynski, was incorporated into the evidence compiled for his court trial and, consequently, became a record by virtue of the processes required to authenticate and verify its reliability and its subsequent use.[2]

Figure 5.1. Cabin-as-record: The cabin of 'Unabomber' Ted Kaczynski sits in a storage facility in California following its removal by the FBI from its original site in Montana.

Records and documents

With a recordkeeping perspective on documents, we don't just look at the individual item as in the previous chapter, but we look at it in a more systemic way, finding connections and links to other documents, to processes and to sequences of documents as enablers. Records, as already pointed out, need to be connected to doing something. Using the example of a video store card containing a barcode, the card in isolation is a document, but my card is what enables me to use the store through an interface to their system. As I use it,

---

[2] Ted Kaczynski conducted a personal campaign against computers, genetic engineering and environmental damage in the United States between 1978 and 1996. When he was apprehended in April 1996, his cabin in Lincoln, Montana, yielded up to 700 items of evidence and was moved from its location and made available as evidence in his trial.

it becomes a record because it creates a link to an authentication process I needed to go through to have the card issued, so the store knows where I live so they can chase me up with fines for overdue videos, and also they know that I can pay the fines when I incur them. It enables the store's systems to link the location of a specific video to me when I borrow it and to track that video when it is due back. The card of its borrowers and the records they become enable the store to manage preferences and the number of videos, to monitor the most popular videos, to conduct inventories of stock and so on. Without my card I can still use the store, but I need to conduct the authentication process every time to enable the store to connect me to the specific videos that I might want to borrow. So, the card by itself is a document, but it is a document that enables me to do something, and seen from the larger perspective of what it allows me to do, it becomes a record – something that creates linkages and associations with actions, data about actions, and other documents.

But we can't always rely on documents. The video card might be stolen, for example, or it may be a forgery. High profile instances of fake or fraudulent documents are well known. They include the notorious Hitler Diaries from 1983,[3] and a less globally known example, the fraudulent Commonwealth car driver's log which was used in an attempt to discredit one of Australia's High Court judges.[4] To prove a document reliable or fraudulent, that document has to be reconnected to the circumstances of its creation and the chain of actions undertaken on it subsequent to its creation. In other words, it has to be viewed as a record and, in order to perform these critical roles, we have to be able to *rely* on it.

There is a difference between legal evidence and recordkeeping evidence which is only just beginning to be widely understood within the archival profession as a result of research during the 1990s. As we saw in the previous chapter, a legal document has to be recorded – that is, it needs to exist at a point of time in a particular form and it needs to be able to be retrieved. Legal documents involve the document being more or less 'fixed'.[5] In British-derived legal systems documents can be 'proved' in court, which means not that it is factual proof but that it can be tested within legal rules of evidence. A record as an authentic individual item of evidence within recordkeeping approaches however, is provable because of the way it has been managed (see Definition 1 below).

---

[3] Of course we could take a different approach to the fraudulent records and use them quite legitimately to tell a different story. For example, it is quite possible to regard the Hitler Diaries as a fake in the context of not being the diaries of Hitler, but in another context, the business context of gulling *Der Stern*, these sixty-two volumes are quite legitimate records.

[4] In 2002 one of Australia's High Court judges was alleged, under parliamentary privilege, to have trawled for 'rough trade' among young male prostitutes in an official car. These allegations were supposedly upheld by the logs of the Commonwealth car driver. The logbooks and extracts from logbooks which were the supposed evidence of these incidents turned out to be forgeries.

[5] David S. Kaufer and Kathleen M. Carley, *Communication at a Distance*, New Jersey, Lawrence Erlbaum and Associates, 1993, contains a brief discussion of fixity of communications (pp. 100-101) which is placed within the ecology of communicative transactions, a very useful way of viewing this attribute.

AS/ISO 15489, Australian Standard Records Management, Part 1 – General, 2002

7.2.2 Authenticity

An authentic record is one that can be proven

a) to be what it purports to be,

b) to have been created or sent by the person purported to have created or sent it, and

c) to have been created or sent at the time purported.

To ensure the authenticity of records, organizations should implement and document policies and procedures which control the creation, receipt, transmission, maintenance and disposition of records to ensure that records creators are authorized and identified and that records are protected against unauthorized addition, deletion, alteration, use and concealment.

Definition 1. An individual communication object as an authentic record

Reliable records and records as contingent objects

The evidence in records does not disappear over time if they have been maintained as evidential objects, but the records often do disappear, or may never have been properly evidential in the first place In order to investigate, examine or assess a set of actions using records it makes no difference whether the actions were taken yesterday or 220 years ago, providing the records exist – both in terms of being made and also of being retained. Records, however, are not always properly made and retained. For example, an investigation into Gulf War illnesses found that:

> [The U.S. Department of Defense] medical recordkeeping for the Gulf War was grossly inadequate. There are no clear records of even basic information, such as the vaccine records of the men and women who served in the Gulf. It is unclear whether such records were ever kept or whether they were destroyed because they were not felt to be a high enough priority to warrant space on the military cargo planes returning to the United States after the war. Many of the medical records from the war are also missing … Finally there was no DoD recordkeeping on the range and extent of exposures present in the Gulf. All these factors seriously hinder any research efforts to establish a cause and effect for the health problems that followed the Gulf War.[6]

Such records clearly lack reliability (see Definition 2 below).

---

[6] *Report of the Special Investigation Unit on Gulf War Illnesses* (to the U.S. Senate, September 1, 1998), available at: http://www.globalsecurity.org/intell/library/congress/1998_cr/s980901-gulf.htm

AS/ISO 15489, *Australian Standard Records Management, Part 1 - General, 2002*

7.2.3 Reliability
A reliable record is one whose contents can be trusted as a full and accurate representation of the transactions, activities or facts to which they attest and can be depended upon in the course of subsequent transactions or activities. Records should be created at the time of the transaction or incident to which they relate, or soon afterwards, by individuals who have direct knowledge of the facts or by instruments routinely used within the business to conduct the transaction

Definition 2. Reliable recordkeeping processes

Reliable records need to be able to be recalled for any number of purposes, including to:

- understand what has been done previously in the course of completing the actions,
- check if something was done correctly,
- answer questions asked subsequent to the actions that took place,
- justify actions,
- provide precedents for acting consistently,
- provide assurance to people external to the action that those actions were appropriate,
- enable external scrutiny to show what happened in particular instances, and
- enable the information content of the record to be reused as required.

Records therefore have a dual role. They have to be able to act as evidence of actions and they have to be able to 'memorialize' or stand as a representation of action which can be recalled.

Records are, however, a construct, always virtual, consisting of the physical object and its relationships, links and contextual information, defined as much by the processes applied to their management as by the physical object itself. Organizations and individuals make decisions about what they accord records status to. For example, in many organizations drafts are not managed as records; only the final copy is. But in a legal office, where the business of the office is document production through negotiation between parties, drafts take on a different significance and are usually managed as records. Once an organization has determined what to manage as records, those data, documents and information identified as being records need greater protection through the application of routine processes to ensure reliability, authenticity, integrity and usability.

But how do organizations or individuals make that determination? The environment within which the transactions are taking place usually determines the choices, and often they are quite instinctive choices, which can be analysed logically. Consider the following case.

In making a purchase from a shop or supermarket, the transaction results in the issue of a receipt to you, the customer. What do you do with the receipt? Every day we make this decision. Usually we just scrunch the receipt into a ball and shove it in with the shopping to be thrown out along with the plastic shopping bag once the groceries are unloaded into our cupboards. The receipts detail our purchases in an itemized way. We could use this to cross-check our purchases, check that the sum total we were charged by the supermarket was appropriate and perhaps use it as a source document feeding into our financial management system to monitor our daily, weekly or monthly expenditure. This accumulated financial record then feeds into our personal budgets and the systems and calculations we may make in preparation for submitting a tax return to the government. If we are seeking reimbursement for the expenditure, we need the receipt to prove that the transaction did take place and to identify what was bought. In that event, our receipt will interface with our employer's financial system.

In this simple, everyday example, decisions on whether to keep the receipt as a record are clearly determined by the actions that are required after the initial transaction. The receipt might be needed to hold the supermarket accountable for their charging if the total amount charged is in error. The receipt might be aggregated into monthly household accounts to monitor budget expenditure. External requirements may be invoked; the need to claim something from an employer means that the record might be kept in a particular way, the need to maintain evidence of purchase for cumulative records to enable submission to the tax office, or to substantiate claims if a tax auditor queries items. All these factors, consciously or unconsciously, assist us as individuals to determine whether to scrunch the receipt up into a ball and throw it out along with the used shopping bags, or whether to retain it for further purposes. If we don't have the record, we can then do no more than assert an action and can probably not proceed on any of the potential further actions, such as filing a claim or maintaining a budget.

These are exactly the same processes that are applied, although consciously, when determining what should be kept as records of any activity. Critical to the determination is an understanding of the transaction, what is going on and what impacts are being brought to bear on the transaction from all over the place. The processes which make up the decisions to read, keep, or throw away a receipt are in fact the same as those for creating, capturing, controlling and maintaining the minutes of the Cabinet meetings in 1910, or in determining today whether a country will go to war.

This highly contextual nature of records is critical. The decisions about what to keep as a record are contingent upon the actions and the context of the decision itself. This feature of records serves as a great frustration to some: there is no one 'right' answer to the questions of what records to make or retain. It depends on the circumstances, the organization, the environment of the organization and the actions that are required subsequently. In relation to the U.S. Department of Defense example which began this section, there may be no right answers as to how the records should have been made and retained, but the report makes it clear that the investigators found many of the wrong ones.

Situating the document in records systems

In addition to being totally contingent on the requirements of an individual or organization, records carry complexity built into determining for management purposes where the boundaries of the record will be drawn. When managing electronic documents we need to identify the complexity of the boundaries of the document in its environment in order to decide what we are managing. Within the World Wide Web, for example, is the document the whole web of documents, the web site, or the web page? In the same way we have to consider the boundaries of a record. A record can be a single item or a group of items. Determining the extent of what will be managed as a record is an application of the contingency characteristic discussed above. It is best illustrated by example.

Aggregating documents into transactional records[7]

Consider the common process of dealing with Ministerial Representations, which are letters to parliamentary representatives responsible for specific portfolios or sets of functions. In this case, the constituent, Mrs Joan Bloggs, writes to the Minister for Roads.

- Mrs Joan Bloggs, pensioner, writes in to complain about the dangerous state of an intersection, where a neighbour's child was knocked off his bicycle, and to demand traffic lights be installed;
- the letter is registered and forwarded to the relevant section for traffic lights to respond to with a brief about style, timing etc;
- a draft reply is prepared and returned with the original to the Ministerial Correspondence section;
- the Ministerial Correspondence section fill out the standard covering minute to the Minister and send it to her with the original letter and the draft reply;
- the Minister signs the reply, which is copied, and the signed reply sent to Mrs Bloggs, and the copy is put away.

Questions:
- how many documents do we have here?
- how many items are there?
- how many records are there?
- which ones are captured or should be captured as records?

In this example, the decision points can be seen to be about the level of aggregation. In a recordkeeping view of the world all the documents in this example are records, but we have a choice about whether we manage them separately or whether we manage them together as the record of one transaction – the result of a single query by Mrs. Bloggs. In the event the work processes established to deal with such queries will determine where each individual organization draws the boundaries. Commonly all these individual records would be

---

[7] This example is derived from a teaching exercise devised by Anne Picot in a Monash University training course for National Archives of Australia in 1998.

managed as an aggregate – the record of the transaction with Mrs. Bloggs. The individual records contribute to the aggregated record. A sequencing process takes place.

This example also raises the question of duplication. In the example, it is possible to imagine that the relevant section dealing with traffic lights will maintain a copy of the letter and their draft response, most likely placed with other such responses on traffic lights in that vicinity, that the Ministerial Correspondence section will maintain a copy of the letter, the details received from the traffic lights section, their minute sheet and their draft reply, and additionally the Minister's own office may keep a copy. Each one of these is a perfectly valid record, residing at different parts of the organization. Such complexity is introduced by the ease with which our current technologies allow the creation and retention of copies. In a nineteenth-century work process to manage such a request, copies may have been retained locally, but the labour involved would probably not have been justified, and the record itself moved around the organization accumulating each step of the process. In our more complex modern world, each of the individual records will need to be addressed in order to work out whether or not to keep them, and if so, for how long. It is likely that the final record with all the results of the contributions from various sections will be the 'full and accurate' record, telling the complete story of the transaction and will be the one targeted for longest retention. It may be that the other records created along the way by the contributing sections are retained in order to accumulate a set of cumulating records on traffic lights, to establish precedents, to monitor progress, to be accountable for the response. Depending on the way each is maintained in relationship to other records, each will have a different business purpose, and a different future use, hence a different retention requirement.

Duplication is not an issue in recordkeeping. Each of the contributing parties is conducting independent but related transactions. By its nature a transaction has more than one part; it must involve at least two parties, each of whom has a valid reason for considering their part of the transaction a record. While other information disciplines fret about duplication, this is not a primary recordkeeping concern, because it is so integral to the nature of a transaction.

In this example, the processes of accumulation have been discussed. Organizations and individuals accumulate aggregations of documents and records to suit their requirements. Common ways of sequencing include:

- serial: documents similar in form and used repetitively for the same kind of administrative purpose are placed together;
- sequence: documents arising from a sequence or chain of actions are placed together; and
- dossier or case file: documents, irrespective of form or action sequence are placed together because they relate to, for example, a person, place, event, piece of property.[8]

---

[8] Based on the categories detailed in Public Service Board, *The Registrar's Handbook*, Canberra, Commonwealth of Australia, 1955.

Each of these sequencing arrangements creates a set of relationships between the individual records within the sequence. In archival science, this set of relationships is referred to as the archival bond – 'the network of relationships that each record has with the records belonging in the same aggregation'.[9] Creating the archival bond or establishing the relationships between records, their creators, and the actions that are taking place commences with the deliberate sequencing of records. This, however, is just the beginning of the complex set of relationships that a record accumulates during its existence and involves a consideration of the contexts in which it needs to be understood. One of the characteristics of a record previously mentioned but not described is that of usability (see Definition 3).

AS/ISO 15489, Australian Standard Records Management, Part 1 – General, 2002

7.2.5 Usability
A usable record is one that can be located, retrieved, presented and interpreted. It should be capable of subsequent presentation as directly connected to the business activity or transaction that produced it. The contextual linkages of records should carry the information needed for an understanding of the transactions that created and used them. It should be possible to identify a record within the context of broader business activities and functions. The links between records that document a sequence of activities should be maintained.

Definition 3. A usable record, whether an individual item or an aggregation of items

To be able to use a record we need to be able to interpret it. If the record is only required for personal reference, the extent of the descriptions included with it can be very vague – for example, I know that the pile on the left-hand side of my desk relates to work that needs attention. I know the order, I have placed things into an implicit order, but woe betide any cleaning processes that attempt to 'tidy' without appreciating this order. If, on the other hand, I want to share the results of my actions, to distribute the actions or even to make sure that I can find them after a period of time, I need to make a greater effort to make this implicit knowledge explicit, available to someone else. I would need to place my documents into a context so that someone else will know what requires doing, or is able to access the material. Within a small group of people, this can still be reasonably ad hoc – we all know what the other is doing and share an understanding of our business. If I wished to communicate beyond the domain of my immediate group, I would have to make more information explicit – I would have to identify who I was, what organization I work for, what authority I have, what the action is, what the background to the action is etc. If I want to communicate with an audience that is world-wide and with multiple disciplinary interests, then I have to identify myself in relation to country, discipline and traditions. It is like the old positioning game we played as children: 'Barbara Reed, Bondi, New South Wales, Australia, Australasia, Asia-Pacific Region, Southern Hemisphere, The Earth, Milky Way, The Galaxy....'.

---

[9] Luciana Duranti, 'The Archival Bond', *Archives and Museum Informatics*, 11, no. 3/4, 1997, pp. 215-216.

For a record, we have to work out how far it must 'reach' in determining the boundaries of what information we have to provide with it to enable it to be understood in the contexts it will be used. In the paper world, much of this information could be assumed by physical placement – the record lived in my office; I work for this organization, therefore anyone coming to the record would know those things. This implicit knowledge disappears in the electronic world, and so direct attention is needed to ensure this implicit knowledge is made explicit.

Extending the reach of records over time is exactly what archival systems are traditionally designed to do. They provide us with ways of interpreting actions and records relevant to the time at which they were created, but not necessarily apparent or understandable to us today. The language of the records may have changed, or the scope of the function may have altered. Documenting these things systematically over time in an environment where there are many records series from multiple organizations is the business of archival systems. But these issues are becoming increasingly important to document contemporaneously, knowing that there will be interpretations required to make records accessible beyond organizational boundaries, particularly in the electronic world where physical and organizational boundaries can no longer be assumed.

Records do not exist in isolation. Whether the links are explicit or implicit, records always exist in a network of documentation, people and business activities. They have always done so. But how you view records depends on the stance that you take in looking at them. So, for management purposes, we need to take a view that is bounded by the organization and the work that needs to be facilitated. From a recordkeeping professional point of view, we might augment that reasonably narrow and focused view, knowing that certain records will be critical for accountability, reuse or tracking activities for long periods. In those circumstances we might intervene to ensure that those records are given the metadata or descriptive information needed to carry them through their projected lifespan (see the section on metadata below). If we are taking a larger analytical look at organizations, interdependencies and broader social interactions (as is often the case with archival perspectives) we might view the aggregations much more broadly and see the recordkeeping system extending across organizational boundaries and out into complex social patterns of relationships.

Not all of these relationships, networks and linkages need to be defined at the point of capturing the record. Layers of additional data can be added at various times to extend the reach of the records as they pass from one domain of action to others, for example, out of the immediate domain of the record creator into the broader domain of the workgroup and then on to the organization. Much of this additional layering of data will occur as we treat records as increasingly composite entities analyzed according to their ever-growing aggregations.

At the point of capturing records into a formalized system, the first of these aggregations or linkages are made. The process known as classification formalizes the linking of records together. Here we need to associate a document with prior transactions and enable it to be linked to everything of relevance that will happen from the point of capture onwards. How we classify or group is a consequence of the sequencing activity determined appropriate for the records. Whether we want to link records together to detail all actions on a single case (e.g. the payment of unemployment benefits to Barbara Reed) or all actions on a set of transactions (e.g. instances of payments of unemployment benefits) or by topics (e.g. all procedures and policies relevant to the administration of unemployment benefits), depends on the contextual environment of how the work is actually undertaken. Determining how the classification will work is therefore dependent on every individual workplace, and needs to be tailored to fit each workplace. While there are general rules that are applicable across all organizations, each will also need to attend to the detail of how work actually happens.

Without formalized rules and specific guidance as to exactly how grouping or categorization is applied, the way in which grouping takes place is open to a great deal of individuality. For example, take the common pack of cards – how would you group within this? Answers would range from grouping by suits, by colour, by number etc and each answer would be quite correct; but, depending on the purpose, one arrangement may be more suitable than another. For any grouping or categorization of information there can be many methods of classification.

For recordkeeping purposes, however, the arrangement of records into categories designed to reflect the business that is going on provides significant strategic advantage. Grouping this way enables the link between the transaction and the record to be dominant, thus providing a major part of the contextual linking we need to understand the record over time. Records grouped by functions and activities are able to be managed as an aggregation sharing specific characteristics such as managing assignment of the control over who can access particular sets of information. For example, in developing a proposal to create a joint venture business, the records reflecting the stages in considering proposals, determining feasibility, ensuring disclosure and deciding whether to go ahead, would all be highly commercially sensitive, and only those who were directly involved in the process would have access to them. Access is directly controlled by who is doing what and in relation to what business. The use of these close connections to the business going on embeds records into the business, as they should be, as enablers of the business, integral to the conduct of the action. We can also string other recordkeeping triggers and controls onto classification by functions and activity, for example, closer integration of workflow with records, automatic attribution of records 'point-of-capture' information, or specification of disposal actions.

While the case for classifying records by function/activity is compelling because of the power of the additional functionality it enables, many systems exist which use other forms of classification, often based on modifications of the subject classification inherited from librarianship. Such classification focuses on retrieval and has a content orientation. For such purposes, subject classification is a powerful tool. However it does not enable the multiple process functionality of functional classification.

These approaches are quite different ways of doing different things. Again, using the analogy of grouping a pack of cards, none of the approaches are wrong; they are just different. The classification technique adopted will depend on the prime objective being served. If it is recordkeeping, then the function/activity classification approach provides much greater process control. If, on the other hand, the retrieval issue is primary, then subject classification is of greater relevance.

There is no reason why more than one approach should not exist together, to provide the best of all worlds. Multiple classifications are made increasingly possible by the creative use of technology. With such technological assistance to provide links, the physical placement of the record into a classification order is not necessary. Virtual links and associations are easier to make, enabling multiple readings of the record in different contexts to coexist. Removed from the physical requirements of the past, where records could physically only be in one place at a time, richer layers of relationships and associations can now be made.

Defining the classification language which will define the way records are linked together in aggregations, either virtually by association or physically as entities, requires formal documentation. Such schemes exist as much to codify rules as to formalize the language appropriate to the organization at a particular time (for example do we agree to use the term 'street kids' not 'abandoned children' or 'homeless youth'). In defining agreed language to be employed in classifying records we are also defining an organizational view of what our organization does and what our society finds an acceptable way of referring to what it does. While the conscious philosophizing on the political and socially situated nature of language is rarely dwelt upon in the definition of classification schemes reflecting organizational language, these things clearly reflect a social representation of function/activity, a dimension of our job as recordkeepers that we should be aware of.

Initial classification takes place at the time of registration or capture. This causes the weaving of the web of relationships between records to commence. But classification processes continue throughout the record's existence. A record can be reused and connected with further records, in the course of the same or different transactions, accumulating a variety of associations, links and classification terms. The classification tools supporting the organizational expression of function/activity are dynamic tools, reflecting changes to language and requiring the uncoiling of complex concepts embedded in terms such as information technology, information management, communication, and the embracing phrase information and communication technology. In keeping with the notion of managing the 'reach' of the record, discussed above, multiple classification taxonomies reflecting larger environments in which the record must be comprehensible also have to be taken into account – for example, a government organization may have a requirement for records to be nested into or linked up to a whole of government taxonomy of function which is additional to the organizational level. Regardless of the complexities, the functions and activities undertaken by an organization which change over time and the business practices themselves remain at the core of recordkeeping classification processes.

Recordkeeping is about maintaining connections over time, so changes to classification schema and records associated with particular terms at specific points in time are needed to provide the context of the record. This is equally true of schemes applied in current business environments as it is to those managed over time. Language as the expression of concepts is culturally bound and culturally sensitive. For recordkeeping purposes, we need to be able to reconstruct the language used, while connecting to current usage. So, for example, we need to know that the now offensive terms used to refer to indigenous people in Australia in the nineteenth-century systems of government and church were quite routine, or that the nineteenth-century use of 'street arabs', with its now politically incorrect nuances, is a previous generation's equivalent to our 'street kids'. Over time this use of language places records and their descriptions within a social and cultural context important to their meaning.

Determining aggregation levels, sequencing and classification for recordkeeping is not simply a matter of ensuring retrieval but it is, above all, a way of conceptualizing and organizing work. Another aspect of it is keeping control over where a record is at any particular time, both as a management control to ensure that work is being done, and from a retrieval perspective – being able to get to a record when it is required.

But this view only works where recordkeeping is embedded in work and the management of records is integral to the way work gets done. This tradition of recordkeeping is known as pre-action recordkeeping, where workflows drive records and the work being done. Registry systems (see Case Study: registry systems below) were a powerful tool for pre-action organizational control. Many of the workflow and document management technologies of the last decade have been attempting to reintegrate the capacity of pre-action recordkeeping into the workplace which was set loose of all controls with the advent of office automation technology. This tradition of recordkeeping is not universal. It is most notably not a part of recent United States tradition for records management. (It is also worth noting that it is the United States that has provided us with most of our office automation technologies). There is, of course, a balance to be managed between excessive control and no control at all, and how organizations achieve this balance is determined by their broader environment of regulation, industry and organizational culture.

Case study: Registry systems

Many of Australia's ways of approaching recordkeeping come from our history as a colony of Great Britain. As such we inherited a system of recordkeeping known as the registry system. This system was the basis for government recordkeeping for over 200 years. While it mutated over the course of its period of influence, the essential characteristics of the registry system exerted the basic recordkeeping influence on generations of Australian recordkeepers. Analysis of its essential features shows great relevance to the translation of recordkeeping thinking into the electronic world. Indeed, technological advances are enabling us to return to many of the basic precepts of these systems.

In the registry system, a centralized work unit managed all incoming and outgoing correspondence and the dissemination of the work throughout the organization. In the earliest form of the system, the nineteenth-century docketing system, incoming correspondence was registered sequentially on receipt into registers of incoming correspondence. In some systems, the numbering sequence commenced again at the beginning of every year, in others, the sequential registration number continued for the life of the series.

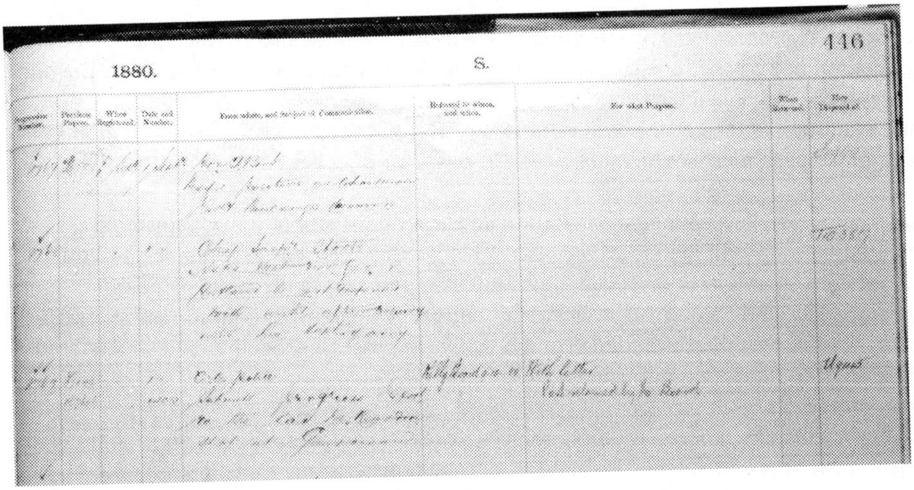

Figure 5.2. An Inwards Correspondence Register of the Chief Secretary's Office, Victoria, 1880. The left-hand columns show the sequential registration of correspondence and the right-hand column records the 'top-numbering' of each item when another related item was received.

The registration process involved assigning the next available number, recording the originator of the correspondence, the creation and/or receipt date, a précis of the document and an annotation of where the correspondence was sent for action. It was also indexed by topic and/or author in separate volumes. Depending on the system, a set of transmission registers or annotations in the incoming registers noted to whom the correspondence was sent for action, often including the time and date of transmission. On completion of the action, copies of outbound letters were made into a set of Outwards Correspondence Letter Books, variously produced by hand copying, press copy technology or later carbon paper, and indexed in separate indexes to outwards correspondence. Depending on the sophistication of the system, outwards correspondence might be independently registered with sequential numbers, including a reference to the inwards correspondence to link the transactions together, or, in larger systems, separate sequences of outwards correspondence might be maintained, often segregated by the name of the office or the topic of the correspondence. This separation was necessitated by limitations of the technology available – only one person could be working with a particular volume at any one time, so segregating the volumes allowed more than one copy to be worked on at any one time.

Ideally, the inwards and outwards correspondence was linked in the registration books which were annotated with correspondence numbers to the outwards correspondence, providing a method of tracking action. The physical document moved around the organization, collecting annotations or authorizations which were usually physically recorded on the correspondence itself, but all were sent through the dissemination system controlled by the Registry, thus enabling a continuous representation of the stages of the work to be compiled in registers within the transmission system.

Once action was completed, correspondence was sometimes stored in the strict numerical order determined by the register, but were often sorted into physical containers reflecting a subject, or the provenance of the correspondence (e.g. aborigines, or police). Thus the physical storage of the correspondence often reflected yet another means of accessing the correspondence, a means which provided the basis for the later development of files.

Where a piece of correspondence linked to an earlier transaction, it was registered sequentially as normal, the index was used to locate the prior correspondence and the previous correspondence was located, physically connected to the latest piece of correspondence and the register was linked with its new later location (top numbering). The two (or more) items then travelled through the work processes together and were stored together at the conclusion of business.

In such systems, the index is the first point of access. From there the registration numbers of the relevant correspondence is found. From the registers, one finds the linked transactions and, tracking the top numbering through, the latest entry determines the physical location of the correspondence as indicated in Figure 5.3.

Sequence of correspondence with Jones
Physically stored in Outward Correspondence registers

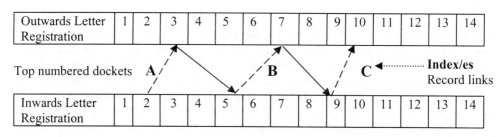

Physically stored as sequences of documents bound in volumes, or as a variety of 'topic' sequences

Figure 5.3. Nineteenth-century docketing system (with top numbering)[10]

---

[10] Diagram adapted from Chris Hurley, 'Relationships in Records (4) – Electronic Series – Rediscovering the Mystery', *New Zealand Archivist*, Summer 2002, p. 8.

In this example, there are at least five sequences that can be identified:

- the inwards registration sequence (the specific correspondence with Jones is not the first in this sequence)
- the transaction sequence A B C
- the outwards registration sequence (again non-sequential for the correspondence with Jones)
- order of the index entries
- order of the copies of the letters to Jones in the outwards correspondence books.

Each of the sequences in Figure 5.3 can be recreated for the management of the correspondence with Jones and it may itself bear little relationship to the sequence in which the collected correspondence of Jones finds itself physically stored.

Such systems were labour-intensive and time consuming to run, but they offered tight control on tracking of work and location of correspondence. As government administration diversified, so did the formal attribution of functions to specific branches or departments of government. Each department then assumed responsibility for the incoming and outgoing correspondence relating to its own functions. Cross-agency flows of physical correspondence were common enough to evolve into independent transmission systems, known as blank cover series, which controlled this flow and the responsibility for action. As the volume of correspondence grew, some of these practices became too time-consuming. So, for example, the practice of maintaining outward correspondence books lapsed after the advent of typewriters and carbon copies, making possible the storage of the outward correspondence relating to specific inwards transactions.

Over time, the individual registration and tracking of documents became onerous and the notion of the topic bundle or file became the dominant locus of control. Incoming correspondence continued to be indexed and, in some instances, was still registered, but index pointers referred to the specific file onto which correspondence was placed. The file, as a physical aggregation, replaced the registration system of individual documents virtually placed together through the registers. The file then was registered; it contained the physical information detailing the movement of the action around the organization and through continued annotation of the next action officer noted on the file cover and on file movement cards maintained centrally, the work was tracked and the location of the file at any one time was able to be traced.

Metadata

The above case study is in this chapter because nineteenth-century British and Northern European systems for the registration, aggregation, classification and tracking of documents (and even earlier systems in parts of Europe) were built around recordkeeping schemes that have many similarities with emerging recordkeeping metadata approaches. In such systems the document can be validly considered in isolation, although it does not exist independently. It has a set of information that describes it – the document-level application of metadata schemes discussed in the previous chapter.

Sometimes this document-level metadata is 'point-of-capture' metadata. Point-of-capture metadata in modern approaches establishes the initial picture of the document by making a record of that document (memorializing it). Links are made between the record, the creator and the business context that created it. The metadata typically describes such things as the creator of the document, the time or date of its creation or receipt, the business transaction or activity it forms part of, often expressed within a classification code. Various specifications for records metadata exist and all start with this point-of-capture level of information.

But for a document to be considered as an authentic, reliable and usable record (see Definitions 1, 2 and 3 above), it needs to be connected with information which describes in richer detail the tapestry of actions it has taken part in, such as what has happened to it, how it has been used, who did what and in relation to what business activities. We need to be able to ask (and often answer) a host of questions, including why a record was formed in the course of doing something (in a business activity sense), and whether the person forming it was authorized and able to undertake the action at the time the action took place.

Being able to link a document with attendant details of what is going on is a major part of the transformation of a document into a record. This type of metadata can be distinguished from point-of-capture metadata by calling it process metadata, although, of course, in recordkeeping they are brought together within the one scheme, a consistent pattern for the application of both types of data elements.

These process-based layers of information about the document make them records by providing continuing contextual links, as we saw in the nineteenth-century example above. In effect, what the record process metadata does is to connect the document to a particular set of actions on an ongoing basis, establishing relationships with other documents. This involves embedding and disembedding actions as the document moves into different contexts. By the use of process metadata documenting and describing the actions taking place a document (or any object about which metadata is being kept) is disembedded from its immediate contexts and can be re-embedded (captured) into new contexts within files, dossiers, series, the archive of an organization and in archives.

The establishment of connections to actions and relationships with other documents are what is referred to in the phrase 'capture of records' in this part of the book. The capture of records is the process essential to bringing objects into a recordkeeping system of control. Once captured (also referred to in other traditions also as being 'set aside'[11]), ongoing

---

[11] This terminology emerged through the work of Luciana Duranti in a University of British Columbia research project, 1994 -1997. For an overview of this project see Luciana Duranti and Heather MacNeil, 'The Protection of the Integrity of Electronic Records: An Overview of the UBC-MAS Research Project', *Archivaria*, 42, 1996.

systemic recordkeeping processes can be invoked to ensure the characteristics of records are maintained.

Depending on the formality of the records system, capture can be as simple as the deliberate assignment of a record to a folder (either physically or virtually on a computer). At this most simple of capture levels, the deliberate act is of significance – it indicates intent to treat the record as a record. Evidence of intent can be as informal as assembling emails in folders, putting children's drawings, school reports, or other documentation together in one place over time, or physically putting papers into a labeled manila folder thus creating a proximity association. In simple systems such as these there is no guarantee that necessary recordkeeping metadata will be available. There is still a metadata scheme present involving such consistently applied data elements as file or folder name. It is, however, a weak form of capture because the bonding of the documents within the folder is easily disrupted by altering the contents and their order within the receptacle without any maintenance of data recording this fact.

To ensure more formal capture and the possibility of a fuller range of recordkeeping processes that make the links between items more or less indelible, registration usually occurs as described above, creating a unique identifier which provides a fixed reference for connecting both point-of-capture and process metadata to the registered object. The registered object itself varies. It might be a draft document, a document that has been created, a document that has been received, a file, or, in archival systems, a registered series of files or other objects. In systems that use registration processes, no further recordkeeping actions can be taken on the object until it is appropriately registered, and registration can only take place once for each object. While the contents of the object can be altered or changed, the metadata can record this along with links to other registered objects of which it is part. Thus a document, as a draft, as a sent document, as part of a file, or as part of a series of records, could involve a number of unique, but linked, registration numbers depending on how the system is configured.[12]

The establishment of initial point-of-capture and process metadata with registration identifiers that can connect data to an object is, then, a beginning, not an end, to metadata application processes. The application should also be directed at the carriage of documents through time and not be a once only occurrence. The record-making metadata is perpetually accumulating around an object.

---

[12] If the registered object is a document being drafted, for example, multiple contributors and multiple creators may work on versions of it. It is a matter of active decision-making as to which versions are captured as records, decisions which, as seen in the example of Mrs Bloggs' letter, are dependent on the nature of the action taking place. In some processes, such as the drafting of legal contracts or highly accountable transactions, every version will be managed as a separate, but connected, record. In other transactions, such as developing a letter to a vendor for purchase of stationery, only the final letter may be declared as a record. This is a contingent, context-dependent decision like so many others in recordkeeping.

Multiple threads of action take place and each one provides a potentially different way of reading the record. Using the example introduced in the first chapter of the photograph of children in the water, central to the Children Overboard case, the photo, when located within the context of HMAS Adelaide's immediate transmission, is evidence of the bravery of individual serving personnel. If placed in the photograph album of an individual sailor, it becomes a personal record of the event. If the same photo, now without the metadata containing the captions contextualizing it, is a record in the Minister's office, it tells a very different story purporting to prove that asylum seekers were throwing their children overboard. In the published versions, the photo becomes part of the collective memory through dissemination of the official 'untruth'. It's the same photo, but the contextual metadata provided about the photo – either explicit or provided by location – enables us to tell many different stories about it, each one occurring at different points in time, each one providing its own sequential yet recursive reading of events.

It is not enough, then, for a record to be an object created in the course of doing something, a characteristic of records identified in the introduction of this chapter. The capturing process needs to take the object, which in a recordkeeping system can be any object, even a desk in an inventorying system, as we saw in the introduction, more or less indelibly linking it to the actions and other objects that surround it. In the process of managing records something new is likely to be formed involving new registration processes. The draft registered document can become the registered document, then part of the registered file, then part of a series of files, then part of the company's archive, and then part of archives elsewhere. In the introduction to this chapter it was pointed out that records are far more than simply physical things. They are the physical thing bound to information which provides all the contextual detail surrounding their creation and ongoing management. In technical terms the record is the object and its associated metadata and the scheme for recording information on all the contextual detail is known as recordkeeping metadata.

If this logic is applied, the distinction between data, documents, information and records becomes easier to explain. Data, documents and information can be created, received and maintained in the transaction of business. But they may not be managed as evidence of actions in the same formative way that those same elements would be if they were managed as records – they may not record every change to the data with the time, date and name of the person making the change, and they may not record all instances of access to the data. That does not mean that some evidence of action elements cannot be reconstructed if required using for example audit logs, but where the possibility of reconstruction is not integral to the management of the information, document or data, they are not being managed as records.

In relation to data, documents and information, the process of making something a record (establishing its evidential nature) by retrospectively tracing all these things is often undertaken where they are required to prove something. Retrospectively identifying all these elements by tracing what has happened to data or a document is, however, a very expensive exercise. What is preferable, if analyses reveal that the need may well arise to use documents or data as evidence, is to enable these processes to be put in place up front, to identify which resources need this layer of protection to enable them to act as evidence of action, and to manage them in this 'record' way from the time of their creation.

Part of the complexity of formative records management is that records can reach and cross, or not cross, thresholds of formality at different times. This is particularly observable in personal papers, where the formalizing layer to create systems to facilitate contemporary systems may be completely lacking, with records rather moving directly to a higher level of aggregation as the whole of the records of an individual or family. At a later date the degree of formalization that has been established might disintegrate as the person moves house or dies and relatives split the records up amongst themselves. This does not make personal papers any less records, but it means that the logical elements of contextualization are often hard or impossible to determine. Nor does this make them different in type from government records, as the U.S Department of Defense example earlier illustrates, and the issues of relocation and inheritance are common phenomena in all circumstances where records exist. Electronic recordkeeping approaches in fact may be expected to, in time, minimize this difference when personal records systems, modeled on specifications of recordkeeping requirements, become available.[13]

Recordkeeping requirement analyses allow flexibility in finding ways to implement appropriate recordkeeping. Using appropriate specification of the structural elements of what is required and the stringing of one or multiple technologies to deliver the functionality frees us from the physical view of records. It also allows degrees of flexibility to be introduced to suit particular organizational, industry or individual needs. In keeping with these ideas, different ways of defining and articulating recordkeeping metadata are being articulated. These are being expressed in terms of recordkeeping metadata standards, and are structured in XML schema. By expressing the dynamism of records and recordkeeping processes in ways that are accessible to technologists and systems designers, the prospect of integration of recordkeeping into business systems of all types and into vital areas such as electronic transactions and service delivery becomes more realistic. But not every recordkeeping metadata standard takes the process-oriented approach; many often stop at defining metadata for the record at point of capture. The ability of recordkeepers to understand requirements and to rethink how to apply records capture and management in diverse and ever-changing technologies will shape the record of the future.

Access

The primary aim of maintaining records is to enable them to be usable and accessible over time with all their reliability and authenticity intact for as long as they are required. For recordkeeping, retrieval is not simply about finding and presenting a document, but involves enabling access to a record, that is, to a document in context, revealing the recordkeeping relationships and the string of associative links, enabling the telling of many different potential stories, that a single record brings with it, as illustrated by the 'Children

---

[13] Sue McKemmish, 'Evidence of Me...', *Archives and Manuscripts*, 24, no 1, 1996.

Overboard' photograph. This is an increasingly complex issue. Often access is viewed as a one-dimensional professional function, concentrating on enabling a user to find the appropriate content required, but in reality it is quite a complex process.

All access takes place within a set of conventions regularized by law or regulation which will be different for each jurisdiction and for each organization. As discussed in chapter 2, these laws and conventions tend to have grown up in a piecemeal fashion depending on just how much openness of the archive a government or society is willing to support. For recordkeeping access is not always an axiomatic right. There are legitimate reasons for restricting access to records, which, after all are reflections of the business that is going on. Such reasons might include delicate negotiations in a commercial setting, proprietary information over which there are intellectual property rights, and personal information, which is protected by privacy codes or legislation.

Access involves both internal and external access. Internal access controls who can see the records within the bounds of the organization or group which is immediately responsible for it. For example, only those with legitimate purpose can see personal files or plans for reorganizing the organization. External access is that access permitted or prescribed by law by third parties – an individual not party to the particular transaction, but who may be the subject of the transaction or is simply interested in knowing how something was done. Third parties can include those responsible for monitoring the actions of the creating body, such as ombudsmen or parliaments. The more open society is about its transactions, the more freely access to internal records is granted to third parties.

The notion of internal and external is a simplistic reduction, of course. What happens in the event of a joint venture or discussions leading up to a collaborative approach where two or more separate bodies agree to cooperate and permit access to records, even sharing information systems to enable this? What of the increased availability of material on web sites? These examples are intended to open up the concept of access as not quite such a straightforward process, and one that is becoming increasingly complex in the world of remote connections and electronic transactions.

Managing appropriate access depends on layers of controls. Firstly, access is, like almost all recordkeeping processes, contingent on what is being done. It relates immediately to who is seeking access and for what purpose. Thus the same person may have different roles, each one of which brings different authorizations for access. For example, in a university environment, I could be a staff member, a researcher, a student and alumnus, all at the same time. Depending on what I am doing when I request information, the access that I am granted will be different. If I am the subject of the record – for example, a student wanting to know about my results – I have some rights to information about me and my record. But if I'm a staff member administering a course, I have rights to a wider section of the university's records base – I might need to get to class lists, have access to systems managing assessment details for many students, access support systems for teaching delivery and course development and so on. If I'm a researcher, my connection to the records I am seeking is not the same as someone involved in doing business, but rather to query some aspect of business. I need to apply for permissions to gain access, which will be considered according to institutional rules, and I may, if successful, be granted permission to current records under freedom of information legislation and organizational policy, or under archival policy, if I'm seeking older records. If I'm an alumnus, my rights might be courtesy-based only, enabling me to use the library, view the documents about the Alumni Association, and pursue whatever discretionary forms of access are provided to me. In each instance, the role I am playing determines what I am able to access, and what rights or user permissions I might be given within the systems.

Managing individuals and their roles, then, is critical to what records I can see. But managing individuals and roles is increasingly complex. How do you know I am who I say I am in a virtual world? The instances of identity theft are now common enough to be the subject of Hollywood movies. This is a problem facing all information professionals and all organizations, and sophisticated technologies are emerging to address these issues, for example, public key infrastructure. The management of such complex technologies involving public and private keys, third party certification, encryption, etc., brings new recordkeeping problems to the fore. These are, as yet, little explored, and the technology and techniques may change. However, as things stand at present large areas of recordkeeping concerns are exposed.

More traditionally, records themselves are allocated some security ranking to protect their status when they are actively being used to undertake business. Some of these rankings are specific to particular organizations, for example Department of Defence security ratings. But commonly, records might be classified confidential or commercial in confidence. Applying such restrictions should have time limits associated with them and processes in place to review and downgrade (or upgrade, if necessary) such restrictions. Less formal security can be allocated to a record within a segment of an organization – this record cannot be seen by anyone outside our group, for example – without the formal allocation of security levels.

Where external access to records is by permission or application, processes for making such decisions are required. Such is the case in administering freedom of information legislation, for example. In such cases, the process can create a new record. Parts of the original record may be blocked from access, where other parts may have access allowed. This process is known as redaction and a redacted record is in effect a new record.

There are distinctions to be drawn about what type of access is available. In some cases, there will be requirements to restrict knowledge, even the knowledge that a record exists. In other cases access may be given to the fact that the records exist, and also permissions to view the content, but not for any permissions to change or alter the record. Determining terms and conditions of access is an important part of the process.

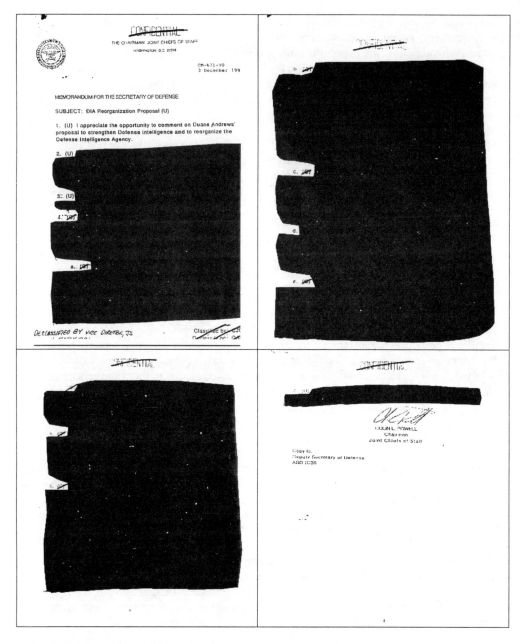

Figure 5.4. A substantially redacted record! This version of a 1990 memo from the Chairman of the U.S. Joint Chiefs of Staff, Colin Powell, was released in response to a Freedom of Information request.

Appraisal

This chapter has already discussed appraisal in some detail, as appraisal in a non-technical sense means evaluation and the thrust of what has been written has been directed at the processes of evaluating what records to capture as records. The example of the supermarket receipt and the example of Mrs Bloggs' letter of complaint to the Minister of Roads worked through the processes of determining what records to keep, but they also considered how long to retain them. In most archival traditions in the modern era only the second half of this statement – how long to retain them – is technically considered appraisal, but in the Australian recordkeeping discourse, appraisal is becoming a wider process.[14]

Traditionally appraisal has been considered as a technique of selection from an extant body of records. Most often it has considered the application of a set of evaluation criteria (including records based ones such as volume, completeness, fragility, or uniqueness) to determine whether records will move into the archival domain (see the next two chapters). In redefining appraisal as a broader process, the Australian definitions have expanded the points of application of the conscious decision-making about the existence of a record, bringing the concept into the ambit of this chapter. Appraisal can now be seen to apply at a number of points, at various times, and to different levels of aggregation. Appraisal is no longer solely associated with reviewing the physical record. It becomes a more abstract, analytical process bringing in wider organizational and social contexts at all points of decision-making. The critical appraisal points are those of:

- capture – determining what records to vest with additional protection of recordkeeping processes to carry them through time;
- reach – determining how far the records should be intelligible outside their immediate domain of capture (and this process keeps on going in an iterative fashion, to enable records to be understood over time, as well as over physical/virtual space);
- migration – determining what records should be maintained in a usable format over time and through system changes; and
- destruction/retention – determining which records to retain and for how long, itself a multiple decision-making process inside whatever structure is relevant, be it a small group, a larger department, a whole organization or the more traditional archival approach involving retention beyond organizational boundaries.

Appraisal decisions occur constantly during the management of records. It is not a linear process but an iterative and recursive set of processes. Each appraisal decision is informed

---

[14] Appraisal is defined in the AS 4390, *Australian Standard on Records Management* 1996 as 'the process of evaluating business activities to determine which records need to be captured and how long the records need to be kept, to meet business needs, the requirements of organizational accountability and community expectations'. This definition was controversial at an international level and the term appraisal does not appear in the AS/ISO 15489 based on the earlier Australian Standard. However, the processes are described as 'Determining documents to be captured into a records system' and 'Determining how long to retain records'.

by the context of the action that is taking place and the expectations of individuals, organizations and society for records to exist.

As Frank Upward has noted, 'If I need a blood transfusion I am, for the moment, a major stakeholder in the quality of blood-bank recordkeeping processes. It is irrelevant whether I have access to the records, or even 'value' them. My needs are part of the multiple uses of such records. In a democracy we are all stakeholders in recordkeeping whether we value the records or not.'[15] He could have added that, at times of crisis, we suddenly value records, expecting them to be there and to have been built within quality processes of formation.

As with the question of what are reliable records, discussed earlier, there is no correct answer to many appraisal questions. All determinations of what to create and what to keep are subjective and bound by the contexts of their decision-making. This element of subjectivity, inherent in the decisions taken, clearly points to the need for reliable records about the appraisal action so that there is accountability for the decisions made. Appraisal actions can be supported by documentation in the form of functional analysis, recordkeeping requirements analysis, business process analysis in the context of current systems or textual justifications to argue the case for retention of records beyond the immediate business needs or beyond the boundaries of the system which created them. The procedures involved in this new approach to appraisal are detailed in records management standards in Australia which are being developed on an ongoing basis, working from the parent international and Australian standards on records management referred to elsewhere in this chapter.

The major outcome of applying appraisal processes is the existence of a record which is capable of being managed for as long as it is required. At a certain point in time, as determined in applying appraisal decisions, records can be destroyed. In these days of cheap electronic storage, the computing answer is to 'archive' everything (that is, dump it onto an extractable medium and remove it from the current systems while still keeping it accessible). While the cost efficiency arguments of the paper era, involving cost benefit analyses of hundreds of metres of valuable office space tied up in unnecessary storage is rendered invalid with advances in storage technology, costs for maintaining, accessing and managing ever-growing volumes of digital data are yet unsubstantiated, but will probably consume even more hidden resources than the old paper storage systems unless conversion and migration strategies start being regularly applied within systems design processes. Even if computer storage for the long term becomes technically and financially viable, the processes of appraisal will continue to be critical recordkeeping activities for determining what to capture and in maintaining accessibility to records over time.

To ensure access to records for as long as they are required now involves the introduction of some newer processes as archivists and records managers grapple with the challenges of electronic recordkeeping. Records that are technologically dependent and stored in proprietary formats and systems often need to outlive the systems and formats in which

---

[15] Frank Upward, 'Functional Analysis, The Continuum and Census Returns', unpublished draft, 1997.

they were recorded. Paper is a forgiving technology. Electronic or digital technologies are far less tolerant of systems design failings or neglect over time. Electronic data formats are very short-lived – what everyday system can read a Wang file stored on a 5½ inch floppy disk from the 1980s?

Migration, the process of ensuring that the data formats in which records are stored are kept readable by moving into new data formats able to be read by current technology, is one of the strategies being applied to manage short-lived systems and data formats. This strategy enforces processes for automatic migration from older to newer versions of software. There is some discussion on whether migration actually creates a new record, and whether that new record in a new format can be regarded as possessing characteristics such as integrity and authenticity. However, the current pragmatic thinking is that where the record is maintained in its original format, linked to the new format, with records documenting the process of migration and a statement of the veracity of the migration, this will satisfy requirements.

An alternative strategy to migration is the process of conversion. This process changes the data format in which the record is created into a standard format for storage purposes at the point of capture of the record into the system, requiring a process intervention at the point of capture. A common format used for this purpose is the Adobe PDF format. Adobe PDF is itself a proprietary format, although its specifications are widely and publicly available meaning that it should be possible to construct ways of reconstructing the viewing of the format into the future. Other formats are also being explored in this search for an appropriate archival data format. All data formats are time-bound and will need strategies for migration into the future.

A third set of options for managing access to obsolete data formats is not process-based, but technology-based. This involves variations of the practice of invoking parts of creating programs, called viewers, into the current software to enable representation of the record in the creating software, a protocol invoked on request for access to the specific record. Such strategies themselves are subject to obsolescence, as is everything to do with electronic data.

As the Australian Archives once said in a submission to a parliamentary commission, 'Storage is the frontline of preservation for the media on which records are stored. Through it, there are links to practically every other element of the records continuum'.[16] The longer the records in systems need to be managed, the more important it is that the management processes continue to continue.

---

[16] Australian Archives, 'Submission to the Australian Law Reform Commission', 1997, section 2.3.1

Conclusion: Records as static objects or dynamic objects

It is convenient, but simplistic, to think of records as complete entities once they have been captured into a sequence, either by formalized processes or by the juxtaposition of items into a folder or other container. There is a point of fixity at the threshold of a document becoming a record. This fixity, from a legal viewpoint, is important, as we have seen in relation to the definition of legal documents. It reflects the result of the action, clearly located at a point of time linked to its creator and able to be rendered to view. But, for recordkeeping, this point of fixity is merely the beginning. Just capturing the record object doesn't invest records with the characteristics identified above. To do that, records have to be able to tell the story of exactly what has happened to them during the course of their existence. They need to reflect who has accessed them, in what circumstances, whether redacted versions of them have been created, whether multiple renditions in different formats have been made, what associations with other records have been made, whether they have been migrated, when and with what guarantees of success, when they are due for destruction, when their security access is reviewed and so on. These additional contextual details are provided by the processes that manage records – the recordkeeping processes, which themselves must leave a record of the action. These are the processes which provide the means of achieving the critical characteristics of records – authenticity, reliability, integrity and usability.

In the words of Sue McKemmish, 'The record is always in a process of becoming'. Even knowing the users of a record – who has seen it – alters the meaning of the record. Each one of the elements outlined above varies the meanings of the record by placing it into a network of traceable actions. Records, then, by their nature are not fixed; they are fluid, ever-forming, but paradoxically they aim to fix the elements that structure their formation. There are points of stasis in the record, but from those points the network of connections continues to radiate outwards for the whole of the existence of the record.

Recognizing the processes of recordkeeping as a critical component of the record alters the way we build systems and deploy techniques to ensure its management. For the most part, today, software systems and functional specifications available for managing records are still primarily managing the record as a static, fixed entity and have yet to refashion themselves for this dynamic, ever-building notion of a record.

Recordkeeping methods in different cultures differ, however, and one single methodology cannot be presumed. Nevertheless, it is interesting that the international consensus as expressed in ISO 15489, the International Records Management Standard, has moved professionals towards a more proactive process-oriented view of recordkeeping. Exploring the reasons underlying the process orientation is vital to rethinking recordkeeping in the electronic age. Some of the practices that we have traditionally associated with recordkeeping have been continued through custom and the reasons for doing them get lost. Yet in some strange way many records managers and archivists are beginning to argue that electronic recordkeeping involves the rediscovery of old practices including the need for metadata schemes and the need to set up registration, classification, workflow and aggregation processes not dissimilar to those of the past. The practices, however, will be implemented in new ways within complex technological environments where multiple options for achieving objectives exist. Recordkeepers need to understand clearly what the purpose of particular processes are, what practices need to be maintained at all costs to defend the critical characteristics of records, and what practices can be changed, altered or even abandoned.

Readings

- ISO 15489, *International Standard on Records Management*, Geneva, International Organization for Standardization, 2001.

- Rich Lysakowski and Zahava Leibowitz, 'Titanic 2020 – A call to Action', Woburn, Mass., Collaborative Electronic Notebook Systems Association, 1999, available at: http://www.censa.org/html/Publications/Titanic2020_PDFv3-03-22-2000.pdf

  This article was written for a general audience and has a populist slant, but presents some interesting statistics and figures on the implications of software dependence for organizations.

- Sue McKemmish, 'Are Records Ever Actual?', in Sue McKemmish and Michael Piggott, eds, *The Records Continuum: Ian Maclean and Australian Archives First Fifty Years*, Clayton, Ancora Press in association with Australian Archives, 1994; available at: http://www.sims.monash.edu.au/research/rcrg/publications/smcktrc.html

  This article explores the notion of record as a construct, rather than a physical entity.

- John Brunker, *Recordkeeping Implications of Online Authentication and Encryption Processes,* Paper presented at the workshop: 'Email as a government record – transferring from paper to e-record ', National Library of Australia, 25 September 2003, available at:
  http://www.naa.gov.au/recordkeeping/rkpubs/fora/03misc/auth_encryp.pdf.

  This guideline is one in a sequence developed by National Archives and is one of the few documents currently available to commence exploring of the recordkeeping issues in encryption and authentication technologies.

The fundamental characteristics of records have been redefined during the last decade in a number of collaborative projects which have sought to identify those things that made records different and, therefore, requiring management techniques different from those used to manage other information resources. Projects of importance in this redefinition include:

- University of Pittsburgh: Functional Requirements for Evidence in Recordkeeping, 1992-1996, http://web.archive.org/web/20001024112939/www.sis.pitt.edu/~nhprc/.

  In a supremely ironic example of the fragility of electronic records, the web pages containing the working papers of the project were inadvertently destroyed. However the papers of this project can be seen through the Internet Archive.

- The Long-term Preservation of Authentic Electronic Records: Findings of the InterPARES project, 2002, http://www.interpares.org/book/index.htm.

  The first phase of the InterPARES project resulted in detailed analyses in the areas of authenticity, appraisal and preservation. It is an international research project and has evolved from earlier work by Luciana Duranti, at the University of British Columbia in Canada, applying techniques from diplomatics to electronic recordkeeping. The InterPARES project is still active at the time of writing this chapter.

CHAPTER 6

The archive

Hans Hofman

Introduction

In the early sixteenth century the last independent Duke of Guelders, Charles of Egmond, travelled through his countries trying to keep them together, defending them against all sorts of enemies, seeking if possible to expand them. His efforts in ruling, maintaining and administering his little empire led to the creation of records. These records were made to keep track of or claim his rights, to list the obligations he could not afford to miss, to record the partnerships he was trying to build, to appoint people to important positions, to collect the money he was always short of, and to keep track of other business. In his continuous fight with the Burgundian-Austrian emperors he had to defend his position as a duke and ruler in his own right. In doing so he produced documents that could support his claimed position. Some of these documents were essentially made up, for example the false genealogies that go back to Charlemagne. Such claims were often the way local rulers supported their power and authority.

Memory and truth were bent and adapted to fit needs, a practice that reminds us that recordkeeping is not an end in itself. The distinction between personal and official documents was not seen as particularly relevant and personal, ducal, and governmental issues were intermingled. During the reign of Duke Charles these records were not kept in one place, but were dispersed over his many castles. A very small part of them travelled with him and his accompanying staff. Although the dukes had a kind of chancellery that took care of writing and dispatching letters, deeds and other documents, there is no evidence they had a registry, unlike for instance the neighbouring duchy of Kleef.[1] They certainly had no records policy or program. The fact that they kept documents and records was based upon the need to have evidence of their rights and to maintain control of their sovereignty.

In the Gelders Archief, located in Arnhem in the current province of Gelderland, the remnants of Duke Charles's archive can be found, together with the archives of his

---

[1] Note that I use this example to give an impression of what happened in previous times. The 'recordkeeping' practices of the dukes of Guelders may very well not be representative of those times; the notion, however, is there.

predecessors.[2] The records of all dukes since the twelfth century are considered to be a *fonds*, and, as such, they represent the archive of the sovereignty of Guelders, before it was absorbed by the Habsburg empire in 1543. It is, in fact, a conglomerate of bits and pieces of the original archives and is the result of many adventures involved in moving them back and forth. Parts of the archive still rest in other places, including Vienna and Brussels. Although the dukes did not use the term 'archive' or 'records' or even the Dutch equivalent 'archief', they probably had a notion of the concept, as they were obviously aware of the purpose of preserving at least some of the documents they created and received.

A corollary to the archives of the dukes may be found in the papers and records of the President of the United States of America. Before the Presidential Records Act (PRA) of 1978 all presidential papers and records were considered to be personal papers. These 'personal' papers were housed in presidential libraries. Each president has his own library, often located in his hometown. The PRA introduced a distinction between personal and presidential records. The personal papers concern his activities as head of the presidents' political party or personal matters. The presidential part relates to constitutional, statutory, or other official or ceremonial duties.[3] The requirement for such a law illustrates the intricacies and complexity of the different sets of records that are created in fulfilling public positions. But how conscious and careful are the actors involved at the White House about the differences? The Iran-Contra affair during the Reagan administration with Oliver North destroying official records, the subsequent Armstrong v. Bush (PROFS) case on preserving emails and office automation documents, and, more recently, the preservation of all the Clinton emails, prove that reality is not that simple.

Previous chapters discussed the creation of documents and records. This chapter will focus on that grouping of records considered an archive. This exists at the level of an organization or any other identifiable record-creating entity, such as a person or group of persons. The relationship between an organization and an archive will be explored, taking both the organization and its records as a starting point. The notion of an archive as an entity on its own will be explored. Should it be seen as a physical entity or as an intellectual or virtual concept? Is it an organic or deliberate construct? What is the relationship between an archive and a recordkeeping system? And, what is the identity of an archive?

Notion of an archive

Outside the archival discipline, particularly in information technology usage, the notion of an archive has come to mean 'older information' that is no longer directly needed in

---

[2] In order to try to avoid confusion I will use archives in this chapter as a plural of archive, not as the equivalent of archival institution. Names of archival institutions, such as National Archives, will begin with capitals.

[3] Further information on these laws and records can be found at www.archives.gov/records_management. The records of both the Congress and the Supreme Court are not covered by any statute, except for the Constitution, hence they are not federal records. Nevertheless, both bodies deposit their records in the National Archives, but retain legal custody.

business, but is still considered to be of some value and therefore kept and stored offline. Projects aiming to archive the World Wide Web are examples of such an approach, directed by the wish to safeguard volatile information for a longer period than originally intended, so other people in the future may know what was available at a certain moment on the Web. This is not the recordkeeping meaning of the word 'archive'.

In general there is a need for people and organizations to keep a record of their activities, their obligations and their rights, which results in the whole of their related documents, which we call 'an archive', being retained. Archives refer to information or documents that emerge from the official or personal activities that are carried out by an organization or person. It excludes documents or other information that have been deliberately collected for some reason, for example libraries that collect publications. The difference is the nature of the preserved or archived information and the way it is selected and managed. For an archive, both the business context in which records are created and human interaction play an important role in identifying and understanding them.[4]

In the nineteenth century a growing awareness emerged about the nature of the archive in relation to organizational or personal activities and about how to deal with it. This was most clearly expressed in the Dutch manual of Muller, Feith and Fruin, which was a codification of contemporary theoretical archival thinking. In their manual an archive is defined as 'the whole of written, drafted or printed documents, ex officio received or created by any agency or one of its civil servants, as far as these documents are destined to remain under that agency'.[5] This approach takes the physical entity as it was transferred to an archival institution as a starting point. It was based, in large part, on the concept of '*fonds*' as defined in French archival theory earlier in the nineteenth century. *Fonds* is defined as 'the whole of documents/records, either of government organizations or of a physical or natural person, automatically and organically brought together because of the very functions or activities they perform'.[6] This concept has helped to focus the activities of archivists and is still one of the main principles of archival science. The fact that *fonds* is not seen as a conceptual notion, but directly connected to the physical entity that is preserved, has caused problems in describing archival records, series or other aggregations, and the organizations and business functions from which they originate. The awareness that the physical entities

---

[4] In Judith Ellis, ed., *Keeping Archives*, Australian Society of Archivists, 1993, records creation is defined as the 'act of accumulating records or incorporating them into a recordkeeping system' (p. 3). This would mean that records only exist in a recordkeeping system of some kind. This is not now quite in line with the new ISO 15489 *Records Management Standard*, clause 7.1 'Principles of records management programmes', where it is proposed that organizations determine what records should be created and in what form and structure. 'Records creation' in this sense is actually an act of appraisal, which determines which of all documents created in the business process should be kept and become records. It is the beginning of the archive in its 'limited' meaning.

[5] S. Muller, J.A. Feith, and R. Fruin, *Handleiding voor het Ordenen en Beschrijven van Archieven*, Groningen, Erven B van der Kamp. 1920.

[6] *Manuel d'archivistique: Théorie et pratique des Archives publiques en France*, Paris, Seupen, 1970, p.22-23. In French: 'Un fonds d'archives est en effet l'ensemble des pièces de toutes nature que tout corps administratif, toute personne physique ou morale, a automatiquement et organiquement réuni en raison même de ses fonctions ou de son activité'.

called archives have in most cases a multi-provenancial character, has led to the now widely accepted view that the administrative or record-creating environment should be described separately from the physical entities in a repository. It is the multiple relationships between both categories of descriptions that are crucial.

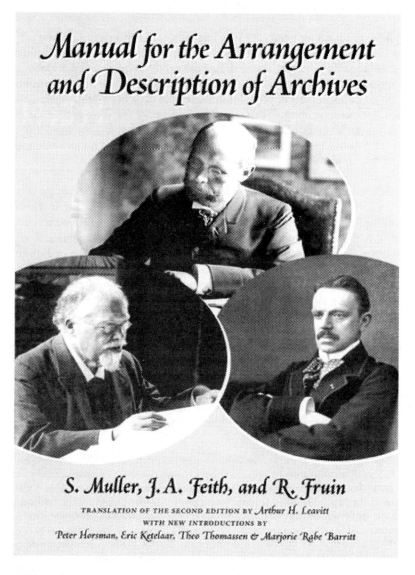

Figure 6.1. A 2003 English edition of Muller, Feith and Fruin's *Handleiding voor het Ordenen en Beschrijven van Archieven*. First published in 1898, its codification of the concept of 'fonds' remains a key principle of archival science.

There are many other definitions of an archive, for example, the two definitions in *Keeping Archives*:

1. the whole body or group of records of continuing value of an agency or individual
2. an accumulation of series or other record items with a common provenance, or a distinct organization, body or purpose.[7]

Both definitions are retrospective and take a rather physical approach. The first one seems to be more a conceptual notion like the term 'record group', but restricts it to those records that have continuing value, that is, the result of appraisal and selection. Other definitions go back to theorists like Papritz, Jenkinson, Schellenberg, Brenneke, Duchein and others.[8] They all have slightly different views which reflect their different cultural backgrounds.

In its pure form one could see an archive as the whole of records received and/or created by one organization or individual. Reality, however, is more complex. As in the example of the Dukes of Guelders, an archive can be the accumulation of the papers and documents of a sequence of counts and dukes, or of the 'organization' called the Duchy of Guelders, starting in the eleventh century.[9] Although the records of each of the dukes can be considered as an archive as related to a period of government, this distinction is not made. Instead, the records are considered as being of one institution. This is because the interrelationships between these 'archives' are so close, and some series, such as accounts and protocols, are ongoing and continue beyond the death of a particular duke to be actioned by his successor.

In archival literature an archive is mostly seen as containing those records that have continuing value, so the scope and meaning of the term are limited. This does not mean that archives can only be found in an archival institution: it includes also those records that are still with the record-creating organization and have continuing value. This view encompasses the idea that an archive will always be the result of recordkeeping activities. The notion of 'continuing value' can mean simply that records are kept for some reason, however minimal.

The Dutch manual considers an archive as an organically created entity. The idea behind it is that the rules for creating an archive cannot be determined by the archivist or the person inheriting custody or control of the material, or by anyone not involved in the conduct of

---

[7] Judith Ellis, op. cit., p.462. The term '*fonds*' is not defined, as it is not a concept really used in Australia.

[8] A. Brenneke, *Archivkunde*, Leipzig, Koehler & Amelang, 1953, p.7; Sir Hilary Jenkinson, *A Manual of Archive Administration*, Oxford, Clarendon Press, 1922; T.R. Schellenberg, *Modern Archives,* Chicago, University of Chicago Press, 1956. And there are dictionaries of differing quality which also try define terms like archives, records and *fonds*, for instance Angelika Menne-Haritz, *Schlüsselbegriffe der Archivterminologie,* Marburg, Archivschule, 2000, and *Dictionary of Archival Terminology,* 2nd ed., Munich, K.G. Saur, 1988.

[9] Until 1386 the Dukes of Guelders were the Counts of Guelders.

the business that created the records. As a consequence the archivist must study them retrospectively to understand the nature of an archive as it is passed down to him or her. This view has changed in recent times under the influence of new insights mainly based upon the increasing impact of information technology, to now emphasize a more pro-active attitude and approach towards records creation.

In the recently published ISO 15489 *Records Management Standard* there is no definition of an archive, only of records and of a records system.[10] This could be interpreted to mean that an archive is seen as an entity post facto (after the creation), or, alternatively, one could say that the standard is about the 'process' of building an archive, since it discusses the creation of records and their management. The end result will inevitably be an 'archive'. The term was not used in the ISO Standard because it has different meanings in different cultures, and archives management was specifically excluded from the standard. Nonetheless, behind this approach there is a notion that an archive consists only of records worth preserving, possibly forever, and transferring to an archival institution. As such an archive would be the result of a series of activities in managing records, that is, the product of a recordkeeping or records system.

This raises the question of whether the records system itself, including its content, can be seen as the archive and its container The answer is yes, but only for those records that are seen as worthwhile to maintain and manage in the system. It is the moment of capture that incorporates such a decision, informed by the moment of creating a document/record and then of appraisal.[11] In this sense the archive is not a static conceptual notion but rather a more dynamic entity, always in the process of becoming and thus the result of deliberate action and decisions..

The recordkeeping system is the 'place' (locus) where records are kept, managed, and made accessible, and, as such, is part of the context of records. The system may be one system, or a range of systems that operate within an organization, either separately for each of the departments or business units or in close collaboration with each other in a distributed environment. The systems should at least be governed by one recordkeeping regime that includes the policies, strategies, rules and methods of the organization.

Because records are created and accumulated in the course of business activities their nature is evidentiary and, as such, they can serve accountability, evidential, and historical purposes. However, it is the context that determines to what extent and in what sense they

---

[10] ISO 15489-1 *Records Management Standard* (2001), Clause 3 'Terms and definitions'. Records system is comparable to a recordkeeping system.

[11] Eric Ketelaar for instance identifies 'an archive' as the result of the process 'archiving' which has its own historically determined structure. See F.C.J. Ketelaar, *Voorwerp van Archiefwetenschap* (paper given at the University of Leiden on 23 October 1993), Houten, Bohn, Stafleu, ⚧☙■ Loghum 1993, pp. 15-19. For the different phases of an archive, see also Eric Ketelaar, 'Tacit Narratives: The Meanings of Archives', *Archival Science*, 1, no. 2, 2001, pp. 131-141. He distinguishes 'archivalisation', 'archivisation', and archiving as three sequential stages. 'Archivalisation' is the 'conscious or unconscious choice … to consider something worth archiving'; 'archivisation' refers to the creation stage of documents; 'archiving' is the capture of documents into a system.

are trustworthy. Were there specific reasons for creating the records? Were they, for instance, created to cover up things or to commit fraud? Are they manipulated, or indeed are they just representing what happened and evidence of business activities? A falsification, for instance, is a record of the very act of falsifying, not of the activity that it tries to represent. However, such records will tend to lack information about that hidden process of manipulation of memory. Fraud or manipulation of records is not always undertaken for evil reasons. For example, in The Netherlands during the Second World War false records were created about birth, marriage and death of Jews to provide them with an Aryan ancestry and thus to mislead the German occupying authorities. In general, because of the lack of any direct contextual information of the falsification process, it will require forensic investigation to expose it. Nonetheless, it may be possible that decisions are made based on the false information, and, in that sense, the information belongs to the business activity in which it is used, and, as such, is evidence and a record or part of a record.

So far, the notion of an archive can at least be seen as:

- a conceptual notion of all the documents created and/or received by one record creator in conducting his business (encompasses 100% of records that are received and created)
- those records of an organization or individual that have continuing value
- a conceptual entity in the process of being formed by an organizational recordkeeping system
- a physical entity being the result of a chain of activities (recordkeeping history) of one or more record creators as transferred by the final owner to an archival repository (encompasses the 5-15% of records that are seen as having archival value; these can be the result of either a deliberate decision, or of one or more accidents, or of both).[12]

Archive in context: Organizations and business activities

Both the organization and the recordkeeping function have their own dynamics and this often results in 'archives' that have a complex structure. An organization is responsible for carrying out functions or activities that may change over time. Some functions or activities may be transferred to another organization, or they may simply end; others may be added and the processes by which they are carried out may change. Possible causes for change may be changing legal mandates or organizational structures, the introduction of new technology, opening of new markets, and so on. As a result, the boundaries of an archive are not always clear-cut. Some related records will follow the transfer of a function to another organization; others will be received because of the addition of a function. So from this perspective, an archive is the result of a dynamic process, the 'making' of the archive. The way the archive is organized depends on bureaucratic rules and practices which may differ between organizations and, at different levels, between cultures.

---

[12] T.R. Schellenberg (op. cit, p. 16) sees an archives as those records that are selected for deposit or deposited in an archival institution.

In addition to the dynamics of organizational structures and functions, the recordkeeping function itself is selecting, structuring and describing the records, and in doing so is shaping the archive. Recordkeeping activities are governed by the business processes they serve and their governing rules and procedures may change over time in line with changes to the functions and business processes. Changes to recordkeeping activities will also influence the structure and content of the archive.[13] The result of recordkeeping activities (and sometimes of accidents, neglect or administrative change) is that eventually only a small part of all received and created records (the conceptual archive) will survive – around 5-15% of the whole. What survives is the result of a series of decisions, determined by all kinds of considerations and criteria. In a sense we could see an eventual 'archive' as the result of a three-step selective process: recording, capturing and selecting for further preservation. Each of these steps involves decisions on what has to be recorded, captured or selected, and why. Several actors are involved in taking these decisions, not only the creator, but also the records manager and the archivist, and, at some distance, the auditor, the politician, the historian, and the user. They all are involved in the building of organizational and societal memory.

Figure 6.2 provides a simple representation of the relationship between agents, business activities and records.

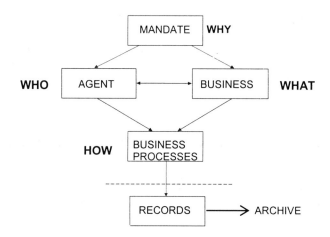

Figure 6.2. The main entities in relation to an archive

---

[13] It is interesting in this respect to notice that in the anglophone countries the word used in this respect is 'records creation' and that archivists in The Netherlands speak of 'archiefvorming' (literally 'archive building' or 'archive creation'). On the one hand the focus is on creating the components (i.e. records) and capturing them, on the other, the focus is on building the whole. In the former case the recordkeeping activity has to be added to records creation in order to maintain the records, while in 'archive building' it seems to be more or less implicit. Is this apparent difference in the use of words reflecting a different cultural view on archives? Dutch archivists use the singular form, 'archief', referring to the whole of documents of one organization or person or group of persons.

The diagram can be read in two directions, from top to bottom representing that business activities are carried out by agents and create records, and the other way around, showing that records reflect business activities and transactions carried out by agents and as such provide evidence of them. Recordkeeping and subsequent archival management deal with the resulting records. They organize, structure, describe, select and dispose of the records. Obviously, when relationships between agents and business functions or activities change, records are influenced. This can also happen when the way functions are carried out – the business processes – change.

From the point of view of an organization or an individual, the flow of documents and/or records that follows from carrying out activities may be seen as more or less organic. Without receiving or creating documents, it is hardly possible to do business or be part of society nowadays. So, without business processes and agents, there will be no 'archive'. Technology and the organizational culture, that is, the way people work, co-operate, and communicate, will influence the business processes and agents. The policies, rules and procedures for recordkeeping will determine the archive.

Needs of organizations

Organizations do not keep records for fun; they keep them because they serve a purpose. Probably the best approach to the identification of the boundaries of an archive is to identify the reasons behind its creation. These are well known in archival theory and can be found in the ISO 15489-1 *Records Management Standard.*[14] The reasons are:

- to enable business processes;
- to deliver services in a consistent, efficient and accountable manner;
- to provide consistency and continuity in management and administration;
- to meet legislative and regulatory requirements;
- to protect the interests of the organization and the rights of employees, clients and present and future stakeholders;
- to provide evidence of business, personal and cultural activity; and
- to maintain corporate, personal and collective memory.

These drivers all essentially relate to enabling business activities, to meet legal requirements (for example, accountability), to protect interests and to maintain one kind of organizational memory. The extent that these reasons apply in an organization depends on the nature of business and, in some cases, is based on risk analysis. Some business areas require greater attention to creating and keeping records than others. The pharmaceutical industry, for instance, is strongly governed by legal and regulatory requirements, while government organizations, especially in democratic states, need to be open and accountable

---

[14] ISO 15489-1 *Records Management Standard*, Clause 4. 'Benefits of records management'.

for their decisions, activities and actions in order to comply with rather abstract notions such as 'good governance'.

It is not the individual record that is relevant in meeting the recordkeeping requirements, but aggregations of records up to the level of all available records of an organization – the archive. Business actions, protection of interests and rights, and evidence can be derived from one record, but in most instances the case will be stronger with, and the organization better served by, the whole set of records. The links between records provide meaning and are an important part of evidence. So, as discussed in previous chapters, the archive is already relevant when it is in the process of being made and, as such, it has a broader meaning than the traditional historical sense that many people attribute to it. At the individual level, a record also derives part of its authenticity, integrity and understandability from its relationships with other records, that is, as part of a larger whole.

Archive in changing organizational structures

Many types of organizations exist, from very small ones to huge multinational organizations. Large organizations are divided into smaller and smaller units, until a level is reached which creates an environment for carrying out a business process efficiently and effectively. The way organizations are structured and activities are carried out is determined by the nature of the business, the available technological infrastructure, funding and people. Making clothes, for instance, has changed over time because of technology. Those changes have had an impact on organizational structures. In the Middle Ages a tailor was usually a one-man enterprise, while during the Industrial Revolution large factories and mass production of clothes emerged. The information technology and communications revolution and the viability of networks of different and dispersed units have enabled clothes to be made in cheap-labour countries and then shipped to developed countries for further handling, packaging and selling. Each major change in technology enables new kinds of organization and new ways of communication. Each new invention also adds to the growing complexity of society. This was equally true for the advent of printing, the steam engine or computing technology.

At present the hierarchical structures of large bureaucracies are being replaced by more horizontal network structures, due to new technologies. A current example is the emergence of chain management, where business processes that are closely related, but carried out by different organizations, are seen as a chain. In health care, for instance, a chain of processes starts with the general practitioner and moves to medical specialists, hospitals and rehabilitation services. Each is closely related. In such cases it is becoming more and more important to have an overall management instead of individually managed sub-processes. Another example of emerging chain management is in the area of criminal justice. To date there are big projects under way in Canada and the UK which envisage a complete reorganization of the whole chain of criminal justice, from the police through courts, corrections, to the parole board and community supervision.[15] This approach involves many organizations, each with its own responsibilities, rules, procedures, and processes. That means that the underlying information architecture and infrastructure has to be adapted to enable interoperability and efficient and proper handling of criminal cases. The current approach is to create an overlaying structure that enables the communication and exchange, while the existing systems stay in place and may only be slightly adapted.

Other possible organizational structures can be found in distributed organizations and virtual organizations. Distributed organizations are in many ways still physical. They consist of business units located at different places, for example multinationals that carry out their activities in different countries. The new communication channels (intranet and extranet) allow better co-ordination of these activities and around the clock work processes. Virtual organizations consist of different nodes at different places which are also connected through the web, but the actual performance takes place in the virtual space of the web. These 'organizations' can be temporary depending on the nature of the activities. They may have physical locations, but that is no longer a key issue.

Many questions arise from these developments. For example, what is the business process? Will every participating organization manage its own records? What are their 'own records'? What is the archive? Will it include all files which have gone through the whole chain, or will each file be subdivided into sub-files of records and will each organization still have its own 'archive' of sub-files? What interrelationships between files exist? What influence will this all have on the notion of the archive? Will the focus of the archive shift to the business function?

Clearly, such new structures and processes have a deep impact on information and recordkeeping practices and processes. A stronger role for recordkeeping will be necessary to ensure the reliability, authenticity and accountability requirements throughout the whole chain of processes. Recordkeeping functionality will probably need to be integrated into the business process much more than has been usual to date. Moreover, it raises questions about responsibility for the whole chain. Will it be a shared responsibility? Will that change in other organizational structures, for example in more horizontal structures? The position of the records manager will be affected in that he or she will need to be much more involved in directing, advising, monitoring and evaluating processes and records and also in ensuring that recordkeeping rules and practices, including access rules, are co-ordinated and aligned. The challenges are huge. One of the big challenges is the cultural aspect, the people – managers and staff – who have to collaborate in different ways.

Organizations will adapt during their existence to the changing environment in which they act. The interrelationships between organizations and the division of responsibilities will change with new insights, and for political, economic, or other reasons. Organizations are not stable entities and will evolve over time. That applies to a single organization during its existence, but also more generally to organizations as a phenomenon. It makes it difficult to

---

[15] See their websites: UK – www.csjonline.gov.uk and www.cjit.gov.uk; Canada – www.sgc.ca/iji-iij/index_e.asp.

identify what the limits of an organization are and at what level we may need to consider the archive. There are many different ways of looking at an organization. Is it the logo, the name, the activities, the structure, the funding, the boss, or a combination of those aspects, that determines the boundaries of an organization? In organizational theory there is no one single view and it is possible to have different views of one organization, depending on what perspective one takes.

What, then, is the record-creating entity? Is it, for instance, a whole ministry or is it a department or business unit or all of these? What delimits the organizational unit and therefore the archive? Is it the fact that an organizational unit has decision-making power, or is it the fact that it has a budget responsibility, or the responsibility for carrying out certain activities or functions, or is it a mixture of these factors? Organizations cluster functions and activities for reasons of efficiency or effectiveness. Functions or activities are related to each other, for instance, the area of transportation or of agriculture, or for achieving a certain goal, for example, making profit as a trading company or a manufacturer. The enhanced possibilities of communication supported by information technology enable broader views, other ways of co-ordinating activities and functions and new perspectives on archives. This also destablilizes the notion of a function. How will these new views and approaches influence the relationship between primary functions, those delivering the core business, and supportive functions, such as activities like financial planning, human resource management and records management? What will become the focus of, or the basis for, recordkeeping management? Will it be dependent on the business function as reflected in the chain of processes, or will it still be the organizational point of view? How well will our archival systems cope with these new developments? Should they reflect a business function performed in more or less sequential organizations through time as comparable with a more horizontal sequence of simultaneously existing processes? How does this 'archive' of one function relate to other functions carried out by the organizations involved? Or will the notion of an archive still be connected to the responsibility criterion that governs an organization, as it is now? Or will this new development make it necessary to adopt a multiple focus with both the function and the organization together and with the different layers of aggregation that can be distinguished? This makes the notion of the archive even more virtual.

Information technology enables us to separate the procedural and contextual metadata from the records, so it will be possible to represent the different views in a virtual way without constantly rearranging the records, as would have been necessary in a paper environment. An effective metadata strategy should support this approach. Recordkeeping software applications should therefore include this functionality, enabling multiple views on the records in the system and on the business context in which they are created and used (the archive being formed).

The view or perspective that one takes also has a relationship with the layers of aggregation that can be distinguished. This applies to organizations, functions and records. These layers of aggregation reflect the interrelationships of records as evidence of business activities. This notion may be compared to an ecosystem where one could take each singular meaningful element as the point of interest or entry point, e.g. a tree, an animal or rock. But equally the entry point could be a cluster of coherent elements, like a certain area with its fauna and vegetation, composition of soil or rock, climate conditions and so on and their delicate interrelationships. It does not matter what entry point is taken – a tree, an animal, an insect, the climate or the soil – they are all intrinsically interrelated and interdependent. Each tree or rock, or any other entity, can in turn also be broken down into its molecular or even sub-molecular parts. It is an extensible, fluid notion, because each part or cluster can be an ecosystem on its own, but, at the same time, it also will be part of a larger cluster. We could see the whole of the earth as one ecosystem. Each view is valid, as it has its own merits, and is dependent on the needs of the analysis being applied – each level of aggregation is never a purpose in itself. A similar approach can be applied to records and business activities. The previous chapter also discusses this idea in the positioning of the record and its meaning.

Administrative traditions and practices

Not only is there a relationship between organizations, their business activities and the records they receive and create, but there is also a relationship between administrative practices and records management.

Most current administrative practices in organizations are built upon nineteenth-century thinking and approaches. Organizations are still basically hierarchical in structure and, within this framework, policies, procedures and rules regulate the way employees work and communicate and how they create and handle information and records. Registries, like the earlier chancelleries, are the centres of control of the documents and records in an organization. They identify, register, track and maintain the records that are received and created. They also determine what form documents should have in a particular situation or for a particular purpose. Through such policies and methods, organizations try to achieve a level of uniformity in creating records, in using documentary forms, and in their style.

As records play an active part in any business process, they reflect this process and its underlying procedures, and the organizational structures that enable and structure it. In a paper environment the records themselves may have the notes of the handling process written on them. In a digital environment these workflow and procedural notes will be registered in a separate system. This separation of the workflow – business process – and document requires a mechanism to ensure persistent linkage between the two which ensures the evidential value of these records. Since an archive is the accumulation of these records, it will and should mirror these administrative processes as they took place through time. These bureaucratic regimes establish what should be registered and captured or not. With the emergence of new technologies this tight network of control has loosened and many records exist outside the recordkeeping system. The rules have not kept pace with technological developments. Registries are still mainly based upon procedures suited to paper records, with the result that many electronic records are not under appropriate recordkeeping control. As a consequence, the archive will be incomplete, because only a small portion of records, possibly possessing insufficient evidential value, will be captured.

With different recordkeeping traditions, organizations in Europe, Australia, Asia and North America may respond differently to meeting the new challenges.[16] Countries with long traditions of recordkeeping practice, such as those in Europe, and, to a lesser extent, Canada or Australia with their close links to colonial England, may rely on these long-standing practices and procedures, because they have proven themselves, and may rely on people to follow them. The level of 'formalness' represents one of the behavioural and cultural aspects critical to devising appropriate recordkeeping rules and procedures.

It is, however, very questionable whether such rules-based practices will withstand the revolutionary impact of new technologies. Reliance on consistent human behaviour may prove even less sufficient in an environment where organizational boundaries are becoming more unclear, transparent, and open. The somewhat anarchic nature of the new communication technologies, such as email, also undermines the top-down enforcement of rules and policies and, as a consequence, the consistent application of them. Increasing mobility of people in job functions also has an impact. Where, in the past, people commonly worked their whole life within one organization, they now stay, on average, about three years. This transience undermines proper and robust recordkeeping practices. Other approaches are required. Recordkeeping requirements and functionality have to be integrated more in application software systems. Where possible recordkeeping activities have to be automated. A recordkeeping regime may also need to cross the boundaries of one organization in order to achieve the required consistency and to fulfil the recordkeeping objectives in a chain of business processes. Although existing recordkeeping principles may stay the same, they have to be applied in more pro-active ways.

As indicated, the focus of recordkeeping attention may shift to the function and the business process. We are still in a transitional stage, however, and can make assumptions, but in the end reality may be different. We may identify some tendencies that can help in positioning recordkeeping. On the other hand we are also still in the position to play an active role in these changes!

Record-creating entity and records management policies

Organizations should define, document and maintain a records management policy. It is important that the highest level of management endorses such a policy. This is not new. Bureaucracies have long had organizational policies to keep control of administrative rules and procedures and the records that will be received and produced.

How strict these policies are depends not only on business and legal requirements and on risk assessment, but also on cultural aspects and traditions. In Germany, for instance, they will be different from those in Australia. The long-standing Prussian administration consists of solid rules for creating, registering, and organizing records, which fit with Prussian

---

[16] David Bearman, *Electronic Evidence*, Pittsburgh, Archives and Museum Informatics, 1994, pp. 261-263.

tradition and are in line with the existing conventions for communication and the view on government.[17] In general, government organizations will have recordkeeping policies that are different from companies; small businesses will have policies, if they have any at all, that are different from those of big multinational companies; pharmaceutical companies will have different policies from those of the automotive industry; organizations in general will differ from private persons; and so on. Government organizations are much more open to outside control, laws and regulations. Accountability is an issue and the public demand for openness of governments is, increasingly, a factor. The way recordkeeping is carried out will differ between democracies and dictatorial states. So societal, cultural, and/or legal context exerts great influence on recordkeeping practices and, subsequently, on the archives. Business companies generally only preserve their records if needed for legal reasons or for conducting their business.

In general, an organization deals with records in two ways: it may determine what records should be made and kept, and also what should be done with the records and how they should be managed, e.g. access and appraisal. The practice of including decisions about what records should be made in policy considerations reflects a shift in thinking based upon the impact of information technology on record creation and recordkeeping. The nature of digital records requires a much more pro-active attitude to avoid the risk of losing information and records. Measures, therefore, have to be taken in the design stage of information systems.

The objectives of a recordkeeping policy are to ensure that authentic, reliable and usable records are created in line with business needs. Those records also need to be kept and managed as long as required. Recordkeeping policies should be translated into recordkeeping programs that include rules, criteria, methods, comprehensiveness, systematic procedures, and requirements about capturing, appraising, organizing, maintaining, preserving, and accessing the records received and created. In order to understand an archive and what it purports to be, it is necessary that this recordkeeping program or 'regime' is properly documented.

In the real world, however, recordkeeping practices have their 'own life'. The human factor and the inherent cultural context influence the application of rules and requirements, so it is necessary to monitor implementation, a role sometimes undertaken by auditors or inspectors. At each operation there may be mistakes or failures, or even deliberate action to subvert the rules. This applies to the creation, the capture, the selection and the management of records. Will all records that should be created, be created? Will all records that are created, be captured? And, finally, will all captured records be properly managed, selected, and if necessary, disposed of, or, alternatively, preserved as long as required? Evidence about these actions is, indeed, found in the 'archive'. In an electronic environment rules, criteria and requirements may be more easily incorporated into systems, either business or records systems, but, even there, human behaviour may not be restricted

---

[17] Examples of this Prussian system can be found in Angelika Menne-Haritz, *Geschäftsprozesse der Öffentlichen Verwaltung: Grundlagen für ein Referenzmodell für elektronische Bürosysteme.* Schriftenreihe Verwaltungsinformatik, Nr. 19, Heidelberg, R. v. Decker, 1999.

by these rules and their implementation in system constraints. There will always be a gap between the ideal and the real situation. It is up to an organization, that is the responsible person(s) and its records managers, to keep that gap as small as possible.

It is, therefore, important to assign the right responsibilities to appropriate people, and, subsequently, to keep them accountable. This does not apply only to records managers, but to all employees of an organization. Initially, somebody with appropriate authority should be given overall responsibility. This person takes care of matching the internal organizational and business needs with external requirements, that is the legal context or co-ordination with related institutions, or the market, and of translating the results of this analysis into a recordkeeping policy. In this sense, the archive is positioned at the crossroads of internal and external needs. The extent to which this is relevant depends on the nature of the business in which the record-creating entity is involved. This activity will be ongoing, because the organization and the organizational context will change. Therefore the recordkeeping policy and subsequent documents need to be regularly revised and updated. It is important that this is done in a policy cycle consisting of four main activities: defining and establishing; implementing; auditing; and reviewing.

One element of the recordkeeping regime is to identify the information systems that enable business processes and to assess to what extent they have or should have a role in recordkeeping. Decisions involve determining whether or not recordkeeping functionality has to be integrated in a business system or kept separate in recordkeeping systems. Relationships between these systems have to be identified and if necessary established. To what extent, for instance, can, and should, recordkeeping metadata about the business process or workflow be extracted from other systems?

Another element is the need to assess how long records should be kept, not simply for a single business process, but also for the organization as a whole. The needs of a single business process will be different from those of the organization. Here the concept of an organizational or internal corporate memory is relevant. Recently there has been a tendency to see records or the archive as an important information source that should be part of knowledge management policies. One aspect of recordkeeping policies at the organizational level may include the issue of unlocking this information asset. Integration of the archive into the other domains of information is then necessary, so it becomes part of a wider view. Multinational companies or government organizations, for instance, have intranet environments with huge amounts of information, of which records could and will be part as well. The rather vague notion of 'content management' is often seen as a possible approach to manage and make the information sources accessible. It makes us aware of other possible approaches that may have a relationship with recordkeeping, such as knowledge management, information management, document management, and so on. These may not be well-defined domains, but they tell us about how other disciplines are looking at information resources and their management. It is therefore important to position recordkeeping in relation to them.

Relationship between organization and recordkeeping system

The following diagram presents a view on the relationship between an organization and its recordkeeping system.[18]

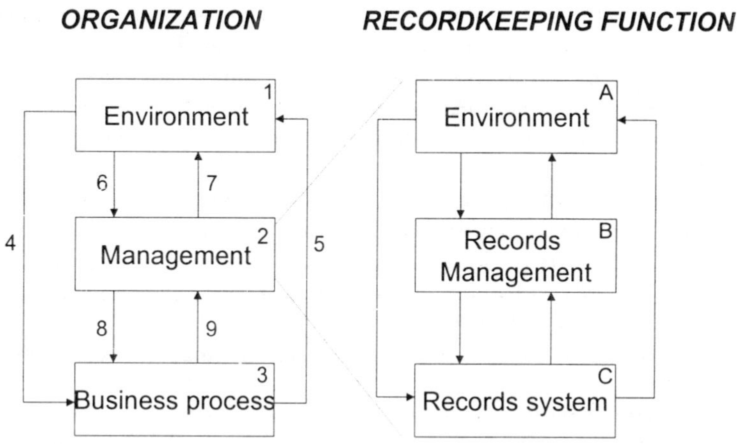

Figure 6.3. Relationship between organization and recordkeeping function

In this model two main processes and their interrelationships are expressed, the business process (box 3), its management (box 2) and the relationships of both with each other and the environment or the context in which they work (box 1). The model represents a management view of the business process and allows us to identify how management is co-ordinating both with the environment and the core business (the left-hand diagram). This model can be applied at different levels, for instance looking at one specific business function, or at all business functions together. That depends on the need.

In the left-hand diagram records management is a part of 'management' (box 2), in the right-hand diagram it is seen as a business activity on its own (boxes B-C) in its own context. The record-creating business processes and their management are now part of its 'environment' (box A).

The numbers, boxes and lines may be summarized as follows:

1. The environment in which an organization works, including its business partners or competitors or other government organizations, the regulatory environment, the technological environment, research and so on.
2. The management activities that will direct the business activities in box 3. It encompasses the translation of regulatory requirements, changes in the market, user

---

[18] Based upon A.C.J. de Leeuw, *Organisaties: Management, Analyse, Ontwerp en Verandering* [*Organizations: Management, Analysis, Design and Change*] Assen, Van Gorcum, 1982.

requirements, technological developments, and so into policies, strategies, procedures, methods, taking into account the available infrastructure to carry out the activities in box 3. These management activities depend, at least in an ideal situation, heavily on the information systems that are available, such as a recordkeeping system. They also evaluate the feedback from the business process or processes being managed (arrow 9) and have a thorough picture of the layout or 'structure' of the business process or processes. Management is impossible without good knowledge of what is occurring.

3. The actual activities that are carried out with the input coming from the environment (box 1) and with an output. The way activities are carried out depends on procedures, staff, available technological infrastructure and so on. It is one or more business processes.
4. The input can be a request for a permit, information, or for products.
5. The output is the result of one or more business processes and can be a permit, information, or physical products. Output can be at the level of a car or a spare part.
6. Requirements, laws, regulations, information about new developments, for example in information technology, or trends.
7. Inquiries, surveys, marketing, public relations, advertising, other communication with the environment.
8. Directions, guidelines, policies from management to staff.
9. Reports from the business processes, evaluation of the performance, accounts, information, records.

The same goes, mutatis mutandis, for the recordkeeping function. Records management is managing the records in the records system, based upon the requirements of the organization and the wider context (e.g. legislation, cultural tradition, and so on). This also includes the notion that management of records should have its own records, for instance part of the records management process (box B) is the development and implementation of classification schemas. Such tools will go into the organization as part of the organization (box A). Output of the records system will be records.

Individuals and families

Individuals or families, as well as organizations, create archives. People take part as individuals in social life and communicate with each other, with government, or with public or private organizations. In doing this they create and receive documents, such as letters, requests and forms, some of which they may choose, or be required, to retain for some time. A passport, a licence, a permit, an appointment booking are all examples of documents that should be kept at least for the time they are valid. There are other more informal documents, however, that people want to retain for shorter or longer periods. These may be kept for reasons that are emotional, such as memory of precious moments or landmarks in personal life, for example, about childhood, weddings, or special occasions, correspondence with good friends or lovers. Not everybody will have the same requirements; it depends on the feelings and character, or on societal, employment and public roles people may have had. Politicians, scientists, writers or other persons with a certain professional or public background tend to leave an archive of some sort consisting of their personal documents. In previous centuries such personal archives also contained many official records as well, and, as discussed earlier, the distinction between personal and public spheres is not always clear. Personal papers are sometimes a valuable addition to official records and can often provide an inside look into what happened. Maintaining these documents may not always be intentional, but may happen accidentally, or through passive neglect where the existence of documents is forgotten.

This private archive-building is not restricted to individuals, but may involve families. Each generation of a family will leave its own 'archive' behind. Such family archives can be seen as a cluster of personal archives, but they contain also other common and continuing series of documents, such as those about financial issues, the management of a real estate and/or other properties. Another type of archive is one that represents different families who have lived in the one manor or castle or house. So-called estate archives are quite common in Europe and represent the history of a castle, estate or manor and the families who lived there. It is obvious that none of these families themselves set out to build such an estate archive, but it happened, because the management of the properties, the real estate and finances provides the continuing common thread through all these sub-archives. Succeeding generations of families build upon existing documents that serve as evidence and memory of what happened before.

An example can be found in the archive of the castle Bergh, located in the eastern part of the Netherlands. It contains records from the twelfth century through to the early twentieth century, up to the point that the castle, or what was left of it, including the archive, was bought by an industrialist. Many generations of the lords, and later counts, of Bergh lived in the castle and left records of what they did and owned. They also had juridical and seigniorial power in ruling their county. When the direct line of descent ended in 1712, a distant relative and member of one of the German principalities, Hohenzollern-Sigmaringen, took over. In the late eighteenth century and throughout the nineteenth century no count lived at the castle and only the administration of the properties was undertaken. Bergh became a subordinated administration of the main office in Sigmaringen. In 1842 the existing, rather loose system of recordkeeping was replaced by a rigid Prussian registry system, one that was implemented in the many locations in central and eastern Europe where the Southern-German principality of Hohenzollern-Sigmaringen had forest and agricultural properties. The change in ownership, over time, had a big impact on the recordkeeping system and the forming of the archive. It is interesting to see that the local Dutch administrator or steward in Bergh himself continued with the existing recordkeeping practice for his own (official) correspondence, while the core official administration changed. A Prussian administrator changed that practice in the second half of the nineteenth century.

The common element in defining this archive is the estate and properties and their administration. The archive (about 200 shelf metres) reflects not only the rise and decline of a family and how they gathered properties in the Low Countries, but also the different recordkeeping regimes. It further illuminates the question, what is the archive? For instance, should the records created and received in the nineteenth century be considered as a sub-archive of the main administration in Sigmaringen, where the whole estate was managed and where one can find also records about Bergh? Does the occurrence of different recordkeeping regimes constitute different archives? If it is not one archive, it can at least be seen as a sequence of archives that share an 'archival bond' at the level of 'archives'. During the centuries a shift occurred from the family to the properties they owned and these became the binding factor of the archive (or perhaps archives). Although many of the properties were sold in the nineteenth century, they were partly bought back again in the twentieth century. Even now they are still managed as a whole by a foundation. So the 'archive' continues to be formed. Does that add another 'archive', that of the foundation? What decides this and what is the criterion? Different views are possible.

Perspectives on the archive and the process of archiving

In examining the nature of 'the archive' at least two perspectives are possible. The first one is a *prospective view* that looks at the process of creating or 'building' an archive in an organization. This perspective requires the focus to be on creating, capturing, and selecting records. The other one is a *retrospective view*, which looks back and tries to characterize and determine the nature of the archive that has been passed down through time, using archival description. The latter was, as indicated, the starting point of a theoretical discourse in the nineteenth century, on which we still build. The impact of new technology, including its impact on preservation of information, increasingly in digital form, demands that we take a more prospective view on records creating and, as a consequence, on 'archiving'. One consequence of this is more emphasis in archival theory and practice on the contextual factors that influence the creation and use of records and, subsequently, of archives.

Another change is the broadening of the scope of the term. Originally and traditionally the term 'archives' was used for written evidence. With the emergence of electronic records, definitions both of records and archives have been adapted to include also new media and, more specifically, new documentary forms. Photographs, videos, audio-recordings, films and so on, are all means of recording and were already included as possible records, but, with the introduction of new technology, new forms emerge, such as multimedia documents, web sites, geographical information systems, complex databases and distributed environments. These new types of documents allow even more multiple views in multiple contexts. When and how do we capture these?

In another context, what would be the equivalent of an archive in an oral tradition? One has to be careful here, because it is risky to apply Western cultural notions to an oral culture, but there seem to be some analogies. In an Australian Aboriginal community the storyteller was the Elder, vested with the authority to hold and transfer the legacy of the ancestors. At different stages of life, accompanied by certain ceremonies or rituals, community members received parts of that legacy in line with what they at that moment needed and were allowed to know. Gradually they became inaugurated into the specific secrets of the tribe until they reached the ultimate stage of tribal wisdom at an advanced age. Are the different stories here the 'records', each representing a fact of life or some knowledge about how to survive, or knowledge about the spiritual origin and identity of the tribe and its members as well as of the human kind? Each 'record' may also have some physical token – a rock, a ridge of mountains, a tree, a shrub, a billabong, an animal – in the natural environment nearby, as a kind of reminder. Or is it the other way around: does the natural environment represent the evidence or reminders of the Dreamtime that is interpreted and explained in stories? Are these physical traces then the 'records'? Can Uluru, for instance, be seen as a whole 'archive', since it is the source of many related stories? Should the stories in this respect thus be seen as 'metadata', enabling the retrieval and understanding of the traces of Dreamtime? The storyteller may be considered the 'recordkeeper' or the mediator between the present and the spiritual universe of which everybody and everything is part.

Figure 6.4. Uluru: an archive of physical traces of oral records?

Each Aboriginal tribe has its own 'archive' of stories, which at the same time both represents and provides the identity that members of a tribe share. Since some of the stories are held in common with other tribes, it reflects a common identity with these tribes as well – the Dreamtime. How static or dynamic is this set of stories? It may not be a closed 'archive', so stories will be added, adapted, and perhaps even forgotten, although tradition is strong. These stories, like records, also have a certain order and interrelationship, which are related to the process of becoming inaugurated into the knowledge and secrets of the tribe.

Within this there is an idea of 'old things are good', or the sanctity of tradition, which emphasizes the relationship with the ancestors, and which has almost disappeared in Western culture as a consequence of the ideas of the European Enlightenment and the impact of the French Revolution at the end of the eighteenth century. It has been replaced by the idea of continuing progress and the dominance of the new and the future. It would be interesting to examine whether there is a relationship between this fundamental change in thinking and the view on archives.

So despite the conceptual notion of 'an archive', the entity called 'archive' which we will have in the end is the result of a series of processes, decisions, and circumstances. One could call that the process of archiving, but that may include too much intentional behaviour and may forget the accidental aspects. The question then becomes the extent to which such an archive represents what an organization has been doing in performing its functions and activities and all the changes therein and how reliable or authentic that representation is.[19] The very fact that an archive is the result of both business activities and subsequent recordkeeping activities does not necessarily make it an accurate reflection of what happened.

Hedstrom describes the role of archivists as intermediaries between past and present and the way they present archives as part of that interface.[20] She identifies two areas where archivists have power over what will be evidence of the past – the area of appraisal and the decisions about what to keep and what to destroy, and the area of presentation of what is kept to users, with all the issues around describing and representing archives. Her argument is that archivists should be open about the decisions they make in managing records and archives. The so-called impartiality or neutrality of archives as sources to learn about history, often claimed by archivists, is now contested, debated and highlighted. Although her discussion of the subject is limited to appraisal, an archival activity discussed in the next chapter, it can and should be extended to the decisions made in the recordkeeping environment. The filter of mediation always has to be visible. Only if records managers and archivists give a proper account of their actions by documenting decisions about appraisal and description will future users be able to interpret and understand the archival sources correctly. The role of contextual metadata and archival description is to explain and to make explicit the origins and the related characteristics of records and their aggregations, such as series, archive and/or archives. In that sense it is not only possible to provide more than one view, but also important to make clear upon what the view is based.

---

[19] I am not going into the difficult and ephemeral issue of truth, since that does not fit within the framework of this chapter. The term 'trustworthiness', however, is more appropriate in the records and archives context.

[20] Margaret Hedstrom, 'Archives, Memory, and Interfaces with the Past', *Archival Science*, 2, 2002, pp. 21-43.

Identity of an archive: Boundaries and meaning

In attempting to identify and explore the concept of an archive, one could easily drown in the flood of literature that exists, which has certainly during the last decade taken the shape of a tsunami. One of the reasons is that one is not only looking at the archive one is looking at, but also at its components, the records, and, furthermore, the wider context of which it is part, both in the area of organizations and business activities and in the broader area of society and cultural heritage. So, one could ask, does an archive have an identity, and, if so, what relevance does it have? In summary, the identity of an archive is derived from the source of its creation, its provenance. This provenance is based on both the organization and its business activities. The records that constitute an archive come from one source: an organization, a cluster of related functions or activities, a business process and so on. Because an archive provides evidence of how an organization has performed certain functions and activities, of organizational and functional changes, and of recordkeeping activities and decisions, it is a relevant entity, worthy to be identified and distinguished.

An identity also assumes boundaries. For records it is the perspective or need that determines these boundaries, rendering these boundaries a flexible notion. The perspective or point of view somebody wants to take in examining records and archives directs the aspects one will or may see. An archive can be seen by itself as a record of an organization and its business activities, and of the way the organization created and sometimes intentionally 'manipulated' this information source into what will be passed down to future generations. In this sense it will be an extension of the notion of the record as described in the previous chapter, where the boundaries of a record are related to 'the contexts in which it needs to be understood'. Pushing this further, a view may consider all the records of the Commonwealth of Australia together either as 'the record' or the archive. The commonality behind it is the federal government as a whole. It is all about the issue of aggregation and to what extent it makes sense to identify and use a certain aggregation. The nineteenth-century notion of an archive as a physical entity has shifted in the late twentieth century to a more virtual or conceptual notion. A clearer distinction has also been made between records and record-creating organizations or business functions, like in the series system.

In the end an archive is more than can be found in archival institutions and less than what is produced in organizations or by individuals during their existence. It is clear that one cannot understand the concept of the archive without examining, or at least acknowledging, the relationships with other levels of aggregation or dimensions. Because of these other dimensions it is possible to position and to identify the archive. The archive as a moment in spacetime offers a perspective on records of an organization or an individual. This view is enabled by the related contextual metadata that described the different characteristics of that archive. It is, however, only one view, and even that can be contingent, that is, determined by cultural tradition or existing recordkeeping practice.

The archive is located in the transition area from the inner organization towards the outer world, from the individual through the organization to the community, from business activities and function towards participation in society, and finally from evidence and organizational memory (i.e. archive) towards collective memory. Furthermore the archive can be seen as a node in a web of relationships with respect to records, clustering records into a larger meaningful whole and embodying them on the one hand, and as a building block in collective memory on the other. In that outer world the archive is a source of distinct origin and specific nature, based on social and business activities, and is as such part of a 'universe' of information. It works in two directions, however. The outer world will influence the records creation and the forming of the archive. So the cultural and social context has to be acknowledged as well. In this respect the existing predominant view on the role of archives, what they represent and the issue of evidence has been challenged lately as too narrow. Through time new layers of meaning must be added to keep the archive understandable. Each new layer will reflect a new perspective that in turn represents a certain view on the world. Each is not only explaining the past, but, often implicitly, also the present and adding new views. The consequence is that a single finding aid is not sufficient, and many access tools or entry points, each expressing a different virtual view, will be needed. Such an approach will also support better user services. It also may replace the traditional approach that seems to assume implicitly that only one view is possible.

Recent insights emphasize that in many cases the attitude of records managers and archivists was not always neutral and was often influenced by factors such as power, deliberate actions and biased views. The nature of an archive is determined by the fact that it is the collective set of records that bear evidence of social and organizational activity. As an entity it also bears evidence of recordkeeping activity and behind that of political and cultural contexts and the exercise of power. These two dimensions are essential in understanding an archive or '*fonds*' as an entity. However, issues like truth – if it is ever knowable – reliability, trustworthiness and authenticity cannot be derived from a record alone; they can only be derived from the record in its context – both the business context in which it was received or created, and the context of other records in the same case, process or archive. The focus of archival theory is therefore on the whole of records at different levels of aggregation, either in a case file, a series, a single archive or multiple archives.

In taking the archive as the focus, the view will mostly be retrospective. It is the result of a series of activities, and in using the archive or its components we are examining the traces of these activities. In a paper world it is the physical 'entity' that can be seen on the shelves of a repository. In the case of digital information, the archive is a more volatile and virtual entity that only can be known by its describing information, i.e. metadata. In both cases the components of an archive may be stored at different places, but, in the case of paper, those parts may be easily considered, and often are, as an 'archive' in itself.

The prospective view concerns the intention to create a valuable information source within the organization which is part of the whole information asset. Within the context of the record-creating organization the relationship with other information sources has to be established. How can it be accessed and used together with library resources, for instance?

Archives also become part of the intranet environment and the World Wide Web, as the ultimate arena for all sorts of information, where in the past they were in the separate domain of the archives. The role they play in that new situation is still that of the authoritative source of information. In this perspective the interaction of the organization with other organizations or persons in society is also reflected. The binding element is the identity of an organization, or, increasingly, of a business function, at whatever level each acts as an independent, accountable and accepted entity in the pursuit of doing business, achieving objectives and communicating with other entities. When the archive is closed and transferred to an archival institution, it has the context of other archives and is part of societal memory, often called cultural heritage. In that context it will be further described to keep it meaningful across domains and time.

From this many questions arise. What will be the influence of current developments on the identity of an archive? In the electronic context there is already the shift from a physical, easily recognizable entity to a virtual archive. What does that mean? In the Australian series system an archive seems to be a virtual thing related to physical or digital series of records that reflect the performance of functions. It is the control system that enables the query to view all the records of an organization, both in the record-creating environment and the archival institution. To what extent will the individual behaviour of civil servants be reflected in or influence the 'archive'? The loosening of the organizational grip on recordkeeping and the weakening of bureaucratic regimes and rules have their impact on record-creating and subsequently on the forming of archives. Will an archive become a 'collection' of individual approaches of recordkeeping – more like a kind of 'personal archives' – representing personal communication networks in carrying out business activities?

Where or how will the organizational needs then be represented? It is obvious that current developments show an increasing tension between the needs of organizations with respect to continuity, accountability and coherent actions on the one hand and the individual behaviour of staff members on the other. Although such a tension has always been an issue, the bureaucratic regimes could usually contain and regulate this. The emerging networked environment, together with social-cultural developments of increasing individualism create new challenges that still have to be resolved, not only in the recordkeeping domain.

We are left with a multidimensional view of an archive. In the following examples different views are reflected, which are all valid, some more, some less, some of which overlap, but they show the many perspectives of this object. They embrace the archive as:

- a conceptual notion of all records of one organization or person;
- a reflection of organizational or personal activities (in a certain period of time);
- one/another level of aggregation of records;
- an organic relic of record-creating activities;
- the result of recordkeeping activities;
- the *fonds* (completed archival entity, considered worth preserving);
- a conglomerate of records from multi-provenancial sources;

- a representation and evidence of the performance of a business function;
- a deliberate, intentional construct of the ruling class (exercising power);
- a node in the web of relationships between records, agents and activities;
- a node in the web of relationships between information resources;
- a building block of societal memory; and
- a record of an organization's or individual's behaviour (both in activities and in managing the information about them).

Concluding remarks

Traditionally an archive is seen as an entity that contains the records of a record-creating organization or individual which are worthwhile for long-term preservation. Archival institutions and archivists have established and operated with that notion. Recordkeeping was and is seen as the 'area of records'. Recent developments in archival theory have placed the notion of an archive using a broader, fuller, and more dynamic perspective which takes into account the many additional dimensions and allows a better understanding and, consequently, better use. It has also connected the archive with records better. It is not only progress in archival thinking that has caused these new insights, but also the emergence of information technology and its impact on the nature of records and the processes in which they are created and used.

This development may also have consequences with respect to organizational structures – that is, the relationship between records management and archival management and the respective organizations that are responsible for them. The transition from the record-creating organization into the different and broader domain of cultural heritage seems to represent a gap that still has to be bridged. The growing interconnectivity made possible through information technology makes organizations, however, more aware of each other and will change the interaction. The relative isolation of both the records management and the archival domain that was possible until now has to be replaced by a new relative openness that requires this activity to be an active part of the larger whole. Finding the right balance, if ever, between maintaining the identity and being part of and partner in that larger whole is a challenge. The same goes for embedding the archival institution and the content it preserves in the cultural heritage domain.

New information technology has triggered the development of a new paradigm in archival theory. The two-dimensional and physical way of thinking has been replaced by a three- and even four-dimensional universe. This new paradigm allows us to view the archive from different viewpoints, and to better acknowledge the many perspectives, embedded in the interrelationships between organization, business function, recordkeeping process, and evidence or memory. This relates not only to electronic records but also to paper-based records. In that model the archive represents the dimension of organizing records into a corporate or personal memory. It is the result of organizational or personal recordkeeping activities based on certain objectives, views, and policies. The broader perspective of society will also influence these objectives.

One of the consequences of this new approach is that the focus has moved from the entity 'archive' itself to the context in which it has been created and will be used. Although the entity is still there, it is no longer a 'fixed' and, in a paper-based environment, often physical thing, but more a virtual or conceptual state in a fluid sequence from a single record to societal memory. Depending on the context it may be viewed differently. Such a notion of an archive enhances its value, but is also not limited to the archive. There are different levels of granularity, but they only get meaning from the context in which they are used. Each level represents evidential value, not only of business activities, but also of recordkeeping activities and subsequently the memory-building process. The context will evolve through what is called 'spacetime', and influence the use of records and archives, adding new layers of interpretation and meaning.

The outside view is also that one can distinguish between different levels of aggregation reaching out into an expanding universe, from record, file, series, archive, collection of archives to information universe, or from function, system, organization, business sector or domain, society to global community. The archive is inextricably linked to its origin, but that origin is not a fixed view either. The example of the dukes of Guelders has shown that. Both one duke and the duchy are valid as a viewpoint. It does not matter.

The complexities of physical archives have troubled archival discussion for decades, and definite solutions have not been found. The clearer distinction between archive and its context of provenance, as made for instance in the Australian series system, helps to resolve these issues. The possibilities offered by information technology, furthermore, help in managing the information about the records themselves, and about their contextual information and complex interrelationships.

The process of 'building' an archive or corporate memory is implied in the ISO 15489 *Records Management Standard*, which identifies the necessity of having a records management policy that governs record-creating. On the other hand different cultural and related bureaucratic traditions have led and will continue to lead to different approaches of record creation and recordkeeping. Finally, an archive can be viewed from multiple perspectives in multiple contexts. The challenge is how to maintain an archive in such a way that this multifaceted view is possible over time and for future generations without the loss of the intrinsic relationships that it carries.

Readings

Post-modern thinking in an archival context

Archival Science, 2, 2002.

This is a thematic issue on 'Archives, Records and Power' edited by T. Cook and J. Schwartz. It contains introductory material and further exploration of post-modern thinking in an archival context.

Fonds

Michel Duchein, 'Theoretical Principles and Practical Problems of *Respect de Fonds* in Archival Science', *Archivaria*, 16, 1983, pp. 64-82.

Terry Cook, 'The Concept of the Archival *Fonds* in the Post-Custodial Era: Theory, Problems and Solutions', *Archivaria*, 35, 1993, pp. 24-37.

These articles discuss the principle of 'respect de fonds' and the tension between the physical entity, the fonds or archive, that has to be described and the often multi-provenancial character of its content.

Bureaucratic regimes

David Bearman, 'Diplomatics, Weberian Bureaucracy, and the Management of Electronic Records in Europe and America', *American Archivist*, 55, Winter 1992, pp. 168-181. Also published in David Bearman, *Electronic Evidence: Strategies for Managing Records in Contemporary Organizations*, Pittsburgh, Archives and Museum Informatics, 1994, pp. 254-277.

Bearman has given a short comparison between the different ways bureaucracies in the US and Europe are working and the influence on recordkeeping.

Angelika Menne-Haritz, 'What Can Be Achieved With Archives?', *The Concept of Record: Report from the Second Stockholm Conference on Archival Science and the Concept of Record, 30-31 May 1996*, Stockholm, Swedish National Archives, 1998, pp. 11-26.

Menne-Haritz makes a clear distinction between the record as part of a business process, the primary purpose, and the record as an information source in doing research, the secondary purpose. At a higher level this can be applied to an archive as well: the archive in the 'forming phase', still growing and changing, reflecting the business of an organization or a person, and the archive as the information source, an entity or object on its own. As such it will have a 'new' life in another process, or series of processes, being managed, described, used, and interpreted. In this sense it will accumulate new meanings in new contexts of use.

CHAPTER 7
The archives

Sue McKemmish, Barbara Reed and Michael Piggott

Throughout time human societies have built memory palaces, including keeping-places for the collective archives of a tribe, dynasty, political or commercial empire, city state, religion, community, industry, family, or nation. Drawn from the records that form the personal and corporate archive of the individuals and groups that make up the particular society, records are selected for permanent preservation on the basis of prevailing ideas about their continuing value. In chapter 2 Adrian Cunningham explores how the keeping of such records has been institutionalized in different times and places, and how 'the nature of the prevailing power relations and the particular roles archives play as contested sites of power struggle … determine the forms and functions of archival programs'. Chapter 2 also canvases the societal purposes behind this institutionalization. Impulses to institutionalize records of continuing value as archives are also explored in chapters 9-12 with reference to issues of governance, accountability, power and memory.

Beyond the boundaries of organizations, and individuals, archiving processes are involved in the transformation of the individual or corporate archive by 'placing' them into a larger archival framework that enables them to function as accessible collective memory. In chapter 1 we explored how, in relation to the Children Overboard affair, the archive of a ship, department of state, office of a minister, media company, individual and family might become part of the collective archives of the government of Australia, the business archives of Australia, or a state or national collection of the personal archives of Australians. They are thus transformed from 'evidence of me', the corporate entity or individual, into 'evidence of us' – components of our collective memory. Chapters 4-6 concern the creation, management and use of documents, records and the archive, and the way in which they function as evidence and memory of individual and corporate entities. This chapter focuses on the archives and the role of the archivists who manage them (styled collective archivists in this chapter).

Societies institutionalize their collective archives according to their own evidence and memory paradigms, which also shape archival notions of reliability, authenticity, and trustworthiness.[1] They establish frameworks for the selection, collection, arrangement and description, preservation and accessibility of their archives that are closely linked to the power configurations and structures for remembering and forgetting of particular times and places. This chapter explores frameworks that have evolved in Western Europe, North America and Australia – i.e. in Western archival science – to appraise, describe, preserve and make accessible our collective archives, the evidence of us, and the principles, systems and methods developed by the profession, which has evolved from the nineteenth century to manage the archives on behalf of their communities.

Although conceptually, the archives of a society comprise all of the records ever created, the accumulation of the individual and corporate archive(s) of the people and groups that make up that community, in archival keeping-places we find only the records that form the extant portion of the archives, being no more than Verne Harris's archival sliver – a sliver of a sliver of a sliver.[2] The keeping-places may be physical or virtual from the Metroon of the city state of Athens, temple of the mother of the gods, and its equivalent the Aerarium (later Tabularium) in Rome, to the great library of Alexandria, the Han Dynasty's Bureau of Historiography, the medieval religious archives housed in the great mosque of Damascus or the Vatican in Rome, the Tower of London archives of medieval England, the Indies Archives in Seville, the French National Archives, the world's first centrally controlled national archival system, the archival repositories of the national archival institutions of today, or the networked archives of cyberspace, to the archives of orality that may exist only in the minds and stories of the remembrancers.

Archival systems, frameworks and scalability

The term 'archival system' has most often been used to refer to specific systems that exist to manage and document records of continuing value under the control of an archival institution. This formative view of archival systems focuses on the processes needed to ensure that records are accessible and that their meaning is available over time. Systems of this type are discussed in this chapter as background to a more extensive discussion of recordkeeping and archiving processes associated with description, appraisal, preservation and access that are applicable within a broader archival framework.

From a records continuum perspective, the concept of an archival system also encompasses a framework-setting role, involving the administration of ownership, custody, access rights and responsibility for all records within a particular jurisdiction, including those of continuing value. The framework is set at a high level by legislation, regulations, standards, rules and policy, but the implementation of the framework occurs simultaneously at different points, at all operational layers within the framework encompassing each of the

---

[1] For an insightful discussion of this issue, see Ann Laura Stoler, 'Colonial Archives and the Arts of Governance: On the Content in the Form', in Carolyn Hamilton et al., eds, *Refiguring the Archive*, Dordrecht, Kluwer, 2002.

[2] Verne Harris, 'The Archival Sliver: A Perspective on the Construction of Social Memory in Archives and the Transition from Apartheid to Democracy', in Hamilton, op. cit., pp. 135-151.

layers of the archives, archive, records and document, that is in all dimensions of the records continuum. A key difference between life-cycle and records-continuum approaches is that each stage of the life cycle is conceptualized as a one-dimensional space in which recordkeeping or archiving processes take place from the perspective of that stage alone. The records continuum defines recordkeeping and archiving as multidimensional. When operating in any one dimension of the continuum, all the other dimensions are present, although the particular focus may be creation, capture, organization or pluralization. From this viewpoint, collective archivists focus on pluralization, operating in one dimension of a multidimensional space. The theoretical underpinning of this view of recordkeeping spaces is explored in chapter 8.

Archival frameworks also operate at a social level. The network of individual archival systems makes up a community of practice that operates to preserve an aspect of the social or collective memory of society. This use of the concept of archival system does not just refer to specific descriptive systems or regulatory regimes, but also includes the archives/records profession with all its complexity – incorporating professional training, resourcing and the health of the profession as a whole – and interactions with other institutions serving similar long-term social expectations of preserving collective memory.

Within an increasingly complex Internet-enabled world, the records continuum concept of an archival system can be seen as a system that operates to impose controls that need to apply beyond the boundaries of one agency. From this viewpoint, an archival system manages an aggregated layer of records existing outside the physical boundaries of a single agency, and encompasses multiple individual agencies, often from disparate layers of government, private organizations and individuals. Applying archival techniques to managing records arising from cross-agency services or 'joined-up' services has yet to receive much professional attention, yet within the records continuum model, such trans-agency controls locate the techniques for managing records at the pluralized (collective archives) layer of operation.

In addition to multiple meanings, the notion of archival system is scalable. Thus it is perfectly reasonable to discuss an archival system that is implemented within one agency, in Australia often referred to as 'in-house archives', of which BHP Billiton or many of the university archives would be examples. Such systems are as legitimately archival systems as those that manage the same set of concerns for the whole of government or multiple agencies within broader constructs. Such organizational archival systems regard sub-elements of their organizations as agencies within their archival systems and apply concepts developed to manage across their defined agencies.

Often understanding 'archival systems' is made more complex by the fact that multiple interpretations may coexist within one institution. Teasing out some of these strands does not diminish any of the roles, but might help explain why some of our overseas colleagues consider that Australian recordkeeping approaches ignore (or in extreme cases by imputation actively reject) the cultural role. Positioning an archival institution or program as regulator for agencies within its domain involves it in setting up an archival framework in the broad sense described above for application at agency levels. The archival institution or program is a cross-organizational body, but its rules are applicable at lower levels of aggregation. When archival institutions and programs collaborate with other institutions and programs dealing with collective memory, they are also operating in a pluralizing dimension.

The term archival systems thus can be used to encompass multiple meanings, some of which have been identified here. These interpretations are not necessarily contradictory or incompatible. However, it is necessary to 'place' or locate discussions of archival systems so as to identify what the scope and effect of strategies adopted can be.

Much of our professional practice, both in Australia and overseas, currently locates discussions about archival systems in the sense of the rules and frameworks established to regulate agencies, as well as the pluralizing processes in place in those domains to identify, manage, describe, appraise, preserve and make accessible records of continuing value, within specific jurisdictional or domain boundaries. How these notions of archival systems may play out in future in a post-modern world and across domain boundaries is explored further in the final section of this chapter. In these early sections we explore the evolution of such archival systems to this point in time, focusing on how associated processes have been reengineered and repurposed in Australian records continuum management frameworks, with particular reference to the Australian series system and the advisory and regulatory role played by government archival authorities in Australia.

Trusted systems and pluralization

Ideally, in either a physical or virtual sense, archival systems are said to function as trusted systems and collective archivists as trusted third parties. It has become axiomatic in Western archival science to assert that, in order to fulfil their function – to preserve and make accessible authentic records of continuing value to society – archival systems and keeping-places need to be independent from the recordkeeping places and systems of the individual or corporate archive. How this can be realized is contested ground.

In the past, the independence and exteriority of the archives have been implemented by physical segregation of collective archives in fortresses, temples or public buildings, the monumental nature of which symbolize the status and power of the records they house, the limitation of the roles of records creators, records managers or corporate archivists, and collective archivists to different stages in the life cycle of the record, the development of separate archival systems to arrange and describe records in custody, manage their preservation and provide approved users with access to them, and the establishment of independent institutions explicitly mandated to fulfil the archival role. The degree of independence of such archival institutions in most jurisdictions, and the capacity of the archival professionals they employ to act independently of their political, economic and religious masters, have been the subjects of continuing debate.

More recently, particularly in response to the challenge of preserving authentic records in electronic systems, new ways of fulfilling the archival mission have emerged, and non-custodial and post-custodial archival frameworks are being developed and debated.

In the custodial model, records of continuing value are transferred to archival repositories once they are no longer needed by their creators. There they come under the guardianship of archivists whose role was for many years depicted as that of neutral, impartial custodians responsible for preserving complete, closed, static sets of records, neither taking away from, nor adding anything to, the archives once in their care. The archivists who worked in the nineteenth and early twentieth centuries were not necessarily faced with choices about what to keep and what to discard. They merely gathered into their repositories the records that had survived. Their main task was to arrange and describe them and to make them accessible to historians and scholars. But the twentieth century saw an explosion of recorded information in all forms, and the emergence of public access frameworks governed by suites of administrative laws, including coordinated freedom of information, privacy and archival legislation. Inevitably collective archivists became involved in assessing the continuing value of records, decision-making about what to preserve and establishing public access regimes to records regardless of where they were housed.

Russian nationalist Vladimir Zhirinovsky has demanded that the 1867 sale of Alaska be nullified.

Figure 7.1. 'trusted systems…trusted third parties.'

Increasingly, particularly in relation to their role in appraisal, but also in relation to other archiving processes, the model of the impartial collective archivist only involved with the records once they are no longer current has been called into question. Although still subscribing to the ideal of archives as trusted systems and archivists as trusted third parties, and to the view that there is an essential exterior role to be played in relation to collective archives, post-modernists have pointed to the impossibility of archivists playing the neutral, segregated role defined for them in the older model, and to the futility, especially in an electronic online world, of relying on physical custodianship of records as a key means of assuring their preservation and ongoing accessibility. Archival writers like Brothman, Brown, Cook, Harris, Hedstrom, Hurley, Nesmith, Upward and others have argued that recordkeeping and archiving professionals, whether they work with corporate records or collective archives are inevitably an integral part of the record and archive making and keeping process. They see the records, the archive and the archives as in part the product of archival methods of appraisal, description, preservation and access, and archivists as active participants in forming and continually transforming the archives. Tom Nesmith, for example, suggests such a role for archivists in his definition of a record as

> an evolving mediation of understanding about some phenomenon – a mediation created by social and technical processes of inscription, transmission and contextualisation

and archives as

> an ongoing mediation of understanding of records (and thus phenomena) or that aspect of record making which shapes this understanding through such functions as records appraisal, processing, and description, and the implementation of processes for making records accessible.[3]

Similarly the view that archives are static, fixed, and closed has been challenged by new ideas about the dynamic nature of records, and the dust never settling on the archives:

> As my colleague Sue McKemmish has argued, records are in a constant state of becoming. They are stretched into new shapes and structures during the filing and aggregating processes that form them, and by disposal and new administrative patterns, which alter their physicality and the control and attention that they receive. Even disposition is cyclical and never final. Records no longer extant or moved elsewhere can still be observed in the place they once occupied in spacetime through data about their life history or their connection with events. Even if they cannot be observed, their place in spacetime is always there. Records can even have multiple lives in spacetime as the contexts that surround their use and control alter and open up new threads of action, involving re-shaping and renewing the cycles of creation and disposition.[4]

---

[3] Tom Nesmith, 'Still Fuzzy, But More Accurate: Some Thoughts on the "Ghosts" of Archival Theory', *Archivaria*, 47, 1999, pp. 136-50; quotes from pp. 145 and 146.

[4] Frank Upward, 'Modelling the Continuum as Paradigm Shift in Recordkeeping and Archiving Processes, and Beyond – A Personal Reflection', *Records Management Journal*, 10, no. 3, 2000, available from: http://www.sims.monash.edu.au/research/rcrg/publications/Frank%20U%20RMJ%202001.pdf. Quote from p. 4 of online version.

Records continuum theorists and practitioners in particular have formed the view that archival frameworks for the ongoing preservation and accessibility of records of continuing value need to be in place throughout the life span of the record, and that archiving processes of appraisal and description need to be integrated with other recordkeeping processes. They conceptualize recordkeeping and archiving functions operating throughout the life of the record in four contemporaneous dimensions relating to their creation as documents, capture as records, organization as individual or corporate archive and pluralization as collective archives.

In other senses too, the archives are never fully formed or closed. They are always being reshaped by different readings, interpretations, and contestations:

> The archive – all archive – is figured. Acceptance of this in South Africa has shaped fundamentally the argument – and the processes built upon it – that the country's archives require transformation, or refiguring. The figuring by our apartheid and longer pasts must be challenged, and spaces must be opened up in the archives by a transforming society.[5]

The archival profession is only beginning to explore how these insights might shape their future practice. Writings on the societal context of functional appraisal have gone some way to explore the implications for appraisal policies and strategies if records managers are not just passive keepers of documentary detritus and collective archivists do not conform to Jenkinsonian notion of neutral, impartial custodians of inherited records. But these shifts have far-reaching implications for *all* aspects of archival thinking and practice. From this perspective, in developing and implementing their frameworks, systems, standards, policies, strategies, and schemas, archivists are not fashioning and using neutral or impartial tools, methods and processes, they are building social structures of remembering and forgetting.

Description

In the custodial model, archivists were concerned with what Jenkinson termed the physical and moral defence of the archives. The physical integrity of the archives was protected by archival storage and preservation processes, as well as guarding the unbroken chain of physical custody. The moral defence of the records – ensuring that records were preserved in the context of their creation and would thereby retain their qualities as evidence of the functions and activities of the organizations or persons that created them – was governed by a set of rules for archival arrangement and description, devised by early archivists such as Jenkinson, and the Dutch team of Muller, Feith and Fruin.[6] These rules were based on principles of archival arrangement and description developed in France and Germany, and

---

[5] Hamilton, op. cit., Introduction, p. 7.
[6] S. Muller, J. A. Feith, and R. Fruin, *Manual for the Arrangement and Description of Archives*, 1940 translation of the second edition by Arthur H. Leavitt (New York, reissued 1968), originally published in Dutch in 1898.

on practical experience of dealing with records in series, which were closed and complete in custody with no further transfers of similar records anticipated.

The rules were more or less appropriate to the type of jurisdictional and functional arrangements, organizational structures and recordkeeping processes of their places and times, as well as being shaped and limited by the available technology. Conceptually they drew on an understanding of the nature of an individual or corporate archive (*fonds*) as a physical artefact that could be reconstructed on the shelves in the repository and 'inherently reflect the functions, programmes, and activities of the person or institution that created them'.[7] The archive or *fonds*, being

> the whole of the documents of any nature that every administrative body, every physical or corporate entity, automatically and organically accumulated by reason of its function or of its activity,[8]

was seen as having both exterior and interior dimensions, the former relating to the external juridical and functional structures in which the records were accumulated or created and the latter to its internal recordkeeping structures. Archivists implemented the rule of *respect des fonds* by segregating the records of different creators in the repository, and arranging these physical groupings to *represent* the external structures in which each particular archive had been formed, thus also reflecting the functions and activities of the records creator. Within these structures, individual record series were then ordered to *recreate* internal filing structures. Archivists described the resulting *record groups* in archival finding aids, their overall aim being to produce a physical manifestation of the *fonds* on the repository shelves and a surrogate in the archival finding aids.

The variant German *provenienzprinzip* (principle of provenance) operated at a different level of the organizational hierarchy, that of the administrative unit that created the records, and was associated with the *registraturprinzip* (principle of registration order) as implemented in pre-action registry systems. The Germans believed that the functions and activities of records creators were best reflected in registration or filing order not administrative structures, drawing on their understandings of how the recordkeeping processes which govern filing order themselves are based on the activities of the records creator. Subsequently,

> *Respect des fonds* and the German variants were blurred in their translation by Dutch and English archivists into the associated principles of *provenance* and *original order*, and ... various permutations of these principles developed in North America. The external dimension of the *fonds* came to be equated with the principle of *provenance* and to be defined as the grouping together in the physical custody of the archives of the records of a single creator. The internal dimension of the *fonds* came

---

[7] Terry Cook, 'The Concept of the Archival *Fonds*: Theory, Description, and Provenance in the Post-custodial Era', in Terry Eastwood, ed., *The Archival Fonds*, Ottawa: Bureau of Canadian Archivists, 1992, pp. 31-85, quotation from p. 35.
[8] Ibid, p. 40.

to be equated with the principle of *original order*, and was defined as maintaining records in their filing or sequence of action order. Over time *respect des fonds* and the related principles of *provenance* and *original order* as thus elaborated came to be considered as the fundamentals of archival science … Archivists became trapped in systems that attempted to represent records and their context by freezing them in time. And they became wedded to the cataloguing notion that archival data consists of the description of the physical objects thus 'created', the formed *fonds* or *record group*. They were like the early photographers who captured on film incomplete streetscapes, ones from which all moving objects had 'vanished', or else immobilised their subjects for long enough for them to be 'frozen' on film.[9]

Nevertheless, these principles, while the product of a positivist and intrinsically conservative world view in place at the end of the nineteenth and beginning of the twentieth century, have remained cornerstones of archival management, and, as re-imagined in the latter part of the twentieth century, continue to have great practical utility in archival practices in the twenty-first century.

In times when administrations were relatively long-lived and stable, organizational structures were simpler and flatter, and archival institutions dealt mainly with records of past administrations, taking them into custody once they were closed, it was reasonably straightforward to identify the boundaries of a *fonds*, and nominate a single records creator. However, this was no longer the case when the dynamics of social institutions changed, administrative structures became more volatile, organizations became larger, more complex and more highly structured, archival institutions came to be concerned with modern records (*fonds* in the process of becoming, rather than already formed in any sense), more than one records creator came to be associated with a single *fonds,* and they and any number of successor organizations might be responsible for transferring to archival custody sub-sets of records belonging to the same *fonds* at different points in time. Archival systems based on the old rules of arrangement and description became increasingly dysfunctional as archivists struggled to solve insurmountable problems associated with scalability, defining the boundaries of a *fonds*, and creating a one-to-one relationship between a *fonds* and a records creator.

Major initiatives relating to the standardization of archival description within the custodial model focused initially on improving the quality and accessibility of archival finding aids, and facilitating data exchange between archival institutions relating to their holdings. At international level, ISAD(G), the *General International Standard of Archival Description,* was developed with these purposes in mind. Early versions essentially followed the cataloguing model described above, combining records and context data in one logical record. More recently, based on much the same approach as ISAD(G), the Encoded Archival Description standard (EAD) was developed in the United States as an XML mark-

---

[9] Sue McKemmish, 'Are Records Ever Actual?', in Sue McKemmish and Michael Piggott, eds, *The Records Continuum,* Clayton, Ancora Press in association with Australian Archives, 1994, pp. 187-203, quote from p. 189; also available at:
http://www.sims.monash.edu.au/research/rcrg/publications/smcktrc.html

up language to enable archival finding aids to be made accessible via the Internet. The latest developments in relation to ISAD(G) and EAD aim to provide richer descriptions of provenance, linked to descriptions of the records in archival finding aids in order to facilitate user searches. Based on the library concept of authority files, the *International Standard Archival Authority Record (Corporate Bodies, Persons, Families)*, ISAAR (CPF), as its name suggests, provides a standardized way of describing records creators of various kinds, while the Encoded Archival Context (EAC) standard enables the sharing of archival data about provenance entities. Although EAD and EAC in particular look to a future in which archival users will access digitized versions of archival holdings online, they are still closely tied in to custodial models and the record group.

Reconceptualizing archival systems: The Australian 'series' system

It was Australian Peter Scott and his colleagues in the then Commonwealth Archives Office (CAO), predecessor of the National Archives of Australia, who broke the nexus between moral defence of the archives, physical arrangement and custody. Scott was one of the first to challenge the view that the *fonds*, in terms of either its exterior or interior dimensions, can be represented through the physical arrangement of records in an archival repository, rejecting also the corollary notion that the description of records and their contexts should mirror the physical arrangement of the record group. Scott believed that it was only possible to comply with the principle of *respect des fonds* by what he termed 'context control systems', archival descriptive systems that document records and their contexts in terms of the relationships between records entities and context entities. His argument rested on an understanding of the *fonds* as a logical, not a physical construct. It was Scott's great insight that the multiple and layered contexts in which records are created, managed and used – their juridical, functional, organizational, procedural and recordkeeping system contexts – can only be represented 'on paper' or intellectually. As a consequence, the Commonwealth Archives Office abandoned attempts to represent the *fonds* in the physical arrangement of records on the repository shelves. Instead Scott set out to build a system that could represent the logical, virtual and multiple relationships between records and their contexts of creation and amongst the records themselves. His genius lay in the separation in the system's structure of knowledge about context from knowledge about the records, and the system's capacity to establish relationships between contexts and records, thus anticipating the use of relational databases in archives systems by twenty years.

In an exploratory essay on the reconceptualization of the archival *fonds*, Terry Cook urged archivists to:

> liberate themselves from the constraints of the 'custodial era' with its focus on physical groupings of records, and to embrace instead the implications of the 'post-custodial' era with its conceptual paradigm of logical or virtual or multiple realities.[10]

---

[10] Terry Cook, 'The Concept of the Archival *Fonds*', op. cit., p. 38.

Figure 7.2. Peter Scott, pioneer of the 'Series' system, was an archivist, and New South Wales Regional Director at the Commonwealth Archives Office/Australian Archives from 1963 to 1985.

He summed up Peter Scott's pioneering contribution to this endeavour thus:

Scott's fundamental insight was that the traditional archival assumption of a one-to-one relationship between the record and its creating administration was no longer valid. He also demonstrated clearly that administrations themselves were no longer mono-hierarchical in structure or function, but ever-changing, complex dynamisms, as were their record-keeping systems. He therefore developed the Australian series system approach as a means for describing multiple interrelationships between numerous creators, and numerous series of records, wherever they may be on the continuum of records administration: in the office(s) of creation, in the office of current control, or in the archives. Scott's own focus was on interrelating records and their immediate creator(s). Australian archivists are now testing enriching this contextuality by adding other multiple relationships based on formal functions and the larger ambient provenance contexts beyond those of the immediate creator ... Scott's essential contribution was to break through (rather than simply modify) not just the descriptive straight-jacket of the Schellenbergian record group, but the whole mindset of the 'physicality' of archives upon which most archival thinking since the Dutch *Manual* had implicitly been based. In this way, as is finally being acknowledged, Peter Scott is the founder of the 'post-custodial' revolution in world archival thinking. Although he worked in a paper world, his insights are now especially relevant for archivists facing electronic records, where – just as in Scott's system – the physicality of the record has no importance compared to its multi-relational contexts of creation and contemporary use.[11]

In spite of the widespread view amongst North American and European colleagues that Scott had abandoned archival principles along with the physical record group as implemented in the traditional model, he did not in fact reject the need to preserve records in their contexts of creation, but rethought the objectives behind the principles of *respect des fonds*, provenance and original order in a modern context.

Scott's conclusion that the physical arrangement of records in the repository and the documentation of records in their context should be separate processes has had far-reaching implications for archival description and archival systems. The object of description ceased to be the creation of a surrogate ('word photograph') of the physical grouping of records in the repository. It became instead the creation of knowledge representations in the archival system of contextual and recordkeeping entities and their relationships. The location system was a separate segment of the archival control system, linked to but not dependent upon the descriptive regime embodied in the archival descriptive system. Indeed in a further and equally revolutionary break with tradition, Scott's system allowed for the description of records not in the custody of the archives.

Following the German *Registraturprinzip*, Scott identified the series as best representing the physical process of records accumulation, defining it in his seminal 1966 article as:

> a group of record items, which, being controlled by numbers or other symbols, are in the same sequence of numbers or symbols, or which, being uncontrolled by numbers or symbols, result from the same accumulation or filing process and are of similar physical shape and informational content.[12]

However, archival systems that follow Scott do not necessarily have to adopt the series as one of their descriptive entities or as the highest level of physical control for records. The hallmark of Scott's system is not in fact the series, but its capacity to represent dynamic and

---

[11] Terry Cook, 'What Is Past Is Prologue: A History of Archival Ideas Since 1898, and the Future Paradigm Shift', *Archivaria*, 43, 1997, pp. 38-39.
[12] Peter Scott, 'The Record Group Concept: A Case for Abandonment', *American Archivist*, 29, no. 4, 1966, p. 498.

multiple realities through the analysis and separate documentation of contexts, records and their relationships. According to Chris Hurley, it was Scott's borrowing of the principles of synchronization from linguistics to solve the problem of changing relationships between entities that 'enables the Australian ('Series') System, uniquely, to deal with asynchronicity and to document live recordkeeping systems concurrently, and not just to document the detritus of dead recordkeeping processes as other archival descriptive methods must do.'[13]

The other groundbreaking aspect of the system developed by Scott, as identified by Hurley, was its application of the recordkeeping processes normally associated with registry systems to the description of recordkeeping systems and their contexts. Unlike many descriptive systems evolving elsewhere and most contemporary archival descriptive systems, which are essentially modeled on a cataloguing approach, the Australian 'series' system is an archival recordkeeping system, a registry of recordkeeping systems. It is this functionality that makes such systems particularly relevant to the long-term preservation of records in electronic systems.

In the Commonwealth Records Series (CRS) system as implemented from the late 1960s in the CAO, organizations and agencies became the focus for descriptions of context, and series and items for records. The relationships of critical interest were the creating/created by, controlling/controlled and transferring/transferred by relationships that exist between agencies and series, the controlling/controlled, and predecessor/successor relationships that exist between agencies, and the controlling/controlled, predecessor/successor and generally related relationships that exist between record series, for example the controlling/controlled relationship between series of correspondence registers and correspondence files respectively, or the generally related relationship between the series of indexes, inwards and outwards correspondence registers in a registry system. However these particular taxonomies of context and records entities and types of relationships are not essential components of the Australian series system, as it is possible within any given implementation of the system to define taxonomies appropriate to the particular jurisdiction. Other applications based on the principles of Scott's system have implemented additional context and records entities and defined new types of relationships, for example the Public Record Office Victoria and the City of Sydney incorporated functional entities and their relationships into their applications in the 1980s, and recent redevelopment of the system in the National Archives of Australia and the State Records Authority of NSW also incorporate functional entities and introduced the types of relationships that exist amongst functional entities, and between them and other types of entities represented in the system. This is a particularly important aspect of the system, given the complex relationships associated with electronic records. [14]

---

[13] Chris Hurley, 'Scaleability', unpublished paper written for the Australian Society of Archivists Descriptive Standards Committee, 2002.

[14] See, for example, Chris Hurley's series of articles on 'Relationships in Records' particularly 'Part 1: What, If Anything is a Relationship' and 'Part 2: How Do I Own Thee? Let Me Count The Ways', both available from http://www.sims.monash.edu.au/research/rcrg/publications/index.html.

Separating out the entities to be documented and enabling them to be continuously and cumulatively linked provides the basis for an archival system of great precision and far greater flexibility than was perhaps intended by its inventor. Making continuous documentation a recordkeeping process, as Peter Scott did, provides archivists with a powerful tool to keep records meaningful over time. Records change, split and move. Agencies change, restructure and shuffle functions. Activities and transactions are redefined, and business processes reengineered. The language that we employ to describe functions and activities and the records that document them changes too, thus the meanings inherent in the descriptions change over time, and documenting these changes is a critical aspect of keeping records usable and accessible over time.

Because the system represents records and contexts entities and their interrelationships through time, the organizations and people involved with records can be assigned multiple roles – and not only those associated with the creation, ongoing management and control of the records, and transfer to archives as provided in the original CRS implementation. There is no reason why other parties to the transactions the records represent, stakeholders and users could not be represented if required. Moreover, because the system is infinitely scalable, within each of the entities, various levels of aggregation can be documented. As long as a consistent set of definitions of the levels of aggregation is clear to those implementing the system, the linkages enabled through the separation of relationships from entities enables multiple views to be encompassed. This is proven in practice, as the system has been applied to organizations outside the national federal framework. Local governments, private organizations, state archives, and archives of all sizes have implemented the system. The system copes with multiple interpretations of levels of aggregation, depending on how those implementing the system define their world and which features they opt to represent. A local government council, for example, might wish to describe all the administrative units making up the council in its system, whereas from the point of view of the state archives, only the local government councils themselves need to be documented. In both systems the council would be represented as a context entity, but acting at a different level of aggregation. The two systems interlock by relationship. The notion of nesting through relationships can be accommodated in this endlessly flexible system.

Although some of the potential for further development of Scott's system is only now beginning to be realized, its original purposes went beyond those of traditional descriptive systems to support the role that the CAO was carving out for itself under the first Commonwealth Archivist, Ian Maclean. Under Maclean, the CAO defined its role in terms that went a long way beyond the physical custody of old records. It looked to exercise its responsibilities across the recordkeeping continuum, i.e. in relation to recordkeeping processes from the time of records creation. At the same time, it was carefully positioning itself in relation to the management of current Commonwealth records and needed an archival system that would support its intervention in relation to current recordkeeping processes in Commonwealth agencies, as well as managing records already in its repositories. The subsequent development of the series system in the national archives reflected a view of the type of archival system needed to manage the disposal of unwanted records from current recordkeeping systems, to assure the smooth transmission of records of continuing value from agency systems of control to archival control, and to manage subsequent archival program action, e.g. conservation action or administration of access, as well as support arrangement and description.

In relation to the accessibility of archival records, the system is itself the archival finding aid. While other, specialized finding aids may be developed, the archival system and its outputs provide the most complete finding aid, especially in today's Internet environment. The National Archives of Australia's record search tool,[15] for example, provides an interface to the archival system, as does the Archives Investigator tool[16] used by the State Records Authority of NSW and the City of Sydney archives, both of which use variants of the Australian series system. Another key feature of the system is that it supports ongoing descriptive processes that enable the addition of broader layers of context by the addition of new relationships over time. Additional information and detail about the records can also be continually added, including audit trails of the ongoing archival processes of appraisal, description and access themselves. In ideal implementations, this would involve the documentation of every management event relating to the records, be that appraisal decisions, destruction authorization, physical location management, access permissions, use of the records, or conservation and preservation treatment implemented. Each of these processes would be documented by recordkeeping process within the archival system, and the records generated in this way would be persistently linked to the archival records being processed, thus helping to assure their authenticity.

Applications of the system which extend its capacity to embrace material not in archival custody enable close links to be established between current recordkeeping systems and archival systems, and open up the possibility of re-purposing and reusing the metadata created in either environment. Historically, possibly as a pragmatic response to lack of staff resources, Australian archivists have resisted the notion of archival reprocessing and listing of records as they were transferred into custody. Wherever possible the systems used by the creating bodies – paper indexes and registers, and more recently records management applications – are inherited by the archives as the best way to access records at item level. The full potential of creating recordkeeping and archiving metadata once and reusing it many times for different purposes in current recordkeeping and archival environments is yet to be fully explored.

In more recent times, Chris Hurley has taken on the Scott mantle and provides inspired guidance on realizing the full potential and power of the Australian series system. His writings and innovative practice have extended the conceptual basis and principles of the system to encompass the challenges of describing context and records entities and their complex, multidimensional relationships in the virtual world of the beginning of the twenty-first century. His further development of the conceptual framework of the series system includes two layers of contextual entities, higher level ambient entities representing organizational structures, jurisdictional or functional groupings, or functions themselves, corresponding to the French view of the external dimension of the *fonds*, and lower level

---

[15] http://www.naa.gov.au/the_collection/recordsearch.html
[16] http://www.records.nsw.gov.au/investigator/investigator.htm

German-like provenance entities representing records creating units and activities. Most recently he has developed the concept of parallel provenance, which may prove to be as groundbreaking as Scott's severing of the nexus between arrangement and description. We will come back to the potential utility of the concept of parallel provenance to represent the perspectives of different stakeholders in the archival systems of the future at the end of this chapter.

Appraisal

Appraisal is a relatively new archiving process. As referenced above, until comparatively recently, archivists took into custody surviving records. Their role was one of collection rather than selection, garnering rather than winnowing, and it was carried out in isolation from the role of records creators. Such an approach to appraisal is reflected in the work of Sir Hilary Jenkinson, Deputy Keeper of Public Records in Britain, and a major influence on the development of modern archival science. When Jenkinson wrote his *Manual* in 1922, there were some early indications of the explosion of records to come, but Jenkinson's writing reflects unease with the notion of active intervention in the determination of what should become archives.[17] He clearly saw such a role as contradictory to his view of the impartial archivist, engaged in the moral and physical defence of records entrusted to his keeping. In Jenkinson's opinion any process of selection was best left to the records creator, who was well placed to identify the records required to document their activities and retain sufficient evidence of their accountable decisions.

In some areas, particularly in relation to the personal and family archive, this garnering role is still being played out. However, from the mid twentieth century in government and business settings, archivists were increasingly drawn into decision-making about what records were worthy of preservation. With increased literacy, the reach of documentary systems into the life of every person in all their roles, both personal and work-related, and the explosion of technology from photocopiers to email, ever more records were being created in our society. Archivists, charged with maintaining meaningful and accessible representations of our society through its recorded transactions, could no longer extend their ongoing protection to all records. Choices had to be made about what to maintain.

Initially, appraisal policies and processes were developed for implementation by archival institutions at the point when records creators proposed their transfer from their stores of active or semi-active records. Writing later in the twentieth century, when the necessity of appraisal as an archival function could no longer be denied, T.R. Schellenberg reflected the evolving practice of the National Archives and Records Administration of the United States relating to identifying, bringing into archival custody and preserving a set of records that met criteria primarily relating to their value for cultural and historical research purposes.[18]

---

[17] Hilary Jenkinson, *A Manual of Archive Administration*, 2nd ed., London, Lund, Humphries, 1966 – a revised version of the original 1922 edition.
[18] T. R. Schellenberg, *Modern Archives*, Chicago, University of Chicago Press, 1956.

These so-called secondary values were seen as being beyond the interests of records-creating bodies as they were likely to be self-serving, and only concerned with the primary values of their records as evidence of their activities insofar as they supported their current responsibilities.

Although Schellenberg-type approaches to appraisal are still implemented in many jurisdictions around the world, in the latter part of the twentieth century, particularly in electronic contexts, appraisal has been redefined in various ways, including the Canadian system of macro-appraisal, and the holistic functional approach taken by the Netherlands national archives in the PIVOT project, outlined below. In Australia, records continuum writings reconceptualized appraisal as a set of continuous, recurring and integrated processes within the four dimensions of the records continuum. These iterative processes determine what documents to capture as records, what records need to be contextualized beyond the boundaries of a single system into an organization-wide archive, and, in relation to the collective archives, what needs to be further contextualized to retain meaning and context beyond the boundaries of the individual or corporate archive. This view of appraisal is not uniformly adopted within the archival profession, and most of the literature that supports writing on appraisal broadly relates to final disposition arrangements focusing on what material will be brought into archival custody and controlled by a third party – an archival institution – operating within the custodial model.

Tensions in archival practice

Appraisal is perhaps the most vexed issue in archival practice in the early twenty-first century. In the absence of much early theoretical writing, pragmatic and practice-based approaches became the core guides to archivists facing the dilemma of what to keep. It is only in the last twenty years or so that the profession has begun to question the validity of many of its earlier approaches and to articulate better theoretical justification for appraisal practice. The tensions in practice are played out in relation to a number of critical areas, with the balance between and mix of various approaches constantly shifting.

While a selection versus collection distinction may seem mere semantic quibbling, under its apparent pedantry there is a substantial issue. Do archival institutions collect material – that is play a garnering role, or do they select – a winnowing role? In whichever role, the aim is to build representations of their jurisdiction, be that private sector, government or community-based. But, conceptually, the collection model creates a more separate role for the archival institution – it exists outside the realm of the groups and individuals engaged in the social and organizational activities that result in the records. The selection model has increasingly become more about partnership, working with records creators and records managers or corporate archivists, rarifying and narrowing down that which will survive into the future. The tools, relationships and roles of the various interested parties vary, depending on the implicit or explicit positioning of the archives in relation to this issue.

When it comes to research versus representation, are archives primarily a rich, value-added resource for future research use? Or are archivists mainly concerned with doing their best to reflect the social transactions embodied in records that come within their jurisdiction? Again, archival institutions do both, but it is a question of where the balance lies in determining their tools, roles and responsibilities.

Are archives, archival institutions and archivists neutral or socially situated? As mentioned above, in the comfortable past, archivists portrayed themselves as something akin to neutral brokers – not engaged with the day-to-day transactions that were embodied in records and thus able to take an objective, external view of importance or significance. Criteria for appraisal decision-making in this world view were fuzzy. Clarifying these criteria, particularly in the light of more complex social theory, post-modernism and professional responsibility has rendered this approach untenable. Acknowledging that all actors in a society are bound by the views of that society, including those charged with making appraisal decisions, has been part of archival professional discourses overtly since the 1980s.[19] With that recognition comes the reflection that the best that archivists can do is to acknowledge their position in the social reality in which they live, articulate their assumptions and work within those documented boundaries.

The view that archivists are imposing individual, institutional and social biases on the determination of what will be archives further reinforces the understanding that archivists involved in appraisal decision-making are an intrinsic part of the record-creating process and has implications relating to the accountability of the profession, and the transparency of accountable decision-making and reappraisal. In an environment where we acknowledge, and even welcome, the notion that a specific appraisal decision is the result of a set of socially positioned and ideologically conditioned understandings, the requirement to clearly document the decision-making processes becomes more critical. Appraisal decisions need to be contestable, both by other stakeholders who are concerned about what records are retained in perpetuity, and also by the recordkeepers of the future.

Reappraisal is the process of revisiting the appraisal decisions of the past. This is a vexed and contentious issue. Each generation will have different views and different priorities on what to maintain as archives. Should we impose the views of current generations on the decisions of the past? Resources available to archival endeavour change with time. Sometimes, the relatively abundant resourcing may permit identification of larger amounts of archival records, while tight resources may dictate a more restricted capacity to maintain archives. These considerations also argue forcefully for a clearly documented approach to appraisal. Where documentation is clear on the requirements, reasons and decision-making, the business of reappraisal is currently regarded as justifiable.[20] The decisions of the past, while different from those that may be imposed today, can themselves tell us much about the past. For example, the fact that there was a deliberate, if never explicitly documented, attempt to excise the records of our convict past from the archives of some Australian

---

[19] As, for example, in the writings of Hans Booms, Terry Cook, Verne Harris, and Tom Nesmith.
[20] This has been much debated in Australia following contentious reappraisal programs undertaken primarily by the National Archives of Australia. In the discussions leading up to the framing of the Australian Society of Archivists statement on appraisal, it seems that there is widespread support of the notion that careful and conscientious reappraisal is acceptable.

states, is itself a significant statement about post-convict colonial society. The views of any social group are not static, however, for the active search for convict ancestors is now a part of much family history and the uncovering of such an antecedent is no longer a matter of shame, rather something of significance to family and even national identity.

Appraisal methods

In Australia the collecting of archives was practised in the manuscript departments of the National and State libraries, in a mixture of settings in universities including the university library, and in the larger museums, regional libraries and historical societies. Their collections were seen very much as research resources complementing (and often acquired in company with) rare printed items, pictorial material, ephemera and sometimes even an oral history interview. They related to individuals and non-government societies and organizations. The most highly prized documentary forms included items from personal papers such as letters and diaries, choice single document 'treasures' valuable as an exhibition item or book illustration, and detailed minutes from a boardroom or trade union central committee. As well, sometimes so-called formed collections of manuscript items were taken in, usually compiled by single-minded people of learning and discrimination for whom all cultural heritage materials were of potential interest. Methods of acquisition could involve lengthy negotiations and cultivation of a relationship with the creators/owners of papers, occasional purchases at auction, and acceptance of gifts via tax incentives schemes.

Decisions about what to accept or target for collecting were typically made against the background of the parent institution's collection development policy, anticipated use perhaps backed up by an academic subject expert's recommendation, and a concept of significance (national/state, historical, cultural). Especially when large sums were needed, and definitely when special funds from government or a foundation might be needed, these decisions would be made by senior executives or even managing councils. Usually however, collection managers with titles such as manuscripts librarian or curator, special collections would draw upon deep familiarity with the strengths and gaps of their existing collection and make an informed appraisal. Their professional mindset and staffing restraints ensured that overall collecting was reactive, researchers' discoveries, death notices, house moves and company collapses being common triggers, balanced by occasional programs targeting sectors, themes or larger priorities.

In the government sector, the common appraisal methods entrenched in North America, Australia and elsewhere for much of the second half of the twentieth century were strongly influenced by the work of Schellenberg and the United States National Archives. They followed a passive, reactive approach in which appraisal processes were applied to records when they were considered closed, after the business that they were documenting was complete. Legislative frameworks for government archives supported the selection of records of continuing value and their transfer to the archives by mandating that records creators must seek the approval of the archival institution before destroying records. In relation to private and personal records, archival institutions offered various incentives to potential donors of records. The archivists then applied a checklist-based methodology to determine whether the particular set of records meet established, often quite loosely defined, criteria to become archives. Typical elements of such checklists included:

- the status of the record creating body;
- whether the records defined policy, or acted as authorization on how a program or policy was to be delivered, as opposed to comprising the voluminous material relating to the instances of implementation of the policy or program – sometimes known as case files;
- the authority of the documents, that is, whether they were drafts, finals, etc.;
- whether the records documented rights or obligations of individuals or organizations;
- whether the records were duplicated elsewhere or maintained in another form;
- whether the records were self contained, that is not requiring reference to ancillary indexes or registers to understand them; or, if not, whether the ancillary records were also extant and available for transfer;
- whether the records were in an arrangement that would facilitate their future use;
- whether they were complete;
- considerations of the volume of material and the age, and relative rarity of the types of records.

This type of approach was critiqued in an iconoclastic blast from David Bearman in his 1989 publication, *Archival Methods,*[21] which accused archivists of failing to meet their stated objectives of providing a reasonably representative record into the future by several degrees of magnitude. While there was, and to some extent still is, professional disquiet about the claims in *Archival Methods*, it served to reinforce niggling doubts about the effectiveness of existing appraisal methodologies. Combined with the increasingly obvious failure of this retrospective methodology to cope with records created in electronic systems, it challenged the archival community to rethink its approach to appraisal.

A number of archivists had been similarly questioning traditional appraisal models. Terry Cook explored the inadequacies of our approach to documenting 'case files'[22] which tended to embrace an ad hoc and selective approach to these voluminous records, which Cook argues would be better documented by concentrating on documenting the framework of the actions and then identifying those cases which actively challenged the accepted social framework in some way, thus establishing an appraisal methodology seeking to particularly to identify and document the 'the key hubs or "hot spots" in the citizen-state interaction'.[23]

Such thinking led Cook to the formulation of a macro-appraisal model which was implemented as the practice of the National Archives of Canada in the 1990s. The theory behind macro-appraisal emerged from a critique of the deficiencies of traditional appraisal theory and strategies, including their records-centric world view, their reliance on

---

[21] David Bearman, *Archival Methods*, Pittsburgh, Archives and Museum Informatics, 1989.

[22] Also called 'particular instance papers' or files containing personal information.

[23] Terry Cook, *The Archival Appraisal of Records Containing Personal Information: A RAMP Study with Guidelines*, Paris, UNESCO, 1991; available at:
http://www.unesco.org/webworld/ramp/html/r9103e/r9103e00.htm

taxonomies of values as reflected in the checklist presented above, their fragmented, bottom-up approach, their inability to cope with the inevitably vast quantities of records given the timing of their application, and their irrelevance to records created in the electronic environment of the modern office. The new theory was also informed by a major shift in thinking about the role of the archivist related to what has been termed the Canadian rediscovery of provenance, and its exploration of what Cook described as the 'conceptual relationships between creating structures, their animating functions, and the resulting records'.[24]

Macro-appraisal seeks to shift the focus from appraising the record to appraising the context in which the record is created from a holistic, top-down perspective. Archivists 'seek to understand why records were created rather than what they contain, how they were created and used by their original users rather than how they might be used in the future, and what formal functions and mandates of the creator they supported rather than what internal structure or physical characteristics they may or may not have'.[25] The main aim of macro-appraisal relates to 'documenting the process of governance' where governance includes 'cognizance of the dialogue and interaction of citizens and groups within the state, the impact of the state on society, and the functions or activities of society itself, as much as it does the inner workings [of] government or business structures.'[26]

At the same time as the Canadians were experimenting with macro-appraisal, the Netherlands was facing a crisis in appraisal brought about by new archival legislation which changed the transfer period to archival custody from fifty years to twenty years. An estimated 600 kilometres of records needed attention in a very short period of time, and in that environment, combined with explicit criticism of the records management of public sector bodies, a new approach to appraisal was urgently required. The PIVOT project (in Dutch, meaning Project for the Implementation of the Reduction of the Transfer Period) implemented a methodology based on the intensive analysis of government's policy goals, policy instruments and the actions taken to implement policy, leading to an assessment of the long-term value of the actions. When documented and approved, this assessment acts as an appraisal tool for dealing with the retrospectively accumulated records of government, and also as a tool for proactive recordkeeping practice in agencies. The approach, particularly on appraising actions of government rather than records, was controversial, but a collaborative approach with various communities seems to have appeased these concerns. The project has been extended a further five years, bringing its completion date to 2006, at which stage an estimated 50,000 government actions will have been documented. The translation of the project work into current records practice has not been as immediate as

---

[24] Terry Cook, 'The Concept of the Archival *Fonds*', op. cit., p. 63.
[25] Terry Cook, 'Mind over Matter: Towards a New Theory of Archival Appraisal', in B. Craig, ed., *The Archival Imagination,* Ottawa, Association of Canadian Archivists, 1992, pp. 38-70.
[26] Terry Cook, 'Beyond the Screen: The Records Continuum and Archival Cultural Heritage', keynote address at Australian Society of Archivists Conference Melbourne, August 2000, p. 10, available at: http://www.archivists.org.au/sem/conf2000/terrycook.pdf.

was hoped, with additional layers of analysis at agency level being required to implement the functional analysis structure into current business processes.[27]

Another approach to appraisal had as its key tool an organizing analytical framework of core institutional functions. It came from Helen Samuels of the Massachusetts Institute of Technology. Her thinking was initially focused on science and technology and on multi-institutional documentation strategies, but in the early 1990s her thinking as a university archivist had matured to produce *Varsity Letters*. Its analysis of generic organizational functions to one side, a key feature was its use in highlighting which functions and subordinate aspects were, by their nature, poorly documented through records and therefore should be 'artificially' documented through such means as oral history.

Though Australians learnt first hand from Samuels, who visited here in 1985, her style of functional appraisal didn't take, and the question of why is to be added to the lengthening research agenda of Australian archival history. Though developed for universities, it was said it could be adapted to hospitals, museums, banks, courts, churches, and businesses, a claim untested here. Possibly, being intended to supplement traditional archival practice, it could not compete with a more radical functional approach incorporated in the broader recordkeeping philosophy of the records management standard AS 4390 which emerged in the mid 1990s.

In Australia government archivists have developed a set of practices called functional appraisal based on detailed analyses of the functions and activities of agencies following the DIRKS (Designing and Implementing Recordkeeping Systems) model.[28] The analyses are undertaken by agency recordkeeping staff while records are still current, following the guidelines provided by archival institutions, and serve both appraisal and records classification purposes. Outcomes include business activity classification schemes, disposal arrangements and authorizations relating to all records, and decisions about which functions, activities, and which records document them, are of continuing value. Government agencies submit extensively documented recommendations on appraisal and disposal actions to the relevant jurisdiction's archival institution, which has the final authority on appraisal decisions. Although the articulation of 'collecting' or 'acquisition' policies by archival institutions goes some way to explaining the basis for decisions about continuing value, there are significant questions about what animates their appraisal decisions.

---

[27] R.C.Hol and A.G.de Vries, 'Pivot Down Under', *Archives and Manuscripts*, 26, no 1, 1998; A.E.M. Jonkers, 'Macro-appraisal in the Netherlands: The First 10 years 1991-2001', *Journal of the Society of Archivists, Estonia*, 4, 2003.
[28] A variation of this is included in ISO 15489. Fully articulated methodologies to support the application of the methodology have been developed by the National Archives of Australia, *The DIRKS Manual: A Strategic Approach to Managing Business Information*, March 2000, available at: http://www.naa.gov.au/recordkeeping/dirks/dirksman/dirks.html, and State Records NSW, *Strategies for Documenting Government Business: The DIRKS Manual*, June 2003, available at: http://www.records.nsw.gov.au/publicsector/DIRKS/final/title.htm

With the new focus on functional/macro-appraisal, the collecting model inevitably came under notice. Three lines of criticism and reconsideration were opened up. One challenged collecting archivists to focus on their ultimate purpose and the logic of a recordkeeping perspective. This view argued that what one collected (desirably not 'stuff for stuff's sake') and how it was collected should only be determined after one had asked why, the strong implication being that merely to answer that one collected, for example, personal papers to support historical research was not good enough. One of the strongest positions was articulated by Chris Hurley, who proposed, as has Sue McKemmish, the development of functional requirements for socio-historical evidence and related 'literary warrant'. The advent of electronic records within the personal and private sectors also highlighted difficulties in the passive and end-of-life-cycle approach to collecting as traditionally practised.

At the same time, the examples of macro-appraisal and the Canadians' 'total archives' philosophy highlighted both how poorly coordinated efforts to document Australian society were and how little jurisdiction-wide analysis was undertaken in directing targeted collecting. The National Library attempted to redress the former in the early 1990s using the looming centenary of Federation as the pretext, and in 1999 the archival community, which had strong reservations with the way its focus was marginalized by the Library, worked through the National Scholarly Communications Forum to convene a national summit of their own called 'Archives in the National Research Infrastructure'. It called for national documentation strategies and research. Although little concrete has emerged to date, a broader awareness of the scope of the national documentary universe is becoming known and knowable through new gateways to trade union and business archives and descriptive appraisals in the professional literature. Some collectors of business archives are also experimenting with state-wide mapping approaches, such as adapting the so-called 'Minnesota method', to better identify sectors for targeting before individual firms within them are approached.[29]

Finally there has been a maturing attitude towards earlier collecting efforts, too easily derided as 'hunter-gatherer' efforts, which grabbed indiscriminately for any old stuff. Historical studies are beginning to appear which attempt to understand their motives, constraints and cultural and institutional contexts. Sue Fairbanks in particular has investigated the social warrants which lay behind the highly personal collecting of the foundation archivists at Australia's two largest university collecting archives and the most renowned collector to head the National Library, Sir Harold White. These ideas have much potential for fruitful further research, in White's case additionally so, as he, more than any other figure, represented the unitary custodial version of the 'total archives' vision, which of course faded when legislation established the library in 1961.

---

[29] J. Ellen et al., 'Making Archival Choices for Business History', *Australian Economic History Review,* 26, no. 2, 2004, pp. 185-196.

Preservation

As we have seen, in the custodial models developed in a physical world, preserving the archives involved setting up safe stores of archives, undertaking physical preservation processes, ensuring an unbroken chain of physical custody, and implementing arrangement and descriptive processes that represented the context of the record in the physical manifestation of the record group in the repository and its surrogate in the archival finding aid. Although under challenge from new approaches, particularly to appraisal and description, this model continues to hold sway in many programs concerned primarily with paper records. However, in a virtual world, these means of archival preservation are no longer relevant, and it becomes essential to rethink the principles that underpinned them. In particular, physical preservation is no longer primarily about the conservation and storage in archival buildings of material objects, but is to do with the processes and routines established in electronic systems, the deployment of metadata, and the system functionality involved in continually rendering a record in a way that maintains its essential characteristics, its 'recordness', strategies pioneered by Bearman in the mid-1990s as part of the University of Pittsburgh's project on the Functional Requirements of Electronic Recordkeeping.[30]

Much of the more recent research relating to the preservation of digital objects has been undertaken by the digital library community. Within the archival community, a number of research projects are exploring various strategies for preservation of electronic records. Broadly speaking, these strategies can be identified as migration, emulation or encapsulation strategies. Migration strategies seek to identify critical points of software dependency when electronic records and their associated metadata must be transferred into a later software version. Emulation strategies seek to preserve records in their native creating format and create or invoke viewers which render the records in readable form, on demand, in the newer software and technology environment. Encapsulation strategies are actively exploring the use of XML to wrap all layers of records aggregation, from record object to *fonds*.[31] One of the most extensively implemented models for managing electronic record objects is to be found in the Public Record Office Victoria's VERS (Victorian Electronic Records Strategy) project. Established in the mid-1990s as a project designed to deliver implementable means of managing electronic records for long periods of time, the initial VERS research adopted some strategically sound directions, including the adoption of XML schema and Adobe PDF formats as preferred formats for the metadata and contents formats. In perspective it can be seen that VERS was a practical implementation of part of the MEO (metadata encapsulated object) envisaged by David Bearman in 1995.[32]

---

[30] University of Pittsburgh, School of Information Sciences, Functional Requirements for Evidence in Recordkeeping (1996), and Metadata Specifications Derived from the Functional Requirements: A Reference Model for Business Acceptable Communications (1996).

[31] See the work of the NARA Project being undertaken by the San Diego Supercomputer Center; available at: http://www.sdsc.edu/NARA.

[32] David Bearman and Ken Sochats, 'Metadata Requirements for Evidence', 1995; available at: http://www.archimuse.com/papers/nhprc/BACartic.html.

All these technological preservation strategies will be informed by the work of the InterPARES international research project, which is specifically directed at the preservation of authentic records in electronic systems, with reference to policies and frameworks for records and archives management, the requirements of reliability and authenticity, and the systems and processes involved in the appraisal, creation, preservation, and description of electronic records.[33] As the InterPARES team comprises researchers and practitioners from many parts of the world, its research increasingly draws on understandings drawn from a range of archival traditions, including archival diplomatics, archival science, records life-cycle world views, and, increasingly, continuum perspectives.

In the diplomatic tradition, records were said to come into existence when their elements were inscribed on or affixed to a medium and they were 'set aside' for preservation by their creators. Their defining characteristics included a fixed content and documentary form, an archival bond with related records, and an identifiable context – documentary, procedural, technological, provenancial and juridical. In order to assure their authenticity, it was necessary to preserve their identity – in terms of these characteristics – and their integrity, that is, to demonstrate that their unique identifying characteristics had not been tampered with or changed. Amongst other things, it was essential to ensure that they continued to exist as physical objects as they were created. Judgments about their reliability and authenticity rested in part on consideration of whether the physical object that embodied the record had been changed in any way that might affect the identity or integrity of the record. In that context, preserving the original record, comprising a representation of an act or a fact inscribed on or affixed to its physical carrier or medium, and maintaining and being able to demonstrate an unbroken chain of custody over the record as a physical object, were critical processes in assuring a record's authenticity. Such processes become redundant when dealing with electronic records as, although they share the key characteristics of a traditional record – their stable content, fixed documentary form, archival bond with other records and identifiable context – they cannot be said to continue to exist as physical objects as they were originally created. The acts of storing, retrieving and re-presenting electronic records using hardware and software applications involve continual processing of the digital components that come together to make up the record, and transformations of the record's content, structure and appearance. InterPARES researchers have therefore concluded, as did Bearman before them, that preservation of original records in electronic systems is not possible. Rather, what needs to be preserved is the ability or functionality required to continue to reproduce an electronic record from its digital components. They are endeavouring to build a model of a system capable of achieving this goal. The development of new descriptive frameworks and metadata tools is a critical part of this project.

---

[33] International Research on Permanent Authentic Records in Electronic Systems, (http://www.interpares.org/).

Frameworks for public access

Frameworks for public access to archives date back to antiquity. Rome's first public archives was founded about 509 B.C. in the Aerarium, or treasury, of the temple of Saturn. As in its Greek counterpart, the Metroon, the records housed in this archives could be consulted by all citizens. In terms of the antecedents for the frameworks for public access presided over by the national and state archives of today, a decree issued in June 1794 by the revolutionary government of France gave the National Archives jurisdiction over the records of government agencies, provinces, communes, churches, universities and noble families. This decree created the world's first centralized national archives system. As Adrian Cunningham reports in chapter 2,

> The same decree also proclaimed the right of public access to these records, thus establishing the first modern instance of archives fulfilling a legal role as protectors of the rights and entitlements of the people and as instruments of accountability and transparency in government.

Some northern European countries had an open access model from the late eighteenth century, but it took almost two more centuries for much of the Western world to emulate these strategies with the introduction of freedom of information, data protection and privacy legislation. In Australia, the impetus to adopt freedom of information regimes at National and State levels was a broad-sweeping set of administrative reforms in government commencing in the late 1970s. What commenced as a coherent access regime mirroring archival access regimes in freedom of information access regimes has now became a fragmented regime, with individual legislation derived from particular requirements (e.g. privacy, health information privacy, the advent of the Internet) driving the development of legislation, without much sense of a unified access regime. State and Territory governments passed individual legislation in all these areas that was partly, but not completely compatible with the national legislation, creating overlaps and also gaps.

Despite the lack of a unified and coherent access regime consistently applied across all of Australia, access to information is much freer now than it has been at any time in the past. The secretive culture of much of the government bureaucracy has, at least in theory, been eroded by the new environment of accountability and transparency, in which citizens can access information more freely and possess rights of amendment and correction over information held about themselves. Access to information, concepts of privacy and rights and responsibilities in relation to access to records and information is a contested, socially negotiable space, with attitudes changing over time in relation to specific circumstances and social norms. This increased complexity and broadening of the public access regime has democratized access to records and has removed administration of access from being purely the domain of archivists located in archival institutions to being a responsibility of each and every organization. In this environment, determining the role and responsibility for access provision to records and information is being contested between multiple disciplines, and archives and recordkeeping professionals are rethinking their roles. As in the other areas of archival endeavour discussed in this chapter, metadata frameworks and tools are playing a critical role in these developments.

Metadata frameworks and tools

The records continuum approach to recordkeeping and archiving illuminates the weaving of the patterns of recordkeeping from initial frameworks to ensure that records are created, through processes that ensure selected records are made accessible to others through broadening of the reach of the record within and beyond organizations, and its capacity to be understood and be meaningful in contexts other than the initial creating environment. Archives are, in our discourse, those records with the broadest social reach – those accessible beyond the boundaries of an organization, whenever and wherever that may occur. To enable this, to establish the preconditions for archives to exist, recordkeeping and archiving processes must occur at multiple and iterative points in the lifespan of a record, not simply within the boundaries of an archival institution, or indeed within a specific jurisdiction or domain.

Essential to the further development of recordkeeping and archiving processes of the kind explored above is the development of metadata management frameworks and schemas that specify the types of standardized information or metadata that integrated archival and recordkeeping processes operating within broad archival frameworks would need to capture in order to fulfil their purposes.[34] Latest developments include the recently issued ISO TS 23081, *Information and Documentation – Records Management Processes – Metadata for Records*, and an Australian Standard, currently in development, which aims to harmonize existing Australian metadata schemas.

The purpose of the ISO document is to provide guidance in understanding, implementing and using recordkeeping metadata and establishing metadata management frameworks, not to specify a mandatory set of recordkeeping metadata (metadata schema). The ISO defines metadata as:

> data describing the context, content and structure of records and their management through time. As such metadata is structured or semi-structured information that enables the creation, registration, classification, access, preservation and disposition of records through time and within and across domains … metadata can be used to identify, authenticate and contextualize records and the people, processes and systems that create, manage, maintain and use them and the policies that govern them.[35]

---

[34] A metadata schema provides semantic and structural definitions of metadata, including the names of metadata elements, how they are structured, and their meaning. Archival descriptive standards and records system specifications can be envisaged as traditional forms of recordkeeping metadata schema.

[35] International Standards Organization, ISO 23081: *Information and Documentation – Records Management Processes – Metadata for Records*, Part1: Principles, 2004, p. 7.

The new Australian Standard will be developed within the overall framework of the ISO and draw substantially on the Australian Recordkeeping Metadata Schema and existing standards developed by the National Archives of Australia, State Records Authority of NSW, the Public Record Office Victoria and South Australian State Archives within the framework it provides. [36]

The Australian Recordkeeping Metadata Schema extends the Australian series system concepts of context, drawing on records continuum thinking relating to a record's complex and dynamic social, functional, organizational, procedural, and documentary contexts of creation, management, and use through spacetime, and informed by the insights of Chris Hurley and Terry Cook. The contextualization provided in the Schema enables the linking of records to ever-broadening layers of contextual knowledge in order to carry their meanings through time. By way of qualification, it should be stated that the richness, complexity, diversity and idiosyncrasies of the contexts in which records are created, managed and used cannot be fully represented in models and schema. They can only ever represent a partial view of the dynamic, complex and multidimensional nature of records and their rich webs of contextual and documentary relationships. Within these limitations, the Recordkeeping Metadata Schema reaches towards ways of representing records and their contexts as richly and extensively as possible, to develop frameworks that recognise their mutable and contingent nature, as well as the role of recordkeeping and archiving professionals (records managers and archivists) in their creation and evolution, and to attempt to address issues relating to time and space.

In the Recordkeeping Metadata Schema, contextual knowledge takes the form of layers of descriptive metadata about:

- records at any layer of aggregation;
- the people or agents involved in creating, managing, and using records;
- the organizational and social structures in which they interact;
- the activities and transactions in which the people or agents are engaged, and related social and business purposes and functions;
- the recordkeeping functions, activities, and transactions which capture, manage and make accessible the records of these activities and transactions;

---

[36] Sue McKemmish, Glenda Acland, Kate Cumming, Barbara Reed and Nigel Ward, *Australian Recordkeeping Metadata Schema, Version 1.0, 31 May 2000*; available at:
http://www.sims.monash.edu.au/research/rcrg/research/spirt/deliver/index.html; Sue McKemmish, Glenda Acland, Nigel Ward, and Barbara Reed, 'Describing Records in Context in the Continuum: the Australian Recordkeeping Metadata Schema', *Archivaria*, 48, 1999. See also the recordkeeping metadata standards issued by the National Archives of Australia,
(http://www.naa.gov.au/recordkeeping/control/rkms/summary.htm), State Records Authority of New South Wales (http://www.records.nsw.gov.au), Public Record Office Victoria,
(http://www.prov.vic.gov.au/vers/standards/pros9907vers2/default.htm), and State Records of South Australia (http://www.archives.sa.gov.au/management/standards.html#South_Australian_Recordkeeping_Metadata_Standard).

- the complex, multiple, and dynamic relationships between all of these entities; and
- the warrants or mandates which govern all of this social and organizational activity, including metadata about social mores, laws, business policies and rules.

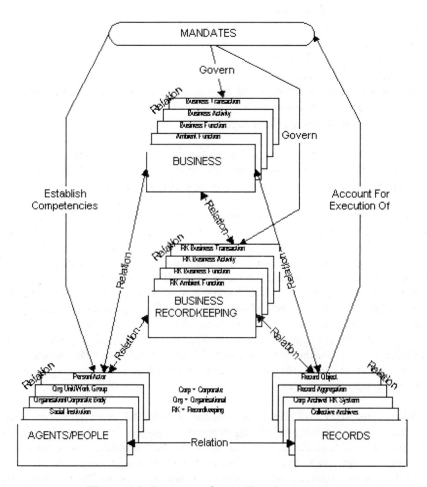

Figure 7.3. Coverage of recordkeeping metadata

The Schema defines metadata that describes records (record objects, record aggregations, corporate archive, collective archives), people or agents (as-actors, as-organizational units, as-corporate bodies/organizations, as-social institutions), business and recordkeeping business entities (functions, activities, and transactions) by:

- indicating their level of aggregation (for records) or place in the hierarchy (for agents and business entities) (Category Type);
- uniquely identifying them (Identifier);
- naming them (Title);
- locating them in time (Date);
- locating them in space (Place);
- classifying them by function (Function);
- describing their interrelationships and governing mandates (Relation and Mandate);
- providing for a descriptive note (Abstract); and
- specifying relevant language (Language).

The business, business recordkeeping and records entities also have unique descriptive elements, e.g. the records entity has metadata elements that describe in detail recordkeeping and archiving processes and capture a record of recordkeeping actions.

The standards evolving in the national standards arena in Australia, as well as in Commonwealth and State jurisdictions, essentially implement sub-sets of the metadata defined in the Schema within different jurisdictions and at different points in the lifespan of the record. The Commonwealth Recordkeeping Metadata Standard, for example, specifies the kind of metadata that should be captured in a records management application at the time a record is created and within its immediate context of creation and management. It has been developed as part of a suite of policies, standards and guidelines, issued by the National Archives of Australia and designed to regulate current recordkeeping by Australian government agencies. Similarly, the State Records Authority of NSW, the Public Record Office Victoria and the State Archives of South Australia have developed recordkeeping metadata standards for implementation by State government agencies in their current recordkeeping systems.

Research initiatives which will provide models and tools for the future development of metadata frameworks and tools include the international project, InterPARES2, and work at Monash University in Australia, in partnership with the National Archives of Australia, State Records Authority of NSW and the Descriptive Standards Committee of the Australian Society of Archives. The Clever Recordkeeping Metadata Project aims to build metadata frameworks that will operate throughout all dimensions of the records continuum to support the creation of documents in the context of social and organizational activity, their capture into records systems, organization within the framework of a personal or corporate archive, and pluralization as collective archives.[37] The InterPARES 2 Description

---

[37] Create Once, Use Many Times – The Clever Use of Metadata in eGovernment and eBusiness Processes in Networked Environments, funded by an Australian Research Council Linkage Project

Research Team is building a Metadata Schema Registry, which describes and analyzes existing metadata schemas and archival descriptive standards and is exploring the applicability of such existing standards to the management of electronic records in the artistic, scientific and egovernment communities.

Initiated in 1999, InterPARES, the International Research on Permanent Authentic Records in Electronic Systems Project, is an example of the kind of multidisciplinary, multinational collaborations that will underpin archival systems of the future. A collaboration between international researchers from multidisciplinary backgrounds from Canada, the United States, Australia, Belgium, China, France, Ireland, Italy, Japan, Netherlands, Portugal, Singapore, Spain and the United Kingdom, InterPARES aims at:

> Developing the theoretical and methodological knowledge essential to the long-term preservation of records created and/or maintained in digital form. This knowledge should provide the basis from which to formulate model policies, strategies and standards capable of ensuring the longevity of such material and the ability of its users to trust its authenticity.[38]

Internationally, recordkeeping professionals have also established greater research connections with professionals from other disciplinary backgrounds to investigate areas of commonality in preserving digital information, information resource discovery and metadata.

Archival systems of the future

The capacity of the frameworks and tools for archiving discussed in this book to address the challenges of forming collective archives that serve the archival purposes of democratic societies in a globalized world is being called into question by a number of writers. Challenges have been issued for example by Terry Cook, Tom Nesmith, Verne Harris, Sue McKemmish and Michael Piggott,[39] for archivists to examine whether their professional frameworks and practices really operate beyond the level of the individual or corporate archive, or are capable of encompassing the world views of all the parties to the transactions the records document and providing meaningful access paths to all stakeholders.

While it has become commonplace in the post-modern archival discourse to acknowledge the role that recordkeeping and archival professionals, their theories and practices play in the politics of memory, in forming and re-forming the archives, and impacting on what is

---

Grant, Chief Investigators: Sue McKemmish, Anne Gilliland-Swetland and Adrian Cunningham (http://www.sims.monash.edu.au/research/rcrg/research/crm/index.html).
[38] http://www.interpares.org
[39] Cook, 'Beyond the Screen', op. cit; Michael Piggott and Sue McKemmish, 'Recordkeeping, Reconciliation and Political Reality', in *Past Caring: Proceedings of the Australian Society of Archivists Conference, Sydney 2002*; Hamilton, op. cit.; Nesmith, op. cit.

remembered and what is forgotten, these understandings have resulted in few changes in archival practice in the key areas of appraisal and description:

> Archival science and practice as they have evolved in European/Western traditions, privilege the records creators, their contexts, world views and value systems. Although the records creator is just one of the parties to the transactions captured in the records, current practice tends to treat other parties to the transaction as objects of the activities and subjects of the record, rather than as parties to transactions, in its appraisal, description and access activities and processes. The notions of ownership, custody, privacy protection and access rights that underpin appraisal, description and access policies are also deeply embedded in European/Western traditions and constructs. ...
>
> Application guidelines for functional analysis and appraisal, as presently embodied in international and national standards, in the policies and practices of lead Australian archival institutions – and indeed of archival programs like macro-appraisal in Canada, and the Pivot initiative in the Netherlands, all take as their main point of reference the mandates of a particular time and place and the world view of the regime in which the archival program operates. So, for example, when analyzing the functions of governments and government agencies in Canada or Australia, the frame of reference is primarily the black letter law and legal mandates of those regimes.[40]

To return to the story of the Children Overboard as told in chapter 1, from the perspective of the government archivist, using the DIRKS methodology as practised in Australia and embodied in the ISO standard, the administration of immigration and customs might be identified as an ambient function of successive Australian federal governments. Linked to that might be business functions such as the implementation of migration policy or border protection, and business activities that are associated with the processing of applications for visas, permanent residence or refugee status, and the detention and repatriation of illegal immigrants. The language used in classification schemes and thesauri resulting from such functional analyses would reflect such world views. And access to the government archives relating to the Children Overboard affair would be controlled by the public access regime established by the Commonwealth government and only accessible via the interfaces established by the National Archives of Australia. Similarly, the media and personal archives we identified in chapter 1 would be classified and indexed according to the perspectives of the relevant business archives or manuscript library, and would be accessible under different access regimes and through separate interfaces. As to the voices of the refugees themselves, few if any archival institutions in Australia would see it as their role to seek to record their experiences.

But what if we took a different point of reference? What if our archival frameworks and systems could accommodate the perspective of the boat people themselves as parties to these functions and activities? What if we developed methods that could transcend the third dimensional boundaries that limit functional analysis to consideration of the regime's

---

[40] Piggott and McKemmish, op. cit., pp. 116-117.

mandates and purposes in the regime's own terms? If we took a fourth-dimensional approach to defining possible ambient functions, we might reference the global mandates associated with international courts, labour organizations, and human rights commissions, and that all too human desire for justice. Then the business functions and activities associated with these ambient functions might be described in the language of illegal detention, abuse of human rights, and institutionalized child abuse:

> And if we used such counter-functional analyses or global, through-time frameworks as the basis of appraisal decisions, and assignment of descriptors in archival systems, how differently might we appraise and describe the records of what in one context might appear to be fairly routine records relating to the implementation of a responsible and accountable immigration policy, but in another might be seen as evidence of abuse of human rights?[41]

In relation to public access regimes, we might also build pluralizing frameworks that provided integrated access to records and archives across jurisdictions and institutional boundaries.

It could be argued that one of the reasons that methodologies can be readily developed and applied at the level of the corporate or individual archive is that the corporate body or individual has a physical existence and is supported, well or not, by statements about itself and its authority to act, including mission statements, mandates, reports and records required by regulation. Beyond this, we are into the realms of social and political analysis – an area in which archivists have no special skills or experience. It becomes a question of determining what social or political theory is appropriate for adoption. Can there be apolitical appraisal at this abstracted level? And, if not, who gets to decide which view should prevail? There has been considerable implicit criticism of the approach of the ex-East German government's implementation of a documentation strategy with an overtly political agenda. But perhaps having an explicit political agenda behind an appraisal regime enables better contextualization of the appraisal decisions and thus a more accurate reflection of the society at that point. On the other hand, perhaps the corporate and individual focus of appraisal decisions in the DIRKS model itself provides sufficient reflection of our society at this point in time, in the same way that the fate of convict records referenced earlier in this chapter is a representation of societal concerns at that time and place?

In the continuum the archival profession has a conceptual framework that enables simultaneous multiple views of recordkeeping 'realities'. In relation to description, the Australian series system and more recent initiatives like the Australian Recordkeeping Metadata Schema, both currently being developed as national standards, set up frameworks

---

[41] Ibid, p.118. This is particularly so in relation to detention of refugees' children. See the Report of the UN Working Group on Arbitrary Detention (Chair Justice Louis Joinet), June 2002. Opinions differ, of course: see, for example, the response of the Minister for Immigration, Philip Ruddock, to the Joinet report (Press Release MPS 46/2002 of 7 June 2002) and Amnesty International's position (http://www.amnesty.org.au/whats_happening/refugees/resources/fact_sheets/mandatory_detention).

for capturing layers of rich contextual metadata, and multiple contexts of creation, management and use. Although most implementations privilege the role of the records creator in the transaction, represent the records creator's context rather than the contexts of other parties to the transaction, and draw on functional classification schemes and thesauri developed at the level of the corporate or individual archive, the frameworks provided by these systems could enable alternative readings of our society, to ensure that the voices of the 'disempowered' are heard.

Thus the descriptive methods and tools developed in the series system and emerging recordkeeping metadata standards enable archivists at the beginning of the twenty-first century to go beyond Scott's original vision of sequential multiple provenance to what Chris Hurley has recently named 'parallel provenance'.[42] Recognizing that the documentation created within the New Zealand national archives system largely reflects the cultural views of the Pakeha majority, but living in a society in which biculturalism is more than mere rhetoric, Hurley began to question how the views of the Maori could be accommodated in systems defined by Pakeha standards and to seek a set of alternative, equally valid ways of viewing and documenting the records. He is currently exploring how the Australian series system and related metadata schema developments, with their powerful relational characteristics, might accommodate such differences, enabling alternative readings of the records and their contexts to be added by different communities of stakeholders. It is possible within these frameworks to represent records from different perspectives, from the point of view of the creator, other parties to the transaction, and other stakeholders, in and through time, from individual, community, corporate and societal perspectives. The tools to construct representations of parallel recordkeeping universes – for example, the universe of border protection and prevention of illegal immigration and the parallel universe of illegal detention and human rights abuse – are already to hand.

It is possible to re-imagine archival systems of the future that:

- manage the records of multiple groups and individuals beyond the boundaries of the personal or corporate archive;
- represent in multidimensional contexts of creation, capture, organization and pluralization – juridical, organizational, functional, procedural, technological and recordkeeping;
- provide multiple views of parallel recordkeeping universes;
- continuously and cumulatively weave relationships between records and related people, organizational structures, functions and activities to assist in preserving their evidential value and enable multiple access paths to records and their meanings; and
- keep records relating to all recordkeeping and archiving processes persistently linked to the records they form and transform.

---

[42] This development is in many ways a logical outcome of Hurley's thinking and writings over many years on archival description, the significance of functions and relationships, and multiple provenance.

Such archival systems would have great potential utility in relation to the preservation and accessibility of electronic records of continuing value, as well as to the management of current records. The locus of the archives system might exist as an interface to archival records held by an archival institution, but it might also link to all records, publicly available or not, of continuing value or not, still maintained in the recordkeeping systems of individual agencies. In this sense, the collective archives could be preserved and made accessible in virtual space. Custodial arrangements and issues of where the record is physically located would cease to be of prime importance.

In the end, given the potential for recordkeeping and archiving frameworks and methodologies to encompass the world views of all the parties to the transactions the records document and to provide meaningful access paths to all stakeholders, the challenge, if archivists choose to accept it, is a political rather than a professional one:

> It is fundamentally about the role of archivists and the archival profession in a democratic society. And the sharp point comes when we consider what, if we presented such parallel views, it would mean for appraisal. Is it time for … archivists working within continuum frameworks to take up this challenge, to complement the considerable achievements in establishing accountable recordkeeping regimes in the third dimension by building fourth-dimensional frameworks that enable records to realise their full potential as accessible collective memory and 'enablers of democratic empowerment'?[43]

Conclusion

Our traditional theory and practice has been derived from a physical world where archiving processes tended to apply only in custodial archival keeping-places. Australian archival practice in the 'series' system broke that physical nexus, and subsequent evolution of practice within the records continuum framework has extended the boundaries of archival systems as discussed in this chapter. Rethinking our practice for the complex digital world of the emerging global society raises tensions with traditional articulations of archival theory and practice. Some of the emerging thinking on archival systems explored in this chapter suggests ways in which archival theory and practice might evolve in a dynamic, contested and post-modern world.

---

[43] Piggott and McKemmish, op. cit. p. 119, with the final phrase coming from Adrian Cunningham, 'The Soul and Conscience of the Archivist: Meditations on Power, Passion and Positivism in a Crusading Profession', *Argiefnuus/Archives News*, 43, no. 4, 2001, pp. 167-77, quotation from p. 173.

Readings

- Terry Cook, 'Mind over Matter: Towards a New Theory of Archival Appraisal', in Barbara Craig, ed., *The Archival Imagination. Essays in Honour of Hugh A. Taylor*, Ottawa, Association of Canadian Archivists, 1992, pp. 38-70.

  This article proved one of the most influential on archival appraisal in the 1990s introducing the concepts of macro-appraisal, positioning the archival role in sociological contexts and providing a new set of models for archivists to explore in relation to appraisal work.

- Chris Hurley, 'The Australian ('Series') System: An Exposition', in S. McKemmish and M.Piggott, eds, *The Records Continuum: Ian Maclean and Australian Archives First Fifty Years*, Clayton, Ancora Press in association with Australian Archives, 1994, pp. 150-172; also available at: http://www.sims.monash.edu.au/research/rcrg/publications/chtrc1.html.

  Chris Hurley's explanation of the Australian series system provides an overview of this means of conceptualizing records description across records of all ages and locations. This system has been particularly relevant to Australian archivists when thinking through frameworks for electronic recordkeeping, inheriting descriptive information from other organizations and in dealing with relationships.

- Sue McKemmish, 'Are Records Ever Actual?', in S. McKemmish and M.Piggott, eds, *The Records Continuum: Ian Maclean and Australian Archives First Fifty Years*, Clayton, Ancora Press in association with Australian Archives, 1994, pp. 187-203; also available at: http://www.sims.monash.edu.au/research/rcrg/publications/smcktrc.html.

  This article articulated the dynamic and ever changing documentation/interpretation of records, moving the archival profession's conceptualization of a record far from the concept of a static object as record contained in most of the literature of the time.

- Michael Piggott and Sue McKemmish, 'Recordkeeping, Reconciliation and Political Reality', in *Past Caring: Proceedings of the Australian Society of Archivists Annual Conference, Sydney, 2002*, available at: http://www.sims.monash.edu.au/research/rcrg/publications/piggottmckemmish2002.pdf.

  This paper explores the social and political dimensions of archives and recordkeeping, as active shapers and reflections of politically situated decision-making about the documentation of modern society.

- Sue McKemmish. Glenda Acland, Nigel Ward and Barbara Reed, 'Describing Records in Context in the Continuum: The Australian Recordkeeping Metadata Schema', *Archivaria*, 48, 1999, pp. 3-43.

Using the conceptual basis of the Australian series system as a starting point, this article describes the development and potential applications of a multiple entity recordkeeping metadata set which encompasses social and organizational activity, people or agents who do business and the records which are the by-products of such business.

• Carolyn Hamilton, Verne Harris, Jane Taylor, Michele Picover, Graeme Reid and Razia Saleh, eds, *Refiguring the Archive,* Dordrecht, Kluwer, 2002.

The contents of this book push archival thinking into a post-positivist critique based on Jacques Derrida's deconstructive perspectives. It also provides numerous essays providing a reinterpretation of a colonial experience embracing previously marginalized groups, and a number of essays that push at the boundaries of what the archive might be.

CHAPTER 8
The records continuum

Frank Upward

Introduction: The storage of activity-based information

Anthony Giddens in his book *Sociology* defines a science as the 'systematic methods of empirical investigation, the analysis of data, theoretical thinking and the logical assessment of arguments' to develop knowledge about a subject matter. Giddens' subject matter is human societies, and he has pushed his discipline towards more in-depth studies of the way societies are shaped by individuals and their memory traces, including studies of the structures they set in place. Central to his notion of memory traces is the storage of information, including its forms of representation and modes of retrieval and dissemination.[1]

Modern archival theory has only sporadically tapped into the wealth of theory that can be drawn from an overview of information processes relating to the storage of information. In terms of the most basic patterning of knowledge in archival science, as most twentieth-century archivists would have perceived it, the emphasis has been upon the objects dealt with in daily activities (the documents and records that comprise the archives) and the management of the places of archival custody for those objects. In the last fifteen years, however, there has been a gradual deepening of what could be described as activity theory from the perspective of the archivist – theory concerned with the continuing storage of recorded information about the actions of people in society, including the establishment of memory banks out of those transactions and their subsequent use. The clearest indication of this is possibly this book itself. In chapters four to seven of this book a number of writers work together using a common method for knowledge development based on the relationship between human activities and document systems (chapter 4), records systems (chapter 5), systems for the corporate or individual archive (chapter 6), and systems for archives as a plurality (chapter 7). In chapters 9-12 authors variously tease out recordkeeping-based activity theory in relation to topics such as the law, memory, accountability and power.

---

[1] Anthony Giddens, *Sociology*, 3rd ed., Cambridge, Polity Press, 1997, p. 12 contains the cited definition of science. The role of recorded information in shaping society is discussed in Giddens' book, *The Constitution of Society*, Cambridge, Polity Press, 1984.

In this chapter I give an updated account of a model for the records continuum first published in 1996. The model itself has helped many of the authors of this book in terms of providing a common orientation for the casting forward of different perspectives. In what follows I point to the spacetime distancing theory within the model, how it connects both to 'classical' object approaches to archival theory and to 'postmodern' process approaches including studies of the making of culture. I then develop a spacetime meta-narrative of archives in different eras, looking at the storage of action-based information in different eras and trying to begin to draw attention to the accelerating and expanding universes of the archivist.

Spacetime distancing and information management processes

In describing an action-based information processes continuum in this section I depend upon Giddens' structuration theory of time-space distanciation and its four interacting regions, the first closest to an action, and the fourth in the further reaches of spacetime. These four regions are:
- intersections of regions and a spatial spread away from the immediate contexts of interaction,
- routinization which provides a temporal spread away from immediate contexts of interaction,
- time-space distanciation, and
- forms of the societal totality.

These can be translated into an information processes model as set out in Figure 8.1. The arrow in this drawing indicates Giddens' structuration theory translated into information management terms, in which the way we act when creating documents affects the way information can be captured, organized and pluralized, and our technologies and techniques for the latter processes affect the way we create information.

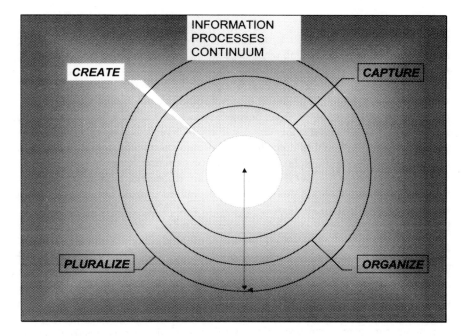

Figure 8.1. An information processes continuum expressed in terms of Giddens' four regions of time-space distanciation.[2]

Giddens' regions and their corresponding relationship with the four dimensions of the information processes model are set out below:

- *The intersections of regions and a spatial spread away from the immediate contexts of interaction:* This region of intersections (represented as a hot-spot in the model) is one of interiority and of immediate interaction between individuals. It is an intersecting region because the individuals are themselves affected by influences from the other regions. Change can only be initiated by actions in this intersecting region. The creation dimension is examined as a region in chapter 4 of this book. In terms of techniques and technology, creation issues relate to such things as the management of the format and structure of documents. It is, from a sociological perspective, the dimension of doing things, whereas the other dimensions represent zones of influence upon actions.

- *Routinization:* Routines for communications between individuals provide a temporal spread away from immediate contexts of interaction, disembedding the interactions

---

[2] The information continuum has been modelled separately by me, Barbara Reed and Don Schauder; four continua have been added in the manner of the records continuum model. I have also transferred the approach into less-tested models for data management and publication. See Frank Upward, 'Modelling the Continuum as Paradigm Shift in Recordkeeping and Archiving Processes, and Beyond – a Personal Reflection', *Records Management Journal*, 10, no. 3, 2000.

from those immediate contexts, which enables them to be carried out more widely in the society. This is comparable to the routines for records capture, pointed to in the second dimension of the model, when documents are disembedded from their immediate contexts of creation, and embedded recursively into new ones. Chapter 5 of this book examines capture as a region where data or documents are captured as evidence that can be reliably used by others who access and use the documents, especially by others involved in the business processes that led to the creation of the information. Routinization is the dimension in which records systems can be said to have their locus. It should be noted here that capture, as an information management activity like organization, and pluralization involves action, hence the recursive return to the first dimension as recordkeeping objects are embedded, disembedded and re-embedded into new contexts. Archivists are sometimes seen as dealing with relics of the past, but their actions are themselves part of continuing creation/recreation processes.

- ***Time-space distanciation***: This refers to the carriage of behavioural patterns into the wider reaches of space (e.g. the corporate man in a blue suit) and time (e.g. the 'IBM' man stretching through the twentieth century). In recordkeeping this first shows up clearly as a process in the third dimension of the model, the formation of an archive, an organized body of records of an individual, a function or an organization (even a formation of ideas as in the work of Michel Foucault[3]) that has a capacity to be carried through time and into other spaces. Forms of spacetime distancing via organizing an archive are examined in chapter 6 of this book. This is where documents and records are organized so that others not directly involved in the business processes themselves, but with oversight or other responsibilities within an organization with ownership or access rights over the record, can access and use what has been created and/or captured. It is the region of the corporate or individual archive. People involved in its construction may not have detailed knowledge of the business processes themselves or may not have been engaged in those processes, so, if they and others similarly outside of the action region are to access and use the documentation, the material needs to be organized in ways that suit their needs and understandings, and unpredictable needs and understandings need to be serviced by thesaurus-controlled subject or functions indexing. Modern technologies related to this region include systems that establish organizational connectivity such as Intranets. Access is available to a defined 'organization' or community of users with a growing emphasis upon portals to help negotiate a way through sites.

- ***Forms of the societal totality:*** This region involves even greater distancing from the region of creation than the previous two. In Giddens' theory there is a problem of scalability. Giddens would conceive of a societal totality in many ways. It could be twenty people who have clubbed together with a common interest, a corporate organization, a nation state, or even a 'global society'. In the process model, this region is present as the plural dimension where archives of individuals and organizations

---

[3] See, for example, Michel Foucault, *The Archaeology of Knowledge*, London, Routledge, 1995, Part 3, pp. 79-131, which discusses the archiving of statements within a discursive formation.

would be logically brought together in some way. The same problem of scalability remains. Is a large multinational corporation an institution or an organization? Is a government archives best located in the third dimension or the fourth? If a national archives institution, for example, is under the control of a parliamentary institution, surely it is an organizational entity? If it is a statutory body its purposes have been institutionalized and have probably been protected from administrative interference, making it 'fourth-dimensional' in terms of the model. On the other hand, is its role truly plural if it does not extend beyond government records? Chapter 7 of this book looks at how archivists have attempted to handle the complexities of archival totalities and begins to raise issues for rethinking the 'scalability' issue. It is a region of pluralization because the potential uses for archives are multiple as are the 'social totalities' that can constitute potential use groups. The modern tools for this are the Internet and web-browser technologies, building upon portals to gain access to a plenitude of sources. It is the dimension in which archives systems can be said to have their locus.

Time is ever-present within Figure 8.1 through the use of the word continuum. It is Bergsonian time in which there are billions of moments and movements out from the moment, with no privileging of past, present or future moments.[4] This rippling out can occur in any time in response to any acts of creation, but the inward pressuring of structuration theory, the way our information processes affect the creation of information, will always be spatially and temporally specific to the moment in accordance with what is available to us and what we choose or are forced to use. This is in accordance with the theories in Anthony Giddens' concept of duality of structure, represented in the diagram above by the two-way arrow. Duality of structure should not be read as representing stable development of archives in accord with a linear life cycle; it in fact hides a multiplicity of structuring influences, so even the term duality is a gross simplification. The lifespan of archival documents can be quite chaotic; influences on our actions can come from many points in a continuum; and the lines in the diagram represent thresholds that may or may not be crossed in the same way that Michel Foucault's thresholds in discourse (of which there are also four) behave:

> The distribution in time of these different thresholds, their succession, their possible co-incidence (or lack of it), the way in which they may govern one another, or become implicated with one another, the conditions in which, in turn, they are established, constitute for archaeology [of knowledge] one of the major domains of exploration. Their chronology, in fact is neither regular, nor homogenous.[5]

The four dimensions, however, place an analytical template over the flux of actual occurrences.

---

[4] For a discussion of Bergson's theories of time in ways of special relevance to archivists, particularly those of film, see Gilles Deleuze, *Cinema 2: The Time-Image*, University of Minneapolis Press, 1989.
[5] Michel Foucault, *The Archaeology of Knowledge*, London, Routledge, 1995, p. 187. Foucault's four thresholds for knowledge formation are positivity (statements), epistemologization (e.g. models), scientificity (rules for making statements) and formalization.

Recordkeeping-based activity theory and a records continuum model

In 1996 I published a model which superimposed a recordkeeping-based archival grain on the processes continuum set out above (see Figure 8.2). The model was designed to help build a form of activity theory for archivists out of their concern with the relationship between recordkeeping and accountability. It draws upon writings of its time about the relationship between archival studies and business processes, especially analyses built upon teasing out the functions activities and transactions of records creating agents.[6]

The axial elements in Figure 8.2 look complex, but they do no more than represent the most basic general categories by which accountability can be discussed: who [identity] did what [transactionality], what evidence exists about this [evidentiality], and how can it be recalled from documents records and archives [recordkeeping containers]. The four continua encapsulate what I am calling, in this chapter, recordkeeping-based activity theory. This could also be called 'new provenance theory'. Within such theory the following elements are encompassed:

- transactionality related to records as products of activities;
- identity related to the authorities by which records are made and kept, including their authorship, establishing particularities of the actors involved in the acts of records creation, the empowerment of the actors and their identity viewed from broader social and cultural perspectives;
- evidentiality related to the records as evidence with integrity and continuity; and
- recordkeeping containers related to the objects we create in order to store records.

---

[6] The development of the activities approach is discussed at the time of its emergence in Frank Upward, 'Institutionalizing the archival document: Some theoretical perspectives on Terry Eastwood's Challenge' in Sue McKemmish and Frank Upward, eds, *Archival Documents: Providing Accountability through Recordkeeping*, Clayton, Ancora Press, 1993, pp. 41-54.

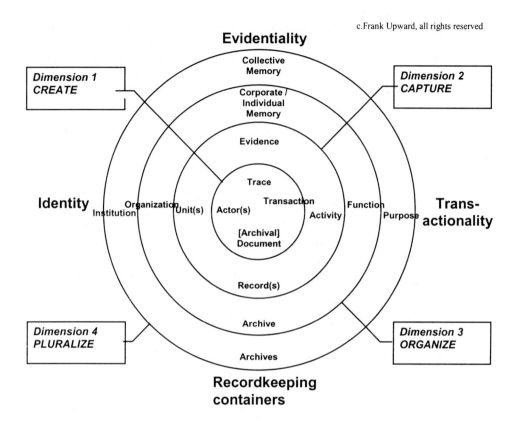

Figure 8.2. The Records Continuum – a spacetime model.[7]

The records continuum model, as the Canadian archivist Terry Cook once noted, is like a plastic sheet.[8] It is topological, by which I mean it is designed to provide an invariant way

---

[7] First presented in Frank Upward, 'Structuring the Records Continuum, Part 1: Postcustodial Principles and Properties', *Archives and Manuscripts*, 24, no. 2, 1996, pp. 268-285; and 'Part 2: Structuration Theory and Recordkeeping', *Archives and Manuscripts*, 25, no. 1, 1997, pp. 11-35.

[8] Terry Cook, 'Final Commentary Session of the Appraisal Seminar', Monash University, Melbourne, 16 March 1999, p. 2. Cook provides a summary of what I am trying to illustrate in this chapter. He said that the model 'provides a model for integrating the public archives and private manuscripts traditions and many archival traditions as well – Australia, Europe, and Canada's total archives approach. But more than that, through the four dimensions and the four axes, there is movement. There is a movement inward from the fourth dimension to the first dimension. And also through the dimensions, looking at the continuum as a plastic sheet, you can think across space and time as well as across the axes. It incorporates records and record-keeping, records products and records processes, nouns and verbs, being and becoming, if you like'.

of looking at any spacetime complex of the records continuum.[9] It gives us a common way of putting forward different views and perspectives. Defining the terms used in the model would be counter-productive to its purpose, except when one is using the model to look at how it relates to specific recordkeeping occurrences and activities. Particular definitions that archivists give to the terms are especially spacetime dependent and the model is meant to provide a tool for comparing and contrasting key similarities and differences in such definitions, not for resolving any disputation. Those wishing to understand the terms further can use dictionaries – and their own experiences – to assist (although, of course, even these definitions have a spacetime component to them, no matter how hard lexicographers might try to iron these out).

The relationship between structure and action, the structuration theory, and Giddens' theories outlined above, can be seen within the records continuum model. One can look at the relationship outwardly, indicating how the plurality of archives is shaped by individuals and their actions, or inwardly, indicating how institutionalization processes and the normalization of memory shape our actions. Chapters 4-7 were set out within a linear explanation, but to understand structuration theory one would have to also read the chapters in reverse order to appreciate the effect (if any) that the way we pluralize archives has upon the way we create documents. To imagine the full operation of the records continuum, however, one would also have to read the chapters in totally non-linear ways, imagining the complex relationships that exist, or could exist, between the points in the four dimensions of the model. Structuration theory might seem complex to the uninitiated, but a practising archivist might be excused for wishing that the issues were as simple as the two-way relationship between what we do and the frameworks for our action. Nevertheless the drive of archivists to influence the way documents are created and records captured has had a major influence on the archival profession over the last decade and has led to a situation where many archival authorities produce excellent recordkeeping advice to the agencies within their jurisdictional control.[10]

---

[9] The prime practical area where topology is of greatest use is in psychoanalysis. It is a major strut in the work of Jacques Lacan for example. It involves a form of analysis which aims at stretching minds into more operative shapes. Lacan's best-known example of topology is in his doughnut and needle example in which it is argued (with good biological evidence) that femaleness and maleness are complexes of the same shape. It is a conscious, but serious, joke that the model as presented is all circles and lines, as doughnuts and needles. The first prototype I presented was all lines, but it was later pointed out to me that the model could do with some feminizing. For a less tongue-in-cheek exploration of the records continuum model as Rorschach test, see Frank Upward, 'The Records Continuum and the Concept of an End Product', *Archives and Manuscripts*, 32, no. 1, 2004, pp. 45-47.

[10] In Australia all state and national government authorities provide advice, with the Commonwealth government and the New South Wales, Victorian and South Australian authorities, in particular, having invested time and thought into the nature of that advice, which is available publicly on the web sites of each of these agencies.

The records continuum model, object, and process

In developing a continuum model out of the recordkeeping-based activity theory of the mid 1990s I was conscious of the need to cater for both an object approach and a systems-based process approach to recordkeeping. In broadly the same timeframe as I was developing model 2 of the records continuum, Canadian archivists whose work I was reading were addressing the object and process approaches in detail. Luciana Duranti was unpacking what, for want of better terms, I will call the classical recordkeeping object approach within archival science and had just completed a review of archival science published in the *Encyclopedia of Library and Information Science*. Terry Cook was preparing his process-orientated treatise on the development of archival ideas in the twentieth century. In this section I consider some perspectives that can be drawn from these works.[11]

Duranti, a Canadian academic with a formative background of studies in Italy, has opened up for many English-speaking archivists discussions of Latinate recordkeeping theories and has presented her own scholarly perspectives on Italian emphases upon the science of diplomatics. Her accounts of archival science can take a reader (well, this one anyway) back into the influence on western thinking of the Graeco-Roman classical tradition, in general, and Aristotelian general metaphysics, in particular, with its emphasis upon the study of the essential aspects of concrete particulars (the aspects which mark them out from other things), the identification of the general attributes under which the particulars fall (their classification), and the impact of spacetime on them (their physics).[12]

She provides a form of study which looks at the characteristics of archival documents, archives and recordkeeping and archiving processes, concentrating on the impact processes have on the recordkeeping object itself. This includes the way documents are linked and aggregated into maintainable bodies of records (the archival bond of the type explored in chapter 5 of this book) and, more contentiously in electronic environments, the way they are protected from change or alteration after they leave the maintaining care of their creators and pass into the hands of archival institutions (the archival limit). She pays particular attention to the themes of the authenticity and reliability of records, documented by Duranti as being a concern in the earliest Italian archival practices as evidenced by the Justinian codes of old Rome.

During the twentieth century Italian archival theorists such as Casanova, Lodolini, Carucci

---

[11] I am not attempting to encapsulate the ideas of Cook or Duranti, although, inevitably, I do intrude on their arguments. My concern is with using their reviews as a take-off point for presenting ideas about the records continuum – perhaps that should be an archives continuum, or a recordkeeping continuum as the points of separation are indistinct. The items of special interest for this section (and also for my review of spacetime complexes of the records continuum later in this chapter) are Terry Cook 'What is Past is Prologue: A History of Archival Ideas since 1898, and the Future Paradigm Shift', *Archivaria*, 43, 1997, pp. 17-63, and Luciana Duranti, 'Archival Science', in *The Encyclopedia of Library and Information Science*, 59, 1997, pp. 1-19.

[12] This summary is based on the coverage of general metaphysics in Michael J. Loux, *Metaphysics, A Contemporary Introduction*, London, Routledge, 1998.

and Duranti herself have continued to explore the making of archives within the particularities of Italian and other experiences.[13] Casanova, in Duranti's account, was the first to discuss archival practices as a science at length in 1928. He helped codify (for Italian archivists anyway) themes and theories relating to records as the natural product of actions, the need to keep whole-of-action accounts rather than partial ones, and the bonding of documents together into an organized archive as a result of controlled aggregation processes.

A classical reading of the model is a reading done at this general metaphysical level. It identifies very broad categories and sets out relations that exist between these categories within five continua. The concrete particulars, the things, are what the model describes as the continuum of 'recordkeeping containers' – *the [archival] document, the record, the archive and the archives*, all of which share a shape, but are different complexes of that shape. The shape itself is stretched, altered and expanded within spacetime as physics would expect of it. The potential of all recordkeeping objects to become public documents, part of the plural world beyond the organization and the individual, is indicated in the model by the square bracket around archival in the first dimension of the container continuum. The influences of archival bonding processes upon recordkeeping actions are present in the exterior dimensions of capture and organization, influences upon things that are done to the object extending its attributes and changing its nature as a thing.

In tracing the model as a way of thinking back to Aristotle I am not claiming lineage for it, but I am pointing to the recurring need of different eras to discover the general metaphysics of recordkeeping anew for their times and technologies. Aristotelian *'being qua being'*, the thing in all that marks it out as that thing, will always be of interest to those who manage information objects of any kind, but the model moves from this perspective to the postmodern one of becoming as becoming. As chapter 5 of this book, for example, indicates, the continuing addition of process metadata means that the archival bond, the links between records are constantly being remade within spacetime. There are no end products in an archival institution, no settled and stable beings, only many which, for the time being, are neglected and forgotten (and some that may be perpetually neglected and forgotten?). Recordkeeping objects are marked out by their processes of formation and continuing formation, not by their intrinsic nature.

The second study I consider in this section, that by Terry Cook, is a study of the ideas about the becoming of archives that archivists have put forward during the twentieth century. In a detailed account he challenges aspects of the classic view of archives as an end product in the custody of archivists, arguing that the archivist is gradually metamorphosing into something 'post-custodial', no longer viewable as a caretaker or freezer, in the Latinate view, of a resource that others have formed and maintained.

---

[13] For a review from an Australian perspective of the Italian approach see Livia Iacovino, 'Common Ground, Different Traditions, An Australian Perspective on Italian Diplomatics, Archival Science and Business Records', *Archives and Manuscripts*, 29, no. 1, 2001, pp. 118-138.

He asks archivists to move from the object, the thing in a general metaphysical view, and create a more dynamic relational view of the processes that form the object, including the archivists own ongoing involvement in the formation of archives as a sociocultural resource. He connects post-custodial thinking to postmodernity, especially in its renewal of an emphasis upon provenance as the study of the dynamic relationships between records creators, functions and 'records', the essence of a postmodern view of becoming. Cook makes it clear he is not discussing the complete abandonment of the archival institution as a physical reception point for archival objects; he is rather identifying an enlarged framework for thinking about custody and the options available for implementing it.[14]

To view Cook's post-custodial intent through the model, and also to see links through to postmodern thinking within the post-custodial ideas that sprang to life during the early to mid 1990s in works such as his, one has to lift one's eyes above the recordkeeping containers continuum and read the circles and lines in dynamic relational fashion, questioning the meaning of points and interconnecting them in different ways. Open-ended and multiple approaches to custody can be discussed via the model once the recursive involvement of all dimensions in the construction of archives in this more random manner is applied. Particularly important is the recursive involvement of action in the first dimension, the only place in the model which accommodates what is being done. Why can we not act in such a way, for example, that archives are formed instantly in conjunction with document creation? The other dimensions are shaping dimensions, regions where both the attributes that shape our action and external evidence of those actions reside, in accordance with structuration and construction theories in sociology (see the next section of this chapter). Can we get these other dimensions sufficiently firmly in place as influences upon action to enable the establishment of microseconds of old archives? Or will we continue to create one-dimensional documents, two-dimensional records, or three-dimensional archive formations for decades, even though our technologies enable four-dimensional approaches?

A postmodern reading, of course, would also raise doubts and questions at every point, intersection and relationship within the model. What is the trace? Does it exist as evidence? How does recordkeeping evidence relate to legal evidence? How does evidence relate to memory? Who really is the creating agent? The individual or the organization that employs them? What is the difference between the individual as a 'corpus' (a whole legal entity, a legal recognition that gave us the word corporation) and as an actor? How well do created documents reflect actions?

And, of course, there are also the large questions of subjectivity and involvement raised by Cook. The archivist (when wearing the hat of the archivist as pointed to within recordkeeping-based activity theory) is enmeshed in a sociocultural role by a focus on recordkeeping objects, the continuing processes of their formation, and the ongoing role archivists can play as actors in appraisal processes or as actors establishing mechanisms for

---

[14] Cook, 'What is Past is Prologue', op. cit., p. 48.

·capturing, organizing and pluralizing records and having these adopted widely. Archivists in this mode need instruments of analysis that correspond to the functioning and mode of change of those objects, to the processes that stretch and shape data and documents into archives – this was among the reasons for developing the model. How were (and will be) documents created, captured as records, organized as part of a corporate or individual records store, or brought into the plurality of the world of public documents? Have the processes supported evidential needs and retrieval needs to make them not only accessible to corporate, individual or public memory but worth accessing for evidential purposes in the first place? These are questions that archivists – including and perhaps especially those in reference rooms – should be asking of their systems, strategies and activities on a daily basis.

The very act and deed: a French excursion

One of the emerging themes outlined by Cook, a shift from records-centred approaches to one where the emphasis is upon the 'very act and deed' (as typified in the work of the Canadian archivist, Hugh Taylor[15]), is worth special consideration within any discussion of recordkeeping-based activity theory. Is the process-object approach outlined to this point supporting Cook's contention or not? Is it really a move away from a records-centric approach? Or is a recordkeeping-based approach inevitably records-centred? In many ways the rest of this book answers that question (recordkeeping approaches are expansive and can be centred in many different ways), but the records continuum model outlined above provides a yes and no answer. Relationally one moves to many points in the records continuum model and beyond. Everything is peripheral, and nothing is central, although our focus can pause in spaces between points in the model or at the points themselves. But the act and deed is diffuse. The act is present in the horizontal axes representing the identity of the agents and the transactions they are involved in. The deeding of the act to the future (and the past) is present in the vertical axes, the storage of recorded information and the evidentiality of that which is stored (the qualities of recorded information as evidence and its ability to be recalled as memory). The dimensions represent the recordkeeping and archiving processes involved in that storage. Yet the anchoring continuum is that of the recordkeeping containers themselves. It is precisely the actuality that archivists are always returning to recordkeeping objects as represented in the model by the containers axis that marks them, and their everyday actions, off from others. Recordkeeping objects can be de-centred, but for the methods of archivists they are always central. An archivist's 'gotta do what an archivist's gotta do' as Sue McKemmish and I once noted – by which we meant that through all the subjectivity and questioning of the ash of evidence, archivists have to concern themselves with whether archives are evidential.[16] This, of course, does not mean that we do not do other things as well.

---

[15] Hugh Taylor, '"My Very Act and Deed": Some reflections on the Role of Textual Records in the Conduct of Affairs', *American Archivist*, 51, Fall 1988, pp. 456-469.

[16] For a discussion of the issue of evidence within archival theory see the discourse between Verne Harris, 'On the Back of a Tiger: Deconstructive Possibilities in Evidence of Me', and Frank Upward and Sue McKemmish, 'In Search of the Lost Tiger by Way of Sainte Beuve: Reconstructing the

It is a view that twentieth-century French literary philosophers seemed to have understood much better than some archivists of that century. One way of illustrating, questioning, and clarifying the act and deed theme in archival theory, in fact, is through references to French literary philosophy in the age of Deleuze, a complex of spacetime which can be said to have become identifiable as an age sometime after the student revolutions in France in 1968 and to be still expanding and collapsing across thresholds, particularly in academia in North America and Australasia. It is typified in English discourse as postmodern, although its major participants would dispute this label.

Records and archives in this era and place began to be regularly portrayed as models for the study of discourse. The purest model for discourse in Jean Francois Lyotard's intriguing work *Figures of Discourse* (1971), for example, is not the literary document, but the archival document – 'something which inscribes itself in a record book, in an account book, in public records, though in an inscription that is always re-actualizable, eternally present (Husserl) in a journal'.[17] Jacques Derrida, on the other hand, pointed to speech as the model for discourse and ridiculed the failure of philosophers to develop forms of analysis that went beyond philosophical dependence upon the spoken word, which, unlike text, is more readily interrogated. In speech words can be questioned, probed and used interactively, but documents have an undiscoverable interiority and any analysis has to contend with the impossibility of regularizing understandings of words across space or through time. Derridan views about the interiority of the act have their locus in the first dimension of the model. Documents will never tell us all we may like to know, which Derrida explores in depth in his book *Archive Fever*.[18] Husserl's eternal presence, on the other hand, exists outside of that interiority, in the way actions are disembedded into records.

Of the gang of French muggers of the intellect of this era, as they are sometimes called, the one that has so far had the greatest impact upon ideas development in the English language is ironically an exponent of depersonalization, Michel Foucault. He explored the external presence of documents in discourse, not their interior mysteries. Unsurprisingly, Foucault, 'the new archivist', and Derrida, the questioner of interiorities of text, were antagonists at times.[19] Foucault constructed a new positivist shape in the place of the nineteenth-century historicism. In his histories and philosophical statements he applied records-based models for discursive formations (the sort of archival approach set out within studies of the aggregating and bonding of records in Duranti) to the study of literary documents. He took

---

Possibilities in Evidence of Me', *Archives and Manuscripts*, 25, no. 1, 1997, pp. 8-43. The 'gotta do' reference is to p. 35.

[17] For an English translation of 'Sur une figure de discours', see Jean-Francois Lyotard, *Towards the Postmodern*, New Jersey, Humanities Press, 1993. The quotation is from p.18 of that book.

[18] Jacques Derrida, *Archive Fever: A Freudian Impression*, Chicago, University of Chicago Press, 1996.

[19] Deleuze described Foucault as the new archivist in his book *Le Nouvel Archiviste,* Paris, Fata Morgana, 1972. Derrida describes his arguments with Foucault (a one-sided view of them of course, given that Foucault was dead) in 'To Do Justice to Freud: The History of Madness in the Age of Psychoanalysis' of which an English translation is in Arnold I. Davidson, *Foucault and his Interlocutors*, Chicago, University of Chicago Press, 1997, pp. 57-96.

attention away from individuals and their work. Yes, you could know things, but they were about the processes of formation, about cultural making. In studying ideas, for example, he looked at the way recordkeeping processes classify them into pigeon-holes within disciplines and the way this controls discursive formations (the way ideas run together in a pack, or, in records terms, as a file). Archiving processes take these pigeon-holed ideas and build up specialized discourses that close off alternatives in a series of power-plays in accordance with the wishes of the pack masters. On the other hand the archive also builds into an unmasterable plurality of ideas. There is always the possibility that something from that plurality can 'irrupt' (flow outwards) to confound the existing unity of power-based discursive formations. Foucault argued that the document is a monument. The 'trace' is a memorial to action and one can study ideas in ways that bypass their interiority of thought. You assess the past by acts and deeds, not by words on the page, even when your subject matter is the history of ideas. He recommended this method, built out of an examination of recordkeeping and archiving processes, as a way of thinking and operating in our diverse spaces in his book, *The Archaeology of Knowledge.*[20]

Iposteguy contemporaneously sketched Foucault, this exponent of recordkeeping-based activity theory, for Gilles Deleuze's book *Le Nouvel Archiviste,* as someone who gave the past and present life together (see Figure 8.3). Foucault as an historian came close to Cook's ideal functioning of an archivist set out in the last sentence of his review of archival ideas. Using the words of Carruthers, Cook looks to archivists to be capable of 'making present the voices of what is past, not to entomb either the past or the present, but to give them life together in a place common to both in memory'. There is a crucial caveat here however. Foucault had archive fever. He ignored individual voices. He was a new positivist, a framer of era-based 'facts' from the archival formation processes, using archival method to study the suppressions that trust in the voice and control over memory introduce when they form a controlling archive. He studied the 'facts' of the operation of power in discourses, the evidence that was not in the document, but external to it in the use made of the document. In the terms of the records continuum model, he looked at acts and deeds in terms of the suppressions involved in the capture and organization processes, and saw in the archive enslavement through the control of diversity – and in its plurality the potential for liberation because of the impossibility of the suppressors ever mastering its diversity.

---

[20] I have referred to *The Archaeology of Knowledge* only in this section. Foucault wrote later theoretical works extending his view of the archive of discourses, but did not greatly disturb the ideas about the archive, recordkeeping classification, and documents that he had set out in this book.

Figure 8.3. Iposteguy's sketch of Michel Foucault as the new archivist.[21]

Paul Veyne, one of the historians who internalized Foucault, put this in very concrete terms.[22] You do not look to explain Roman gladiatorial contests in terms of the love of bread and circuses (as he had once done). You study the specificities of occurrence of the acts, resisting the temptation to work from the precept that the acts can be generalized across time in terms of constants in human nature. You ask yourself different questions, when you are studying the 'very act and deed', such as, why did gladiatorial fights only take place within the Roman Empire? The act and deed theme raises the crucial historical question asked of all documents by Michel Foucault: what can we learn from the specificity of their occurrences? Archival method is a major protector of an historian's capacity to answer that question, whether they are historians of ancient Rome or of the 'War on Terror' in the twenty-first century.

From the viewpoint of theories about the spacetime complexes of the continuum, the results of Foucault's use of archival method in turn provides archivists with a way of exploring in their own discourse how different complexes of thought from the past can both cling to us and dominate our thinking, and how, at some time or another, new complexes can be expected to burst through and disrupt the dominant complexes. In that aspect of his thinking Foucault was very much a continuum philosopher, a person who juxtaposed ideas from any era and sought to understand the specificities of particular complexes of ideas in their occurrence. It is to different spacetime complexes that I now wish to turn.

---

[21] Gilles Deleuze, *Le Nouvel Archiviste*, op. cit., p. 48.
[22] Paul Veyne, *Writing History: Essay on Epistemology*, Middletown, Wesleyan University Press, c1984.

Spacetime distancing and the expanding universe

The preceding sections have made introductory references to general metaphysics. I now want to make use of one of the earliest metaphysical approaches to the spacetime continuum set out by Samuel Alexander in his 1920 book, *Space, Time and Deity*. Alexander worked out from the idea that the spacetime continuum represented the totality of all that exists, a totality that was infinite and expanding. Descriptions of things can be true in their time, but not in other times. Everything around us was, and is, a complex of an expanding continuum. Alexander's work was part of one of the most fundamental paradigm shifts in modern human thinking in which time is not viewed as a separate dimension, but as an integral one, a shift that at the same time in history was enabling Einstein to develop his theories of relativity.[23]

Spacetime theories in cosmology and general metaphysics have continued to expand since then, as continuum theory itself would expect. At the beginning of the twenty-first century physicists are starting to toy with notions of creating universes in laboratories, universes which will not displace our own, existing in their own spacetime. In metaphysical philosophy the spacetime continuum as an explanation of the totality that exists is still expanding, although its significance is disputed fiercely.[24] Over the last thirty years or more spacetime continuum thinking has also begun to intrude into the studies of recorded information. In Michel Foucault's work, for example, the archive, a singularly diverse entity, controls our thinking, but ironically can never be mastered in its entirety, so is always poised to disrupt the discursive formations it has constructed. In sociological parlance (from Giddens), human behaviour and the communities we live in are time-space distancing complexes shaped by the way we store recorded information. In the archival profession, Eric Ketelaar has begun to open up similar debates by asking the question is everything archive?[25]

In the next part of this chapter I use the spacetime continuum as a meta-narrative in the manner of Alexander, attempting to demonstrate the expansion of the archival universe to the point where its diversity has become the source of many complexities. My aim is not to compete with Adrian Cunningham's chapter earlier in this book, but I give a perspective that can be read back into that chapter. My concern is with establishing a story about recordkeeping activity theory in different times and places. I gallop through pre-modern unities, discuss the development of diversity within modernity, and then point to what Jean

---

[23] Alexander's book explains the spacetime continuum as the totality of all that exists via evolution of materials to organisms to the development of consciousness, and the relationship between human consciousness and the objects that surround us, or at least that is how it is described in Quentin Gibson's classic short introductory book, *Facing Philosophical Problems*, Melbourne, F. W. Cheshire, 1961, pp. 36-37.

[24] For an introduction to general metaphysics see Michael J. Loux, *Metaphysics,* op. cit. Loux ends his book with a joke about the continuum in metaphysical philosophy: 'Like the other debates we have considered the controversy over temporal persistence has great staying power' (p. 231).

[25] Eric Ketelaar posed the question 'Is Everything Archive?' in a seminar paper delivered at Monash University, 5 August 2002.

Francois Lyotard called the postmodern condition – the disjointing impact new technologies are having upon us.

Pre-modern and modern archives in Europe

The deeply human concern for the establishment of an archive first showed up in cave paintings, dance, song and storytelling as artistic preservation tools for the carriage of survival information through time. Once societies began to trade with each other, recordkeeping concerns were added to the arts of the earliest communities. The archival pursuit, the recording of transactions and the retention of that recorded information through time, is a keystone for all forms of knowledge management. With the development of script scribes became ubiquitous, and civil and military administration became more complex. You cannot recruit, maintain and deploy large armies without records. They are necessary to establishing trust in trade relationships and in contracting the arrangements between citizens and between citizens and government. They are necessary for levying and collecting taxes. They were also needed for planning, carrying out, and maintaining public works.

The centre of the emergence of recordkeeping dependent societies is usually seen as the Middle East. Places now known as Iraq and Egypt feature in the stories of records and archives in the ancient world. Recent archaeological discoveries suggest similar changes to social structures as a result of recordkeeping were occurring in South America and Asia at this time. The brief flourishing of Greek democracy in Athens in the fifth and fourth century B.C. produced philosophers like Socrates, Plato and Aristotle. Within this chronology, script seems to have spread like a wildfire and immediately unlocked the potential in much pre-existing thought.

The Greeks gave us the word archive (from *archeion*) which provides a one-word picture of the archive as the keystone in the arch of governance, but right from these origins the archive was one of two entwined macro-pursuits for knowledge management from which all other disciplines have sprung. The other macro-pursuit is represented today by librarians. The Greek archive might for a brief time have kept records of the Athenian city state, including of the Senate, a place for the registration of agreements between citizens and the maintenance of magistrates' records, or it may have been limited to magistrates' records. From the outset there was a competitor, the Metroon, the recorded information held in the religious temple, the source or mother of the Greek metropolis.

If the history of the governance role of the archive in Greece is a little mysterious because of its interconnections with the Metroon, the role of the archive is said to be much more clearly present in the Roman archivum, a tool of the law and the market-place supporting governing processes and the transactions between citizens. It was not a public office; it was *the* public office protecting the authenticity and reliability of documents. Here there is more solid archaeological evidence and even some documentation in the form of the Roman Justinian codes. It held documents that furnished proof of events and controlled the skein of relationships between citizens, governments and their daily business. It was a proving ground of those documents, giving authenticity and reliability to them. According to a common view of the archives, found in writing as different as the archivist Luciana Duranti's review of archival science and Jacques Derrida's book *Archive Fever,* deposit in public places guaranteed the reliability and authenticity of records as witnesses of action. Unbroken custody in that safe house was believed to ensure the continuity of these valued attributes.[26]

Gradually the recordkeeping and archiving processes in Latin-dominated Europe began to divide and split. The proving processes began to be transferred to the form of the documents themselves. After a period of documentation chaos, the so-called Dark Ages of Europe where respect for knowledge survived only in English monasteries – or so the story goes – archival documents began to re-exert their control on some European communities, emerging as legal instruments in their own right. The professions of the jurist and the notary appeared and an area of professional study was opened up with the establishment of Padua University in 1158. Meanwhile the recorded information of the temple followed a similar pattern of emerging professional studies when, in the same era, a religious university was established at Avignon, then the papal city. It could be argued that this separation in knowledge formation within two universities was the beginning of the process of the separation of church and state in Western societies, but it took many centuries for the chink to become a major fissure. The notary tradition for many centuries depended on creating documents which witnessed events before God, and before the ruler as representative of God.

In the sixteenth and seventeenth centuries consolidated records offices began to accompany the growth of a new form of governance, the nation state. The new state archives, in the words of Duranti, directed their endeavours at 'authenticating actions, protecting patrimonies, educating present and future generations, and preserving historical events independent of their age'. An approach to past actions was beginning to be consolidated which clearly reflects, in starkly political terms, what Jacques Derrida describes in Freudian terms as the power of the archive to impress, repress and suppress. The desires and will of the rulers of the state became the major shaping forces of their content and the source of their economic sustenance.[27]

European expansion and colonialism in the nineteenth century, and the creation of disciplinary formations within Western processes of knowledge formation, led to major transformations in the study of recordkeeping and archiving processes and to the development of modern archival theory. The nineteenth-century colonial dominance of Northern European countries (Great Britain, Germany and the Netherlands) was substantially built upon the domestic establishment of powerful forms of recordkeeping, forms of recordkeeping which were cast adrift from the archives as an institution and were dispersed throughout bureaucratic organizations within their records. Through recordkeeping processes controlled by registries that maintained reliable data about

---

[26] Luciana Duranti, 'Archives as a Place', *Archives and Manuscripts*, 24, no. 2, 1996, pp. 242-255; Jacques Derrida, *Archive Fever,* op. cit., pp. 2-3.
[27] Luciana Duranti, 'Archival Science', op. cit., p. 2, and Derrida, *Archive Fever,* op. cit.

documents and the links made in the course of business between documents, the administrative processes were able to settle into routines that allowed for control at a distance. This regularized decision-making through accessible administrative precedents, enabling records to build like coral on the sea floor.

In England these routines were controlled by registrars, and it was a pattern that spread readily out to their colonies. By the early twentieth century, registry systems could be found in many organizations throughout the English-controlled world, including general administrative registrars in government departments, specialized ones in hospitals, and organizations dedicated to registration such as land titles and transfer offices and registries of births, deaths and marriages. Registration processes enabled governmental structures to be far-flung, extending across the nation state and across the globe.

Meanwhile the archives as custodial institutions were losing contact with current recordkeeping processes. Nation state archives were becoming a holder of end products, studied by historians and other researchers after they were perceived to have outlived their administrative life. In these historically orientated institutions, nineteenth-century archivists developed the studies of archives into a forensic science, which in turn had a synergistic relationship with the emergence of history in the nineteenth century as a major professional discipline.[28]

Archivists used diplomatic science, palaeography and emerging historical research methods to study documents with an emphasis upon the process of archive formation in the past and puzzled over how to set out in their depositories the records as the skeletons of organizations.[29] The continuing expansion of nation state archives meant that there were a growing number of laboratories at their disposal as the nineteenth century proceeded. Significant results were produced from them. The French, immersed in their studies of the large dispersed accessions of material from the *ancien régime*, developed influential ways of respecting the fullness of the resource itself (*respect des fonds*). The palaeographer, Natalis de Wailly recommended in 1841 arrangement methods in which the first

---

[28] T.R Schellenberg, *Modern Archives, Principles and Techniques*, Melbourne, Cheshire, 1956, pp. 174-175.

[29] S. Muller, J.A Feith and R. Fruin's manual is the classic reference for this metaphor. They compare the archivist's task with that of a palaeontologist, where you fit the scattered bones together to represent the skeleton of what had once existed. It was published in 1898; by 1910 it had been translated into German, Italian and French, indicating its cross-cultural significance in mainland Europe. The second edition was translated into English in the late 1930s (*Manual for the Arrangement and Description of Archives*, New York, Wilson, 1940) but there is no practical sign that English-speaking archivists fully caught to the significance of its very first rule – that first of all you should catch your archive (the archive of the corporate entity as a legal fiction) – until Peter Scott in Australia during the 1960s developed a system for doing so (see chapter 7 of this book). It is one of the great paradoxes of archival theory that while European theory discusses the archive extensively and builds from that notion, English-language literature has tended to ignore it and its formation as a way of organizing ideas, and those who have emphasized it, such as David Bearman in his work on capturing the corporate archive in electronic recordkeeping during the 1990s, are likely to be seen as eccentric thinkers.

determinant was the order imposed by the originator of the records. Others in Europe similarly discovered that it was often sufficient to reproduce the order of the originators. The principle of 'original order' became ingrained in archival methods A related principle to emerge from the study of archives was that of provenance which in relation to Northern European theory is more aptly termed provenience (respecting the source). After the Prussian State Archives was set up in 1874, for example, the principle of retaining recordkeeping order was pushed through to the extent of creating classification-based spaces in repositories for the records of particular agencies where future transfers of records would be maintained in their order of creation (the archives as mausoleum?).[30]

In Europe, government archivists in many countries spent the first half of the twentieth century digging deeper into the tracks they had begun in the previous century. It was a period of largely separate national developments, where archivists in each country established their spacetime truths while imagining they were universal truths. The French codified the implementation of *respect des fonds* within the *Manuel d'archivistique,* formally published in 1976 but based on continuing explorations of theory and practice recorded in internal manuals from the 1840s. A German monograph of the mid-twentieth century, *Archivkunde* (Leipzig, Koehler & Amelang, 1953), based on lectures by Adolf Brenneke, continued to carve out the distinction between records and archives that nineteenth-century German archivists had developed, distinguishing between records that are still in the hands of creators and those that are in archives, pointing to the significance of research use of archival material, and developing distinctive ways of classing archives. In Great Britain, Sir Hilary Jenkinson produced his *Manual of Archive Administration* after World War 1, which, with a little revision, remained that nation's master statement on the subject for half a century. The Dutch codified their practices at the end of the nineteenth century in Muller, Feith and Fruin's classic *Manual for the Arrangement and Description of Archives.*

All works were culturally insular, with the partial exception of the archetypal traders of the period, the Dutch, where the work of the Germans and the French were taken into account. At times the insularity reached majestically arrogant levels, as when Jenkinson, early in the twentieth century, argued before a Parliamentary Commission that in relation to archives there was not much the English could learn from continental Europe.[31]

All the manuals contributed to archives as a forensic science, as ways of studying past complexes of recordkeeping, but their institutional and descriptive nature meant they were not in close contact with current complexes. Jenkinson, for example, was content at least in the first half of his lengthy career with leaving the formation of the archives to the civil servants that created them. His manual, however, included lengthy sections on how archives were formed in different eras, an essential understanding for moral defence and for

---

[30] This account is derived from the works of Schellenberg and Duranti, cited above, and my teaching notes.

[31] He referred only to Belgian practices in his argument and demonstrated that he knew little about European practices. See Andrew Horder's Master of Arts thesis, *The Context of Jenkinson's Manual,* Monash University, Faculty of Computing and Information Technology, 1998.

maintaining the integrity of the records but one that is hollow if current practices are not similarly studied. The utility of Muller, Feith and Fruin's manual, Dutch archivists have recently concluded, tends to peter out for records created after the Treaty of Utrecht in 1815, and, broadly, all forensic manuals can be expected to be of questionable use beyond the latest solid layers of acquisitions the archival institutions contributing to it had received.[32]

Modern archives in the U.S.A. and the concept of heterotopia

The concept of the heterotopian archive in the works of Michel Foucault, who coined the phrase, is a complex one already set out above in terms of its essential features. Foucault believed that in Europe the formation of disciplinary boxes for knowledge had closed off many alternatives and he directed attention to the need to liberate knowledge from the archive as it had been formed within the discursive formations themselves. He pointed to the many different shapes for thinking within that archive, shapes that are too complex to be fully observable within any analysis but are ironed out by recordkeeping and archiving processes. Foucault was writing about literary text, but, in doing so, he was applying the method of an archivist, exploring how ideas build in the same ways that the 'fonds', the archival resource, builds.

Foucault spent the last part of his life in the United States, where he is supposed to have found his heterotopia, diverse ways of thinking where the potential for difference is difficult to suppress and options for the future remain more open. In much of Europe the dominant emphases had been upon regularizing understandings of the shape of the archive as a resource, using forensic approaches to government recordkeeping within reasonable expectations that governments would be interested in this process. In the United States the justifications and actions for providing resources to archives formation were directed towards a plurality that broadened attempts to attract finance to a function that was not automatically present within governmental funding processes.

United States archivists, of course, did mount governmental records-based arguments. One shape for archival thinking that developed came from writers like Margaret Cross Norton, the Illinois State archivist (1922-1957), a strong exponent of the need to avoid divisions in our concepts of archives and records. She challenged the hegemony of nineteenth-century derived styles of historicism, arguing her case at both theoretical and pragmatic levels. The paperwork explosion of the twentieth century was a prime concern for Norton. Pragmatically she contended that the view of an archivist's work as historical would limit the financial support state archives programs would receive. Theoretically she argued that it is a fallacy to treat archives only as historical records, as a cultural resource, arguing that archives could be thought of in 'moments old' form. The archival resource came into

---

[32] Frank Upward, 'In Search of the Continuum', in Sue McKemmish and Michael Piggott, eds, *The Records Continuum*, Clayton, Ancora Press, 1994, pp. 115-117, expands upon the summary given here.

existence from the time information was recorded.[33] At even deeper non-Nortonian theoretical levels this raised the possibility of the archivist adding a clinical role to their forensic one, supplanting the division between the recordkeeper and the archivist that the nineteenth century had constructed.

The 'moments old' archives became part of the diversity of U.S. thought and practice, but the development of a clinical role for archivists, which such a proposition supports, was cut short in the 1950s at the height of archivist/records manager theorizing. A pragmatic consensus was reached that the most suitable strategic relationship with records management was through life-cycle models in which the maintenance of the current record was handed over to the developing professional grouping of records managers, albeit with the archivist having a say in disposal scheduling. A baton-changing relationship was established in which archivists remained in their accustomed position, picking up responsibilities for the archives when administrators had finished with using them as records in their daily activities. The archival institution was at the end of the cycle within the dominant life-cycle models, open to receiving the end product of the disposal processes.[34]

The maintenance of the separation between current archival documents and those in archival custody was irrelevant anyway. The 'moments old' archives conceptualization did not have any substance in the United States, at least in European terms as a means of protecting the integrity of the record. During the second decade of the twentieth century government recordkeeping processes ceased to manage documents and records within registries. Business records management processes were adopted in government as well as business within which people became used to filing material after it was actioned, whereas the best practices in Northern Europe were based on pre-action registration. Pre-action systems controlled documents organizationally before action officers got their hands upon them. Without such registration processes there is no stable point for the creation of a reliable and authentic 'moments old' archives. Certainly an archive can be said to be forming from the moment documents are created, but there is total dependence on the integrity and capacity of individuals to see that appropriate material is filed. Post-action approaches to records management are cheap and sometimes nasty, leaving all societies and organizations that follow them open to the actions of people abundantly present in the United States (and all large societies) who, over the years, have been given titles like carpetbaggers, robber barons, greed-is-good advocates and, more recently, mafia managers – those who seize the immediate opportunity to wax fat rather than look to the long-term well-being of business transactions across society.

---

[33]See for example Margaret Cross Norton, 'The Scope and Function of Archives', in *Norton on Archives*, ed. by T.W. Mitchell, Carbondale, Southern Illinois University Press, 1975, pp. 3-24, originally published in 1934, which is full of 'recordkeeping-based activity theory'.
[34]For a discussion of archivist/records manager relations in the U.S. in this era, see Frank B. Evans, 'Archivists and Records Managers, Variations on a Theme', in M.E. Daniels & T. Walsh, eds, *A Modern Archives Reader*, Washington, National Archives and Records Service, 1984. pp. 25-37.

The other major shape to emerge in the United States, one which was equally at odds with much European archival theory, was the collecting approach, and this, given the relative absence of authenticity and reliability discussions, came to dominate much of the discourse. The United States had entered the twentieth century with no nation state archives and an acknowledged need to collect material. The American Historical Association had established separate Historical Manuscripts and Public Archives Commissions. Within one commission the emphasis was on collecting within local communities; in the other the emphasis was on debates over the role of a national archival institution. Government, business and personal papers, meanwhile, were finding their way via collection processes into a diverse array of libraries, places of deposit set up by community groups, government archival depositories in a few states, and business and bureaucratic depositories. The early heterotopian approach has remained dominant as a patterning for archival activity. The notion, strongly present in European twentieth-century archival theory, that archivists do not collect, but are situated in ongoing relationships with records creators, has never been a strong part of U.S. discourse, although it is certainly a strong part of what their archivists do. The words 'collections' and 'collecting' in some ways cling to their discourse like a bath-tub ring and there was little strong use of the terms 'recordkeeping' and 'archiving' from the 1960s until the opening up of electronic records issues three decades later.[35]

The dominance of a collecting vocabulary in the United States suggests that archivists who dealt with personal papers saw themselves very much as collectors, rather than as documenters of the past, as many these days would see themselves. By the 1960s such archivists were beginning to challenge the nineteenth-century principles of forensic archival practice.[36] The aggregation order of personal papers is seldom systemic. Over time they are chucked in garages, boxes or whatever, and shuffled around like cards in a pack. The creating agent, in a sense, might be the person who collected the papers, while the name of those whose papers were being collected might not matter a jot from retrieval and control viewpoints. The papers may contain none of that person's correspondence, only inward correspondence from others and (or) material collected from many sources. From this chaos it is easy to create tables of difference between archivists of personal papers and government archivists. These tables are not really sustainable. Nineteenth-century individuals, like nineteenth-century bureaucracies in fact often maintained their own records systematically. Disorder is a twentieth-century problem and there is no guarantee

---

[35] The United States' National Archives, for example, was established in the early 1930s. By the 1950s it had done a lot of collecting and was ready to begin to regularize its relationship with the Government bureaucracies but had trouble adjusting its vocabulary. The clear example was the publication of *A Modern Archives Reader*, op. cit., where the material relating to the formation of an archive in an organization was lumped together in a section entitled 'pre-archival functions', as if archival functionality resides only in archival institutions. Within that book's account of archival functions the words 'collecting' and 'collections' dominates discussion. On the other hand, Norton's concept of 'moments old' archives was far from dead; it was just going through a period of repression. (See the writings of Richard Cox for critiques of the collecting approach in the United States; Cox has helped keep 'moments old' views alive in the U.S.)

[36] For an account of the 'manuscript' tradition in the U.S., written within the collecting vocabulary, see Richard C. Berner, *Archival Theory and Practice in the United States: A Historical Analysis*, Seattle, University of Washington Press, 1983.

that twentieth-century government records will have been created and maintained systematically. The commonalities between personal archives and government records are seldom addressed in archival literature and it is only in recent years that this challenge has been taken up.[37]

Archivists in the United States began to wear their heterotopian collecting approaches and their concepts of the life cycle of records as a badge of modernity. The 'modern archivist' developed ideas about appraisal, public access and advice to government agencies on the maintenance of records that made the major forensic science function of the European archivist – the listing of records – recede into a wider array of professional functions.

The United States archive is, however, heterotopian and, in the 1990s, electronic recordkeeping issues began to cause reformulations of the spacetime complexes as ideas about recordkeeping and documentation processes, which, in Foucauldian terms, had been suppressed in their discourse, have begun buckling back to the surface. The Nortonian discourse has bounced back within electronic recordkeeping projects, but within electronic systems the absence of registration points to give stability to the systems operation is unthinkable. The documentation drive, rather than collecting drive, can be found in specialized Internet archives of current events and episodes. The United States' 150-year history of battling against carpetbagging in their own society has reemerged within accountability discussions as economists, archivists and regulators look at the catastrophic economic effects of massive corporate collapses at the beginning of the twenty-first century. The War on Iraq, with its public justifications based on hopelessly inadequate and unreliable intelligence information, can only deepen the need for the United States to give even greater thought to recordkeeping-based activity theory.

These changes in the conditioning factors for spacetime complexes of the records continuum reopen perspectives on whether archivists should see themselves solely recipients of material that no longer has primary administrative uses, or whether they can be framers of the archives in the moments after the record is created. They raise issues of the extent to which recordkeeping processes can be transferred into electronic systems. In the nineteenth century recordkeeping processes helped colonial powers conquer vast spaces, enabling distributed bureaucracies to flourish. The processes were based on the flow of work in the organizations and the analysis of its business processes. Modern information and communication technologies refocus attention on flow and business analysis, instantly conquer spatial dispersion, and can provide for immediate formation of archives within networked systems. Registration no longer is a time-consuming manual thing, but an automatic and essential element of the communication process.

Norton's 'moments old' archive may yet reemerge in the United States as a nanosecond approach, in the manner first anticipated within the early and middle stages of the University of Pittsburgh research project into functional requirements for recordkeeping evidence. The technology, David Bearman, one of the researchers, came to argue is no longer the problem. The technology can form archives instantly. Robust systems that meet

---

[37] Sue McKemmish, 'Evidence of Me...', *Archives and Manuscripts*, 24, no. 1, 1996, pp. 28-45.

the nanosecond ideal, however, are not yet designed and operational, although their prototypes can be seen in electronic commerce and research is continuing.[38]

Conclusion

What will archival science (or archival studies, if you prefer) look like when archival practitioners and thinkers are further down the road in tackling the biggest challenge of our era, the instant construction of archives that can be electronically communicated across vast spaces and through long reaches of time? How long will it take to meet that challenge? Will there be new twists to the journey through spacetime and the development of new complexes of the records continuum that take archivists off in different directions, such as the development of our own form of 'M' theory in which records will sit under our information systems continuously constructing themselves within their own universe while not displacing the information systems universes sitting elsewhere in spacetime? Will the bath-tub ring complexes of our past win out, finding new means of expression? Who knows, but the answers and new questions are there somewhere in the ever-expanding universes of our archives. In finding those questions and answering them for our own time archivists will need to move from linear concepts of time and the developmental progress of ideas within it. They will, as was first argued in chapter 4 of this book, have to begin developing a capacity to understand the recordkeeping activities of different eras, past, present and unknown, developing their existing important methods for analyzing archives and in our era, directing them more at the heterotopian archive. Michel Foucault wrote:

> The great obsession of the nineteenth century was as we know, history: with its themes of development and suspension, of crisis and cycle, themes of the ever-accumulating past, with its preponderance of dead men and the menacing glaciation of the world ... The present epoch will perhaps be above all the epoch of space. We are in the epoch of juxtaposition, the epoch of the near and far, of the side-by-side, of the dispersed. We are at the moment, I believe, when our experience of the world is less that of a long life developing through time than a network that connects points and intersects with its own skein. One could say that certain ideological conflicts animating present-day polemics oppose the pious descendants of time and the determined inhabitants of space.[39]

---

[38] University of Pittsburgh, Functional Requirements for Evidence in Recordkeeping, 1992-1996 (http://web.archive.org/web/20001024112939/www.sis.pitt.edu/~nhprc/) provides information on the research project which brought this issue forward strongly in archival discourse.

[39] Michel Foucault, 'Of Other Spaces', *Diacritics*, 16, no. 1, 1986, pp. 22-27, is discussed in ways that archivists should be able to relate to by Edward De Soja in his 'Heterotopologies: A Remembrance of Other Spaces in the Citadel-LA, in *Postmodern Cities and Spaces*, ed. by Sophie Watson & Katherine Gibson, Cambridge, Blackwell, 1995. Bernadine Dodge mentions the concept in 'Places Apart: Archives in Dissolving Space and Time, *Archivaria*, 44, 1997, pp. 118-131, one of the few articles in archival literature to tackle head on themes of space and time.

Archives as a plurality, as a network that connects points and intersects with its own skein of the type that chapter 7 of this book points to, at this moment still seems to be where the future of an archivist's activity theories can be found, pursuing the relationship between recordkeeping and accountability in any era and space.

Readings

- Terry Cook, 'What is Past is Prologue: A History of Archival Ideas since 1898, and the Future Paradigm Shift', *Archivaria*, 43, 1997, pp. 17-63.

- Luciana Duranti, 'Archival Science', in *The Encyclopedia of Library and Information Science*, 59, 1997, pp. 1-19.

  Read what the authors really wrote. Duranti's article is a classic example of masterly encyclopaedic condensation and Cook discusses many shifts in thinking which have not been discussed in Chapter 8.

- Anne J. Gilliland-Swetland, *Enduring Paradigm, New Opportunities: The Value of the Archival Perspective in the Digital Environment*, Washington DC, Council on Library and Information Resources, 2000.

  Another comprehensive cornucopia of ideas, with particular emphasis upon electronic communications and product.

- Sue McKemmish, 'Yesterday, Today and Tomorrow, A Continuum of Responsibilities,' in P.J Horsman, F.C.J Ketelaar and T.H.P.M. Thomassen, eds, *Naar een Nieuw Paradigma in de Archivistiek,* 's-Gravenhage, Stichting Archiefpublicaties, 1999.

  An introduction to the Australian records continuum approach to archival theory and practice.

CHAPTER 9

Recordkeeping and accountability

Chris Hurley

We should have lost memory as well as voice, had it been as easy to forget as to keep silence.[1]

Since 1999, each issue of *Archives and Manuscripts*, the journal of the Australian Society of Archivists, has proclaimed that it is the archivist's mission to 'ensure that records which have value as authentic evidence ... are made, kept and used'. The statement goes on to assert that the work of archivists 'is vital [inter alia] for ensuring organizational efficiency and accountability'. Clearly, it is the intention of this journal's editors, and of the profession whose voice it is, to state that a connection of some kind exists between recordkeeping and accountability. As Tacitus reminds us, however, mere memory is not the same as action (giving voice). There is all the difference in the world between having a recorded memory and doing something about it.

Nevertheless, the nexus is apparent, not only to recordkeepers:

> When we campaign for greater access to information we must at the same time campaign for improved records management. There seems little point in having access to information that is chaotic and unreliable. Clearly there needs to be systematic, complete and dependable record keeping ... Old records may be so chaotic as to render rights of access highly time consuming, if not wholly fruitless. Indeed, in Mexico, where a freedom of information law was enacted in April 2002, a report stated that 'public records, transcripts and notes from important meetings have been purposefully kept from public view, leaving almost no official record of how key decisions have been made. In many cases, official records have been destroyed or taken home by officials when they left office' ... [Therefore] a clear duty must be imposed on the providers that information be complete, coherent and understandable by its target audience.[2]

---

[1] Publius Cornelius Tacitus, *The Life of Cnaeus Julius Agricola*, ii.
[2] Jeremy Pope, 'Access to Information: Whose Right and Whose Information?', in *Transparency International: Global Corruption Report 2003 – Special Focus: Access to Information*, edited by Robin Hodess, London, Profile Books, 2003, p. 19.

Recordkeepers and accountability advocates seem to agree that, in support of accountability, good systematic records must exist and they must be complete, they must be authentic and reliable (dependable), they must be accessible and usable (coherent and understandable).

Effective recordkeeping cannot *per se* ensure accountability. At best, full and accurate records provide an accountability tool, which can be used by those with the power and will to do so. Good records can assist them in their task by preserving memory, but, if the watchdogs keep silence, or are terrified or seduced into it, memory alone cannot achieve results. The most that can be fairly claimed, therefore, is that effective recordkeeping is a necessary, but not a sufficient, condition for accountability.

In a book dealing with the exposure of corruption in Australia,[3] Robert Pullan hardly refers to the role of records and recordkeeping at all. Instead, he concentrates on the widely acknowledged role of an independent and capable media and examines the threat to accountability posed by the undermining of the media by forces of wealth and influence. Another commentator, himself a journalist of note, has drawn attention to the significance of documentation when holding people and institutions to account:

> not even the NSW Defamation Act ... can fully protect the corrupt when public servants drop documents over the transom to a trustworthy and capable reporter. That steady ululation you hear in the newsroom is of reporters wailing into telephones: 'That's all very well, but where are the doccoes?' [4]

Documentation has ever been a powerful tool in the hands of capable journalists when holding institutions to account.

In another recent book, Warwick Funnell, Professor of Accounting at the University of Wollongong, examines the role of watchdogs, particularly auditors, in support of accountability and the emerging threats to their effectiveness. Funnell has no doubts about the nexus between authentic, reliable and accessible documentation and accountability:

> The quality of independence is especially important when governments display a concerted reluctance to provide information which would allow their actions to be opened to public debate. Having to rely upon government-sponsored avenues for answers would contribute little to public confidence. The actions of elected representatives continue to deepen public cynicism and confirm their beliefs about political selfishness and government preparedness to delay, avoid and suppress damaging information, regardless of the cost to individuals. Whistleblowers, whose importance is inversely proportional to the openness of government, attract special treatment from governments despite legislation which exists to protect publicly motivated individuals who find themselves unable to tolerate government deception.

---

[3] Robert Pullan, *Guilty Secrets*, Glebe, NSW, Pascal Press, 1994.
[4] William De Maria, *Deadly Disclosures*, Kent Town, SA, Wakefield Press, 1999, p.xi (foreword by Evan Whitton). The term 'doccoes' is an Australian diminutive for documents.

... Information ... is the life-blood of a healthy democracy. In partnership with a free, popular press, it ensures control over the inevitable arrogance to which governments are susceptible, and which is a threat to the freedoms of citizens, by forcing them to be accountable for their constitutional powers. Accountability in this sense, therefore, is not limited to the narrow financial reckonings of the economist and the accountant. Rather, it is imbued with the elemental values upon which the very existence of a liberal democracy and civil society depend and from which political arrangements derive their meaning. Institutions of accountability create the circumstances in which transcendent social values can take hold and be nurtured ... Almost without exception, the value of each of these institutions of accountability depends upon the quality of independence from the government which it enjoys.[5]

This chapter will not attempt to remake the case for a nexus between poor recordkeeping and lack of accountability. That case is already amply documented in Australia and elsewhere, in official reports such as the 'WA Inc.' Royal Commission[6] into corrupt practices in the commercial dealings of the Western Australian government in the 1980s, and in numerous books, articles, and addresses which have appeared over the last decade.[7] Instead, this chapter will provide an analysis of the different roles and functions of recordkeeping in relation to accountability and evaluate, in relation to recordkeeping as a distinct professional discipline, the worthiness of that profession to carry out those roles and functions.

The Auditor-General of the Commonwealth of Australia once noted in relation to an accountability crisis that:

poor recordkeeping attracts corruption like flies to a carcass ...[8]

Wherever corruption and a failure of accountability are found, an associated failure in recordkeeping practices is, almost invariably, identified as part of the cause. These

---

[5] Warwick Funnell, *Government by Fiat*, Sydney, University of New South Wales Press, 2001, pp. 155-156.

[6] See Bob Sharman, 'The Hollow Crown', *Archives and Manuscripts*, 21, no. 2, November 1993, pp. 196-207, for an analysis of some of the recordkeeping aspects of WA Inc.

[7] For extended treatment by a number of different authors, see Sue McKemmish and Frank Upward, eds, *Archival Documents*, Melbourne, Ancora Press, 1993, and Richard J. Cox and David A. Wallace, eds, *Archives and the Public Good*, Westport, Ct, Quorum Books, 2002. For analysis of ways in which recordkeeping supports accountability, see Livia Iacovino, 'Reflections on Eastwood's Concept of Democratic Accountability and Continuity', *Archives and Manuscripts*, 21, no. 1, May 1993, pp. 30-47. See also Sue McKemmish, 'The Smoking Gun: Recordkeeping and Accountability' at http:// www.sims.monash.edu.au/research/rcrg; Sue McKemmish and Glenda Acland, 'Archivists at Risk: Accountability and the Role of the Professional Society' at http://rcrg.dstc.edu.au/publications/archive1.html.

[8] Sue McKemmish, 'The Smoking Gun', op. cit. He referred to the 'Sports Rorts Affair', involving the use of a whiteboard to keep the only records of a ministerial decision-making process allocating grants to sporting clubs – and their subsequent erasure. When allegations were raised that allocations had been made disproportionately for political advantage, there was no documentation left to review.

conclusions are generally based on somewhat vague, though seldom challenged, ideas about what constitutes good recordkeeping practice. Very often the conclusions rest on little more than observed deviance from 'what used to happen'. While it is gratifying to have the significance of recordkeeping to accountability endorsed in this way, this chapter will question whether recordkeepers are tempting fate by not having more robust, principled and enduring standards to offer when such issues arise.

It must be understood that this subject involves two kinds of accountability. First, there is the accountability of all persons and entities towards other persons and entities in their dealings with each other. This is the common or generic kind of accountability to which good recordkeeping is an important adjunct for the reasons already stated. Then there is the responsibility for ensuring that good records are made and kept. The first accountability is for honest, responsible, upright and transparent conduct of human affairs, and the second is a precise responsibility for making and keeping records which serve the first accountability by providing good, reliable, usable records.

Connections between accountability and recordkeeping are theoretical and principled as well as being pragmatic and contingent. What this means is that the foundations of recordkeeping (itself conducted accountably), which support accountability must encompass high-sounding precepts about what good recordkeeping is as well as reliable measures of performance. No amount of articulating and theorizing about recordkeeping principles will ensure accountable behaviour. As one author on accountability notes, citing the author, C. S. Lewis, with approval:

> I'd sooner live amongst people who don't cheat at cards than among people who are earnest about not cheating at cards.[9]

On the other hand, a focus that is too narrowly upon correct methodologies and techniques and excludes any consideration of the moral principles, which alone can illuminate the purposes for which correct recordkeeping is undertaken, would make it impossible to differentiate between good and bad recordkeeping in any meaningful way. An over-reliance on principle can lead to the kind of inappropriate response which has followed the financial, ethical and other systemic meltdowns of the 1980s and 1990s in Australia, one which makes a beguiling trap for recordkeepers to fall into if they are not careful:

> If we are service providers we write reassuring mission statements that provide to our clients paper guarantees that we are all about best practice, which includes moral behaviour. Or we rush codes of conduct ('cut-out catechisms' according to one commentator) into print ... Codes are being written for politicians and public servants. All manner of service providers, from hospitals to McDonalds, are hawking mission statements and conduct standards to assure clients and customers that best practice reigns ... Finally we have the start now of governments offering ethical guarantees on their policy making.

---

[9] De Maria, op. cit., p. 234.

It seems that when we are not devising these high-sounding feel-good codes of conduct, we are enshrining 'ethical obligations' in law (e.g. the *Queensland Public Sector Ethics Act*), or paying enormous salaries to our official guardians of ethical conduct. ... Genuine community concerns about official wrongdoing have been met by a cavalcade of remedies that appear big on form and small on substance. In the projection of reassurance to a community badly hurt by wrongdoing, you may detect a compulsion to look good rather than to act right.[10]

It is possible, however, for standards of good recordkeeping behaviour to be too pragmatic, so devoid of ethical content as to become mechanical and without direction. Compliance standards must be predictive, testable, and enforceable by reference to the particular performance measures. Above all, they must be uniformly enforced. They must, in fact, be auditable to ensure that they produce results (outcomes) as well as being merely implemented. Recent recordkeeping audits in the Federal and New South Wales governments have laid some weight on agency compliance with methodologies (i.e. DIRKS[11]) and there is no harm in that up to a point, but such outcomes still beg the question: 'Yes, but is their recordkeeping any good?' An answer to that question will not be found by merely testing compliance with a methodology or technique. It can only be found in the ethical purposes for which good recordkeeping is required.

Methodologies and techniques are necessary for good recordkeeping, but they are not sufficient. Process is no substitute for intelligence. The test of whether the recordkeeping is good depends not simply on compliance alone, but also on the ethical purposes for which good records must be kept. Without that, we can know that records are being kept systematically, but not whether they are fit for the purposes for which they are needed. Qualities of completeness, authenticity, and usability must be referenced to the reasons why good records are needed. Only then can the work of the recordkeeper in the role of agent of accountability be tested empirically to determine whether or not they are doing a good job.

Accountability of whom, for what, to whom?

Albert Meijer, a researcher at the Centre for Public Management at Erasmus University, Rotterdam, investigated the consequences of the use of information and communication technologies for political and legal accountability.[12] He identified six elements involved in any accountability situation and four types of accountability, providing a matrix for analyzing the related recordkeeping issues in greater depth than will be possible here. Using his analysis, it is possible to be more explicit about the various ways in which the nexus

---

[10] William De Maria, p. 235.

[11] DIRKS is a step-by-step technique for implementing compliant recordkeeping systems used in the national and New South Wales government sectors (see http://www.records.nsw.gov.au/). The larger purposes served by DIRKS methodology may be found in related recordkeeping frameworks issued by, for example, the New South Wales State Records Authority.

[12] Albert Meijer, 'Anticipating Accountability Processes', *Archives and Manuscripts*, 28, no. 1, 2000, pp. 52-63.

between recordkeeping and accountability can be understood. It is clear, for example, that a distinction should be drawn between recordkeeping as an integral part of any accountability process, regardless of who is accountable and what they are accountable for, and accountability for recordkeeping itself.

The six elements Meijer identifies are:

- an event that triggers the accountability process;
- someone who is accountable;
- an action or situation for which someone is accountable;
- a 'forum' in which someone is accountable;[13]
- criteria by which action can be judged; and
- sanctions which can be imposed.

Meijer identifies the basic nexus between recordkeeping and accountability as follows:

> before the forum can discuss or sanction … it needs to reconstruct what has happened. Information is needed to reduce uncertainties. If sufficient information is available, an accountability forum can make a reconstruction of what happened.[14]

In any situation, who is accountable, what they are accountable for, who they are accountable to, and the criteria by which performance is to be judged must be clearly documented in advance. Records will be especially relevant in documenting the event that triggers an accountability process, and the action or situation under review. This documentation involves a special kind of nexus between recordkeeping and accountability – an accountability not only for the action or situation itself, but a separate accountability for keeping records of such actions and situations. False, misleading, or missing records of any event or situation will hamper the accountability process. So it is not enough to make someone accountable for something and to hold them accountable; someone must also be accountable for keeping adequate records so that the 'forum' can undertake the review and reconstruction which is a necessary ingredient in any accountability process.

In government legislation, this special recordkeeping accountability can take the form of a generic obligation to 'make and keep full and accurate records' or a specific obligation to keep records of accountable actions (e.g. financial records under financial regulations). Meijer discusses an accountability typology identified by Romzek and Dubnick, set out below. Within each of the four types of accountability, Meijer identifies methods which result in higher or lower levels of control or regulation:

---

[13] Accountability forum is defined as the institution which holds organizations accountable by requiring information to reduce uncertainties about the situation which is the object of the accountability process. This equates with significant elements of the role of agent of accountability discussed below.

[14] Meijer, op. cit., p. 54. See also B.S. Romzek and M.J. Dubnick, 'Accountability in the Public Sector: Lessons from the Challenger Tragedy', *Public Administration Review,* 47, May/June 1987.

Type		Examples	Degree of Control
Internal	bureaucratic	• budgetary control • reporting	high
	professional	• peer review • advisory board	low
External	legal	• prosecution • appeal and review	high
	political	• name, blame, shame	low

Figure 9.1. A typology of accountability.

These four types of accountability should be read in conjunction with the accountability triangle illustrated in Figure 9.2. Meijer's analysis assumes that these forms of regulation are fixed in an internal/external matrix. Using the accountability triangle, it is possible to see that the forms of control he analyzes could be viewed differently depending on the role and function being carried out. The degree of control could be altered accordingly.

An example can be found in peer review, or benchmarking, which Meijer concludes gives a low degree of control because it is 'internal'. Professional benchmarking can become 'external', however, when it takes the form of professional standards or codes of ethics which are binding (or, at least, powerfully influential). The examples usually given are doctors and lawyers, but those models are of limited utility when examining the work of recordkeepers. The archetype of the medical or legal professional is a self-employed and, therefore, autonomous entity, whereas most recordkeepers are employees.[15]

A less problematic parallel can be made with engineers, who frequently operate as employees or contractors. They have clear professional codes instructing them in duties which transcend the terms of their employment.[16] It is because engineers subscribe to professional obligations which override contractual or employment obligations in certain instances that they can be said to have autonomy, in the same way that lawyers and doctors are traditionally said to have it. This kind of autonomy is one of the hallmarks of professional status. If recordkeeping is held to be a profession, it follows that it too must have a basis upon which conflicts between professional duty and employment obligations are resolved, without the former always yielding to the latter.

The need for some kind of professional benchmarking is most obvious in, though not confined to, situations where the records support rights, entitlements or accountabilities which Meijer would regard as 'external' to the entity within which the recordkeeper is employed. The need to ensure that police recordkeeping is up to standard to protect the

---

[15] Increasingly, doctors and lawyers too are employees, but the analysis of their professional obligations continues to be made on the increasingly shaky assumption that they are all self-employed.

[16] An engineer obtaining knowledge of structural flaws which might endanger life is under a professional duty to make this known and to ensure that action is taken regardless of any contrary contractual or employment obligations.

rights of both victims and the accused, and in support of justice, is routinely demonstrated. A less obvious example arises when recordkeeping responsibilities and accountability do not lie within the same entity. Records pertaining to someone's accountabilities can be kept by a third party either through monitoring – a log kept by air traffic controllers of an aircraft's movements, for example – or incidentally – meteorological records which excuse a failure in performance owing to inclement weather, for example.

Special consideration needs to be given to the accountability of archivists who have control or regulation over the making, keeping, and disposal of records by others. In this capacity, the recordkeeper acts outside the accountability triangle – as an agent of accountability (similar to a court, an auditor or an ombudsman). This is not the recordkeeper's only accountability, but it is one which often focuses attention on untoward or unsatisfactory professional behaviour on their part. Later in this chapter, it will be argued that archivists in Australia and elsewhere who regulate disposal are almost wholly unaccountable, in any meaningful way, for their administration of appraisal because:

- there is no 'forum' within which they are accountable for appraisal;
- there are no criteria worth speaking of by which their actions can be judged; and
- their own articulations of their responsibilities for appraisal fail to get the balance right between the moral purpose of appraisal and its method of execution.

In this regard it is important to remember, following the pioneering work of Helen Samuels and others, that appraisal is about what records are made in the first place, not just those which are kept and destroyed. A good illustration of the connection between this technical insight and the needs of accountability may be found in a recent work analyzing the Children Overboard controversy in Australia.[17] The author, discussing how accountability became so confused in the subsequent investigation of the events by a Senate Committee that clear responsibility could often not be assigned, comments:

> Mike Scrafton, senior adviser (Defence) ... played a significant role ... Scrafton had been told by Defence public affairs on 10 October that the photographs were of the wrong event, and by Ritchie that there were doubts about whether any children had gone overboard at all.

> Scrafton understood the value of ensuring that a level of ambiguity was retained. When the secretary of the department, Dr Allan Hawke, realised that the published photographs were of the wrong occasion, he instructed that the minister be informed in writing of the problem. The head of Defence public affairs spoke to Scrafton and, instead of providing a formal minute, merely emailed further copies of the photos. In effect, she obeyed the adviser in preference to her departmental secretary. Hawke was informed but did not follow it up. It was still possible for the minister's office to say it had not been advised formally of the error. Advisers could act in protective

---

[17] See Sue McKemmish's summary of this event in chapter 1.

mode; they could determine what advice they wanted and, more significantly, what advice they did not want.[18]

And further on:

The original story was passed by phone from ship to taskforce to ministers. The only written advice was the sentence in the report sent to the prime minister and others on the evening of 7 October. Yet bureaucracy is renowned for being smothered in red tape, overwhelmed by paper. Not this time, clearly. Indeed, so little was committed to paper that it should be a cause for concern.

The taskforce was established after a corridor conversation between Moore-Wilton and Farmer. There were no terms of reference, and a fluid agenda and membership. Asked if a lack of a 'paper trail' was worrying, Farmer responded:

For me, no. I am concerned with effectiveness and with outcomes. That means I am concerned about paper trails where there is a quite appropriate requirement for a paper trail in an audit or other sense, but successive governments have made it clear that they want a public service that is able to be flexible and get the job done. That, for me, does not mean producing huge mounds of paper ...

Not for the modern official the leisurely opportunity to write a note for file recording a conversation with colleagues or ministers and acting as a record if something later became controversial. All that was available were the phone notes of participants, often shorthand scribbles intended as an aide-memoire for the person taking the call rather than as material for the public record ... Adding to the paucity of written information is a concern about which documents are public and therefore 'discoverable' under freedom of information legislation. Combined with email, yellow stickers, and message banks, the changing culture is producing a new style of record keeping ... Historians in the future will have loads of material but – if this case is a typical example – little that tells us how the significant decisions were made.[19]

It is sometimes asserted that accountability is an issue only for governments. Government archivists, it is argued, have the statutory mandate to regulate the activities of official agencies, but no such statutory control operates to oblige private sector or individual enterprises to comply with obligations involving a statutory recordkeeping authority or to submit to that authority.

It is true that government agencies are sometimes governed by a statutory scheme in which another agency (the recordkeeping authority) is given some power to regulate their recordkeeping actions generally and that we will look in vain for a similar situation applying in the private sector, i.e. some authority external to a non-government

---

[18] Patrick Weller, *Don't Tell the Prime Minister*, Melbourne, Scribe Publications, 2002, pp. 75-76.
[19] Ibid., pp. 87-89.

organization with statutory power over its recordkeeping activities. It is sometimes said, also, that recordkeeping in the public sector is governed by statutory regulation whereas the private sector is self-regulating. This distinction is virtually meaningless when analyzing the role of recordkeeping and accountability. Regardless of whether the mandate for recordkeeping is found in statute, in an edict, or in custom, there is no essential difference between the public and private sectors. The origin of the mandate may matter in terms of its effectiveness, but a mandate, whatever its form, lies at the basis of any recordkeeping activity.

The distinction between external regulation and self-regulation in this context is, therefore, false. It is based on a perception that government is only ever an aggregation of discrete entities, never an integrated whole. The correct analogy, for this discussion, is between government (regarded as a single enterprise) and a corporation (also a single enterprise). Both these enterprises are self-regulating. Governments regulate themselves by means of legislation because that is their wont. Private corporations regulate themselves by edicts (policies, instructions, and procedures) emanating ultimately from the board or other governing authority. One of the things that distinguishes recordkeeping legislation is that, unlike most statutes, it does not apply, in the generality of its provisions, to society at large. Instead, archives laws belong to that relatively small group of statutes by which governments regulate their own behaviour and operate to govern the activities of official agencies only – not the activities of society at large. This small group of statutes regulating the activities of government itself includes statutes for the auditing and maintenance of public accounts, laws establishing ombudsmen, anti-corruption laws, and freedom of information laws.

The role of a recordkeeper in a private sector corporation, operating under a mandate issued from the board, is exactly analogous to that of a government recordkeeping authority operating under statute. The range of recordkeeping roles analyzed below could be carried out equally well by a government recordkeeping authority or a private sector recordkeeper – provided an appropriate mandate was given, in whatever form, and the authority thus conferred was upheld when challenged.

The accountability in question therefore is that of the enterprise itself, which confers a mandate on the recordkeeper to act. It may be a government empowering a recordkeeping authority to act under statute, or it may be a private corporation enabling a records management business unit to operate under a decision of the board or an instruction from the general manager. In that sense, all recordkeeping activity in support of accountability is an act of self-regulation. Governments can choose not to make themselves accountable by having weak recordkeeping laws or none at all. Similarly, private sector organizations can choose not to make themselves accountable by neglecting recordkeeping or failing to support it.

If anything, contrary to the commonly held view, it is the private sector, rather than sovereign governments, which is more susceptible to external regulation – recordkeeping requirements imposed as a condition of incorporation upon public companies, for example, are more onerous than requirements placed on public sector corporations.[20] Where statutes bear upon the illegality of certain recordkeeping malpractices, such as the prohibition in the Crimes Act of the destruction of evidence, they operate equally on both public and private sector entities.[21]

In the simplest form of accountability, governments, organizations and individuals are accountable for their own actions or for situations which they have brought about or failed to prevent. A steward or reeve must render account to his master for the conduct of affairs with which he has been entrusted. This rendering, or reporting, involves telling what happened and why. Such tales are more reliable when based on documentary evidence. It is worth noting that, in these simple, binary relationships, a reliable record can be of equal advantage to both parties – master and servant can both find protection by appealing to a reliable record to prove what actually happened.

It does not follow that records will be used ethically or fairly in such situations. Leaving aside obvious malfeasance resulting from the misuse of falsified records to obtain an advantage, it is clear that records kept in support of accountability have historically been seen to be instruments of oppression as much as guarantees of fairness and equity. Good recordkeeping was the basis of Morton's Fork[22] – a byword for procedural unfairness. Amongst the first objects of popular fury in the French Revolution were the estate rolls and other evidence upholding what were perceived to be unfair obligations and taxes under the 'feudal' regime that was being overthrown. The Nazis, like oppressive regimes everywhere, tended to be good recordkeepers because they appreciated how information can be used to ensure that oppressed citizens remain accountable to the totalitarian requirements of their regime.

In this simple binary sense, records are linked to accountability as supports for obligations between two parties – either as master and servant or as two equal contracting parties. This is almost synonymous with the concept of records as 'evidential'. Records embody a statement of obligations subsisting between two parties and provide a history of the satisfaction of those obligations. In this broad sense, records support all human interaction other than the exercise of brute force, plundering, and slavery.[23]

In this chapter, a more complex model will be used, involving a three-way set of relationships. This will make it possible to discuss the roles and responsibilities of

---

[20] Public sector corporations differ in that they are more often subject to freedom of information and privacy type statutes.

[21] Chris Hurley, 'Recordkeeping, Document Destruction, and the Law (Heiner, Enron and McCabe)', *Archives and Manuscripts*, 30, no. 2, 2002, pp. 6-25.

[22] Cardinal Morton was Chancellor to Henry VII in England at the end of the fifteenth century. He squeezed money out of people by consulting tax records. If they had paid a lot, he would say that they were very rich and could afford to pay more. If they had paid only a little, he said they were holding back and could afford to pay more.

[23] Even slavery and bondage, however, have involved paperwork. Indentures were contractual and documented. The papers testifying to an ex-slave's freedom were highly prized. But most of this paperwork dealt with the obligations and entitlements of slave-owners, rather than of slaves.

recordkeepers without specifying whether they are 'internal' or 'external' (as defined by Meijer). Put simply, in every situation of any complexity in which accountable actions involve responsible recordkeeping, it is usually possible to identify three separate players. This is the accountability triangle.

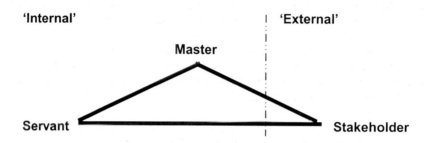

Figure 9.2. The accountability triangle.

Any person or entity involved in an accountability relationship can stand at different points in the triangle, depending on their role and function. Let us take the example of a retail trading company. The company (master) has an accountability relationship with its employees (servants). As with all such relationships, the obligations/benefits can be, and usually are, mutual. Employees have obligations to keep full and accurate records of sales, ordering, stock, accounts, and payments. The company benefits from this because it provides the basis for a successful and profitable business. The company has obligations to keep good records of attendance, salary payments, leave entitlements, and health and safety compliance. Employees benefit from this because it provides the basis for rewards and safe working environment.

External stakeholders, who might be customers, regulators, Government, other companies, unions, or industry groups, can also have relationships built on accountable recordkeeping with both the company and its employees. Another company (a wholesale supplier, for example) will keep records of supply, delivery, invoicing, and receipt of payment with the retail trading company, which will keep corresponding records of orders, receipt, and payment. These records document and make possible contractual dealings between the two entities – to their mutual benefit. While the contract for supply may take place company to company, most of the other 'routine' documentation will be managed using recordkeeping systems established by the company for employees (servants) to use.

The employer obviously has an interest in ensuring that employees faithfully carry out these documentation systems because they provide the documentation the company needs to protect its business. At the base of the triangle, however, the employee (servant) also has a self-interested motive for ensuring that good records are kept. Signing the suppliers delivery docket and making sure a copy is kept for the retail trading company benefits the supplier, by providing evidence of delivery, and the employee, by providing evidence of receipt limiting the employee's personal liability to an action he has actually signed off on.

One can envisage another situation, however, where the triangle can be used to change the roles of those involved. At its simplest, a publicly listed company is the servant of a board of directors operating on behalf of the shareholders (stakeholders).

In relation to the pay-as-you-earn tax system, the Government (master) requires companies (servants) to deduct tax as salaries are paid. In this situation, the employee, who has no choice in the matter, is a stakeholder. A set of mutual obligations and benefits bind the Government and employers in a shared interest in good recordkeeping. The employee (stakeholder) has a similar relationship with both parties: supplying information to the employer which might vary the tax rate and ensure the employer is deducting the correct amount, and completing tax returns to ensure that the employee receives any refund due and is not placed in jeopardy from unpaid tax.

In a government environment, the 'master' may be the Crown or Executive, accountable, in a democracy, to the voters or taxpayers (stakeholders). Records are important in holding governments to account (e.g. through Parliamentary inquiries or in audit reports) and in holding citizens to account (e.g. financial records maintained for tax purposes). Modern governments however take a protean form, and it is necessary to identify the bureaucracy (servants) as playing a separate role. Records of the relationship between the government and bureaucracy serve to make bureaucrats accountable to the executive and to sheet home policy responsibility where it belongs. Many of the accountability failures of recent times have come from the blurring of the roles of executive and bureaucracy and the attendant confused records which result.[24] Similarly, records sustain accountable relations between the bureaucracy and the public, protecting the public from the officiousness of bureaucracy and enabling government to oversee the work of their officials.

Even within government, a whole range of relevant ideas can be grouped around these three roles. The responsibility of governments and bureaucrats, for example, may be to individual citizens (in relation to their personal rights and entitlements, or obligations), or to a larger concept of the public interest or social obligations. Similarly, it is possible for governments to 'externalize' agents of accountability by establishing them with a degree of constitutional independence from the ordinary control that executives have over the bureaucracy. Thus, auditors, ombudsmen, the judiciary, and, occasionally, archives authorities may be externalized by giving them an independent (external) role in recordkeeping accountability within government.[25] Similarly, it is argued, governments have sought to divest themselves

---

[24] Funnell, op. cit. makes the point at p. 22: 'Instead of being the final link in the chain of accountability, governments insert themselves lower in the line, insisting that they are only another stakeholder in service delivery, not the ultimate agent who should be held accountable, and certainly not responsible. Governments may possess the means of dealing with crises in service delivery, but they want to be held accountable not for the crisis itself; they accept responsibility only for their preparedness to take action'.

[25] See the discussion below on the significance of 'autonomy' for recordkeepers undertaking the role of agent of accountability.

of responsibility by outsourcing accountability for services. It is said that you can tell that an Australian Government is really in trouble and unable to solve a problem when it sets up an independent Royal Commission.

Confusion and uncertainty over accountability results when it is viewed solely through the lens of a binary relationship:

> My argument is that current doctrines or guidelines on public management are dangerously confused over the two concepts of 'effectiveness' and 'accountability' as they relate to practices of policy and program management. These two key concepts have a close practical bearing, in that program managers must now, under the rhetoric of the new management regime, account for their results and justify their program's 'effectiveness impact' ... [But] to whom or what is the newly unchained program manager accountable? A fear now dawning is that the deregulated and devolved administrative environment is shaping up as 'an accountability trap' which, despite its best intentions to encourage managers to take risks and be responsible for their operations and be rewarded for good performance, will leave officials open and vulnerable to unpredictable demands and inquiries from administrative review bodies – such as the ombudsman, the Administrative Appeals Tribunal, the auditor-general and of course parliament and its committees – each with different standards of legitimate public risk. These two areas of uncertainty and fear converge, and are two of the main roads leading to that noisy roundabout where so many officials and commentators get lost or come unstuck – the performance indicator junction. The use of 'junction' is appropriate, because 'performance' reflects the theme of effectiveness and of measuring results, while 'indicator' reflects the theme of accountability and of justifying results in some shared policy language or commonly respected framework.[26]

Only when the program manager understands that there are two or more sets of requirements can such conflicts be resolved.

In the private sector, stakeholders can be thought of as shareholders or as the public interest, or both. Internally, the distinction between the board and the officers of the company can be easily fitted into the model.

Viewing recordkeeping accountability through the prism of the triangle helps to tease out the respective roles in which an actor can be found in relation to the obligations and benefits of accountability relationships. These relationships subsist between the parties to transactions (or parties involved in any documented situation). In any such relationship, it is possible for some agent of accountability to be involved. The agent of accountability – the 'accountability forum' in Meijer's phrase – stands outside the triangle in a monitoring or

---

[26] John Uhr, 'Corporate Management and Accountability: From Effectiveness to Leadership', in *Corporate Management in Australian Government*, edited by Glyn Davis, Patrick Weller and Colleen Lewis, Melbourne, Macmillan Education Australia, 1989, pp. 155-156. A similar theme is explored by Iacovino, op. cit.

enforcing role. Agents of accountability are auditors, ombudsmen, and the courts. From time to time, it is proposed that recordkeepers operate, or should operate, as agents of accountability. To explore this proposition it is necessary to consider two questions: what is involved, and are recordkeepers capable of carrying out what is involved?

Recordkeepers as agents of accountability: What is their role?

Accountable recordkeeping must be implemented and undertaken. Set out below is a range of roles which logically can be undertaken in relation to accountability, beyond simply implementing good recordkeeping requirements. In order to be complied with, the requirements must be specified. To be satisfied that they are being complied with, performance must be monitored. To ensure that they are met, requirements must be enforced. The tasks of specifying, monitoring, and enforcing constitute a recordkeeping role and function different from that of implementation. It is time to look at the role of the recordkeeper as an agent of accountability – that is, not merely as an implementer of good practice, but as someone who is responsible for ensuring that good practice is carried out.

While it is possible, and indeed necessary, to separate these roles out for the purposes of discussion, it does not follow that a single authority cannot carry out more than one role. In what follows it will be argued, however, that some roles cannot – or, at least, should not – be carried out simultaneously by the same authority.

It is important that the roles being undertaken are clearly articulated and assigned. Otherwise, it is all too easy, when a difficult case arises, for action to be replaced by speculation over what is the proper role to be undertaken. The agent of accountability can be tempted to escape the consequences of having to deal with a difficult case, or to respond to pressure, by gliding imperceptibly from the role of watchdog into the role of mentor. It can be claimed afterwards that the role was upheld, whereas in fact, one role was abandoned in favour of another in a confused fog over which role, if any, had actually been assigned in the first place. Unless the role is clearly articulated and assigned in advance, this form of conduct lapses speedily into double standards – adopting one role now and a different role later, depending on the difficulty of each case, the power and position of those we are dealing with, or the amount of pressure that is brought to bear.

Ordainer

In this function, the recordkeeper acts in a quasi-legislative role. There is a mandate to issue edicts or binding instructions, which may take the form of regulations or procedural requirements. The person or agency instructed is bound in some way to comply and the logic of the position is that non-compliance is punishable in some way, but monitoring, detection and punishment are not logically roles of the ordainer. Instructions may have general application to all without exception, they may be variable in the ordainer's discretion, or they may be issued to only one person or agency, pertaining either to continuing behaviour or to a particular instance. This role may take the form of a power to forbid, thereby preventing or imposing a veto on action rather than initiating it – the power to approve disposal is an example of the exercise of this role to forbid, rather than prescribe, action.

Preceptor

In this role, the recordkeeper acts a standard-setter. The ordainer intervenes to change things, whereas the preceptor says what needs to be done if things are to change. The preceptor is not, however, the authoritative source of action. The precept may be a standard, allowing for a variety of implementation strategies to achieve a stated objective, or a statement of procedure or method, an inflexible process to be adhered to. It is someone else's business whether or not the standards are actually applied, or even approved. The preceptor is a repository of professional wisdom and experience, which is articulated in an authoritative but non-prescriptive form for others to do with as they please or think best. It should be possible to predict without ambiguity what behaviour will satisfy the requirements of the standard.

Mentor

In this role, the recordkeeper is a source of advice, education, instruction, or recommendations. The recipient of the mentor's attention can take it or leave it. The mentor oversees the activities of another but does not act to assist with implementation of advice or recommendations given. It involves peer review rather than consultancy. The mentor does not specify a standard of behaviour or a benchmark to be achieved. The mentor's role is to offer professional guidance in achieving an outcome defined by the recipient of the mentor's attention. The driver for the one being mentored may well be the need to conform to some standard or requirement, but the mentor is not mandated to ensure that the standard is met, nor is the mentor responsible for articulating the standard. What is offered is professional advice on how the ones being mentored may achieve what they want, for whatever reason, to do.

Facilitator

In this role, the recordkeeper intervenes to assist as a co-participant in the implementation of requirements, advice or recommendations, whether received from the recordkeeper or not. The decision whether to act and how to act remains with the 'client' but the recordkeeper is here a participant in whatever course of action is decided upon. It is immaterial whether or not that course of action is undertaken upon compulsion. The facilitator's mandate is to support, but not to carry out, the client's decision on how to act and provide expert assistance, including tools or infrastructure, in achieving the desired result.

Provider

As a provider, the recordkeeper supplies professional services, possibly for a fee, and, where appropriate, an assurance that these services meet whatever obligations the client has, under statute, standard, or instruction, or whatever self-imposed objectives the client has. The provider relieves the client of much of the work involved in determining what to do or how to do it, but not the accountability for what is done. The recordkeeper may or may not be a provider of choice. In some cases, utilization of a provider's services may be obligatory (e.g. as when government agencies are obliged to lodge their archives with the government's archives authority). It is necessary to distinguish the acceptance of responsibility (e.g. where an archives is responsible for giving public access) from providing services in support of another's accountability (e.g. where the access conditions are decided not by the archives but by the responsible agency). In other cases (e.g. the provision of commercial secondary storage or records management advice) there may be an unfettered choice of providers. Alternatively, the choice of providers may be limited (e.g. to panels of certified providers).

Enabler

In this role, the recordkeeper does not assume the role of providing services but, instead, the tools or infrastructure which are desirable or necessary to meet recordkeeping obligations or needs. Typical would be the role now developing for providers of whole-of-enterprise metadata frameworks, portals, and interfaces within governments and large corporations. These are often presented as beneficial for purposes of information discovery and service delivery, but they have, or can have, other recordkeeping purposes as well – including the documentation and preservation of evidence.

Monitor

Monitoring involves setting up a reporting system whereby information returns are made concerning the conduct of recordkeeping, usually within a government, jurisdiction or corporation. It is not unlike establishing systems of financial reporting from agencies or business units to the centre. It is the role of the monitor to determine what information should be supplied and to establish procedures for regularly gathering and compiling it. A good monitoring system underpins an effective audit (see below). It is not necessary for the monitor to do anything with the information gathered and maintained; that is the role of watchdogs, enforcers, and auditors.

Watchdog

A watchdog takes action when wrongdoing or a departure from standards/procedures is detected. The watchdog's role may range from prosecution, through reporting of deviant behaviour publicly or to a third party, to issuing an instruction to act, desist or vary activity deemed to deviate from requirements. It is very important that a recordkeeper who adopts, or is entrusted with, a watchdog role diligently and frequently exercises this role; reporting annually, or more frequently, without hesitating to report deviance despite the risk of giving offence is one example of this. If the watchdog holds fire except for the most egregious cases, the stakes are raised immeasurably. The role changes from watchdog to whistleblower and the recordkeeper risks all the abuse, ostracism, adverse pressure, and marginalization which is the lot of those unhappy pariahs. It was Sherlock Holmes who observed the special significance of the dog which did not bark. It is in the recordkeeper's own self-interest, therefore, to be a watchdog frequently and relentlessly or not at all.

Enforcer

An enforcer is a watchdog with teeth. Enforcement involves compulsion – the power to direct the actions of others, or detect them in transgression, and to alter their behaviour by punishment or sanction.

Auditor

An auditor evaluates performance against a pre-determined set of standards or benchmarks and reports the results. You either fail or pass an audit. There should be no room for discussion, though there may be negotiation over the auditors' perceptions of fact and their evaluation of extenuating circumstances. It is fundamental that the audit role must be separate from roles such as ordainer, preceptor, provider, monitor, and enforcer. Recordkeeping success is the product of the effective work of the recordkeeper as much as the compliance of the agency or business unit which is the object of the recordkeeper's attention. The recordkeeper's performance is being audited too. In practice, recordkeepers sometimes act as their own auditors, but conceptually this conflict cannot be resolved.

Role	Key ideas
Ordainer	*Quasi-legislative.* Issue edicts or binding instructions. Compliance. Non-compliance is punishable. Power to allow or forbid (e.g. appraisal).
Preceptor	*Standard-setter.* Not intervening to change things, but saying what must be done for things to change. Articulation of wisdom and experience.
Mentor	*Source of advice, education, or recommendations.* The recipient can take it or leave it. Does not specify a standard or benchmark.

Facilitator	*Assistance.* Participate in whatever course of action is decided upon. Carry out the decision and provide expert assistance on how to do it.
Provider	*Service provider.* Supply services and assurance that these services meet obligations. May or may not be a provider of choice.
Enabler	*Provider of tools/infrastructure.* For example, providers of whole-of-enterprise metadata frameworks, portals, and interfaces.
Monitor	*Reporting system.* Collect information on the conduct of recordkeeping. Similar to financial reporting underpinning effective audit (see below).
Watchdog	*Intervention.* Intervenes when wrongdoing or a departure from standards/procedures is detected. Prosecution, publicity, warning. Routine, not discretionary.
Enforcer	*Watchdog with teeth.* Involves compulsion or inflicting penalties – directing others, detecting transgressions, altering behaviour by punishment/sanction.
Auditor	*Evaluation.* Evaluates performance against pre-determined standards or benchmarks. Reports the results.

Figure 9.3. Roles and responsibilities of recordkeepers.

In Sydney, Australia, while this chapter was being written, it was possible to see municipal employees, wearing a sort of flak jacket emblazoned with the fluorescent words 'Enforcement Services', handing out parking tickets.[27] This is funny because of the comic juxtaposition of the ideas of enforcement and customer service. Some roles and functions just do not belong together. It follows that two or more entities must be involved. Our colleagues in the audit world, for example, tell us that the auditor and the standard-setter must always be different entities, for reasons to do with auditing standards, not recordkeeping standards. Leaving aside the special responsibilities of the auditor, whose task it is to evaluate, and, therefore, to hold accountable, the performance of both the business and the recordkeeper, these roles can, in broad terms be divided into two.

Firstly, the recordkeeper can undertake what may be broadly regarded as servicing roles and functions. These involve acting as preceptor, mentor, facilitator, provider, or enabler. While adherence to standards is relevant, both for the provider and the recipient of services, the recordkeeper does not here act as enforcer. In this role, persuasion and education are key tools. The recordkeeper is typically an advocate for good recordkeeping and a persuader. Results depend on the recordkeeper's success in 'selling' accountable recordkeeping. To be effective, the recordkeeper must be politically astute, flexible, client-

---

[27] Soon after these words were written, their titles changed; they became 'City Rangers'.

focused, and insinuating – able to win and hold the support of those who govern and finance the program.

This may be contrasted with what may be termed regulatory roles and functions. These include acting as monitor, watchdog, ordainer, or enforcer. Adherence to standards or requirements is vital for the recordkeeper and the business. In this role, specification, compulsion, regulation, compliance, punishment, and intimidation are key tools. The recordkeeper plays an authoritative role.[28] Results depend on clarity around what is required and credibility that these requirements will be enforced. To be effective, the recordkeeper must be consistent and effective in applying the rules and the level of compliance must be credible.

If these roles are not separated, recordkeepers, instead of operating systematically and plausibly as agents of accountability, will be seen to operate ineffectively and opportunistically – and may in fact do so. A recordkeeping authority which is unclear about its role, or claims to be responsible for both these aspects of recordkeeping accountability, will be seen to slide from one mode into another, with the result that standards are not upheld consistently or effectively. This can appear, and may well be, an opportunistic way of escaping responsibility for enforcing recordkeeping obligations when it is bureaucratically inconvenient to do so. If the authority tackles an agency about unlawful destruction, confused about whether or not it is an enforcer or a mentor, it may begin by threatening punishment and end by mentoring. That may afford a convenient escape from potential bureaucratic difficulty or the consequences of exposing official wrongdoing, but it is no way to uphold accountability.

It is pointless to engage in debate over whether servicing or enforcing are to be preferred. They are both perfectly acceptable implementation strategies, to be taken up or laid aside as required, depending on the role and function being undertaken. In order for recordkeeping accountability to be upheld, there must be a reasonable degree of certainty as to which of these roles a recordkeeping authority will undertake in any given set of circumstances and a barrier preventing it from opportunistically sliding into some other role when the going gets tough. In government, that may involve divesting our archives authorities, who often prefer insinuation to 'thwaking', of some of the enforcement roles if they are shown to be unreliable in or incapable of carrying them out.

It will certainly involve making recordkeeping authorities themselves accountable for consistently and effectively upholding whichever roles and functions they are mandated to carry out. Recordkeepers cannot be left the freedom to decide for themselves which roles and functions they will carry out from time to time and to pick them up and lay them aside at their own discretion. Part of accountable recordkeeping involves specifying the level of performance expected of the recordkeeper in the roles and functions they are mandated to carry out and to audit their performance against those specifications.

---

[28] An English colleague describes this as 'thwaking'.

Recordkeepers as agents of accountability: Can they be trusted?

One of the consequences of being an agent of accountability is that, occasionally, one has to act like one. The making and keeping of records is accountable when it is undertaken in accordance with the requirements of responsible recordkeeping and the behaviour is observed and evaluated in accordance with those requirements. Just as the implementer of good recordkeeping requirements can be made accountable for good recordkeeping, the agent of accountability can, and should, be made accountable for that role.

In most of the publicized instances of a failure of accountability involving recordkeeping, there is a violation of standards by someone else. The Heiner Case[29] is important because, inter alia, it raises questions surrounding the second level of recordkeeping accountability – the accountability of the recordkeeper in the role and function of agent of accountability. Whereas other cases demonstrate how poor recordkeeping on the part of others underlies a lack of accountability, the Heiner Case demonstrates a failure on the part of the recordkeeping profession itself to behave accountably.

In 1990, the Queensland Government ordered the destruction of the records of an investigation begun, but not yet completed, by retired magistrate, Noel Heiner. It is alleged that this represents a failure of accountability and a violation of good recordkeeping practice. What makes the case unusual in the catalogue of similar failures is that, on this occasion, the consent of the Queensland State Archivist was sought and obtained. If the allegations of failed accountability and poor recordkeeping practice hold, then the actions of the recordkeeper as well as the Queensland Government must be condemned. That being so, the issue is not just whether the Queensland Government was at fault for poor recordkeeping practice, but whether the State Archivist was at fault for not holding the Government to account, thus exhibiting poor practice in the role as agent of accountability. The issues are:

- by what standard or benchmark is the behaviour of a Government Archivist, or any recordkeeper acting in the role of an agent of accountability, measured;
- who monitors that behaviour; and
- how can they be made to comply with the requirement that they act accountably as an agent of accountability?

---

[29] The 'Heiner Case' involves the destruction of documents gathered by a retired magistrate, Noel Heiner, in late 1989 during the course of an inquiry into mismanagement at a youth detention centre. The manager of the centre, who was being investigated, initiated legal action to obtain the documents with the intention of launching legal proceedings. The Government denied this application by ordering the records destroyed, obtaining the authority of the State Archivist to do so. It has subsequently been alleged that the documents would have revealed details of inappropriately handled physical and sexual abuse of juvenile inmates (of the kind later found by a Royal Commission to be endemic in Queensland institutions) and that the Government's actions were consistent with a systematic cover-up of these abuses by politicians, bureaucrats, and unions. For more detail, refer to the chapter by Hurley in Cox and Wallace, op. cit.

For many years, the profession at large refused to acknowledge any failure on the part of the Queensland State Archives. The State Archivist's colleagues on the Council of Federal State and Territory Archivists (COFSTA) congratulated her on escaping censure after one of the many inquiries into the case. Not until 1999, after a prolonged and bitter debate on the archivists' professional listserv, did the Australian Society of Archivists (ASA) acknowledge that the appraisal in Heiner was not in accordance with 'professional standards'. At the same time, the ASA drew some conclusions about the role government archivists should play in appraisal and the methods they should employ. Parts of this statement were immediately repudiated by COFSTA.

Figure 9.4. Cartoonist Kevin Lindberg lost his job as a union organizer when he drew attention to the destruction of records of the Heiner investigation. He has pursued the political and recordkeeping implications ever since.

If the 1999 ASA Statement represents a well-founded condemnation of a recordkeeper's failure in the role of agent of accountability, it must be based on either a belated recognition that the benchmark was not met or the formulation of a new benchmark in response to a realization, similarly belated, that, with the benefit of hindsight, standards existing at the time of the Heiner appraisal were flawed. The profession's failure to face up to its own shortcomings, either on the part of one of its own practitioners or of its own standards, might thus demonstrate an inability to accept accountability for their own actions in a mature and professional way.

In its 1999 Statement, the ASA appealed to 'professional standards' of appraisal, but it is difficult to know what professional standards they were referring to and how the kind of generalized statements of principle which pass for professional standards, in appraisal or any other aspect of professional practice, could really serve as a benchmark for judging the actions of the Queensland State Archivist in the Heiner matter. All the Government Archivists of Australia felt confident enough that the ASA was wrong about what professional standards are to dispute the ASA's judgment on material points. This might be evidence of a robust and healthy professional debate, or it might indicate that discussion of these standards actually amounts to little more than an exchange of individual opinions.

If there really were professional standards of appraisal, it would be possible to test the conflicting views of ASA and COFSTA in the open and determine who is right and who is wrong. In the event, COFSTA appealed not to a different interpretation of agreed standards and procedures, but rather to their superiority of experience and judgment. It is clear, however, that accountability can give no weight to the opinions of persons who happen to occupy certain positions, unless those positions are formally mandated to issue judgment and resolve disputes. Opinions can only be benchmarked against a comprehensive, well-articulated, and professionally verified body of precept and practice.

The actions of other agents of accountability – judges, accountants, auditors, ombudsmen, parliamentary investigators – are all measurable in this way. If there is disagreement about the opinion of one practitioner, that need not be resolved by referring to the unverified opinion of another practitioner. The argument that the COFSTA view of professional standards should be accepted because of who they are is no answer. Judges' opinions can be appealed against to a higher court, which determines whether they conform to an established body of precedent and prior practice. Accountants and auditors have elaborate and detailed statements setting out professional requirements and standards, as well as machinery for resolving disputes about alleged departures from those requirements and procedures by individual practitioners.

In the recent Enron Case, an American court found the accounting firm of Arthur Andersen guilty of misconduct in relation to recordkeeping. That was the end of the matter. It would have availed Andersen naught for Price Waterhouse to have said that they thought what Andersen did was OK and that should satisfy everyone because they too were a big accounting firm and their opinion should be respected. Yet that is, in effect, what COFSTA was saying in Heiner. They could say this because there were no standards to demonstrate that what they were saying was wrong.

In establishing such standards or benchmarks, it is not sufficient to set out methodologies and techniques. There must also be an element of principle. Methodologies and techniques, in and of themselves, cannot guarantee a satisfactory outcome. There must be an articulation of why the approved methodologies and techniques are being mandated. Methodologies and techniques do not prevent an outcome that is arbitrary, unpredictable, and untestable. Throughout the long debate amongst Australian archivists on the Heiner appraisal, it was impossible for anyone participating in that debate to validate their opinion because there were no agreed benchmarks or criteria to use. Unlike auditors, ombudsmen, and judges, archival appraisers cannot be benchmarked. They should not be given the autonomy or independence which would underpin a role as an agent of accountability until it is possible to say, by reference to criteria of behaviour established outside the regime in which the recordkeeper works, whether or not their actions in a particular case were reasonable and proper.

One of the things that was wrong with the Heiner appraisal is that it was undertaken in an 'ad hoc' manner. It involved decisions about what to do with the records of aborted inquiries without there being any rules, principles, precedents or procedures which ensured that similar cases would produce similar outcomes on other occasions. It simply represented the Archivist's personal opinion on the day with no guarantee that tomorrow a similar case would be adjudged in a similar way. Even if the opinion was honestly arrived at on the basis of lengthy experience and conscientiously held, there can be no reassurance that the person taking that decision is acting responsibly or accountably. It was never possible to say that the Queensland Archivist got it right because she was treating the records the way such records should be treated and were, in fact, always treated, or that she got it wrong because she was treating them as a special case and different to similar records, and contrary to the appraisal rules.

The political, organizational, social, and administrative environments in which recordkeepers operate mean that their conditions of employment will determine their actions unless they operate in accordance with a set of professional principles explicit enough to provide the basis upon which they can, if necessary, refuse to conform to the political, organizational, social, and administrative pressures to which they are subjected. The answer lies, not in acts of individual courage, but in the accepted application of overriding principles and practices.

This can be achieved, it has been suggested, by according the recordkeeper, acting in the role of agent of accountability, some degree of independence or autonomy – providing for the recordkeeper to answer to a loyalty or responsibility outside the chain of bureaucratic command. This might be to a professional standard, to an external review process, to the legislature, or some other constituent mechanism which frees the recordkeeper, to some degree or other, from the ordinary chain of command when exercising the role of agent of accountability.

The proposition is that archives authorities need the kind of 'independence' that judges, accountants, auditors, ombudsmen and other agents of accountability have in order for them to act effectively in support of accountability in some, but not all, of the roles and functions outlined above. This is closely akin to the characteristic of autonomy, which is sometimes used to define a profession. During the late 1990s, a bitter court battle was waged in New Zealand by stakeholders opposed to the integration of the National Archives of New Zealand into a unit of the Department of Internal Affairs embracing other 'heritage' activities, such as the National Dictionary of Biography and the office of the Government

Historian. Much was made of the need for Archives to be independent, in order for it carry out its role and function in support of Government accountability.

In 2000, a new Government was elected which was opposed to the proposed integration, proclaiming that it intended to achieve independence for the Archives and to ensure it carried out its important role in accountability. The upshot was the establishment of Archives (renamed Archives New Zealand) as a Department of State in its own right. This was hailed by stakeholders as a victory, as vindication of their stand, and as independence for the archives authority. It was, of course, no such thing. The Chairman of the New Zealand State Services Commission was so outraged by these sentiments that he went to the length of issuing a public statement pointing out that whatever else a New Zealand Department of State might be it had precious little independence. Policy was set by Government and practice was subject to various statutory provisions including the State Sector Act, the Finance Act, and the Audit Act. The State Services Commission Chairman was, of course, perfectly correct. No-one with any understanding of the Westminster system of government, even of the somewhat peculiar manner in which it is applied in New Zealand, would describe a government department as independent. Quite the contrary, because the subservience of executive agencies is the hallmark of that dependency which some kind of adherence to the separation of powers requires; truly independent agents of accountability need to be shielded from such subservience. If you really wanted to establish Archives as independent, departmental status, the most dependent and subservient of all, is the last administrative status you would choose. Departments may be bureaucratically powerful, but that is not the same thing.

Abiding institutions of accountability do need to be set apart from other executive agencies with something like independence or autonomy, but that carries with it the responsibility that their practice must be subject to some established norms, standards and procedures against which their own behaviour can be judged. Government archival authorities in most Western democracies do not have this kind of independence. They are almost all mere executive agencies with some statutory powers and responsibilities. Where there is a measure of true independence, as in the Western Australian Records Commission,[30] it is difficult to know by what measure their actions are to be judged because our professional standards and precedents are so paltry.

A reasonable thesis can, therefore, be developed that most government archives authorities are neither fit nor capable of acting independently as agents of democratic accountability in

---

[30] Following recommendations of a 'WA Inc.' Royal Commission into failures of government accountability, new public records legislation split off important aspects of the regulatory function of the State's archives authority and vested those powers and responsibilities in a Commission comprising the State's Auditor, Ombudsman, Information Commissioner, and one other appointee. The Commission reports to Parliament, has significant statutory powers of regulation and oversight, and regulates recordkeeping activities of Government, including those of the State's Public Records Office. The Public Records Office remains an executive agency reporting not to the Commission, but to a government department. There is thus no formal administrative nexus between the Commission and the PRO. The functions of the archives authority have, effectively, been split between the two.

the manner of courts, accountants, auditors, and ombudsmen. This is not to say that archives authorities should not be constitutionally protected in order to carry out their role in support of accountability, but rather to ask whether they are ready to carry out such a role in the absence of a satisfactory articulation of the behaviour required of them, monitoring of their behaviour, and means to enforce their compliance. As one colleague with whom I have discussed these issues put it rather nicely, being asked by recordkeepers for the autonomy and independence they would need to carry out their role as agents of accountability is a bit like being asked by a sixteen-year old son for the keys to the family car.

Even when there is a formal independence, watchdogs are susceptible to subtle pressures to compromise their integrity. Their organizational budgets and personal career prospects lie in the hands of those whose interests a watchdog role sometimes calls upon them to defy. Succumbing to these and similar pressures is called 'regulatory capture'. Such capture can be venal or can be simply the demoralization of good men and women through exhaustion. Many and varied are the ways in which the watchdog can be worn down.

Making ourselves accountable for our own professional behaviour means:

- having our decisions contested and repudiated if we fail to do what we say we will;
- saying what we will do to ensure outcomes which are fair and just to all parties;
- stating those outcomes in advance;
- being able to test whether or not we achieve those outcomes;
- making all recordkeepers accountable for them; and
- stating them in terms which, so far as possible, cannot be misinterpreted or argued away.

Benchmarks are needed by which the behaviour of recordkeepers can be submitted to external scrutiny, peer review, review and appeal, audit, or whatever other process may provide a 'forum' for external assessment of their judgments.

As an illustration of the kind of principled approach which needs to be taken to establishing benchmarking of the behaviour of recordkeepers, here are three suggested hallmarks of good appraisal which might be derived from an examination of the Heiner Case, as well as the Enron and McCabe[31] cases:

1. *Preservation of Evidence Principle.* Accountable appraisal needs to ensure, regardless of any limitations in the laws relating to discovery and the destruction of evidence, that

---

[31] McCabe was a case in the State of Victoria in which judgment was made against the British and American Tobacco Company for the lung-cancer-victim plaintiff. The judge ruled that BAT had deprived the plaintiff of a fair chance to make her case because of their document destruction practices, even though the destruction of documents predated her case. The ruling was overturned on appeal and, in a final attempt to have that reversal overturned in the High Court of Australia, the family of the lung-cancer victim, who had subsequently died, was not granted leave to appeal that reversal.

records that might reasonably be required to establish anyone's rights and entitlements are kept for as long as that requirement exists.[32]

2. *Consistency Principle.* Appraisal should ensure that records resulting from the same functional process are retained for the same period in all circumstances.

3. *Transparency Principle.* Records should be appraised in accordance with pre-determined retention periods which have to be stated in advance.

These and other principles like them are neither novel nor unorthodox. They are now to be found amongst the statements of principle underlying the functional requirements for recordkeeping and recently issued recordkeeping standards. A similarly principled approach was once taught as the foundation stone of true appraisal. Many of them are set out for us in the old books. They are articulated in, or can be inferred from, the recently developed standards on records management.[33]

In *Modern Archives* Schellenberg distinguishes between two underlying purposes of appraisal.[34] He is speaking explicitly about the work of the United States National Archives – a government body operating under statute. Schellenberg acknowledges, however, that the archivist/appraiser in government faces the same challenge as any appraiser – how to 'adjudge' which records should be evaluated for preservation 'for reference and research purposes'. He offers a threefold basis for appraisal:

1. *Primary values.* This is how Schellenberg refers to the business purposes of the 'originating agency' or business unit, in contra-distinction to 'secondary values', which embody the needs of other agencies within the government enterprise, and, by extension, of the government itself, as well as 'private users'.

2. *Secondary values related to content.* Schellenberg refers to 'study, research, or inquiry'. Some people now refer to these as 'informational values'. If records only have primary value to an originating agency or business unit, it follows that secondary values include enterprise-wide, or whole of government, requirements that some records be retained because of their value to the enterprise.

3. *Secondary values related to rights and entitlements.* Schellenberg describes these as 'various rights, privileges, duties, immunities, and the like that derive from or are connected with the citizen's relationship to the Federal government'.

---

[32] Whatever the legal position, one consequence of the McCabe Case has been revision of the rules governing the practices of lawyers in advising on document destruction with regard to possible litigation, not just litigation already on foot. Accountable recordkeeping needs to consider the same issue: should disposal decisions have regard only to strict legal obligations or should professional standards raise the bar higher?

[33] AS ISO 15489.

[34] T R Schellenberg, *Modern Archives*, Chicago, University of Chicago Press, 1956, pp. 115-117.

Schellenberg speaks of secondary values related to rights and entitlements as discretionary. It is therefore conceptually accurate to categorize retention on rights-related grounds under compulsion, such as the statutory prohibition on destruction of records sought during discovery in a court case, under category 2 (secondary values related to content). It is clear from Schellenberg's analysis that he regards the preservation of records based on secondary values related to rights and entitlements as discretionary in the public sector, just as it is in the private sector.

It is to standards, therefore, that both the public and private sectors must look to see what limitations have been propounded on an otherwise unfettered discretion. In a separate chapter, entitled 'Appraisal Standards', Schellenberg quotes from a paper by Dr G. Philip Bauer of the National Archives staff:

> There are innumerable other classes of records that are important to persons in support of their 'rights'. 'There is no end to the list,' to quote Dr. Bauer. 'They arise every time an individual has any sort of dealing with his government. The extent to which, the duration for which, and the place at which a government should preserve such records are matters of public policy ...'[35]

Since the treatment of records on such grounds is discretionary, for both public and private enterprises, it follows that it is only through the application of standards that accountable recordkeeping can be achieved. For recordkeeping to be accountable, it must be conducted in accordance with standards, professional or otherwise, which indicate how accountable behaviour can be identified and adjudged. Such standards must, as Dr Bauer recognized half a century ago, have a policy basis which addresses the ethical purposes of recordkeeping.

The international recordkeeping standard states explicitly that records systems should be managed 'in compliance with ... (inter alia) ... the regulatory environment and community expectations in which the organization operates' (8.2.3).[36] This resonates with the distinction between compliance based on compulsion and discretion outlined above. The ISO standard goes on to say that over and above the minimum periods of retention required by statute, the 'rights and interests of all stakeholders should be considered when determining how long records need to be maintained ... decisions should not be made intentionally to circumvent any rights of access' (9.2):

> Records should be retained to: ...
> c) meet the current and future needs of internal and external stakeholders by:
> 1) identifying the enforceable or legitimate interests that stakeholders may have in preserving the records for longer than they are required by the organization itself ...
> 2) identifying and assessing legal, financial, political, social or other positive gains from preserving records to serve the interests of research and society as a whole...

---

[35] Ibid. pp. 155-157.
[36] AS ISO 15489.

Applying, then, the same analysis that was used to outline how accountable recordkeeping can be implemented, it can be seen how recordkeepers can themselves be made accountable:

Ordinance. The recordkeeper is issued with edicts or binding instructions to behave accountably (e.g. a statutory or employment requirement) which may specify accountabilities which the recordkeeper is obliged to satisfy (e.g. a charter).

Precept. The recordkeeper acts accountably in accordance with standards (professional standards – e.g. ISO) or codes of conduct which are professionally binding (e.g. codes of ethics or professional policy statements).

Mentoring. The recordkeeper looks for sources of advice, education, instruction, or recommendations on how to act accountably (e.g. an advisory or consultative board) or submits to peer review.

Facilitation. The recordkeeper employs accountability experts, conciliators, or negotiators to assist in making the decisions and/or designing systems (e.g. use of consultancy).

Provision. The recordkeeper employs accountability experts or stakeholders to discharge the recordkeeper's own accountabilities (e.g. certification, internal audit).

Enablement. The recordkeeper adopts methodologies, tools or infrastructure developed to implement compliant and accountable behaviour (e.g. checklists, software, quality assurance, generic compliance mechanisms).

Monitoring. The recordkeeper sets, or is set, predetermined measures of performance, qualitative as well as quantitative, and reports to a third party on whether those measures have been met (e.g. charters, business plans, reports).

Watchdogs. The recordkeeper's reports are acted upon and deviant behaviour is corrected by recommendations or instruction (e.g. from oversight committees) or decisions are appealable to a review board with an advisory role.

Enforcement. Correction of deviant behaviour by the recordkeeper is accompanied by punishment or sanctions (e.g. reprimand, financial penalty, removal) or decisions are appealable to a review board with discretionary power to reverse the recordkeeper's action.

Auditor. The recordkeeper's performance as an agent of accountability is audited (e.g. in an auditor's report and response).

These rules and constraints may not be accepted graciously by the owners of records or the employers of appraisers. Recordkeepers may find it hard to urge these principles upon their unwilling masters. A reluctance to be held to account against criteria which recordkeepers may not be able to meet, provides no basis for setting the boundaries on the principles which should underlie appraisal standards. That is a risk management issue for the implementation level and the procedural level in any appraisal program. The point is fundamental. Otherwise, we cease to be a profession and become instead an association of tradesmen.

The whole point of standards is to mark the no-man's land between what we are constrained to do and what we aspire to do – otherwise what we are constrained to do will never change. On a practical level, unless our reach exceeds our grasp, we won't be open to some of the new methodologies and techniques which technology is offering us to overcome the traditional constraints on appraisal. Professional standards based honestly upon true ethical foundations could be rendered into acceptable and flexible implementation strategies under which methodologies and techniques appropriate to accountable recordkeeping could then be crafted.

Readings

- Richard J. Cox and David A. Wallace, eds, *Archives and the Public Good: Accountability and Records in Modern Society*, Westport, Ct, Quorum Books, 2002.

  This is a collection of essays written by archivists and designed to provide 'record-focused case studies' to communicate and promote to a wider audience the significance of the roles records play in constituting society. Issues covered include the politics of custody and ownership, appraisal and destruction issues, access to information, cover-up and non-disclosure, the use and limitations of records in memorializing a nation's past, the trustworthiness of systems and owners of records.

- William De Maria, *Deadly Disclosures: Whistleblowing and the Ethical Meltdown of Australia*, Kent Town, SA, Wakefield Press, 1999.

  De Maria has collected and analyzed seven case studies involving whistleblowers involved in conflict with institutions of various kinds, frequently their own employers. He also attempts a theory of organizational behaviour when confronted with dissent and criticism. Although there is no particular emphasis on recordkeeping and the analysis is uneven, the value of the book lies in the documentation of the organizational instinct to 'save face' which is the true enemy of accountability.

- Warwick Funnell, *Government by Fiat: The Retreat from Responsibility*, Sydney, University of New South Wales Press, 2001.

  The primary thesis concerns the abdication of responsibility by Westminster-style democracies for social and public interest matters. Funnell deals with the post-Keynesian process of privatization and commercialization by governments and the change this has wrought in the relationship between government and governed. In the course of developing this thesis, he documents and analyzes the concomitant attack which has been mounted on agents of democratic accountability, principally auditors and ombudsmen in Australian jurisdictions. His book also documents the evils consequent upon management of public business within an ideological framework allegedly modeled on the private sector.

- Sue McKemmish and Frank Upward, eds, *Archival Documents: Providing Accountability Through Recordkeeping*, Melbourne, Ancora Press, 1993.

  In its time, this was a ground-breaking endeavour. Contributors interweave case studies documenting records-related accountability issues with theoretical expositions. The work has been characterized as representing a 'strand' or position, but several contributors are at pains to link the overall themes set out in the book with archival traditions and demonstrate continuities with traditional theory and practice.

CHAPTER 10
Recordkeeping and juridical governance

Livia Iacovino

... law is a social institution whose primary function is the governance of behaviour.[1]

Introduction

Records play a central role in governance as social mechanisms that help bind societies together. Governance includes 'government' and its laws as in a nation-state or organized community, and 'self-government' as a means of control over personal and group behaviour within a self-governing community. Within this definitional framework, law is only one form of governance. However, the positivist tradition of jurisprudence limits law to rules backed by coercive sanctions in which power and state are co-dependent. Francis Fukuyama, a social and political scientist, reinforces a governance view of society through his analysis of the nature of communities 'formed not on the basis of explicit rules and regulations but on a set of ethical habits and reciprocal moral obligations internalized by each of the community's members. These rules or habits gave members of the community grounds for trusting one another.'[2] Understanding how communities are bound together has become important in a global environment, in which the relationship between sovereign states is being replaced by relationships between individuals, social groups or businesses.

If we adopt a definition of juridical power as encompassing a plurality of legal forms in which state law is only one aspect, law and ethics are two principal governance mechanisms intrinsically linked with recordkeeping, namely:

- recordkeeping forms an integral part of the governance of legal and social relationships (for example, doctor-patient, citizen-state and parent-child within a web of community relationships);
- recordkeeping supports legal and ethical rights and obligations within a socio-legal system;

---

[1] J.E. Penner, 'Basic Obligations', in *The Classification of Obligations*, edited by Peter Birks, Oxford, Clarendon Press, 1997, p. 91.
[2] Francis Fukuyama, *Trust: the Social Virtues and the Creation of Prosperity*, London, Penguin, 1995, p. 9.

- recordkeeping is required to regulate business and social activity;
- recordkeeping provides ongoing evidence or proof of a particular activity; and
- recordkeeping contributes to personal, organizational and democratic accountability which underpins an ethical legal system.

The notion of social relationships as networks that form the basis of a juridical system, in which documents witness the relationships, is a central tenet of archival science. As Luciana Duranti has expressed it:

> No one has an existence outside the network of relationships tying one to the others in one's life. Such relationships are ruled in part by law in all its aspects, and the function of the law is objectified in archival documents.[3]

The 'other part' can be interpreted as normative ethics, that is, ethics as rules that guide human action, and ethical intentions that are evidenced in action, that is through the records themselves.

Archival science, recordkeeping, law and the state

The relationship between recordkeeping and governance cannot be understood in a social, cultural, economic or political vacuum. Communities and sovereign states have evolved on the basis of attempting to regulate the behaviour of their constituents, individually or collectively, through legal systems that have evolved over time and space as they responded to changing norms and values. The development of individual legal rights in Western society in the last century has constrained modern governmental powers and, together with statutory rights of access to public records, has played a significant role in improving legal and political rights of citizens (see also 'Government Obligations and Access to Public Records' below).

Diplomatics and legitimizing state power

Institutions since ancient times have used alleged 'truth' from documents to legitimize their power, for example the papal claim to temporal power in the document known as the 'Donation of Constantine', which the fifteenth century Italian humanist Lorenzo Valla exposed as a forgery.[4] Records as tools for acquiring state power are evidenced in the seventeenth century European 'diplomatic wars' in which property rights were won on the basis of documentary evidence. The principles that grew out of the need to prove the record's reliability and authenticity for property rights and for ascertaining the truthfulness of the facts therein were given a universalized meaning through diplomatics.

---

[3] Luciana Duranti, 'Education and the Role of the Archivist in Italy', *American Archivist,* 51, no. 3, Summer 1988, p. 355.
[4] Heather MacNeil, in *Trusting Records,* Dordrecht, Kluwer, 2000, pp. 11-12.

Figure 10.1. The Donation of Constantine (c. 1240). Emperor Constantine, cured of leprosy by his baptism, places the tiara on Pope Sylvester. The fresco illustrates the medieval belief in the authenticity of the document known as *The Donation of Constantine* by which the church legitimated its power. It was not until 1440 that Lorenzo Valla in *Discourse on the forgery of the alleged Donation of Constantine* used close textual analysis and historical criticism to prove that the document was a forgery.

Diplomatics is 'the analysis of genesis, inner constitution and transmission of documents, and of their relationship with the facts represented in them and with their creators'.[5] It focuses on analyzing retrospectively the nature and characteristics of the document in the context in which it was created. 'Contemporary diplomatics' as exemplified in the writings and research of Paola Carucci, Luciana Duranti and Heather MacNeil extends diplomatics to prospective recordkeeping requirements. The diplomatics approach to recordkeeping is particularly suited to verifying who is legally responsible for an action, whether the records have emanated from a competent authority, who created and who owns the records, the documentary form of the record prescribed by the legal system and whether the records are part of the normal course of business, a major principle in evidence law.

Archival science, which drew many of its principles from diplomatics, continues to remain relevant to law, as records are a source of legal evidence, and to institutions of state, as records document the relationships between individuals and the state. Records are critical in

---

[5] Luciana Duranti, 'Diplomatics: New Uses for an Old Science (Part I)', *Archivaria*, 28, 1989, p. 7.

demonstrating in court that a right or obligation exists, or an obligation has not been performed.

Theory of state and archival science

The theory of state in nineteenth-century European thought was centred on its legal structure, as an all-embracing juridical entity or 'fonds', which provided a framework in which the functions and activities of the state could be conceptualized. It formed the basis of the 'historical method' employed by archival science as a means of classifying records by the juridical body that created them, separating the records of one creator from another, for legal rather than historical purposes. Although the method provided the origin of the classic archival theories of provenance and original order, which became the basis for the arrangement and description of archives, it reveals the central purpose of the archival authority since antiquity – maintaining authenticity of public records through their unbroken custody, a theme of continuing relevance in the electronic records environment. The historical method's system of classification of records provided evidence of the actions of government through the functions and activities of the body creating the records (the state and its laws), and evidence of the government's relationship with its citizens (the rights and duties of the citizens) within the state.

As the regulation of the citizen within the state underlies any legal system, the concepts and developments briefly explored here explain the close relationship of jurisprudential and archival notions in nineteenth-century Europe. However the relationship between the citizen and the state has become more complex and, in many ways, the relationship has been transformed and in some instances removed from the public sphere. The 'privatizing' of public law is an important change that alters a long-standing relationship between citizen and government and the role of recordkeeping in that relationship. For example, corporatized government agencies have limited public obligations, and contractual relationships between government and service providers further remove the citizen from direct access to government agencies and their records (see 'Archives and Modern Government' below).

Public archives

The role of the public archives as a place of authority which endowed records with authenticity over time has its origin in antiquity, and is found in both Eastern and Western civilizations. In ancient Greece the term 'archives', which entailed state power, government and authority, was applied to current records naturally accumulated by public officials in the exercise of their functions. Public record offices held both public and private transactions because, in ancient Greece and Rome, the individual and the state were treated as part of the one body politic. However, separate places of deposit for archives were also established which reflected the need to protect and secure the archives. European states of the sixteenth century did not distinguish between the juridical-administrative-evidential and cultural-historical-memorial value of records. It was not until the development of modern institutional archives in Europe attributed to the establishment of the National Archives of France in 1794 that archives of defunct public bodies were designated as historical sources and as public property severing their evidence-memory unity. However, in Italian archival science it has been argued that the divisions between current and historic archives had no theoretical significance and served as phases for practical organizational uses only. Thus the concurrent value of the document – juridical-administrative-evidential and historical-cultural-memorial – remains constant.

The legislative controls of a public archival authority over both current and historical records are reflected in the powers accorded to it in its enabling legislation. In many countries archival/records legislation initially focused on responsibility for the preservation of historical records transferred into archival custody, with a gradual shift to responsibility for the management of government records through authorized disposal, compulsory transfer and access, to finally ensuring the implementation of recordkeeping standards and practices throughout its jurisdiction. For example, in Australia the State Records Act 2000 (WA) provides for the establishment of principles and standards by which government organizations must manage their records. The sharing of responsibility between archival authorities and government agencies over the totality of governmental record activity, regardless of the age of the records, accords with a continuum view of the record as both evidence and memory.

Recordkeeping and juridical systems

A juridical system

The concept of a juridical system provides a useful way of exploring the notion of regulation and governance of recordkeeping activities. 'Juridical' is a term widely used in civil law systems to describe a legal system in which rules bind social groups and regulate the legal facts dealing with social and legal relationships. It is therefore one way of conceptualizing legal systems. Luciana Duranti says 'juridical thinking is not universal other than as philosophy of the law. Jurisprudence, being the study of a specific juridical thinking, is necessarily conditioned by time and space'.[6] The term juridical system and many associated concepts are found in diplomatics.

Juridical systems as defined by Duranti emphasize codes of behaviour; this is shown in the following passage:

> A social group founded on an organizational principle which gives its institution(s) the capacity of making compulsory rules. Thus a *juridical system* is a collectivity organised on the basis of a system of rules. The system of rules is called a *legal system*. A legal system is a complex paradigm containing many divisions and subdivisions. It can be broken down into *positive law* (as set out in the various legal

---

[6] Luciana Duranti, 'Medieval Universities and Archives', *Archivaria*, 38, Fall 1994, p. 40.

sources – legislation, judicial precedent, custom – and literary sources – either authoritative, consisting of statutes, law reports, and books of authority, or non-authoritative, such as medieval chronicles, periodicals, other books) and all the other *conceptions and notions of binding law* (natural law, morality, orthodox religious beliefs, mercantile custom, Roman/Canon law). *Because a legal system includes all the rules that are perceived as binding at any time and/or place, no aspect of human life and affairs remains outside a legal system.*[7]

A juridical system circumscribes the boundaries in which records have authority, and endows them with trustworthiness and authenticity. Examples of juridical systems include professions, institutions, communities, industry and church groups, family or private social associations which issue rules, codes of ethics or conduct, or standards that provide an important means of ensuring the conformity of its members. They may provide their own sanctions to enforce conformity, for example expulsion from the group or shunning by the profession.

A juridical system also applies to communities or societies that adopt oral recordkeeping. For example, Australian aboriginal communities manifest elements recognizable in any juridical system; they have the prerequisites of being organized groups with the power to enact and interpret law, as well as to impose sanctions when the law is broken. Judicial recognition of the continuing existence of Aboriginal law as the legal basis of traditional rights and interests was recognized in the Australian High Court's decision in *Mabo v Queensland*.[8]

In summary, the juridical system provides a means of ascertaining the legal and moral obligations of organizations and individuals within their respective jurisdictions and reflects a society's norms and values codified in law or other forms of regulation (voluntary or obligatory) at a particular time. The juridical model reflects the unique role that records play in regulating legal and social relationships.

Record reliability and authenticity in the juridical system

The role of record reliability and authenticity in a juridical system is a key element of governance. Within juridical thinking, reliability and authenticity are both necessary for the record to be trustworthy. The reliability of the record is associated with the degree of control exercised over its creation procedures. Authenticity is linked to a record's mode, status and form of transmission, and the manner of its preservation and custody. The juridical system incorporates trust found in the nature and character of society itself, from its informal rules, its community and professional expectations, and its notion of public interest.

---

[7] Luciana Duranti, 'Diplomatics: New Uses for an Old Science (Part II)', *Archivaria*, 29, 1989-90, p. 5. Emphasis added.

[8] *Mabo v Queensland [No 2]* (1992) 66 ALJR 408.

Concepts of record trustworthiness in archival science, which originate from Roman law, are also found in the evidence laws of common law countries, for example, the ancient records and the best evidence rules.[9] In Roman law there were two concepts of particular relevance to trustworthy records, the concepts of 'perpetual memory' and 'public faith'.[10] Public faith in society as a whole is 'community as society' in Aristotelian terms. The relationship of these concepts to recordkeeping principles can be traced to the function of public records as collective memory providing social continuity. The public place in which records were kept formed part of the seat of government and also contributed to the trustworthiness of the records. The Roman law of evidence reinforced the privileged status accorded to government documents and invested them with public faith.

In shifting from Roman law concepts to the common law, substantive differences need to be acknowledged; for example, in Italian law, documents executed between private persons, such as contracts, are public documents if authenticated by a notary and have the same evidential weight as a public record. In the common law system, contracts between private citizens would be in the private sphere, as notarized records of a private transaction are not part of the common law tradition.

Property and record authenticity

The principles of private property as they have evolved in Western legal systems have centred on possession, custody, and ownership. These principles have played a central role in determining whether 'custody' of records, defined as including physical possession, is the only means by which the record's authenticity can be maintained over time. An alternative legal model to the record as physical property, found in both common and civil law systems, is one that focuses on rights and duties that arise as a result of ownership, for example, a company owns its records but has a duty to provide access to its shareholders.

The concept of continuous custody of a record has been central to archival theory and originates from both the common and civil law systems concern that no tampering with the record should have occurred after its creation. Initially the responsibility for integrity rests with the parties to the transaction, who must ensure no interference occurs when the transaction takes place. Third parties, including archival authorities, have certified the authenticity of a record on the basis of the custody rule. In the digital context, a range of solutions is being explored which includes the use of digital signatures to safeguard record integrity, both at the time the transaction takes place as well as once it is archived.

---

[9] Evidence Act 1995 (Cth) s 152, 'If a document that is or purports to be more than 20 years old is produced from proper custody, it is presumed, unless the contrary is proved, that: (a) the document is the document that it purports to be; and (b) if it purports to have been executed or attested by a person - it was duly executed or attested by that person'.

[10] Luciana Duranti, 'The Concept of Appraisal and Archival Theory', *American Archivist*, 57, 1994, pp. 328-344; 'Archives as a Place', *Archives and Manuscripts*, 24, no. 2, 1996, pp. 242-255; and 'Reliability and Authenticity: The Concepts and Their Implications', *Archivaria*, 39, 1995, pp. 5-10.

Evidence law and record authenticity

The transfer of custody of records from a 'creator' to a 'preserver' such as an archival authority is one strategy for preserving the authenticity of a record. Evidence law has had rigorous requirements for best evidence that required a document to have been in 'proper or unbroken custody' to be authentic. Changes to evidence rules in a number of countries have placed more responsibility on the business creators to ensure that electronic systems have been operating correctly and that they have been maintained so as to be accessible, in effect turning businesses into 'preservers'. For example, the Evidence Act 1995 (Cth) ss 146 and 147 relate to presumptions that enable documents, regardless of format, as long as they form part of the records belonging to or kept by a person, body or organization in the course of, or for the purposes of a business, and that are produced by processes, machines or other devices that function properly, to be acceptable as evidence. The rationale for this is that, if a business depends on electronic records, they may be presumed to be reliable and authentic. The presumptions can be legally challenged.

Even though there is a presumption in modern Australian evidence law that established business practices produce reliable documents, there is no guarantee in advance that the records will be admitted or not challenged.[11] In the New South Wales judgment, *Albrighton v Royal Prince Alfred Hospital* it was decided that records made subsequent to a duty to an employer are likely to be reliable as they arise from a professional duty.[12] The law recognized ethical professional behaviour as a contributing factor to the accuracy of the record and thus to its admissibility in legal proceedings.

The best evidence rule, that is the production of an original record, has been a safeguard of record integrity, particularly in the era when hand-copying or re-setting type could produce errors. The rule has been abolished in many common law jurisdictions, but does not completely detract from the need of either party in legal proceedings to prove that the record is what it purports to be and that its identity and integrity have not been compromised.

The juridical dimensions of the records continuum model

European notions of a juridical system have been incorporated into Australian records continuum thinking. Within the records continuum model, the relationship of ethical-legal governance mechanisms and recordkeeping is viewed from the perspective of the continuum of recordkeeping processes that create, capture, manage, preserve and re-present records as evidence of social and business activity for business, social and cultural purposes.

---

[11] For example, presumptions that cover records are included in the Evidence Act 1995 (Cth) ss 146, 147, 150-153, 166, 173 and 183.
[12] *Albrighton v Royal Prince Alfred Hospital* [1980] 2 NSWLR 542.

The four dimensions of Frank Upward's records continuum model can be used as a tool for highlighting where the impact of the law is of particular significance in recordkeeping processes and how socio-legal systems operate in an interconnected and cumulative way at different levels, depending upon whether we are concerned with the document as trace, the record as evidence, the archive as memory, or the archives as collective memory. For example, legal evidence as trace of the action (first dimension) gains greater evidential weight as part of a reliable recordkeeping system (second dimension) and also ensures authentic corporate and societal memory (third and fourth dimensions).

The following table summarizes recordkeeping processes from a records continuum perspective and their juridical dimensions.

1. Create as a document	
as *trace of event*	Legal evidence
as *product of transaction*	Procedures required by law or implied by law Legal consequences Sanctions and penalties
as *product of an actor*	Authorship Legal and professional responsibilities/ethics

2. Capture as a record	
as *evidence*	Rights-obligations
as a *record of activities*	Procedures required by law or implied by law Legal consequences Sanctions/penalties (re retention of evidence)
records level	Evidence laws and compliance (re operation of capture aspect of recordkeeping systems)
unit level	Ownership (intellectual or real) Legal competencies and permissions

3. Organize as memory	
corporate memory	Legal accountability of the organization
as a *record of function*	Substantive laws: universal; industry specific laws; codes/practices
as *archive at organization level*	Reporting responsibilities Legal personality Entity specific legislation Legal and moral competencies

4. Pluralize as collective memory	
social or historical memory	Authentic evidence over time
as *record of purpose*	Legal mandates/missions
as *archives*	Responsible third party: archival legislation; FOI Privacy; access/disclosure laws
at institutional level	Legal mandates/powers Enabling legislation

Figure 10.2. Recordkeeping processes from a records continuum perspective.

Creating documents (first dimension) identifies the impact of legislative requirements on what documents are produced, whether they have the capacity to be used as evidence (that is, any documentary trace of a fact or event which may be admitted as legal evidence), whether the specific documentation of a transaction is required or implied by law (for example, Banking Act 1959 (Cth) s 51 requires a bank to prepare and give to the Reserve Bank information about its banking business and accounts and financial statements in a form specified by the Reserve Bank) and whether there are legal or moral consequences of non-documentation, including sanctions and penalties, for example for the non-return of annual reports as in the Corporations Act 2001 (Cth). In some cases a law will prescribe specifically the data to record, when it should be made and how long it should be kept; for example, the Medical Practice Regulations 1998 (NSW), Reg. 13, 14(1), and 15(1) specify that a record for each patient must be made and kept by a medical practitioner, when it should be made, and how long it needs to be kept, and Schedule 2 prescribes what details the record must contain about the patient.

In other cases, it is simply good business practice to make and keep a record to prove that the action took place. For example, recording the date and time a person is admitted into hospital, the treatment given and by whom and the date of discharge is essential to establishing who was treated (the identity of the patient), when the treatment took place, whether it was part of normal medical practice for the medical condition being treated, who can see the information resulting from treatment and for what purposes, who owns the data and the records once the treatment has ended, and how long to retain the record. Thus the records also support a legal fact by providing evidence that particular procedures were followed and that the events took place.

Even when legislation is not specific about record creation it may be implied. For example, the Trade Practices Act 1974 (Cth) prohibits unfair practices, such as misleading or deceptive conduct or specified false representations, or consumer product information. Section 75AC requires proof of the safety of a product and places strict liability on manufacturers for injury and loss caused by defective goods. Although there is nothing in the Act specifying the making or keeping of records, compliance is dependent on maintaining records dealing with the manufacture and distribution of the product as the only possible defences.

The commencement of issues which cross dimensions include those relating to the document as the product of an actor, such as authorship, legal, ethical and professional responsibilities, and the recipient of the document as the person to whom the communication is directed.

Capturing records (second dimension) is concerned with evidence of rights and obligations. Recordkeeping processes and systems need to be shown to have operated consistently and reliably as part of the normal course of a business to satisfy legal evidence, for example, Evidence Act 1995 (Cth) ss 146 and s 147. Legislation may also authorize the legal acceptability of electronic signatures to authenticate parties to the transaction. Ethical drivers include professional duties and accountability of individuals and groups to ensure that records sufficiently document business activities, noted in *Albrighton v Royal Prince Alfred Hospital* above. Even if the destruction of records is not strictly illegal, the absence of records may make a legal defence difficult. Records may be required in anticipation of possible litigation, because the law implies an assurance that a person can make a claim within a time fixed by law, that is, a limitation period which may in some circumstances be extended. For example in *Syrett v Vorbach*, Dr. Vorbach had destroyed patients' notes as the normal course of his practice, based on guidelines of the Australian Medical Association, and not as a result of a proceeding brought against him by a patient, Rosemary Syrett.[13] She sought an extension of time to bring the action. The plaintiff alleged a breach of contract and negligence in respect of medical advice and treatment received by her in 1984. She argued that her opportunity to pursue her claim had been adversely affected by the destruction of the records. The case indicates that the doctor needed to take into account the nature of the illness (e.g. whether it is likely to reoccur) and needed to have kept the records.

In *organizing memory* (third dimension), the law is interested in the legal accountability of the organization, requiring it to exercise its corporate memory in a number of ways. These include the organization's capacity to control the behaviour of its representatives operating in the first two dimensions, that is, the individuals and groups that constitute an organization. Here the law operates upon company behaviour through processes such as universal legislation (e.g. tax laws), industry specific laws (e.g. Banking Acts) and codes and practices (e.g. the Australian Bankers' Association Code of Banking Practice). The Income Tax Assessment Act 1936 (Cth) s 262A(1) requires companies to keep for five years records that record and explain all transactions and other acts engaged in by the company. While such standards have their origins in the fourth dimension of this model, their impact is felt in the third. Various reporting responsibilities are established both to other bodies outside the organization and internally within the organization. Issues relating to legal and moral competencies are raised. The legal obligations of directors of a company or a professional practice can shape the organization of corporate memory. Greater disclosure of corporate activities is often achieved through corporate governance. Corporate governance includes mechanisms a company has in place to assure shareholders that the company's affairs are being run prudently. Broadly, this is the dimension of organizational

---

[13] District Court of South Australia, *Syrett v Vorbach*, No. DCCIV-99-336 [2001] SADC 46 (30 March 2001).

accountability which affects what an organization should be capable of remembering about its business activities.

Pluralizing as collective memory (fourth dimension) is the all-embracing socio-legal environment of recordkeeping. It includes the notion of collective 'will' and universal well-being, as expressed in ethics theories. Here the law is concerned with the carriage of authentic evidence over time and beyond changes to company or personal identity. Legislation may regulate transmission to an archive. It is the dimension of legal mandates, missions and enablement. Archival legislation can establish an archival institution with third party powers to direct what is preserved and how it is made available. The locus of Freedom of Information (FOI), privacy, access and disclosure laws can be found here, although they also operate at the third dimension as compliance mechanisms. Government frameworks, such as a Public Key Infrastructure (PKI) which includes a hierarchical chain of trusted certification authorities invested with the competence to authenticate the ownership of a public key to support digital signatures, must also be able to ensure a continuity of the trust chain to make electronic transactions accessible over time. For fourth dimension legislation to operate successfully as a means of bringing together the memories of a range of subordinated collectivities or juridical systems, it must have an effect within the other dimensions. If organizations are not compliant, or induced to be compliant, societal framework laws, moral codes and powers of this type are often ineffective.

Legislative compliance requires a framework built on the juridical environment, which takes into account a range of legal considerations. The regulatory environment can be established from positive law and its authoritative sources: statute (legislation) and case law (common law); professional, personal and corporate ethics; and industry codes of conduct and practice as sources of regulatory control that may prescribe recordkeeping requirements explicitly or implicitly, but more importantly controls that are sustained by records as proof of action.

In fact, governance is not so much about what laws regulate or control recordkeeping, but rather about how records support legal and social relationships.

Records, social relationships and legal systems

The role of recordkeeping in underpinning legal relationships is recognized as much in the common law as in civil law systems. Both the civil and common law systems recognize a range of legal relationships, the nature of which determines the rights and obligations of the parties concerned as evidenced in records. Legal relationships may also be classed as socio-legal relationships, insofar as they have social and moral consequences as well as legal ones. They include personal relationships arising out of birth, marital status or family (e.g. the parent-child relationship), public relationships in which a citizen interacts with the government (e.g. the taxpayer-taxation officer (representing the Crown) relationship), commercial relationships involving organizations providing a service to a customer (e.g. the buyer-seller relationship) and professional relationships which provide a professional service, the oldest legally recognized professional relationship being that of the doctor-patient.

The legal system recognizes individuals (human beings) and organizations as legal persons in order to recognize them as holders of rights and obligations and to regulate them, for example, as an incorporated company (which could include a succession of human incumbents), unborn persons or an agency. It also gives a legal person a legal 'personality' to identify the sum total of all their rights and duties.

Socio-legal relationships give rise to records that involve a number of participants or actors, who may be immediate parties to a transaction, or agents representing another party, with a number of different roles. The identity of the participants in the action recorded is, therefore, an essential element of a record, as well as of legal significance.

In archival theory identity has been defined by the corporate entity, organization, legal or natural person that created the records. Person identity is one element of the requirement for record authenticity. The nature of person identity is also tied to community identity, which may be ethnic or religious, as well as professional, familial, or service-related. The nature of community as a means of providing identity, a value system and trust, contributes to the reliability and accuracy of its records. For example, within a medical community, the medical practitioners' registration board acts as a trust channel – a third party to which a patient can turn for verification of a practitioner's professional credentials.

'Identity' elements in recordkeeping and related legal rights and duties

The degree of reliability of the contents of a record depends on how much is captured of the identity of the persons involved in the record's creation, their credibility, their authority (their competencies) and the consent of parties to the transaction. Validation or certification of the parties to a transaction, or of the authors and recipients, depends on controls in the record creation process.

The assignment of legal responsibilities to 'persons' is an indication of their property rights in records, or of their rights to the data or intellectual content in records, or of what they can do with the information. If we add third parties, who have an interest in legal relationships, we can come up with a useful matrix to identify recordkeeping participants in any legal system. In ethics, all the categories would also be moral agents. The example below is from a generic university context.

Writer/actor/physical person: human person at the desk/work station acting in his/her own right in relation to other persons; witness to the facts; relevant to reliability of facts in a record, e.g. a lecturer employed by a university.

Author/record creator/agent: legal actor/juridical 'person' or position having the capacity/authority to act legally in his/her own right; the will to act (the juridical act); the actor who undertakes an act which creates, modifies or maintains a situation; an entity/corporate body capable of acting legally, e.g. a university mandated by statute. The author can only be established by knowing the legal system; juridical agency/agent with mandated functions must be known. Note: author and creator are separate entities in diplomatics and archival science respectively.

Recipient/addressee: the person for whom the record is intended/directed; may, or may not be the recipient of the action, e.g. a university student. Note: The recipient of the communication must be differentiated from the recipient of the action.

Third party: 'one who is a stranger to a transaction or proceeding' (*Osborn's Concise Law Dictionary*, 8th ed, London, Sweet and Maxwell, 1993, p. 323). A person who is not part of the original transaction and thus an independent outsider who may authenticate the record, seek access to, or use the record or data therein either for themselves or on behalf of another third party. This party may be vicariously liable for the transaction. The author and the addressee are the first and second party if they are the actors of the action. The relationship of the third party with other parties in the transaction may be removed by various degrees, e.g. a researcher or a research institution, a regulatory watchdog, an archival authority, or a signature certification authority.

Record or data subject: the person(s) who is (are) the subject of, or referenced in, a record or document; in the subject matter of the document; about whom information has been collected and may have no involvement in the action of the record. In some cases may have provided the data, or be the same person as the recipient, e.g. a student.

The writer of the document, the author, and his/her link to authority/competence, the record subject, the third party, and the legal relationships of these parties are one way of establishing who owns the document, who controls access to it, who can reproduce it, who can destroy it and other rights associated with the data and the record.

'Authorship' as authority is important to both the reliability and the ownership of the record. Authorship can also be defined by the moral permission given by a community. It is linked to authority and competence, the sphere of functional responsibility entrusted to an office or an officer within the juridical system, the legal person responsible for the action. Authorship is also relevant to ownership; that is, records created or received by an organization or a legal entity are owned by the organization or entity; a record sent to someone is in the 'possession' of the recipient, which may or may not equate with ownership. This may, however, be different from the ownership of intellectual property of the record. Copyright law may stipulate who is the author of the moral rights of the work, as opposed to the owners of the economic rights. Ownership also affects control over access to the information in the record, although this could be overridden by statute, for example, access rights to personal data by the record subject under freedom of information or privacy legislation. Thus the author, for legal purposes, may be different from the author identified from the analysis in diplomatics or archival science.

The legal actors that have been added to the matrix (third parties and record subjects) reflect changed business and legal realities, such as the accretion of individual human rights in the last decades of the twentieth century. In the web environment, they may operate as intermediaries or trusted third parties. There is a web of legal relationships that exists between all these actors that have legal personalities. These relationships will determine rights and liabilities of the legal persons participating in the action of the record. In turn, these records support the rights and obligations of the persons involved in the action.

Archives and modern government

In recent years the way services are provided by government worldwide has undergone dramatic change. Many countries have redefined government in terms of its commercial dealings, with private-public sector regulatory regimes working across government and business on an equal footing; for example, in Australia the Trade Practices Act 1974 (Cth) Part IV applies to all business entities, including the business operations of public sector entities. The government-citizen relationship is no longer subject only to public law. However, the public interest purpose of public bodies in relation to citizens is recognized in both legislation and case law. Mason J describes public authorities as 'referable mainly to the character of a public authority as a body entrusted by statute with functions to be performed in the public interest or for public purposes.'[14] A public authority's overriding obligation has been described as to 'act reasonably and in good faith and upon lawful relevant grounds of public interest ... The whole concept of unfettered discretion is inappropriate to a public authority, which possesses powers solely in order that it may use them for the public good'.[15] Public interest and high moral actions expected from government also serve as trust mechanisms essential to reliable and authentic records.

Government obligations and access to public records

Access has been expressed as a separate right from ownership, for example, in Freedom of Information (FOI) laws, and yet it is *a* right of ownership, which owners give up. Ownership is a form of control over information and how it is used. Negative rights of

---

[14] *Sutherland Shire Council v Heyman* (1985) 157 CLR at 456, as quoted in W.D. Duncan, 'Reliance upon Government Information - Select Issues', in *Government Law and Policy, Commercial Aspects,* ed. Bryan Horrigan, Leichhardt NSW, Federation Press, 1998, p. 390, footnote 2A.

[15] H.W.R. Wade, *Administrative Law*, 6th ed., Oxford, Oxford University Press, 1988, pp. 399-400, as quoted in Dan Young, 'Current Issues in Government Tendering and Contracting Practice', in *Government Law and Policy, Commercial Aspects*, op. cit., p. 69, footnote 1.

access which include unauthorized access, including alteration of data, and unauthorized interception of electronic information have been addressed in Australia through state and federal computer crime legislation, for example, the Summary Offences Act 1966 (Vic) s 9A and Crimes Act 1914 (Cth).

Statutory rights of access to government records – FOI and archival legislation – compete with the need to ensure certain kinds of information are kept secret, as well as the individual 'right' to privacy, although the latter has only recently become a primary concern of government. Statutory schemes within government for giving public access to records began with access arrangements for older records in the Archives Acts. This has found expression in the thirty-year rule in most Australian jurisdictions, in Britain and most Western countries. Archival institutions are legal actors with rights and responsibilities to a number of persons (also with Crown immunities), which include the public and other government bodies. However in relation to transactions between the public and government agencies, that is the 'business of government', archival institutions are third parties, as they are not the parties in the transaction, except in their own business transactions. Other generic laws, including FOI and privacy law, are relevant to all government transactions.

Citizens' rights and obligations

The process of acquiring and losing citizenship is a fundamental recordkeeping issue, as personal identity records from birth certificates to passports lead to many other rights within a legal system, for example, free education and medical treatment (although some are available through permanent residency status). The necessity for authentic records that provide these rights is illustrated by the Electronic Transactions Act 1999 (Cth) s 4, which excludes electronic 'copies' of migration and citizenship records because of the high risk of fraud in this area. Reliable government officers and stable government are at the core of ensuring basic citizens' rights. Linked to the right to participate fully in the democratic process are rights to government information, privacy and confidentiality. Other rights are in substantive law, such as taxation, and the activities in which individuals engage with government at local, state and federal levels.

Another legal remedy for citizens includes whistleblowing which has been defined as 'the activity performed by a "whistleblower", who in turn is an employee who publicly discloses unlawful, improper or wasteful activity that is occurring within the workplace.'[16] Whistleblower legislation confers immunities for disclosure of matters relating to the public interest to an authorized person. Protection provided to the whistleblower includes civil and criminal immunity or provision of an administrative process for the disclosure that exonerates from any breach of confidentiality regarding improper public conduct, but not individual wrongdoing. There is also victimization protection, and the whistleblower can commence legal proceedings to recover damages for reprisals under the Whistleblowers Protection Act (Qld) s 43 and the Public Interest Disclosure Act (ACT) s 29. However, the

---

[16] John McMillan, 'Whistleblowing', in *Ethics for the Public Sector,* edited by Noel Preston, Sydney, Federation Press, 1994, p. 116.

personal and financial repercussions of whistleblowing have never máde it an attractive option for those who contemplate this course of action.

Freedom of information

Access to public information is one of the most useful tools for citizens to assert their rights and become informed voters. Under Westminster conventions the traditional method of obtaining government information was by way of a question in parliament put by a member of parliament, or through public inquiries, investigations by parliamentary committees, and statutory reporting obligations. Within the Australian political and legal system, which was the first to do so in a Westminster system, 'the single most important way in which individuals can access government information is by federal and state freedom of information (FOI) legislation'.[17] The Australian Freedom of Information Act 1982 (Cth) formed the model for Australian state FOI legislation and arose from administrative law reforms in the late 1970s and early 1980s designed to improve government accountability. It had three goals: to provide individuals with a general right of access to information held by government; to improve public scrutiny and accountability of government; and to increase public participation in the processes of government decision-making. The principles of government underwritten by case law, and the Australian High Court in particular, have clearly demonstrated the public's 'right to know' the dealings of government as in the 'public interest'. The restriction by the courts on the doctrine of public interest immunity has been important in this regard, for example, the application of the public interest test to Crown privilege in *Sankey v Whitlam* and to confidentiality in *Commonwealth v John Fairfax and Sons Ltd*. In *Commonwealth v Northern Land Council* the High Court limited the restriction on public interest immunity in relation to cabinet documents.[18]

Access via FOI is a notion not based on ownership of information but on political and legal rights. The need for a citizen's right to government information has its origin in the development of government secrecy, a feature of bureaucracy, and the need for greater government transparency, identified by the German sociologist and organizational theorist Max Weber in the late nineteenth century. It is in the political environment of secrecy that the need for FOI arises.

Public access rights have to be considered in terms of their impact on recordkeeping in terms of accountability, that is, administrators being required to provide reasons for decisions, the reality of political interference in watering down access rights, and the relationship of accountability and recordkeeping as crucial in the areas of privacy and access (see below). In an era when the technological means of access should provide every

---

[17] W.B. Lane, and Nicolee Dixon, 'Government Decision Making: Freedom of Information and Judicial Review', in *Government Law and Policy, Commercial Aspects,* op. cit., pp. 104-105.

[18] *Sankey v Whitlam* (1978) 142 CLR 1 [53 ALJR 11, 21 ALR 505], *Commonwealth v John Fairfax and Sons Ltd* (1980) 147 CLR 39 [55 ALJR 45, 32 ALR 485] and *Commonwealth v Northern Land Council* (1993) 176 CLR 604 [67 ALJR 405, 112 ALR 409].

citizen with a right to information to enable him/her to participate fully in society, there is a need to clarify legal rights of access to the records arising from outsourced activities, in particular where client interaction with the provider is high, for example, access to government social services.

Government commercialization and access rights

The administrative law regime, which includes judicial review, administrative appeals and Ombudsman legislation in which FOI is a central feature, may be of limited use in providing access to government information in relation to the commercial activities of government, for example, in Australia 'government business enterprises' (GBEs) are increasingly exempted from administrative law, including FOI, as it is seen as placing them at a competitive disadvantage. Outsourcing or 'contractualization' of public administration has led to the diminution of rights available to citizens for accessing government information. Public rights to records cease in the case of privatization, which involves the selling of assets and entitlements of a government-owned corporation to the private sector, completely or partially. As government functions are further privatized FOI will eventually be limited to a diminished area of government activity.

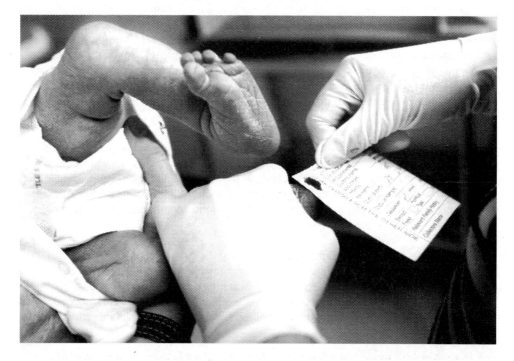

Figure 10.3. In 2004 Victorians were surprised to learn that over thirty years' worth of 'Guthrie cards' – used to collect blood samples from newborn babies for screening for rare diseases – are now owned by a private company.

Privacy rights and obligations

The right to privacy includes the duty not to disclose, and thus diminishes the right to free speech. It is an example of balancing the needs among a number of participants: the record creator, the recipient of the communication, the record subject, the researcher and the public interest needs of law enforcement agencies. The balancing of the right of access to personal information by third parties with the obligation to protect it, like the protection of intellectual property and the right to access creative works, is at the heart of modern privacy law. This is reflected in the Privacy Amendment (Private Sector) Act 2000 (Cth). The main objects of the Act are that:

> s 3(b)(iii) recognises important human rights and social interests that compete with privacy, including the general desirability of a free flow of information (through the media and otherwise) and the right of business to achieve its objectives efficiently.

The protection of privacy is a fundamental principle in recordkeeping practice (see Ethics of Recordkeeping below), which depends on trusted third parties, from archival authorities to professional and industry regulators, as well as the users, who contribute to the web of trust that protects personal information.

Recordkeeping concerns regarding privacy centre on records that may need to be retained to ensure that the rights and obligations of those affected by the business transaction are protected. Privacy regulation does not always accommodate the recordkeeping principles of reliability and authenticity; in particular it may not take account of the record's functional context and the effect of lapse of time on desensitizing personal information recognized in archival access regimes. Of particular concern to archivists internationally is the deletion of personal information that has served its primary purpose. In addition the deletion of inaccurate information may also deny knowledge of the consequences of the use of the incorrect data. An alternative to deletion of incorrect information is to make a notation as adopted in Freedom of Information Act 1982 (Cth) s 50(3): 'To the extent that it is practicable to do so, the agency or Minister must, when making an amendment under paragraph (2)(a), ensure that the record of information is amended in a way that does not obliterate the text of the record as it existed prior to the amendment'.

Ethics of recordkeeping

Ethics involves relationships between individuals, individuals within a community life, how they live as social beings, as moral agents, their acts and motives, and relationships between communities. Recordkeeping as a social activity is concerned with the motivation of moral agents, be they rule-based or personal dispositions, essential to record trustworthiness. As described above juridical systems also recognize the need for moral principles to bind communities together. A community of interest, such as a profession that has developed a set of ethical standards, plays an important part in the regulatory controls over consistent professional practice. Professionals have a special responsibility to avoid or prevent harms beyond everyday responsibilities. The special responsibility is based on two grounds: an implicit contract that a professional has with society and a moral obligation to use knowledge wisely.

A recordkeeping professional has ethical and legal obligations in relation to the accurate capture and storage of the data in the record, its 'stewardship' as property, its legal destruction, its preservation as an authentic record over time, to the protection of personal data from inappropriate disclosure and to providing access to material on equal terms. Individual rights and obligations depend on records as evidence of ethical (or unethical) behaviour, including what is destroyed to cover up unethical or illegal behaviour. The legal obligations are found in FOI, privacy and recordkeeping legislation, and common law duties of confidentiality, contractual and other special relationships, balanced with the correlative rights of access to information.

In addition to legislation, recordkeeping professionals adhere to principles of confidentiality in relation to records in their custody through their professional codes. As stated in the *International Code of Ethics for Archivists:*

> Archivists should respect both access and privacy, and act within the boundaries of relevant legislation. Archivists should take care that corporate and personal privacy as well as national security are protected without destroying information, especially in the case of electronic records where updating and erasure are common practice. They must respect the privacy of individuals who created or are the subjects of records, especially those who had no voice in the use or disposition of the materials.[19]

Archives within globalized networked communities

The delivery of electronic services via the World Wide Web has greatly increased the risk to privacy, of fraudulent manipulation of data and reproduction of records without attribution. Initially there was uncertainty as to the extent to which the existing jurisdictionally-based legal systems were both applicable and enforceable in what appeared to be a 'borderless' Internet. Different countries have taken different paths in relation to regulating web activities through copyright digital agenda acts, privacy and electronic transactions acts. Some countries have passed technology-specific legislation, for example, the United States' digital signature legislation, while other countries have technology-neutral law or 'electronic equivalencies', for example, Australian electronic transactions and copyright law, so that both the tangible old-world product continues to be protected as well as the new one.

Global legislative frameworks have also played an important role in the convergence of Internet law in relation to electronic commerce, privacy and intellectual property. For

---

[19] International Council on Archives, *The International Code of Ethics for Archivists*, 6 September 1996, accessed May 2002 at: http://www.ica.org/biblio/code_ethics_eng.html.

example, in Australia the Electronic Transactions Acts are modeled on the United Nations Commission on International Trade Law (UNCITRAL) model, the Privacy Act 1988 (Cth) draws its principles from the OECD privacy principles, and the Copyright Amendment (Digital Agenda) Act 2000 conforms to the World Intellectual Property Organization (WIPO) 1996 treaties. Despite the passing of specific legislation to accommodate web services in many countries, the legal system tends to trail technology and thus ethical guidance remains an important element of online regulation.

How has global electronic activity affected the regulatory context of recordkeeping? The regulation of recordkeeping in organizations has been largely determined by laws within the jurisdiction in which they operate. These prescribe explicitly or implicitly which records need to be created and retained for business, cultural and other purposes. The organizational perspective of 'regulation' pertaining to a specific industry, as well as laws that are relevant to recordkeeping in general, often in procedural law, rather than substantive law, are still relevant. However, they have to be rethought within the context of 'small government', the globalization of the economy and the limitations of national jurisdiction. These questions are the larger legal, economic and policy issues that need to be kept in mind in relation to recordkeeping in the global environment.

Conclusion

In recordkeeping and archival theory, the nineteenth-century European concept of state had a powerful influence on the adoption of the record creator as the unit of archival description and organization. It was an all-embracing concept of state, which drew its juridical power from a legal system that controlled what was documented, how it was documented, who could have access and how long documents were preserved. In the late twentieth century the state's control was mitigated by citizens attaining political and legal rights which included access to public records and protection from the inappropriate disclosure of their personal information. The current commercialization of government has introduced a number of third parties that have altered the citizen's relationship with the state and their rights to records of government services.

Society has become an inclusive term, encompassing all humanity, and the state is the legal representation of a specific society. Within the juridical view of society, a legal and ethical boundary is defined by the rules sanctioned and enforced by a community which depends on records to enforce the rights and obligations of its members. These communities of common interest include organized interest groups, professional groupings, occupations, industries, multinational corporations, families and like-minded individuals as well as sovereign states. Their driving force is their collective self-interest. As a community of common interest cuts across national and jurisdictional boundaries it has conceptual relevance to global governance, as well as providing a legal and ethical boundary in which internal controls on creators-preservers ensure records are reliable and authentic, and contribute to personal, group and collective identity.

Readings

- Luciana Duranti, *Diplomatics: New Uses for an Old Science*, Lanham, Md, Scarecrow Press in association with Society of American Archivists and Association of Canadian Archivists, 1998.

  This book comprises six reprinted seminal articles on diplomatics which appeared in Archivaria, 29-33, beginning in 1989. It is recommended reading for those who intend to understand the juridical concept as used in diplomatics and the relationship of law to recordkeeping as formulated in archival science.

- Heather MacNeil, *Trusting Records: Legal, Historical and Diplomatic Perspectives*, Dordrecht, Kluwer, 2000.

  Chapter 1 covers the evolution of the concept of record trustworthiness. Chapter 2 analyzes the legal rules governing the admissibility and weight of documentary evidence in common law jurisdictions generally and Canada specifically.

- Chris Hurley, 'Recordkeeping, Document Destruction and the Law (Heiner, Enron and McCabe)', *Archives and Manuscripts*, 30, no. 2, 2002, pp. 6-25.

  Chris Hurley analyzes the recordkeeper's dilemma when the destruction of documents is legal but ethically wrong, although on further analysis may be illegal as it denies potential litigants access to evidence needed to support their case. He suggests a number of avenues to be pursued by the recordkeeping professional.

- Livia Iacovino, *'Things in Action': Teaching Law to Recordkeeping Professionals*, Melbourne, Ancora Press, Monash University, 1998.

  Chapters of relevance are chapter 2 on the records continuum, chapter 4 on law as core recordkeeping knowledge as defined within the juridical concept and chapter 5 on access rights, privacy, property, breach of confidence and evidence law as they relate to recordkeeping.

- *Archives and Manuscripts*, 26, no. 2, 1998.

  This special issue on 'Recordkeeping and the Law' includes a number of themes that are relevant to juridical governance, oral records, and commercialization of government: see Livia Iacovino, 'The Nature of the Nexus between Recordkeeping and the Law', pp. 216-246; Peter R.A. Gray, 'Saying It Like It Is: Oral Traditions, Legal Systems, and Records', pp. 248-269; Simon Fisher, 'The Archival Enterprise, Public Archival Institutions and the Impact of Private Law', pp. 328-366; and Madeline Campbell, 'Government Accountability and Access to Information on Contracted-Out Services', pp. 294-325.

CHAPTER 11
Recordkeeping and societal power[1]

Eric Ketelaar

The struggle of man against power is the struggle of memory against forgetting.[2]

One way of understanding the relationship between memory and power is to conceptualise memory itself as a kind of 'symbolic power' which can be marshalled in much the same way as material power and, to use Pierre Bourdieu's terms, economic and cultural capital are marshalled.[3]

The two quotes at the start of this chapter, one might think, would be more appropriately placed at the beginning of the next chapter on 'Archives and Memory'. However, they also make clear the role of recordkeeping in the dialectic relationship between Power and power. In any society, Power is legitimated through appeals to a collective memory and a collective identity. Individuals can, however, resist such Power by 'emigrating into their inner self' and reverting to their private memories. By sharing these memories within their families and other trusted groups, remembrance of time past will stay alive. The struggle of memory against forgetting will build a collective identity independently from what the prevailing Power decrees.

Individual and collective memories are reflected and represented in 'traces', ranging from the Aboriginal Dreaming to the bits and bytes stored in a computer memory. Many of these inscriptions are the fruit of recordkeeping. Such recordkeeping can serve society as a symbolic power, to be marshalled whenever man has to struggle against Power.

---

[1] This essay is a revised and expanded version of my 'Archival Temples, Archival Prisons: Modes of Power and Protection', *Archival Science*, 2, 2002, pp. 221-238, which was based on my 'Empowering Archives: What Society Expects of Archivists', *Past Caring? What does Society Expect of Archivists? Proceedings of the Australian Society of Archivists Conference, Sydney 13-17 August 2002*, Canberra, Australian Society of Archivists, 2002, 11-27, and on a paper I presented in the seminar 'Archives, Documentation and the Institutions of Social Memory', organized by the Bentley Historical Library and the International Institute of the University of Michigan, Ann Arbor, 31 January 2001.
[2] Milan Kundera, *The Book of Laughter and Forgetting*, Harmondsworth, Penguin, 1983, p. 3.
[3] Jan-Werner Müller, 'Introduction: the Power of Memory, the Memory of Power and the Power over Memory', in Jan-Werner Müller, ed., *Memory and Power in Post-war Europe*, Cambridge, Cambridge University Press, 2002, p. 25.

Power

The Power of the Written Tradition is the title given by Jack Goody to a collection of his essays. In that book Goody, a professor of cultural history and anthropology, continues the arguments he advanced in his earlier writing.[4] Writing, according to Goody, gives power to dominant groups and empowers the dominated. The findings of Goody and others with regard to the profound changes in societies caused by writing, led sociologist Anthony Giddens to propose the importance of the retention and control of information as an essential means of storing power, control and other authoritative resources:

> there is a fundamental sense ... in which all states have been 'information societies', since the generation of state power presumes reflexively gathering, storage, and control of information, applied to administrative ends.[5]

A well-known example is the survey undertaken after the Norman conquest of England in 1066. The survey, epitomizing the royal power of William the Conqueror, created the records providing the input for the Domesday Book. The great book itself, England's first and most remarkable public record, was less a usable record than proof of the power of writing and a symbol of nearly mythical royal power, equal to the power of the Last Judgement – hence the name given to the register.[6]

Power, control and information are not only used by the nation-state. Power is 'an integral and primary aspect of social life', Anthony Giddens posits, while Michel Foucault asserts 'Power relations are rooted in the whole network of the social'.[7] Power and control are exercised whenever an individual or organization, public or private, wants something to be done. Control – in James Beniger's phrase, 'purposive influence toward a predetermined goal' – presupposes power. Control is derived from the medieval Latin *contrarotulare*, meaning, checking something with the rolls, the medieval form of parchment and paper accounts and other records.[8] To check whether the aspired goal has been achieved, information is gathered to assess the current state and to compare that with the intended outcome, or rather vice versa. Information in the cybernetic (= controlling and steering) cycle leads to knowledge, and knowledge serves power. As David Hanlon remarks:

---

[4] These include *The Domestication of the Savage Mind*, Cambridge, Cambridge University Press, 1977, and the influential *The Logic of Writing and the Organization of Society*, New York: Cambridge University Press, 1986.

[5] Anthony Giddens, *The Nation-State and Violence*, Cambridge, Polity Press, 1985, p. 178; *Power, Property and the State*, London, Macmillan, 1981, pp. 94-95.

[6] Michael T. Clanchy, *From Memory to Written Record: England 1066-1307*, 2nd ed. Oxford, Blackwell, 1993, pp. 32-35; Elizabeth Hallam and Andrew Prescott, *The British Inheritance*, Berkeley, University of California Press, 1999, pp. 4-5.

[7] Giddens, *Power, Property and the State*, op cit., p. 50; Michel Foucault, 'The Subject and power', in James D. Faubion, ed., *Michel Foucault. Power,* vol. 3, London, Penguin, 2002, p. 345.

[8] James R. Beniger, *The Control Revolution*, Cambridge, Mass., Harvard University Press, 1986, pp. 7-8.

We cannot fool ourselves into ignoring the ways in which knowledge serves power and how knowledge in the service of power is collected, housed, catalogued and preserved.[9]

Records and archives

That knowledge-power is ingrained in records and archives. The power of archives is as old as the archives. Indeed, the word derives from the Greek *archè*, meaning power or government.[10] 'There is no political power without control of the archive, if not of memory', writes Jacques Derrida.[11] Governing the nation-state depends on the creation and maintenance of records, both for its internal organizalion and for its disciplinary and surveillance power.[12]

But records themselves have power too. Records 'are about imposing control and order on transactions, events, people, and societies through the legal, symbolic, structural, and operational power of recorded communication', Joan Schwartz and Terry Cook assert in their introduction to two issues of the journal *Archival Science* devoted to archives, records, and power.[13]

Surveillance

In the eighteenth century Jeremy Bentham designed a panopticon, a prison where the inmates were kept under constant surveillance (pan-optical) by guards in a central control tower, who could not be seen by the prisoners.[14] Bentham believed the power of the system to rest not only in that it locked up prisoners in their cells, but, more importantly, in the prisoners' self-consciousness of knowing that they were constantly being watched and guarded. Real panopticons have seldom been built, although a famous one was constructed in Tasmania for hardened exiles.[15] The panopticon inspired the architecture not only of

---

[9] David Hanlon, 'The Chill of History: the Experience, Emotion and Changing Politics of Archival Research in the Pacific', *Archives and Manuscripts*, 27, 1999, p. 15.

[10] Archè means also beginning. See Roberto G. Echevarría, *Myth and Archive: A Theory of Latin American Narrative*. 2nd ed., Durham, NC, Duke University Press, 1998, pp. 31-32.

[11] Jacques Derrida, *Archive Fever*, Chicago, University of Chicago Press, 1996, p. 4.

[12] Giddens, *The Nation-State and Violence*, op. cit., pp. 172-192; Giddens, *A Contemporary Critique*, op. cit., pp. 174-176; Christopher Dandeker, *Surveillance, Power and Modernity*, Cambridge, Polity Press, 1990); David Lyon, *The Electronic Eye*, Minneapolis, University of Minnesota Press, 1994; Frank Webster, *Theories of the Information Society*, London, Routledge, 1995, pp. 52-73; Matt Matsuda, *The Memory of the Modern*, Oxford, Oxford University Press, 1996.

[13] Joan M. Schwartz and Terry Cook, 'Archives, Records, and Power: the Making of Modern Memory', *Archival Science*, 2, 2002, p. 13.

[14] Michel Foucault, *Discipline and Punish*, New York, Pantheon, 1975; Mark Poster, *The Mode of Information,* Chicago, University of Chicago Press, 1990, pp. 89-91.

[15] Richard F. Hamilton, *The Social Misconstruction of Reality,* New Haven, Yale University Press, 1996, pp. 175-181.

prisons, but also of libraries. The best-known example is the panoptical reading room of the British Museum built in 1854, which expressed, as its copy the reading room of the State Library of Victoria expresses today, the power of a comprehensive and well-ordered system of knowledge, to be consulted under the strictest surveillance and discipline.[16]

Figure 11.1. The domed reading room of the State Library of Victoria, 2004: the architecture of surveillance applied to knowledge and the invigilation of its use.

Apart from prisoners being locked up in their prison, society itself often became imprisoned. In the eighteenth century, for example, the French introduced the police state with the *lettres de cachet* (sealed letters, in other words: records) that, once they issued by

---

[16] George F. Barwick, *The Reading Room of the British Museum*, London, 1929, and Philip R. Harris, *The Reading Room*, London, British Library, 1979, quoted by Jo Tollebeek, 'Het Archief: de Panoptische Utopie van de Historicus', in *Toegang. Ontwikkelingen in de Ontsluiting van Archieven: Jaarboek 2001*, 's-Gravenhage, Stichting Archiefpublicaties, 2001, p. 88.

royal edict, confined the subject to house arrest or worse.[17] The records were as powerful as the prison. Therefore, the people storming the Bastille on 14 July 1789 cried, according to Charles Dickens' *A Tale of Two Cities* (book 2, chapter 21):

> 'The Prisoners!'
> 'The Records!'
> 'The secret cells!'
> 'The instruments of torture!'
> 'The Prisoners!'

The prisoners were freed; the Bastille prison with its cells and instruments of torture was demolished; the records were liberated! Nearly two centuries later, their power was released anew in Michel Foucault and Arlette Farge's study devoted to the *lettres de cachet* in the archives of the Bastille prison.[18]

Two hundred years after the capture of the Bastille, shouts corresponding to the cries for the Bastille records were heard from the civic groups storming the Stasi offices in Erfurt, Dresden, Leipzig, Berlin and other German cities: 'Security for *our* records', 'I want *my* file', 'Freedom for *my* file'. In the minds of the people, the files of the East German intelligence service were converted into *their* files.[19] 'Police files are our only claim to immortality' writes Milan Kundera.[20] At the same time, the Stasi archives stood for an invisible power – the power of the past and the power of the future, when the Stasi archives would be instruments in the process of political and social transition. This attitude, a seminal Unesco report on archives of repression suggests, was largely influenced by the cultural memory of the use made after the Second World War of the Nazi archives.[21]

---

[17] Wolfgang Ernst, *Das Rumoren der Archive,* Berlin, Merve, 2002, pp. 22-23, 78-79.

[18] Arlette Farge and Michel Foucault, *Le désordre des familles*, Paris, Gallimard, 1982.

[19] Cornelia Vismann, *Akten: Medientechnik und Recht*, Frankfurt am Main, Fischer Taschenbuch, 2000, pp. 307, 310.

[20] Kundera, op. cit., IV.6, p. 87.

[21] Antonio González Quintana, 'Archives of the security services of former repressive regimes,' *Janus*, 1998, no. 2, pp. 13-14.

Figure 11.2. When civic groups stormed the Stasi headquarters in East Berlin on 15 January 1990 they claimed 'Freiheit für meine Akte!' (Freedom for my file!); someone scrawled the slogan on the sentry box.

Entire societies may be imprisoned in what Foucault calls *panopticism*, regimes where power rests on supervision and examination that entail a knowledge concerning those who are supervised.[22] Big Brother is watching you, not by keeping his eyes continually fixed on you necessarily, but by creating and checking your file, or rather – as in Bentham's panopticon – keeping you aware of the existence of a file on you. In East Germany the pure knowledge – or rather the assumption – that the Stasi was keeping records affected people's

---

[22] Michel Foucault, 'Truth and juridical forms', in Faubion, op. cit., pp. 58-59; Webster, op. cit., pp. 69-70.

behaviour.[23] The records exerted their power over people not by being used, but simply by being there – not unlike the intimidating effect of the Domesday Book. In this respect there is a striking similarity between totalitarian and colonial regimes, as Ann Stoler affirms:

> that colonial states were first and foremost information-hungry machines in which power accrued from the massive accumulation of ever-more knowledge rather than from the quality of it.[24]

Documentary surveillance to discipline people is not only a tool of public government.[25] As Giddens stated, 'surveillance in the capitalist enterprise is the key to management'.[26] Every religious, economic, or social organization is dependent upon administrative power, to control (in Beniger's sense), to keep track of what the organization is doing in relation to its members, workers, and clients. Consequently they also survey *and* determine how people behave. Oscar Gandy uses the term 'the panoptic sort' to denote the system of disciplinary surveillance, using a number of technologies, involving collection and sharing of information about citizens, employees, and consumers – information which is used to co-ordinate and control access to products and services in daily life.[27] Such 'womb-to-tomb surveillance' has been called the 'record-prison', as effective as the panopticon.[28] 'Files of files can be generated and this process can be continued until a few men consider millions as if they were in the palms of their hands,' writes Bruno Latour.[29]

Australia had and has its panopticons as well. One of the most tragic examples is that of the government and mission institutions where thousands of Aboriginal children were placed after they had been taken away from their families.[30] In these 'half-caste homes' knowledge-power was exercised. A report of the inspection of a half-caste school in Darwin, dating from September 1936, starts with: 'I. Records. Neatly and correctly kept.' Section II Government begins with 'Discipline apparently presents no difficulties.' Organisation in Section III, is 'unsatisfactory ... Despite written instructions ... the Head Teacher has attempted too much and accomplished very little'. After IV Methods follows (at last!) V. Proficiency and progress of children.[31] The Aboriginal children were locked up,

---

[23] Joachim Gauck, 'Von der Würde der Unterdrückten', in Hans Joachim Schädlich, ed., *Aktenkundig*, Berlin, Rowholt, 1992, pp. 266; James M. O'Toole, 'Cortes's Notary: The Symbolic Power of Records', *Archival Science*, 2, 2002, pp. 56-57.

[24] Ann L. Stoler, 'Colonial Archives and the Arts of Governance', *Archival Science*, 2, 2002, p. 100.

[25] Dandeker, op. cit., pp. 150-192; Oscar H. Gandy Jr., *The Panoptic Sort*, Boulder, Colo., Westview Press, 1993, pp. 60-122.

[26] Anthony Giddens, *Social Theory and Modern Sociology*, Cambridge, Polity Press, 1987, p. 175.

[27] Gandy, op. cit., pp. 1, 15; Poster, op. cit., pp. 91-98.

[28] Arthur R. Miller, *The Assault on Privacy,* Ann Arbor, University of Michigan Press, 1971, quoted by Thomas S. McCoy, 'Surveillance, Privacy and Power: Information trumps Knowledge', *Communications*, 16, 1991, p. 35.

[29] Bruno Latour, 'Visualization and Cognition: Thinking with Eyes and Hands', *Knowledge and Society*, 6, 1986, p. 28.

[30] Rowena MacDonald, *Between Two Worlds*, Alice Springs, IAD Press, 1995.

[31] Ibid, p. 35.

maybe not always physically, but in a system of surveillance and knowledge- power, based on and practised by registration, filing and records.

The archiving gaze

So far we have encountered records as instruments of power. But these instruments have an intrinsic power too. Public and private agents do not merely observe and describe reality; they shape people, events, and the environment into entities that will fit their categorizations and that are recordable. This social reification entails that there are virtually no facts other than those that are contained in records.[32] Archives, writes Derrida, do not only serve to preserve an archivable content of the past. No, life itself and its relation with the future are determined by the technique of archiving. This means that records have power also by what they record, and what they do not record, and how they record. American anthropologist, Michel-Rolph Trouillot, mentions the slave registers which did not include births. This exclusion did not result from carelessness, nor from a need to keep them secret, and it had no ideological reasons. Births were not included simply because registration only made sense when it was sufficiently certain that the children would remain alive.[33] Today in The Netherlands, neither a birth certificate nor a death certificate is made when a baby dies before its birth has been registered. All that will be drawn up is a certificate stating that the child wasn't alive at the moment of declaration.[34] For the registry office, children who die before being registered were never born, just as, because the slave register did not have a column for births, slave-born babies were not considered to exist.

Samuel Kaplan demonstrated the politics embedded in the administrative reports concerning Cilicia, drawn up by French officials after the First World War.[35] All the field officers availed themselves of modes of representation and stylistic paraphernalia that were readily accessible to their intended readers. The rhetorical strategies were chosen purposefully:

> Competing social visions affected the writing of documents. Specifically, these visions manifested themselves in the divergent political agendas that French officials brought to bear when deciding what was included and excluded from the reports.

---

[32] James C. Scott, *Seeing Like a State*, New Haven, Yale University Press, 1998, pp. 82-83; Alain Desrosières, *The Politics of Large Numbers*, Cambridge, Mass., Harvard University Press, 1998; Geoffrey C. Bowker and Susan Leigh Star, *Sorting Things Out*, Cambridge, Mass., MIT Press, 1999.
[33] Michel-Rolph Trouillot, *Silencing the Past,* Boston, Mass., Beacon Press, 1995, pp. 26-27, 48, 51-53.
[34] Eric Ketelaar, 'Archivalisation and Archiving', *Archives and Manuscripts*, 27, 1999, p. 56.
[35] Sam Kaplan, 'Documentation as History, History as Documentation: French Military Officials' Ethnological Reports on Cilicia.' Paper presented in the seminar 'Archives, Documentation and the Institutions of Social Memory,' organized by the Bentley Historical Library and the International Institute of the University of Michigan, Ann Arbor, 17 January 2001.

To understand the power of the record fully, one has to decode its content, structure, form and the recordkeeping contexts. Such decoding requires, in Ann Stoler's forcible expression, reading 'along the archival grain', accepting even the unethical, forbidden, illegal, evil or irrational recordkeeping.[36]

Records reflect realities as perceived by their creators. As James Scott argues:

> builders of the modern nation-state do not merely describe, observe, and map; they strive to shape a people and landscape that will fit their techniques of observation … there are virtually no other facts for the state than those that are contained in documents.[37]

This 'archiving gaze' permeates the record. It is especially forceful when the 'archiver' and the 'archived' belong to different power systems, as, for example, in colonized and occupied territories. Evelyn Wareham writes that 'Records generated by colonial administrations are intrinsically associated with political systems by which local communities were subjected to outside power.'[38]

The 'archival turn' in post-colonial scholarship has led to the rediscovery of the power reflected *in* the records and of the power *of* the records. One of these powers is that colonial archives are not only, as Ann Stoler argues, 'products of state machines, it is less obvious that they are, in their own right, technologies that bolstered the production of those states themselves'.[39]

Records of repression

Records in our surveillance society reveal as much about the administering as about the administered. That is why it is so difficult to keep the right balance between, on the one hand, the requirement to destroy personal data when they have served their primary purpose, including that of serving the legal rights of the data subjects, and, on the other hand, the possibility that the files might get a new meaning and purpose in the future. Many of the files created during and after the Second World War, which are now being used in the processes of restitution of and recompensation for Holocaust assets, should have been destroyed. Such destruction was, not long ago, lobbied for by partisans of 'the right to forget'.[40] Such destruction would have been in accordance with the criteria of data

---

[36] Stoler, op. cit., pp. 99-10; Michael Piggott and Sue McKemmish, 'Recordkeeping and Reconciliation', *Convergence*, Australian Society of Archivists and the Records Management Association of Australia, 2001, p. 337.

[37] Scott, op. cit., pp. 82-83.

[38] Evelyn Wareham, 'From Explorers to Evangelists: Archivists, Recordkeeping, and Remembering in the Pacific Islands', *Archival Science*, 2, 2002, p. 199.

[39] Stoler, op. cit., pp. 90, 98.

[40] Denis Peschanski, 'Les responsablités de l'historien face aux archives sensibles', in Gérard Ermisse, ed., *Mémoire et histoire*, Paris, International Council on Archives, 2000, pp. 136-137.

protection and privacy legislation and of most professionally accepted criteria for archival appraisal. One of the lessons learned is that files created under unprecedented circumstances, or in an extraordinary era – such as during or after war, revolution, natural or man-made disasters, political or economic crises – have to be appraised differently from those created in the course of 'normal' human business. The same applies to the archives of repression. The Unesco report on archives of repression prohibits, when appraising these archives, the use of selection criteria based on their value for historical research; the individual rights of victims of political repression take precedence over historical research.[41] Archives of repression are not only created by intelligence services, armed forces, police, prisons and concentration camps; other repressive institutions are paramilitary bodies, tribunals, psychiatric centres for 're-education', and all sorts of civil administrative bodies.[42] And let us be conscious of the fact that power which creates archives of repression is a very old phenomenon; one of the first (and still existing) manifestations of this phenomenon is the Inquisition.

Figure 11.3. Destroying records to save lives: During the German occupation of The Netherlands civil registration records became records of repression. To prevent the Nazis from using them for identifying people to send to concentration camps or into forced labour, Dutch resistance raided the Amsterdam Central Register of Population, emptied the file drawers and set fire to the records (27 March 1943). Within a week most of the resistance fighters were caught and executed.

---

[41] Quintana, op. cit, p. 17; Caroline Obert-Piketty, 'La Mission d'étude sur la spoliation et la restitution des biens juifs de France', in Ermisse, op. cit., p. 143.

[42] Quintana, op. cit., p. 18.

Records of liberation

Records, then, may be instruments of power, but, paradoxically, the same records can also become instruments of empowerment and liberation, salvation and freedom. The antipodes of the agencies of repression just mentioned are the truth and reconciliation commissions, United Nations-sponsored criminal tribunals, royal commissions and various other fact-finding and judicial institutions. They convert the records of the former 'bureaucracy of destruction' [43] into instruments of atonement, while creating their own records of reconciliation. The Nazis' obsession with recording and listing also made them receptive to the liberating effect of lists, as anyone who has seen *Schindler's List* knows. The detailed recordkeeping system of the Nazis still forms an indispensable source for restitution and reparation. On-going restitution now, a half-century later, to the rightful owners or their children of works of art, diamonds, gold and other Holocaust assets is only possible by using the records made by German institutions. [44] In the same way, the records of government institutions and church missions continually supply the clues for many Aboriginal people in Australia and elsewhere to reunite with their families. [45]

Records can sometimes have the power of a sanctuary. Because the Nazi Nuremberg laws declared everyone to be a full Jew who had four Jewish grandparents, a life could be saved if a person could prove that one of the grandparents was non-Jewish. During the German occupation of The Netherlands, several archivists were involved in forging seventeenth and eighteenth century registers of marriage. They faked a marriage between a forebear of a Jew with a Christian, thereby saving the lives of their descendants. After the war, these faked registers were replaced by the originals, which had been kept hidden – like the proverbial needle in a haystack – in the stacks, sometimes in the company of irreplaceable Jewish archives and Torah rolls. [46]

Sometimes, quite unintentionally, archives may be safe havens. Vitaly Shentalinsky revealed how the KGB archives yielded literary treasures, which had been confiscated from their authors and kept in files as evidence of the writer's alleged treason. These files also contained the original literary texts written down during the interrogations in the Lubyanka headquarters of the KGB, such as Osip Mandelstam's autograph copy of his poem about Stalin ('The Kremlingrag dweller ... Fat fingers as oily as maggots ... And his large laughing cockroach eyes ...'). The poem is annotated: 'Appended to the record of O.

---

[43] Paul R. Barthrop, 'The Holocaust, the Aborigines, and the Bureaucracy of Destruction: an Australian Dimension of Genocide', *Journal of Genocide Research*, March 2001, pp. 75-87, quoted by Piggott and McKemmish, op. cit., p. 334.

[44] Eric Ketelaar, 'Understanding Archives of the People, by the People, and for the People', in J.D. Bindenagel, ed., *Washington Conference on Holocaust-Era Assets Proceedings*, Washington D.C., 1999, pp. 749-761; Greg Bradsher, 'Turning History into Justice: The National Archives and Records Administration and Holocaust-Era Assets, 1996-2001', in Richard J. Cox and David A. Wallace, eds, *Archives and the Public Good*, Westport, Ct, Quorum Books, 2002, pp. 177-203.

[45] MacDonald, op. cit., pp. 72-73.

[46] Frederick C.J. Ketelaar, 'Qui desiderat pacem', *Nederlands Archievenblad*, 90, 1986, pp. 97-102.

Mandelstam's interrogation, 25 May 1934' and countersigned by the interrogator.[47] In Romania between 50,000 and 100,000 pages of literary manuscripts confiscated by the totalitarian regime have been returned to the rightful owners.[48]

Capturing people

Power is control, control is surveillance and recording:

> Control over racial classification, employment, movement, association, purchase of property, recreation, and culture, sport, and so on, all were documented by thousands of government offices. This was supplemented by the record of surveillance activities by the security police and numerous other state intelligence bodies, as well as by large quantities of records confiscated from individuals and organisations ...[49]

In these terms Verne Harris describes South Africa under Apartheid. But it might also have been the description of the German Democratic Republic with its Stasi files, or the Soviet Union with its KGB archive, or Cambodia with the Khmer Rouge archives, or Nazi-Germany, or too many other cases.[50]

In Auschwitz, Dachau and most other concentration camps the Arbeitseinsatz (Labour Assignment Office) was crammed with IBM sorters, tabulators and printers. The office 'tabulated not only work assignments, but also the camp hospital index and the general death and inmate statistics'.[51] Edwin Black's recent book shows how state agencies and private business co-operated in oppression through records. Like other totalitarian regimes, the Nazis were obsessed by registering, counting, making lists, and censuses. Thousands of people were involved in the 'restlose Erfassung' – the term means 'total registering', but also has the connotation of all-embracing seizure.[52] And seized they were, the Jews, the gypsies, the mentally ill, the handicapped. The German census of 1939 supplied the data for the Volkstumskartei, the 'Registry of National Character', which captured Jews and all other people in the German Reich who were considered not to belong to the German Volk. Keeping this registry up-to-date and perfecting it was the main task of the Bureau for publications of the SS Security Office, the Sicherheitsdienst. And where else could such a

---

[47] Vitaly Shentalinsky, *The KGB's Literary Archive*, London, Harvill Press, 1997, pp. 170-175.

[48] Florin Pintilie, 'Modalités de conservation et d'accès aux documents de la Securitate actuellement en dépôt dans les Archives du Service roumain d'information', in Ermisse, op. cit., p. 154.

[49] Verne Harris, *Exploring Archives,* Pretoria, National Archives of South Africa, 2000, p. 8, and 'The Archival Sliver: Power, Memory, and Archives in South Africa', *Archival Science*, 2, 2002, p. 69.

[50] Quintana, op. cit.

[51] Edwin Black, *IBM and the Holocaust*, New York, Crown, 2001, p. 352.

[52] Götz Aly and Karl Heinz Roth, *Die restlose Erfassung,* Frankfurt am Main, Fischer Taschenbuch, 2000 (originally published 1964); Carl J. Couch, *Information Technologies and Social Orders*, New York, Aldine de Gruyter, 1996, pp. 90-92.

registration bureau be better located than in the Archives? Indeed, the Privy Prussian State Archives in Berlin were in charge of the registry.[53]

Figure 11.4. 'Since everything in Buchenwald is administered, classified, registered, recorded in inventories and countersigned ... The bureaucratic order reigns over the SS empire' (Jorge Semprun).[54] Two prisoners managing the detainees' records in the record office of the Political Department (Registratur in der Politische Abteilung) in the concentration camp Buchenwald, 1943.

Controlling memories

In all totalitarian systems records are used as instruments of power, of extreme surveillance, oppression, torture, murder. The records themselves are dumb, but without them the oppressor is powerless. In the hands, however, of a killer 'that exercises his bloody craft behind a desk' (to quote Gideon Hausner, attorney general in the Eichmann trial), the files and registers become instruments of 'a bureacracy of murder'.[55] The records gain fearful

---

[53] Aly and Roth, op. cit, p. 95.

[54] Jorge Semprun, *Quel beau dimanche,* Paris, Bernard Grasset, 1980, p. 358 (quotation is translated).

[55] *The Trial of Adolf Eichmann: Record of the Proceedings in the District Court of Jerusalem*, vol. 1, Jerusalem, Ministry of Justice, State of Israel, 1992, p. 62; Albert Breton and Ronald Wintrobe, 'The Bureaucracy of Murder Revisited', *Journal of Political Economy*, 94, 1986, pp. 905-926.

power in a totalitarian system, the power George Orwell prophesied in his *Nineteen Eighty-four*. In Orwell's haunting science-fiction novel, the Party attests:

> Past events, it is argued, have no objective existence, but survive only in written records and in human memories. The past is whatever the records and the memories agree upon. And since the Party is in full control of all records and in equally full control of the minds of its members, it follows that the past is whatever the Party chooses to make it. (book 2, chapter 9)

The principal character of *Nineteen Eighty-four* is Winston Smith, who works in the Ministry of Truth, constantly rewriting the past. When Smith is interrogated, his torturer asks:

> 'Does the past exist concretely, in space? Is there somewhere or other a place, a world of solid objects, where the past is still happening?'
> 'No.'
> 'Then where does the past exist, if at all?'
> 'In records. It is written down.''
> 'In records. And ----?'
> 'In the mind. In human memories.'
> 'In memory. Very well, then. We, the Party, control all records, and we control all memories. Then we control the past, do we not?' (book 3, chapter 2)

The power of records does not always flow in one direction, in James O'Toole's arresting wording. He discusses samizdat writing in the Soviet Union:

> The victims of systematic oppression may use records to resist the powerful, even in unlikely circumstances. When pressed, they can seize a power that would be otherwise unavailable to them by mastering and controlling the processes of writing.[56]

Human rights

Societal power is a double-edged phenomenon: power is used for restraint and for liberation, for repression and for redemption, power is productive and destructive. Records too are both 'instruments of oppression and domination' and 'enablers of democratic empowerment', as Adrian Cunningham advances.[57] Michael Piggott and Sue McKemmish forcefully demonstrate, in their review of the nexus between recordkeeping and reconciliation, that records have a two-fold power: being evidence of oppression and evidence required to gain freedom, evidence of wrong-doing and evidence for undoing the wrong.[58] This restraining and empowering power of records and archives is an interesting

---

[56] O'Toole, op. cit., pp. 57-58.
[57] Adrian Cunningham, 'The Soul and Conscience of the Archivist: Meditations on Power, Passion and Positivism in a Crusading Profession', *Argiefnuus/Archives News,* 43, no. 4, June 2001, p. 173.
[58] Piggott and McKemmish, op. cit.

complement of the social reification I mentioned earlier. If the fact of oppression appears in the records originally created for surveillance and tyranny, they can also be used for reclaiming human rights and regaining freedom.

We have seen how records act as instruments of power. Oppressed by power, but also countervailing that power, is the basic human veneration of human rights: the right to life, liberty, security of person and property; freedom from slavery, torture or cruel, inhuman or degrading treatment or punishment; and the freedom of any kind of discrimination, because, as the Universal Declaration of Human Rights affirms, all people are equal before the law. Ensuring and securing these human rights has nowhere been expressed more convincingly than in societies in transition from oppression to democracy. In most of the former communist countries, the new democratic parliament has passed laws to compensate citizens for arbitrary and unlawful nationalizalion in communist times. This has led to thousands and thousands of people (in Romania more than 250,000 in a single year – 1998)[59] rushing to the state archives where they hoped the evidence they needed would be kept.[60] In Hungary, Romania and Poland the general public suddenly realized the value of well-kept and accessible public archives and the importance of archival institutions.[61] People wrongly convicted under a totalitarian regime for crimes they never committed are regularly being rehabilitated on the basis of evidence in the archives of their former oppressor.[62] In Spain the Civil War Section of the National Historical Archive in Salamanca, by delivering tens of thousands of certificates, helped victims of the Francoist repression in their struggle for amnesty and indemnity. The already cited Unesco report on archives of repression calls this 'the boomerang-effect' and declares that the archives

> which were essential for carrying out repressive activities, are converted under the new political regime ... into an important means for enabling new social relationships to be established.[63]

Refiguring archives

The political and societal inversion in former totalitarian countries involves a profound reassessment of the role of archival institutions too. Formerly they were identified, and identified themselves, with the regime and the State. Now, as the President of Romania

---

[59] Costin Fenesan, 'Les Archives nationales de Roumanie dans le contexte de la société contemporaine', in Ermisse, op. cit., p. 106; Silviu Vacaru, 'Les Archives nationales et leurs relations avec l'administration publique', in Ermisse, op. cit., p. 84.

[60] Lajos Körmendy, 'Historical challenges and archivists' responses, Hungary, 1945-2000', *Archivum*, 45, 2000, p. 49.

[61] Vacaru, op. cit., pp. 84 , 90, 91; Daria Nalecz, 'Évolution du rapport au secret d'État en Pologne depuis les années 80', in Ermisse, op. cit., p. 110.

[62] Pintilie, op. cit, p. 153.

[63] Quintana, op. cit., p. 10.

said,[64] the rule of law necessitates reversing archival politics, refashioning public archives and refiguring them into archives of the people, 'civic archives'.[65]

Paradoxically, the power of archives of repression and the 'fetishism of the detail' inflating the archives (of Stasi and FBI alike)[66] make them into invaluable empowering sources of collective and individual memories. In totalitarian, dictatorial or repressive regimes

> there is a lack of any legal means of reflecting a plurality of ideas and behaviour. It is only the archives, particularly those of the police and intelligence services which controlled the population, which can reflect the latent social confrontations inherent in these regimes. In contrast to the public image which such regimes have tried to present, their real nature can be discovered in the files and indices of the security services.[67]

Upon independence and liberation, the new societal powers will use and maintain the records of the former regime. Undoubtedly, as the UNESCO report on archives of repression states

> the information they contain is, in many cases, pure invention. But they are authentic documents. In the democratic period, documents of the former regimes will become authentic and valid proof of actions taken against people for political, ideological, religious, ethnic and racial motives.[68]

But the archives have a double-edged power: created and used primarily against individuals and minority groups, they can become, in the hands and minds of these groups, either objects for destruction or new weapons to combat others. Jeff Burds comments:

> One of the greatest obstacles to understanding the history of Eastern Europe during and after the Second World War has been that the memories of the events themselves have been constructed ethnically – which is to say, each ethnic group has recorded their own

---

[64] Gérard Ermisse, 'Les Archives au coeur du débat démocratique', in Ermisse, op. cit., p. 11; Emil Constantinescu, 'Message', in Ermisse, op. cit, p. 25; Virgil Nitulescu, 'Les possibilités d'appliquer les instructions du Conseil de l'Europe en Roumanie', in Ermisse, op. cit., p. 48.

[65] Carolyn Hamilton, Verne Harris and Graeme Reid, 'Introduction', in Carolyn Hamilton et al, *Refiguring the Archive*, Kluwer, Dordrecht, 2002, pp. 7-17; William G. Rosenberg, 'Politics in the (Russian) Archives: The "Objectivity Question", Trust, and the Limitations of Law', *American Archivist*, 64, 2001, pp. 78-95, especially 78-85 describing the refashioning of the former Soviet state archives. The political changes in Central and Eastern Europe also make it necessary to reconceptualize archival principles as the concept of the 'state archival fonds' which treated public and private archives indifferently, according to Charles Kecskeméti, quoted in Ermisse, op. cit., p. 119.

[66] Sonia Combe, *Une société sous surveillance*, Paris, Albin Michel, 1999, p. 78.

[67] Quintana, op. cit., p. 12.

[68] As German archivist Klaus Oldenhage writes, referring to the Stasi archives, the value of archived texts 'does not depend on the moral quality of its creator' – Klaus Oldenhage, 'Was bringt das neue "Stasi-Aktengesetz"?', *Der Archivar*, 55, 2002, pp. 335-336.

versions of the tragic devastation of that era. The postwar phenomena of diasporas and refugee cultures have further splintered memories and perspectives, and subsequently channeled them through the prisms of the Cold War, East and West.[69]

The power of memories

Another example of such memory (and archival) politics is given by Robert Donia who reported on archives and libraries in Bosnia and Herzegovina, where the power of different political factions and individuals dictate the formation and preservation of certain kinds of social memory:

> Key institutions of social memory in Bosnia are gradually moving from the public, state-controlled sector to ownership by individuals and political formations with distinct national outlooks and agendas. The new elites are either creating or reviving distinctive contours in the visual landscape and new policies into archives, museums, and libraries under their control. These transitions-in-progress are partly the result of the international community's policies and resource allocations.[70]

Such appropriation of memories, and of the archives and artifacts which embody memories, happens elsewhere too. One may think of the Pacific Islanders' taboo on records, both those in their personal possession and those preserved by public institutions.[71] The same applies to Aboriginal and Torres Strait Islander records in Australia.[72] In these cases we accept the power of indigenous customs and beliefs to outweigh the principle of equal access to archives. But how far can one go? How much power has the creator of archives, or his heirs? Should one permit the owner of a Rembrandt to use the painting as a dartboard? is the provocative question Joseph Sax poses in his treatise on public and private rights in cultural treasures.[73] Robert Adler demonstrated how the policies and politics of the Kennedy Library to preserve a specific kind of memory are influenced by the power of the Kennedy family. Archivist Bill Joyce, who has been a member of the Assassination Records Review Board, confirmed this by stating that the Board

---

[69] Jeff Burds, 'Ethnicity, Memory, and Violence: Reflections on Special Problems in Soviet and East European Archives'. Paper presented in the seminar 'Archives, Documentation and the Institutions of Social Memory', organized by the Bentley Historical Library and the International Institute of the University of Michigan, Ann Arbor, 7 February 2001.

[70] Robert J. Donia, 'The New Masters of Memory: Libraries, Archives, and Museums in Post-socialist Bosnia and Hercegovina', Paper presented in the seminar 'Archives, Documentation and the Institutions of Social Memory', organized by the Bentley Historical Library and the International Institute of the University of Michigan, Ann Arbor, 15 November 2000.

[71] Monica Wehner and Ewan Maidment, 'Ancestral Voices: Aspects of Archives Administration in Oceania', *Archives and Manuscripts*, 27, 1999, p. 32.

[72] Sue McKemmish, 'Placing Records Continuum Theory and Practice', *Archival Science*, 1, 2001, pp. 333-359 (footnote 47).

[73] Joseph L. Sax, *Playing Darts with a Rembrandt*, Ann Arbor, University of Michigan Press, 1999.

was unsuccessful in achieving access to the papers of Robert F. Kennedy. These files (including much of Kennedy's records as Attorney General in his brother's administration) are located at the Kennedy Library in Boston, though access is maintained through a committee of family members.[74]

Records have power

Records have power, imbued as they are with tacit narratives.[75] Records do not speak for themselves because they merely echo what their creator has meant and what the user of the record wants the document to tell him or her. Records, as John Van Maanen and Brian Pentland concluded in their study of police records

> like any product of a social process, are fundamentally self-conscious and self-interested. What is recorded is never simply 'what happened' because, first, no event can be fully or exhaustively described and, second, all records, as institutionalised forms, represent the collective wisdom of those who are trained to keep them. Records are not factual, neutral, technical documents alone, although while serving legitimate ends they must appear this way, and while serving illegitimate ones even more so. They are designed – implicitly or explicitly – to produce an effect in some kind of audience, which itself actively uses records to interpret events. This is not to suggest conscious deceit or cynicism on the part of either record keepers or users (although ... this is certainly possible). Rather it is simply to acknowledge and open up for analysis the conditions under which organizational records are produced and used.[76]

Reformulating Van Maanen and Pentland's assessment in terms of the power embedded in recordkeeping, one has to acknowledge that the creation, maintenance and use of records are expressions of societal power. It even starts before a document is captured in a recordkeeping system: the conscious or unconscious choice to consider something worth archiving (what I have named archivalization) is an expression of societal power. This is true even for the seemingly innocent technologies of filing, categorization, codification,

---

[74] Robert M. Adler, 'The Public Controversy Over the Kennedy Memorabilia Project'; William Joyce, 'Targeted Declassification: Federal Records and the End of the Cold War'. Papers presented in the seminar 'Archives, Documentation and the Institutions of Social Memory', organized by the Bentley Historical Library and the International Institute of the University of Michigan, Ann Arbor, 14 March 2001. See Sax, op. cit. for other cases.

[75] Eric Ketelaar, 'Tacit Narratives: The Meanings of Archives', *Archival Science*, 1, 2001, pp. 143-155.

[76] John Van Maanen and Brian T. Pentland, 'Cops and Auditors: The Rhetoric of Records', in Sim B. Sitkin and Robert J. Bies, eds, *The Legalistic Organization*, Thousand Oaks, Sage Publications, 1994, p. 53. Van Maanen and Pentland's findings and comparable research by others have been superbly woven in a general recordkeeping context by Ciaran B. Trace, 'What is Recorded is Never Simply "What Happened": Record Keeping in Modern Organizational Culture', *Archival Science*, 2, 2002, pp. 137-159.

labeling and storage.[77] Recordkeepers are 'creating value, that is, an order of value, by putting things in their proper place, by making place(s) for them.'[78] Taxonomies, acquisition criteria, descriptive standards, reading room rules, opening hours, visitors' guides – they all constitute exclusions, inclusions, priorities – a regime of practices which include the 'rules imposed and reasons given' by societal power.[79] This is especially relevant in appraisal – selecting what should and what should not be kept.

Recontextualizalion takes place at every stage of a record's life and in every dimension of the records continuum, under the influence of societal power.[80] Every interaction, intervention, interrogation, and interpretation by creator, user, and archivist is intentionally or unintentionally enforced by power. Each of these activations leaves fingerprints, which are attributes to the archive's infinite meaning. As Derrida remarked in a seminar on 'Refiguring the Archive',

> There is no archive without the signature of the archivists. By 'signature of the archivists', I don't mean the individual signature of the person in charge, but the signature of the apparatus, the people, and the institution, which produces the archive. The signature is a language. The archivist doesn't simply perceive the documents, doesn't simply receive the documents. It organises it, it produces it in a certain way, and in this production implies the language on the part of the archivist.[81]

Subjects of the record

Each activation of the record is an enrichment, an extension. It is not a palimpsest, as in Orwell's *Nineteen Eighty-four*, where the past is written over by the present. The object is open yet enclosed; it is what I have called 'membranic', the membrane allowing the infusing and exhaling of values which are embedded in each and every activation. This works in two directions, into the past and into the future. Every activation adds something to what Kopytoff calls the cultural biography of the object,[82] and what I call the semantic genealogy of the record. Therefore, we can agree with Derrida, who writes that the archive

---

[77] Ketelaar, 'Archivalisation and Archiving', op. cit.; Bowker and Star, op. cit.

[78] Brien Brothman, 'Orders of Values: Probing the Theoretical Terms of Archival Practice', *Archivaria*, 32, 1991, p. 82.

[79] 'Practices being understood here as places where what is said and what is done, rules imposed and reasons given, the planned and the taken for granted meet and interconnect', according to Michel Foucault, 'Government Rationality: An Introduction' [original French version published in *Esprit*, 371, May 1968, pp. 850-874], in Graham Burchell, Colin Gordon and Peter Miller, *The Foucault Effect,* Chicago, University of Chicago Press, 1991, p. 75.

[80] Ketelaar, 'Tacit Narratives' op. cit.; Bernadine Dodge, 'Across the Great Divide: Archival Discourse and the (Re)presentation of the Past in Late-Modern Society', *Archivaria*, 53, 2002, pp. 16-30.

[81] Jacques Derrida, 'Archive Fever in South Africa', in Hamilton et al, op. cit., p. 64.

[82] Igor Kopytoff, 'The Cultural Biography of Things: Commoditization as Process', in Arjun Appadurai, ed., *The Social Life of Things,* New York, Cambridge University Press, 1986, pp. 64-91.

is never closed; it opens out of the future.[83] The archive, in Derrida's thinking, is not just a sheltering of the past – it is an anticipation of the future.[84]

Every activation also changes the significance of earlier activations. Let me give an example. The records created and used by German and Dutch agencies during the Second World War to account for the looting of Jewish assets continued to be used, after the war, by German and Dutch agencies in the processes of restitution and reparation. The same record was activated by different societal powers, for different purposes and for different audiences again and again, as it is today activated in the search for looted and lost works of art and other Holocaust assets.[85] The looting and the registration of the looted property were, of course, an appalling event, but it was through the subsequent uses of the record that the primary registration became really a record of a traumatic experience. This is an application of Freud's Nachträglichkeit; events that occur later may change not just the significance, but the nature of prior events.[86] By extension one may say that current use of records affects retrospectively all earlier meanings, or to put it differently, we can no longer read the record as our predecessors have read that record.

This retrospectivity has important implications. Those who were subjected to the power became subjects of the record created by that power. Formally, they had no voice in the creation and use of the record. However, by retrospective causality, they have to be considered actors in the semantic genealogy of the record and the archive too. Their power should be recognized as much as the power of creators and keepers.[87]

Archivists have power

When the records of the state cross the boundaries of the records continuum's fourth dimension, it entails a reappropriation of the citizens' memories, as Giuseppe Vitiello suggests.[88] This bestows a special responsibility on the guardians of these memories: the archivists. Their role is one of power, as we saw in the discussion of the tacit narratives of the records. They have the *archontic* power 'to inscribe a trace in some external location'.[89] That power, however, is subject to another power: the societal power from outside the

---

[83] Jacques Derrida, *Archive Fever*, Chicago, University of Chicago Press, 1996, p. 68.

[84] Ibid., p. 18.

[85] Ketelaar, 'Understanding Archives', op. cit.; Henny van Schie, 'Joodse tegoeden en archieven: Context in de praktijk', in Peter J. Horsman, Frederick C.J. Ketelaar and Theo H.P.M. Thomassen, eds, *Context. Interpretatiekaders in de archivistiek. Jaarboek 2000*, 's-Gravenhage, Stichting Archiefpublicaties, 2000, pp. 257-273.

[86] Susan van Zyl, 'Psychoanalysis and the Archive: Derrida's *Archive Fever*', in Hamilton et al., op. cit., pp. 53-55.

[87] Michael Piggott and Sue McKemmish, op. cit., p. 116-118. Modern data protection and privacy legislation recognizes the specific rights of data subjects.

[88] Guiseppe Vitiello, 'L'État a-t-il une mission de gardien de la mémoire collective?', in Ermisse, op. cit., p. 67.

[89] Derrida, *Archive Fever*, op. cit., p. 42; Verne Harris, 'A Shaft of Darkness: Derrida in the Archive', in Hamilton et al., op. cit., p. 67.

Archive. Archivists have to yield to that power, because they are members of the society. But if the societal power wielded over archives is abused, jeopardizing universal human rights or the right to integrity of the archival material (and thus their reliability as evidence), then the archivist should use all of his or her power to fight.[90]

Conclusion

To conclude, let us check how our discussion of recordkeeping and societal power corresponds with the meanings of 'power', as listed in dictionaries such as the Oxford English Dictionary. Power is a quality or property, the ability to do or effect or act (the power of speech). Power is also government authority or, more generally, the political or social dominant position entailing control over other people. Power furthermore is a person, body, or thing with influence or strength. Power is energy, or an active property or function.

Records *have* power and *are* a power. They have power as instruments of authority and control: for effecting knowledge-power, control, surveillance and discipline – in too many cases for enforcing oppression as well. The powers in society depend on recordkeeping. But records can also have the power to be instruments of empowerment and liberation. Because of these powers, records are a power, with influence and strength, with a high societal power.

---

[90] The first principle of the Code of Ethics of the International Council on Archives (www.ica.org) reads 'Archivists should protect the integrity of archival materials and thus guarantee that it continues to be reliable evidence of the past'. In the commentary archivists are exhorted to 'resist pressure from any source to manipulate evidence so as to conceal or distort facts'. These principles and the ensuing conflicts of loyalties have been at the heart of numerous cases in Australia and abroad. A few have been treated by Cox and Wallace, *Archives and the Public Good*, op. cit.

Readings

- Christopher Dandeker, *Surveillance, Power and Modernity. Bureaucracy and Discipline from 1700 to the Present Day*, Cambridge, Polity Press, 1990.

  Dandeker, building upon the writings of Weber, Foucault and Giddens, analyzes surveillance (i.e. the gathering of information and supervision of people) as a means of administrative power.

- Gérard Ermisse, ed., *Mémoire et histoire: Les États européens face aux droits des citoyens du XXième siècle*, Paris, International Council on Archives, 2000.

  Proceedings (in French) of a conference of archivists, historians, lawyers and representatives of Unesco, the Council of Europe and the International Council on Archives, on the role of records and records professionals in processes of democratization, especially of countries in Central and Eastern Europe. One of the sessions was devoted to the problems of dealing with the archives of the intelligence services of former repressive regimes.

- Michael Piggott and Sue McKemmish, 'Recordkeeping, Reconciliation and Political Reality', in *Past Caring? What does Society Expect of Archivists? Proceedings of the Australian Society of Archivists Conference. Sydney 13-17 August 2002*, Canberra, Australian Society of Archivists, 2002, pp. 111-119, also available at: http://www.sims.monash.edu.au/research/rcrg/publications/piggottmckemmish2002.pdf.

  The authors challenge archivists to establish accountable recordkeeping regimes by building frameworks that better enable records to function as accessible collective memory beyond spatial and temporal boundaries.

- Joan M. Schwartz and Terry Cook, eds., 'Archives, Records, and Power', two special thematic issues of *Archival Science*, 2, 2002, pp. 1-163.

  A collection of fifteen articles on archival documents as social constructs, on archival institutions as active sites where social power is negotiated, contested, and confirmed, and on archivists having power over memory and identity.

CHAPTER 12
Archives and memory

Michael Piggott

Their memory of the sprightly way Ellison performed an act so wanton of their lives would one day be his death sentence ... No sooner are they on their way than Bligh asks for pen and paper ... His passion is to put everything that had happened to him on paper. He is unsure whether he will survive. He is certain that he cannot trust those with him to tell his story as he wants. He denies them any paper to record their own thoughts.[1]

What does much more to distinguish our specific human from non-human memory is our social existence, and the technological facility which has created a world in which memories are transcribed on to papyrus, wax tablets, paper or electronic screens, that is, a world of artificial memory.[2]

Only now do Antipodeans reclaim ancestral black sheep. Even in the 1970s, as Tasmania's chief archivist told me, respected figures used to rip out pages of convict records bearing their forebears' names.[3]

As with so much preceding this chapter and with archival thinking generally, we must begin with the use of terms. Obviously our focus needs to be directed to *memory*, but the meaning of *archives* inevitably becomes involved. That one second of the reader's time needs to be taken up in this way may seem surprising, because *memory* is heard in daily communication and is used by archivists so confidently and so often.

---

[1] Greg Dening, 'Reading to Write', in Marion Halligan, ed., *Storykeepers*, Sydney, Duffy & Snellgrove, 2001, pp. 35 and 36. For this historian/anthropologist's fuller and beautifully written multidisciplinary account, see *Mr Bligh's Bad Language,* Cambridge, Cambridge University Press, 1992. The mutiny and its multiple aftermaths offer a superb case study of the interplay of archival, published, human and artistic memory, and as the quote hints, their many consequences.
[2] Steven Rose, *The Making of Memory,* rev. ed., New York, Vintage, 2003, p. 387.
[3] David Lowenthal, *The Heritage Crusade and the Spoils of History*, Cambridge, Cambridge University Press, 1998, p. 16.

Archives and memory: An undoubted connection

There are two reasons for this confidence in the repeated use of memory. Firstly, we should acknowledge an influence that has nothing to do with professional concepts and principles. Archivists are not immune to the wide popularity of the term *memory* and its best-known applications, remembering and forgetting. It is a key concept in postmodern discourse in the social and human sciences, and Pierre Nora's invented term 'lieux de mémoire' and its English rendering 'sites of memory' have entered common cultural currency. Memory is also a popular leitmotif in poetry, the theatre, film and fiction. It is also linked to the most elemental phenomena. Look at fire, for example. It hardly needs mentioning that fire and memory have a number of rich historical and psychic dimensions, involving such remembering rituals as candle vigils (community tragedies), bonfires and burning effigies (Guy Fawkes and the fifth of November), eternal flames (war dead), campfires (old timers' yarning) and passing on lit torches (war dead, Olympic Games ideals).

The idea of *memory* is a part of everyday consciousness, a point no better illustrated than in our reaction to disastrous loss of archives such as meaningful personal possessions. Writers are among those who feel this most deeply and express it best. Thus the Polish-Australian writer Lily Brett summarized the loss of photos, personal items of significance and thirty years worth of diaries as, 'All of the ordinary things. Archived moments. Mementos. Memorabilia of celebrations. Recorded pleasure and pride. Remnants of disappointments. Struggles. History'.[4] In similar vein, the Australian storyteller, critic and scriptwriter Bob Ellis described the loss of his home and contents in 1993:

> I noticed that the home videos were going up now, my diaries of last year, my big novel, my own baby photos, the five hundred videos of *The Simpsons* … The purpose of life is to remember, I wrote, quoting Henry Miller, with lordly midget significance in *The Nostradamus Kid*, and here was memory, lobotomised away in flame … Occasionally I went back down to beg the fireman to squirt the memory room of the tapes and diaries and the single photo of me and my dead sister but each time fraughtly, politely, they ordered me away, calling me sir.[5]

Secondly, for archivists, the archives-memory relationship comes with their professional mother's milk. It is in fact a fundamental relationship in Jenkinson's notion of a record, an 'Old Testament' definition from which so much of twentieth-century English language archival thinking ultimately draws. The relationship is there in his famous definition, implied by the purpose for which documents are 'subsequently preserved in … [officials'] own custody for their own information'. Why would anyone bother to do that? Jenkinson explains:

> The official or responsible person … who has to preside over any continuous series of business functions, the manager of a small estate at one end of the scale, the

---

[4] Lily Brett, 'Bonfire of the Memories', *The Age* ('Good Weekend' supplement), 16 November 2002, p. 73, reproduced from her memoir *Between Mexico and Poland,* Sydney, Picador, 2002.
[5] Bob Ellis, *Goodbye Jerusalem*, Milsons Point, NSW, Vintage, 1997, pp. 41-42.

controller of a kingdom's finances at the other, relies for the support of his authority on memory; so soon as writing becomes general in use he adopts the preservation of pieces of writing as a *convenient form of artificial memory*; and in doing so starts a collection of Archives.[6]

Jenkinson reinforced the idea of archives as a memory prosthesis by repeated shorthand references to them as 'written memorials', and by the use of a lovely illustration of business continuity enabled through the corporate memory bank of an official's files. These function so that 'the Administrator, called upon to take up any piece of business, may not be dependent on his own memory, but find a summary of all that has been done in the past on this matter in his files.'[7]

It has been hard to improve on Jenkinson's definition for plausibility and richness in according archives a memory role from the moment they exist as records, though we should acknowledge that the content of some records themselves, such as a file note, photo caption, meeting minutes or diary entry, are (re)constructed after the event. It has become a classic definition and resonates still. In the mid 1990s, the National Archives of Australia directed its new recordkeeping message into government agencies with a 'Keep A Record' poster, illustrated by the image of an elephant. The accompanying text explained:

> They say elephants never forget, which if true, would make them a huge help in keeping records. However, human recall is less reliable so we need to store information.[8]

---

[6] Hilary Jenkinson, *A Manual of Archive Administration*, 2nd ed. London, Lund, Humphries, 1966, pp. 11, 23. Emphasis added. The phrase 'artificial memory' has endured; note, for instance, its use by Steven Rose in the second of the quotations that begin this chapter.
[7] Ibid., pp. 152-153.
[8] *Memento*, no. 1, September 1996, p. 8.

Figure 12.1 National Archives of Australia poster.

And note how one of North America's leading thinkers, Tom Nesmith, defines 'archiving':

> The multifaceted process of making memories by performing remembered or otherwise recorded acts, transmitting such accounts over time and space, organizing, interpreting, forgetting, and even destroying them.[9]

---

[9] Tom Nesmith, 'Seeing Archives; Postmodernism and the Changing Intellectual Place of Archives', *American Archivist*, 65, no. 1, 2002, p. 26.

Jenkinson's explanation for the origins of recordkeeping is limited to its role in overcoming the diseconomies of scale in some timeless administrative business setting. He is silent on the many other early needs for records evident in, for example, astrologers' use of lunar and solar data for predicting future celestial and earthly events recorded by Babylonian, Chinese, European and Arabian civilizations over 2000 years ago.[10] In other settings, when confirming property rights and citing (unwritten) law, indeed whenever access to historical knowledge was called for, communities usually resorted not to charters and the like, even when the technology was available, but to the oral wisdom of elders and remembrancers. Nevertheless, Jenkinson's classic definition, the first of many to refer to or imply a notion of documentary, if 'artificial', memory, accorded with everything else archivists knew. Scholarly and popular texts on the history of alphabets, writing and recorded knowledge confirmed it. So did the origins and meanings of terms: memento, memorabilia, memorandum, aide-mémoire, and memoir.[11] So did simple child-like commonsense. When, in *Through the Looking Glass*, Lewis Carroll has the King assert that he would never forget a particular horror, his Queen warns, 'You will though, if you don't make a memorandum of it'.

While archivists learnt from Jenkinson that records perform a memory-like function and saw how it enabled his Administrator to handle a 'piece of business', in time, via the insights of Max Weber, they also realized that records enabled the official to handle consistently many pieces of bureaucratic business of enormous variety and reach. The kingdom defined the limit in Jenkinson's list of political structures. For the past four centuries, however, very large corporate structures, and preeminently the state, have needed a 'memory' too. The nation-state and its machinery for activities such as taxation, policing, economic planning and delivering welfare programs, found records to be not an artificial convenience but an indispensable and highly accurate enabler of organized recall. The mode of power distribution and scale and technological sophistication of operation conditioned the specific contexts, but the file (functioning as the panopticon as Eric Ketelaar shows in chapter 11) replaced the sea monster as Leviathan's symbols, and in the twenty-first century should probably now be a string of zeros and ones. To put it another way and in an historical setting, we might quote Matsuda's observation on concluding his case study of the capture of Joseph Vacher, a French vagabond murderer in 1897:

[10] See 'In the Shadow of the Moon', *New Scientist*, 30 January 1999, pp. 30-33 and, more generally, Richard Stephenson, *Historical Eclipses and Earth's Rotation*, Cambridge, Cambridge University Press, 1997.
[11] Examples of each are Andrew Robinson, *The Story of Writing*, New York, Thames and Hudson, 1995, and the recordkeeping history text most cited by archivists, M T Clanchy's *From Memory to Written Record,* Cambridge, Mass., Harvard University Press, 1979. For examples of the use of this text by archivists, see Hugh Taylor, '"My Very Act and Deed": Some Reflections on the Role of Textual Records in the Conduct of Affairs', *American Archivist*, 51, Fall 1988, pp. 456-469, esp. 457-460; James M. O'Toole, *Understanding Archives and Manuscripts*, Chicago, Society of American Archivists, 1990, pp. 8-11; and Luciana Duranti, 'The Odyssey of Records Managers, Part 1', *ARMA Quarterly*, 23, no. 3, July 1989, p. 3. For a fuller list of records terms suggestive of memory, see Jacques Le Goff, *History and Memory,* New York, Columbia University Press, 1992, pp. 84-85.

Vacher ... was directly and indirectly pursued by the archives, records, and actors which constituted the memory of the state; memory as a network of administrators, techniques, specialists, and their departments ... he was captured and condemned by the memory of the state. That memory was a composite of bureaucratic logic and the resources and technologies available to a doctor and a judge: investigative networks, files, identity cards, expert in reading bodies and signs, all organized to operate in a world of accelerations and displacements.[12]

Overstating the connection

This broader corporate role for records and Jenkinson's definition so convinced archivists of the connection between archives and memory, however, that the temptations of generalization and ethnocentrism were overwhelming. A little over twenty years ago, George Bolotenko wrote:

It has been said before, but bears repeating: the preservation of documents and manuscripts is the preservation of the collective memory of society, the *summa* of the human past.

In support of this declaration so grandiloquent and suggestive – think of all that *summa* hints at – Bolotenko referenced the French National Archives' *Manuel d'archivistique: Théorie et pratique des archives publiques en France*.[13] In archival discourse twenty years later, *memory* remains one of our most popular explanatory tools.[14] It is deployed as conference themes, for instance, and whenever we try to express in a word or two what the records and archives game is all about. Thus the Australian Society of Archivists (ASA) captures 'The Archivist's Mission' in a couple of sentences, ending by stating that the work of archivists

is vital for ensuring organisational efficiency and accountability, and for supporting understandings of Australian life through the management and retention of its personal, corporate and social memory.[15]

---

[12] Matt Matsuda, *The Memory of the Modern*, New York, Oxford University Press, 1996, pp. 140-141. I thank Terry Cook for first drawing my attention to this brilliant text. A sample of the variety of literature on aspects of the political sociology of recordkeeping include John Tagg, *The Burden of Representation*, Basingstoke, Macmillan Education, 1988, chapters 3 & 4; John Torpey, *The Invention of the Passport*, Cambridge, Cambridge University Press, 2000; Kenneth C. Laudon, *Dossier Society*, New York, Columbia University Press, 1986; Stanton Wheeler, ed., *On Record*, New York, Russell Sage Foundation, 1969; and M. T. Clanchy, passim.

[13] George Bolotenko, 'Archivists and Historians: Keepers of the Well', *Archivaria*, 16, 1983, p. 6, footnote 5 (*Manuel*, p. 89).

[14] Barbara L. Craig has also noted this attraction. See her timely and accomplished overview, 'Selected Themes in the Literature on Memory and Their Pertinence to Archives', *American Archivist*, 65, Fall/Winter 2002, pp. 276-289.

[15] Reproduced on the ASA website (http://www.archivists.org.au), its bi-monthly bulletin, and also presented in ASA publications and submission. For a frank commentary on this 'overly wordy text',

While this formulation was being debated within the ASA in the mid 1990s, a representative group from the Australian archives and records industry issued a position statement on electronic recordkeeping, warning Australia against 'the possibility of losing. …[its] corporate memory, that is, the trail of evidence of action that is provided by records'.[16] In the same year appeared the Australian Standard on Records Management (AS 4390), which stressed the importance of records to corporate, personal and collective memory, a point retained when the standard was adapted for promulgation internationally as ISO 15489.

The memory analogy (for how could the putative equivalence be meant literally?) is an equally popular choice for archival institutions, particularly government and in-house institutional archives. Thus on the reverse of its business cards, Archives New Zealand printed 'Keeper of the Public Record – the Memory of Government', while the National Archives of Australia publishes a magazine entitled *Memento*. Elsewhere it is the same: in Vancouver, for example, the aim of the archives of the University of British Columbia is 'to serve as the institution's corporate memory by identifying, preserving and making available for use the University's permanent records'. In our own professional literature, archives-is-memory has also proven hard to resist. The equivalence features perhaps most strongly among those who describe with approval the archivist's role within the new postmodern paradigm as active shapers or 'co-creators' of collective and corporate memory.

The idea of archival memory is also strongly fixed in archival policy and political sectors, and has been for a considerable time. The analogy has been just as popular via its negative – amnesia, forgetting, erasure and suppression, indeed memory loss of any kind – and is used especially to highlight the challenges of electronic records with their new meanings of erasure and memory loss to exploit. 'Without reliable electronic records', the United States higher education sector was warned in 1997, 'colleges and universities will be unable to manage and defend themselves – they will lose their memories and be at significant risk'.[17]

In fact a generation ago the US Committee on the Records of Government began its report with a concern that 'The United States is in danger of losing its memory'. The spectre of lost electronic records was strongly highlighted, as were concerns about poor records management of traditional paper records. The report foreshadowed repercussions for accountability, administrative efficiency, citizens' rights and entitlements, and also for a notion of corporate memory and for society at large. Government records formed

---

see Adrian Cunningham, 'The Soul and Conscience of the Archivist: Meditations on Power, Passion and Positivism in a Crusading Profession', in Ethel Krieger, ed., *Wresting the Archon from the Arkeion*, Pretoria, National Archives of South Africa, 2001, pp. 167-177 – particularly intriguing as he had a large involvement in the drafting of the statement. See also *ASA Bulletin*, April 1996, p. 34, June 1996, p. 97 and August 1996, p.117.

[16] Australian Society of Archivists, *Corporate Memory in the Electronic Age*, May 1996, p. 4.

[17] Timothy McGovern and Helen Samuels, 'Our Institutional Memory at Risk; Collaborators to the Rescue', *Cause/Effect*, 20, no. 3, Fall 1997, p. 19.

the basis of a national history and an understanding of American government. ...[They] contribute to a sense of community, a national consciousnesses, and understanding of [American] society and culture. Without records, there is no history. Without history, there is no understanding of continuity and change, no national consensus to support government.[18]

In the new century, the relationship continues to have an appeal. The United Kingdom government, when establishing common infrastructure in 2001 for museums, libraries and archives, described in a 'language of purpose' the role of archives to be 'the nation's memory, reflecting our history and national identity'.[19]

Much of this extravagant use has lacked elaboration. One does not expect footnotes on business cards, nor should a publicly-directed mission statement need a glossary of terms. The requirements of press releases often see complexity traded for generalizations and conciseness. But the line: 'we preserve memory ... and that's a good thing' has an in-built risk, which archivists learn the hard way when facing public protests over mishandled or unpopular appraisal which resulted in archival destruction. Of course, as noted below, remembering naturally involves forgetting, yet while we may understand this internal contradiction, we employ 'memory' publicly with surprising confidence. The assumption seems to be that we all know what memory and the archives-memory formula actually mean, needing neither discussion nor definition.[20]

In fact the concept has multiple meanings and archivists' most common modes of use (collective memory, historical memory, official memory, cultural memory, corporate memory, popular memory, social memory and public memory) are not necessarily synonyms.[21] It has a semantic history and a vast literature, and well-established

---

[18] United States Committee on the Records of Government, *Report*, March 1985, pp. 9 and 14.

[19] *Re:source news*, 1, no. 1, March 2001, p. 1.

[20] Brien Brothman, Frank Upward and Sue McKemmish have also commented on archivists' largely uncritical and undeveloped use. See Brothman's 'The Past that Archives Keep: Memory, History and the Preservation of Archival Records', *Archivaria*, 51, 2001, p. 50, and McKemmish and Upward's 'In search of the Lost Tiger, by Way of Sainte-Beuve: Reconstructing the Possibilities in "Evidence of Me ...'", *Archives and Manuscripts*, 29, no. 1, May 2001, pp. 22-42 at endnote 16. For two local examples of superficial use, see Gavan McCarthy and Tim Sherratt, 'Mapping Scientific Memory – Understanding the Role of Recordkeeping in Scientific Practice', *Archives and Manuscripts*, 24, no. 1, May 1996, pp. 78-85; and Bruce Smith, 'Lost Memory: the Paper Drives of World War II', in B. J. McMullin, ed., *Coming Together: Papers from the Seventh Australian Library History Forum*, Clayton, Ancora Press, 1997, pp. 61-68.

[21] On the distinction between 'social memory' and 'collective memory' for example, see Dario Paez et al., 'Social Processes and Collective Memory: A Cross-Cultural Approach to Remembering Political Events', in James Pennebaker, Dario Paez and Bernard Rimé, eds, *Collective Memory of Political Events*, Mahwah, NJ, Lawrence Erlbaum Associates, 1997. Clearly archivists don't believe the differences are meaningful. A case in point is a National Archives of Canada public policy statement approved on 17 October 2001 titled 'Preserving the Archival and Historical Memory of Government'. In addition to the two forms employed in the title, the statement refers to two more: 'collective memory' and 'recorded memory'. See http://www.collectionscanada.ca/06/0620_e.html (viewed 1 October 2004).

subdivisions in which are explored memory's relationship with such themes as commemoration, women, war, bereavement, identity, landscape, politics, religion, the Holocaust, ethics, museums and even specific documentary forms such as photographs and diaries. And we should add, of course, memory's most obvious and troubled complement, the vast canvas of history itself.[22] So extensive is this relationship that it has resulted in classics such as Jacques Le Goff's *History and Memory* and supports its own journal, *History & Memory,* produced since 1989 from Tel Aviv University. When applied to experimental psychology, clinical psychoanalysis and cognitive neuroscience, *memory* opens a second and equally vast field. As Kerwin Lee Klein ruefully remarked, at the beginning of his detailed survey of current research, 'Welcome to the memory industry'.[23]

Through archivists' carefree use of *memory,* several critical questions are ignored. The most basic is whether archives and memory are the same thing. Take the example of a family, grieving the loss of a son during war, lovingly pasting mementos, photos and letters into an album. Is what cultural historians would call 'memory-making', hobbyists see as 'scrapbooking' and cultural theorists 'consignation', in fact, what we would call recordkeeping and archiving? Or rather, do archives facilitate or enable memory-making? If so, how does this role as agent differ from their use as a resource to producers of histories, which are, in turn, often critical to collective memory-making?

And should we accord archives an *exclusive* or *central* role in memory-making within institutions and society? Mission statements notwithstanding, there is no consensus among those who have seriously thought about archives-based memory, and the shades of variation are intriguing. Assertions that archives are 'the documentary base of a nation's collective memory' (Cunningham) and 'the bedrock' of corporate and collective memory (Cox) at least allow for other agents, as does the qualification that archives are 'fundamental (but not exclusive) components of the world's memory' (Wallot). Others have spelt out why even these concessions are inadequate. Most social memory is not captured as records; most records don't become archives; not all archives are seriously resourced for the very long-term. And in any case, records plus this privileged moraine, Verne Harris's sliver of a sliver of a sliver, are but one of many enablers of memory. As Terry Cook put it, galleries, museums, libraries, historic sites, historic monuments, and public commemorations, as well as archives, can support remembering and forgetting, the latter 'perhaps' being the most important![24]

---

[22] Troubled, because while social memory and historical reconstruction happen differently, there are many areas of conjunction, including historians' use of eyewitness recollections, memoir and oral history. See Paul Connerton, *How Societies Remember*, Cambridge, Cambridge University Press, 1989, pp. 13-21, and Kerwin Lee Klein, 'On the Emergence of *Memory* in Historical Discourse', *Representations,* 69, Winter 2000, pp. 127-129.

[23] Klein, op. cit., p 127; another useful summary from the memory industry commentators is Jay Winter's 'The Generation of Memory: Reflections on the "Memory Boom" in Contemporary Historical Studies', *GHI Bulletin 21*, Fall 2000, available at: http://www.ghi-dc.org/bulletin27F00/b27winterframe.html, viewed 24 August 2004.

[24] Adrian Cunningham, 'Ensuring Essential Evidence', *National Library of Australia News*, November 1996, available at http://www.nla.gov.au/nla/staffpaper/acunning5.html; Richard Cox, 'The Record in the Information Age: A Progress Report on Research', *The Records & Retrieval*

Within the cultural heritage sector nationally and internationally, these honest and necessary distinctions are ignored. In the preamble to *Directions for 2000-2002* the National Library of Australia styled itself as 'a place which nourishes the nation's memory', with subsequent elaboration implying this memory also means Australia's history, heritage and culture. Its 2004 exhibition 'Future Memory' also claimed it was 'the designated keeper of Australia's collective wisdom'![25] Around the time *Directions* was issued, the State Library of Victoria equated its collections of 'documentary and published heritage' with 'our social memories'.[26] As for museums, their role in supporting and challenging memory, particularly through collecting and public programs and exhibitions, has long been acknowledged, and they too cannot resist the power of memory as a label.[27] Historical societies, whose collecting embraces material from all three cultural heritage sectors, are also seen by archivists and memory scholars as repositories and shapers of memory.

Distinctions blur even further because, internationally, archives libraries and museums are regarded collectively as memory institutions, something that started back in 1975![28] UNESCO's 'Memory of the World' program, which allows archival and printed materials on its register, is one of many manifestations. Within cultural and memory studies too, scholars bracket the three together. For them, the significant contrasts reside not within heritage institutions, but between orally communicated myths and beliefs on the one hand, and the more physically endurable objects, artefacts and documents on the other.[29]

Report, January 1996, p. 4; Jean-Pierre Wallot, 'Archival Oneness in the Midst of Diversity: A Personal Perspective', *American Archivist*, 59, Winter 1996, p. 24; Verne Harris, 'The Archival Sliver: Power, Memory, and Archives in South Africa', *Archival Science*, 2, 2002, p. 65; Terry Cook, 'What is Past is Prologue; A History of Archival Ideas Since 1898, and the Future Paradigm Shift', *Archivaria*, 43, 1997, p. 18.

[25] *Future Memory: National Library Recent Acquisitions 27 May-1 August 2004*, Canberra, ACT, National Library of Australia, 2004, p. 14.

[26] Cathrine Harboe-Ree, 'Contemporary Collection Policy: A Comparative Study', in *Beyond the Screen: Capturing Corporate and Social Memory*; *ASA Conference Proceedings*, Canberra, ACT, ASA, 2000, p. 35.

[27] As this chapter was being finalized, the Australian War Memorial launched a new exhibition drawing from its sculpture collection entitled 'Shaping Memory'. For a sample of the relevant Australian museum literature, see Chris Healy, *From the Ruins of Colonialism*, Cambridge, Cambridge University Press, 1997, Chapter 3; his chapter on museums in Kate Darian-Smith and Paula Hamilton, eds, *Memory and History in Twentieth-century Australia*, Melbourne, Oxford University Press, 1994; and the articles grouped under 'Museums and Material Vulture' in John Rickard and Peter Spearritt, eds, *Packaging the Past? Public Histories*, Melbourne, Melbourne University Press, 1991.

[28] As noted by David Bearman and Jennifer Trant. See their *Cultural Institutions in a Networked Environment*, Stockholm, May 23, 2002, Archives and Museum Informatics, 2002, available at: http://www.archimuse.com/papers/AMI.stockholm.020524.pdf (viewed 1 October 2004).

[29] The classic articulation of this dichotomy is Pierre Nora's. See his 'Between Memory and History: Les Lieux de Mémoire', in *Representations*, 26, Spring 1989, pp. 7-25, the theoretical introduction to a 7 volume collaborative work which appeared between 1984 and 1994 (although Eric Ketelaar has reminded us in *Archives and Manuscripts*, November 2003, that this translation has its flaws). For an

How archives support memory *differently* from library and museum materials awaits sustained analysis, but the need is all the more urgent because our cultural roles partially overlap, each support research and other use, each offers outreach and public programs, and libraries so often manage archival collections.[30] Undoubtedly the authoritative standing that records enjoy would be a key part of the explanation, such as in family history where birth certificates, property documentation and photos support memory in ways in which orally or print transmitted memory cannot. It is something we will return to below.

As to what each memory institution collects, a broad cultural heritage notion of archives representing society's memory is one of the key planks of the so-called 'social', 'societal' or 'archivalization' school of thinking.[31] It seeks to re-balance what is seen as too strong a concentration on recordkeeping and records and their role in supporting evidence and accountability. It is dangerously out of step with postmodern approaches across all archival functions and conceptions of archival science, at its worst resulting in a context of record creation that is too narrowly defined and a role for the archivist that is too idealistic. Rather than a neutral mediator, this school views the archivist as an active shaper of collective memory. Thus it 'is no longer acceptable to limit the definition of society's memory solely to the documentary residue left over (or chosen) by powerful record creators' wrote Terry Cook, who has also spelt out how this could be achieved via documenting societal governance rather than governments governing, and via documentation which reveals citizen-state interactions and their equivalents in corporations, non-government bodies, institutions and religious and other organizations. The scope of that documentation is also broadly conceived, embracing, as well as the transactional records of administration, 'recorded information in all media'.

---

excellent summary of the project's context and approach, see Nancy Ward, 'Memory's Remains: Les lieux de mémoire', in *History & Memory*, 6, no. 1, 1994, pp. 123-149. Others to contrast oral with material traces are Kenneth E. Foote, 'To Remember and Forget: Archives, Memory and Culture', *American Archivist*, 53, Summer 1990, pp. 378-392 and Richard Harvey Brown and Beth Davis-Brown, 'The Making of Memory: the Politics of Archives, Libraries and Museums in the Construction of National Consciousnesses', *History of the Human Sciences*, 11, no. 4, 1998, pp. 17-32.

[30] Few archivists have been concerned to explore their similarities and differences in relation to memory. One of the earliest was Hugh Taylor, whose 'The Collective Memory: Archives and Libraries As Heritage', *Archivaria*, 15, 1982/83 promised in its title more than it delivered. More recently, Richard Cox has noted there is an issue to address. See his 'The Concept of Public Memory and Its Impact on Archival Public Programming', *Archivaria*, 36, 1993, pp. 122-135 and his review essay 'Making the Records Speak: Archival Appraisal, Memory, Preservation, and Collecting', *American Archivist*, 64, no. 2, 2001, pp. 394-404.

[31] The naming is Terry Cook's. For an elaboration and others of similar mind, see his 'Archival Science and Postmodernism: New Formulations for Old Concepts', *Archival Science*, 1, 2001, pp. 18-19. See also his 'The Records Continuum and Archival Cultural Heritage' in *Beyond the Screen*, op. cit., pp. 9-21. Another member of this school, Eric Ketelaar, has also expanded on these ideas for Australian audiences. See his 'Archivalisation and Archiving', *Archives and Manuscripts*, 21, no. 1, May 1999, pp. 54-61 and 'Empowering Archives: What Society Expects of Archivists', *Past Caring: Proceedings of the Australian Society of Archivists Conference, Sydney 2002*.

In this way, a richer, more representative, societal memory can result, inclusive of the less powerful, the marginalized, those otherwise forgotten. But because political and administrative structures record them only as welfare recipients, law breakers, security threats and so on, archivists are urged to proactively locate their memory by appraising personal and family papers, private sector records, and records in all media including documents which 'move and speak'. In short, it is that bracket of creators, sectors and media the Canadians term 'total archives', embracing much of the documentation libraries and museums also seek.

A broader and more qualified articulation

To summarize, archivists have used the term *memory* in two ways. Firstly, at the micro level of the archival document, they adopt or adapt Jenkinson's artificial memory definition. Secondly, they acknowledge that memory is essentially social and they apply it to entire societies as well as businesses families and other social groupings and institutions. In other words, they accept the broad consensus of sociological findings developed by the French sociologist of knowledge, Maurice Halbwachs (1877-1945), from the 1920s onwards, that individual memory formation is necessarily broader, be that context the family, a social class or and entire society. They see it as encompassing a 'group' consciousness about the past and about events, people and other foci in the past, and they believe that the influence of archival institutions on those consciousnesses is so strong as to justify asserting that an organization's or society's memory *is*, in effect, its archives.

Some of our number also remember to note the importance to memory of other agents such as recorded and orally transmitted information. Obviously then, archivists' standard notion of the memory-archives relationship needs qualifying and sharpening. The memory role of archives and the memory work of archivists are rarely direct and not nearly as dominant as implied in our rhetoric.[32]

A more qualified recasting here should begin by drawing on one of the long-established conclusion of memory studies to accept that all memory is inherently social. The identity of individuals, social aggregates and society at large, their consciousness of sameness and understanding of the world, despite time and physical distance, are sustained and changed by a number of factors that include the ebb and flow of collective memory. In turn, which groupings remember and forget what, how, and why, can be shaped and facilitated by archives, and also by social phenomena such as class, gender and power relationships

---

[32] One of the few case study illustrations of a strongly qualified claim for archives vis-à-vis memory by an archivist is Jeannette Bastian's *Owning Memory: How a Caribbean Community Lost Its Archives and Found Its History*, Westport, Conn., Libraries Unlimited, 2003. Two Australian historians have also recently illustrated the rich interplay of multiple memory agents/sources: Mark McKenna, *Looking for Blackfellas' Point: an Australian History of Place,* Sydney, University of New South Wales Press, 2002, and Tanja Luckins, *The Gates of Memory: Australian People's Experiences and Memories of Loss and the Great War*, Perth, WA, Curtin University Books, 2004.

within families, collectivities and society as a whole. Each question – what? who? how? why? – can be affected by archives and the work of archivists, in combination with monuments, commemoration and landscape. The 'living memory' of orally sustained and transmitted knowledge can also play its part. Finally, the exercise of individual, group and societal memory can be affected by external forces such as disasters (e.g. fire), war (e.g. cultural genocide) and colonialism (e.g. expropriation and repatriation of archives).

Pushing these qualifications further, we should acknowledge that sometimes archives are utterly irrelevant to what is remembered, forgotten and re-remembered. Sometimes memory formation is neutral so far as deliberate or benign shaping or preservation of archives are concerned. Sometimes archives are the prime agent in buttressing, undermining or skewing memory; at other times they do so only in concert with other forms of recorded information, the built environment and public rituals and ceremonies. Sometimes supported by oral sources, people 'remember' one version of the past, while others reject that version due to lack of, or because of contradictory archival sources. More often, archives and their shapers and preservers, which include archivists and archival institutions, impact indirectly via the users such as historians, and documentary filmmakers and their readers and audiences. This, in turn, happens most clearly when the times are favourable historiographically, culturally, politically or demographically.

The qualifications in practice

In turning now to elaborate on the ways archives and archiving shape and sustain memory, it is appropriate to start by choosing a case in which they are utterly irrelevant, although that absence was not without consequences in the 'politics of memory'. Archival silence is central to the historian David Roberts' investigation of whether or not a massacre of indigenous Australians occurred near Sofala, thirty kilometres from Bathurst in the central west of New South Wales in the early 1820s, and how it was and is remembered.[33]

According to a traditional story, still repeated today in Sofala by descendants of European prospectors and settlers, a large number of local Aboriginals were killed at Bells Falls Gorge. Roberts could glean little variation in the story and failed to discover any detail identifying the site. There was a vague possibility that they were shot at and forced to jump from the top of the falls. He searched at plausible locations for physical traces without success. Two things were not in dispute: the enduring presence of the gorge, and – while representatives of the Wiradjuri nation still live in the Bathurst region – the absence of a local indigenous population. Oral tradition eventually fed published recollections from the late 1800s and from the 1930s and attests to the durability of the story. Then, as a new interest in indigenous history emerged in the 1970s, local histories began asserting the

---

[33] David Roberts, 'Bells Falls Massacre and Bathurst's History of Violence: Local Tradition and Australian Historiography', *Australian Historical Studies*, 105, October 1995, pp. 615-633. For his reflections on the reaction to that research, see his 'The Bells Falls Massacre and Oral Tradition', in Bain Attwood and S. G. Foster, eds, *Frontier Conflict*, Canberra, ACT, National Museum of Australia, 2003.

massacre as fact. Eventually, in the most sympathetic accounts by indigenous and white writers, the literal truth was stated with embellishment and sensationalism.[34] These, in turn, have influenced student newspapers in nearby regional universities and New South Wales educational films.

There is now a large body of published academic scholarship based on archival research, confirming the indigenous-settler violence on the frontier of European settlement in nineteenth and early twentieth century Australia. It has been patiently compiled since the 1950s and accelerated from the 1970s. Very much within that trend, Roberts looked diligently through the relevant printed and archival sources documenting government, military and militia activity in 1820s New South Wales. There are incomplete accounts, in part reflecting settler and military reluctance to report encounters with Aboriginals, particularly because their 'dispersal' was officially banned. Because of this, in fact some prosecutions did occur. The surviving historical record does show that in the Sofala/Bathurst region settler/indigenous relations had deteriorated by 1824 to the point where martial law was briefly declared. There was a 'climate of hostility between European settlers and Aboriginal people at Bathurst', concluded Roberts, 'which could well have resulted in such an atrocity'. In other words, though it might have happened, 'the fact was not documented in the contemporary records'.

The disagreement between Roberts, on the one hand, and local European and wider indigenous tradition, on the other, is a microcosm of the central 'politics of memory' issue in contemporary Australia. The representation of the Bells Falls massacre/'massacre' in its *Contested Frontiers* exhibition in the First Australians gallery of the National Museum of Australia has generated considerable debate and controversy, and symptomatic of one of the issues prompting an official inquiry into the museum and its exhibitions philosophy.[35] In its contested bases for historical accuracy, Bells Falls is but one instance of disputes over the past generation involving aspects of Australian aboriginal history. Whether it be native title land rights applications, claims of mistreatment of wards of the state, the motives behind and extent of separating part-Aboriginal children from their families, the aptness of the term 'genocide' to describe what happened in Tasmania, or estimating numbers killed from frontier violence, in all there is clearly visible a clash of two kinds of memory, two ways of knowing and remembering.[36] The presence and interpretation of archival documents was and is crucial to that clash.

---

[34] See Al Grassby and Marji Hill's *Six Australian Battlefields: The Black Resistance to Invasion and the White Struggle Against Colonial Oppression*, Sydney, Angus & Robertson, 1988 and Mary Coe, *Windradyne: A Wiradjuri Koorie*, Aboriginal Studies Press, 1989.

[35] For an account of reaction to the exhibition, see Graeme Davison, 'Conflict in the Museum', in Attwood and Foster, op. cit., pp. 201-214. For the Inquiry report, see *Review of the National Museum of Australia, its Exhibits and Public Programs,* Canberra, ACT, Commonwealth of Australia, 2003, pp. 32-37.

[36] The challenge to emerging (though not uncontested) orthodoxies has centred largely on the conservative intellectual monthly *Quadrant* and the right wing 'think tank' the Institute of Public Affairs, Sydney. On museums and exhibitions, see Rod Moran, 'Paradigm of the Postmodern Museum', *Quadrant*, January-February 2002, pp. 43-49 and Keith Windshuttle, 'How Not to Run a Museum', *Quadrant*, September 2001, pp 11-19, the latter specifically attacking the National

What can we conclude about archives and memory? Far more common than in the Bells Falls case, they share a role in representing, enabling and shaping memory with other cultural heritage 'mediators', recorded oral testimonies and so on. That this actually needs stressing arises because of a mindset of linear logic seen in such phrases as *from* memory *to* written records, and *between* memory and history. The clear implication is that one gives way to the other. Thus Pierre Nora, one of the most influential writers within memory studies, has argued that twentieth-century France is bereft of real lived traditional memory. As a result, modern memory is vicariously experienced through concentrations of objectified memory, tangible substitutes such as records, monuments and rituals.[37] Nora's ideas and framework are far more complex than can be rendered in a single paragraph and a longer paragraph would require mention of changes in the state's commemorative activity (e.g. the role of schools and official memory rituals), representation through mass media, museums and the proliferation of heritage associations. Yet even acknowledging the changes within today's modern 'memorial culture', using the example of France, cannot hide Nora's dichotomy of past society-wide 'environments of memory' and today's 'sites of memory'. In fact, this divide is a very blurred one. As Kirk Savage has pointed out, even traditional internalized memory needs external mediation devices to sustain itself. Even more telling,

> The modern reliance on memory 'traces' does not mean that more ephemeral and less easily documented means of remembering have been abandoned.[38]

In short, the lived natural memory activities of reunions, ritual observances and even meaningful gestures on the one hand, and erecting monuments and developing documentary collections on the other, are not mutually exclusive.

An equally worrying binary is evident in the way archivists have conceived of oral history and oral sources. Thus in his Plenary Address to the Society of American Archivists in 1995, the ICA President Jean-Pierre Wallot made a strong plea for their inclusion in the archivist's frame of reference.[39] Taking an evidentially superior stance against presumed fallacious memories, he argued, could be regarded as Euro-centric and racist. It ignored the fact that seventy percent of the Third World 'have no literacy skills nor written records, but do have a vibrant oral culture and sophisticated oral traditions and oral memories'. Besides, excluding 'from the world's memory storehouses ... the majority of human beings' looked a little foolish in light of the West's approach to court evidence placing oral testimony over

---

Museum of Australia's Bells Falls section of its First Australians gallery. Something of the political context of this debate is analyzed in Stuart Macintyre and Anna Clark, *The History Wars*, Melbourne Melbourne University Press, 2003, chapter 10.

[37] See Pierre Nora, op. cit.

[38] Kirk Savage, 'The Politics of Memory: Black Emancipation and the Civil War Monument', in John R Gillis, ed., *Commemorations: the Politics of National Identity*, Princeton NJ, Princeton University Press, 1994, p. 146 note 6. Patrick Geary has also pointed to the constantly changing interplay of oral and written, individual and collective memory even in early Middle Ages Europe. See his *Phantoms of Remembrance,* Princeton, NJ, Princeton University Press, 1994, p. 175.

[39] 'Archival Oneness in the Midst of Diversity', *American Archivist*, 59, Winter 1996, p. 19.

second-best written records, and the preservation and transmission of Christ's and Socrates' presumed words through oral traditions subsequently recorded.

What failed to get acknowledged in this otherwise commendable cultural ecumenism was that societies based on vibrant oral traditions and memories are not confined to the Third World or the past. They exist on every continent today. Nor is this duality confined to an era that ended in Clanchy's period of interest, 1066-1307. Nor should we think oral and documentary memory cannot coexist within the same individual, organization or society. It would be a mistake also to conceive of oral tradition through Western documentary frameworks which imply, for instance, that it can be captured through audio/video recording.[40] Finally, any Australian text offered under the title 'recordkeeping in society' should be doubly mindful of oral records in view of the presence of the original (indigenous) Australians.[41]

The role conceded to oral memory should also, of course, be extended to print-supported memory. The twentieth century provides a number of illustrations, none more telling than those offered by the history of the USSR and its post-war satellites. Here, with history texts, holidays, museums and the media all harnessed to stage-manage official memory, it was left to dissident underground writers and poets such as Solzhenitsyn to witness and record collective memory. Via their hand-typed, illegal *samizdat* publications, they performed 'the central role ... as keeper of the records, custodian of memory, and truth telling for the nation'. Their individual memory 'became the source for, and representation of, national history'.[42] A similar claim has been made of war. Thus Paul Fussell explains how the influence of the First World War on British life persisted well into the Vietnam War generation. It was the powerful published writing of poets and memoirists such as Siegfried Sassoon, Robert Graves, Edmund Blunden and Wilfred Owen that profoundly shaped the way the Western Front 'has been remembered, conventionalised, and mythologised'. By default, Fussell also reveals how minor was the role of historical records such as soldiers' diaries and letters, even though they were readily available to him (and us) through the collecting activity of the Imperial War Museum, London.[43]

---

[40] See the theme issue 'Archives and Indigenous Peoples' of *Comma*, 2003.1, edited by Verne Harris and Adrian Cunningham, in particular Shadrack Katuu, 'Engaging Orality Within the Archival Discipline: Its Contents and Discontents', pp. 83-102.

[41] Nonie Sharp offers a superb recent illustration in her *Saltwater People*, Crows Nest, NSW, Allen & Unwin, 2002. The oral traditions of one of the saltwater people's clan's most famous representatives, Eddie Mabo (1936-1992), did not prevent him from retaining a substantial 'western' and 'written' archive. See also Adrian Cunningham, 'The Chamberlain and Mabo Papers: Case Studies of Personal Papers of National Symbolic Significance', in particular his reflections on 'what drove a man whose oral culture has no tradition of personal recordkeeping ... to keep extensive records on such a wide range of activities over such a long period of time'. See http://www.nla.gov.au/nla/staffpaper/acunning4.html (viewed 1 October 2004).

[42] See Richard S. Esbenshade, 'Remembering to Forget: Memory, History, National Identity in Post-war East-Central Europe', *Representations*, 49, Winter 1995, p. 74. See also Adam Hochschild, *The Unquiet Ghost*, New York, Viking, 1994 and Connerton, op. cit., p. 15, as instances of the vast literature on this topic.

[43] Paul Fussell, *The Great War and Modern Memory*, New York, Oxford University Press, 1975.

Oral and printed sources do not exhaust the necessary qualifications. Sometimes group or individual memory is supported by archives; nothing more. This is readily illustrated in autobiographies and memoirs, where the most careful recollections trigger the need for archival research. A case in point is the 1988 recollections of the Australian communist Bernice Morris.[44] Her story mines vividly recalled accounts of political struggles supported with cross-references to world events including the 1954 Royal Commission on Espionage, life in China and the Soviet Union as well as in rural Australia, and as a nurse at the Royal Melbourne Hospital. Morris also draws on and reproduces photos, newspaper reports and correspondence between her and her husband Dave while separated, including a period of victimization following his naming during the Royal Commission. She also extensively uses the dossier the Australian Security Intelligence Organisation (ASIO) maintained on her husband for twenty years, which was released to her in the 1980s.

Bernice Morris represents one of many examples[45] of the interplay of personal memory and personal and official archives. The latter inevitably contained contested facts ('the files … rarely recording anything accurately', p. 3). But the ASIO dossier was implicitly trusted by Morris as reliable authentic evidence that her husband was officially perceived as a potential security risk. He was socially and literally 'adversely recorded'; and, as she remembered with bitterness, this recording did indeed result in his being dismissed from a series of workplaces.

The memory activity of Morris and other activists similarly affected by surveillance[46] was not, of course, only that; it was at once individual and collective. Their oral accounts and suspicions of ASIO's gaze were able to be shared and validated through their use of the dossiers released in the 1980s, albeit with deletions. This more public consciousness was strengthened and extended because a considerable number of activists were writers, and

---

[44] Bernice Morris, *Between the Lines*, Collingwood, Vic., Sybylla Co-operative Press, 1988, especially chapters 6-7 which were based almost entirely on files of the Australian Security Intelligence Organisation.

[45] Some examples, such as the autobiography of the early life of renowned historian Manning Clark, *The Puzzles of Childhood*, Ringwood, Vic., Viking, 1989, are based on incredibly detailed recall and a few family photos, although contextualized by knowledge based on library and archival research. Another instance involving photos and an equally staggering memory would be Denis Freney's *A Map of Days*, Port Melbourne, Vic., William Heinemann Australia, 1991. Mark Baker's *The Fiftieth Gate*, Sydney, NSW, Flamingo, 1997, represents a further variation in which the Melbourne academic historian revisits in 1995, with his parents, their birthplaces and sites of Holocaust survival and interweaves their triggered recollections and the results of extensive archival research in Poland, Jerusalem and Germany. Better still in some ways is the example of Timothy Garton Ash's 1992 project in the archives of the East German Ministry of State Security to 'investigate their investigation of me' while he was in East and West Germany in 1978-1983. He pursued the inquiry through his and informers' files and compared these with his own memories, letters, notebooks, diaries and knowledge of the times as an eyewitness. See his *The File*, London, HarperCollins, 1997.

[46] One further example is the Australian diplomat and writer Ric Throssell. Like Morris, he came under the notice of the Royal Commission, obtained access to parts of 'his' dossier and related files, and drew heavily on it and other archival records to produce an autobiography. See his *My Father's Son*, Port Melbourne, Vic., Mandarin Australia, 1990.

through the systematic revelations of historians. The work of both complemented the largely submerged collective memory within the actual dossier biographies.[47]

This group also shared with the wider political left and labour movement the belief that ASIO was part of a McCarthy-like conspiracy to defeat the Australian Labor Party in the 1954 federal election through the establishment of a Royal Commission to investigate allegations of Soviet spying by two embassy defectors, Vladimir and Evdokia Petrov. A number, in fact, were called before or named by the Commission, including Morris and Ric Throssell. Ironically, belief in the so-called 'Petrov myth' was also severely undermined by the release of the Royal Commission archives in the 1980s. The myth 'could not survive historical interrogation', but, as Robert Manne has demonstrated, collective memory does not change because of, or depend on, archives alone. With Labor back in power in the 1980s, this, combined with other social factors and the archives' release, meant that the myth died 'because it had lost its psychic-political purpose'.[48]

To Morris and other left-wing activists, memory and archives were complementary, but they are not always associated so positively. Just as often we see personal recollections and documentary memory contradict each other. Publishers' advertising departments know the value of announcing their latest title as a myth-exploding study based on newly released archives.[49]

But memory and documents can clash with devastating – as well as commercial – consequences. On a largely personal level, from the body of Holocaust hoax literature, we may cite the autobiography of Benjamin Wilkomirski, published by Suhrkamp in 1995 as *Bruchstücke* ('Fragments; Memories of a Childhood, 1939-1948') and quickly and widely translated. It was a harrowing account of a confused, frightened childhood in Nazi death camps which won the author a number of prizes and invitations from Holocaust archives and museums. Not since the publication of Anne Frank's diary had a child's view of Jewish persecution touched so many readers; not for a long time had child survivors felt at last they had a champion to voice their collective memory. But through the late 1990s, the memoir began to be challenged, and despite vehement denials and plausible explanations drawing in part on historical records, it was shown to be fraudulent. The conclusions of investigative journalism, DNA tests and documentation from Swiss and other archives were enough to have the book withdrawn. The phenomenon of conflicting oral histories and creation of

---

[47] See Fiona Capp, *Writers Defiled*, Ringwood, Vic., McPhee Gribble, 1993, in which she traces the investigation of left-wing writers, historians, academics, and organizations in the 1930s-1960s.
[48] For a summary of the Petrov Royal Commission story, see Manne's 'Australian Political Mythology: the Case of Petrov', in John Carroll, ed., *Intruders in the Bush*, 2nd ed., Melbourne, Oxford University Press, 1992. For a fuller account based on extensive archival research, see his *The Petrov Affair*, Sydney, Pergamon, 1987 (Rev. ed., Melbourne, Text Publishing Company, 2004).
[49] Some recent Australian examples are Peter A. Thompson and Robert Macklin, *The Battle of Brisbane*, Sydney, ABC Books, 2000; Paul Burns, *The Brisbane Line Controversy*, Crows Nest, NSW, Allen & Unwin, 1998; and Robert Manne, op. cit.

new identities for orphaned Jewish children of the Holocaust, however, make the entire issue complicated and enduring.[50]

Diary exposes vital evidence in Kelly trial

By **GLENN R. OWEN**
CRIMINAL REPORTER

Startling new evidence, hidden from the world for more than 119 years, has cast new light on the trial of Australia's most notorious bushranger, Ned Kelly.

Documents obtained by *The Age* show Kelly's trial in October 1880 was deliberately cut short before vital, last-minute evidence could be tendered.

Kelly was found guilty and sentenced by Justice Sir Redmond Barry. Two weeks later, he was hanged at the Old Melbourne Gaol.

The documents show that Sir Redmond disregarded a crucial submission by Kelly's defence — that the bushranger could not have been at Stringybark Creek the day he allegedly shot dead Constable Thomas Lonigan because he was in a photographic studio in a nearby town, posing in his armor for a surprise portrait for his mother's 70th birthday.

It is alleged that Sir Redmond, anxious to attend a garden party at Government House on the evening of the trial's second day, curtailed the proceedings in order to give himself time to go home and change.

The Kelly trial was covered for *The Age* by its chief court reporter of the day, Ebenezer Pickett. Pickett, who died at a Mount Dandenong nursing home in 1978, aged 110, kept a secret, detailed journal of his life and times.

This extraordinary diary has only recently been discovered, after Mr Pickett's grandson, Mr Ross Pickett, found it at the bottom of a trunk of old legal memorabilia.

What he found was a scrupulously notated account of Ebenezer's daily activities, written in small, almost indecipherable shorthand. The entry for October 21 1880 reads:

Supreme Court. Warm day. Kelly in dock. Barry seems hurried, forever adjusting his wig and looking at his timepiece. "Why so long, defence counsel?" he asks, becoming more irritable. Assistant counsel enters court, bearing pile of documents. "All will be revealed, Your Honor, in the fullness of time," says counsel. "Time and time enough," quips Barry, in typical fashion. "But time for you [pointing at defendant] is up." I notice tipstaff at back of court, waving at Barry, pointing in the direction of St Kilda Road. "But we have photographs, Your Honor," says counsel. "But I don't have a thousand words," said Barry, half in Latin, to underline his classical education. He orders evidence to be suppressed and, with unseemly haste, leaves the bench. Later, I notice his carriage travelling swiftly away. Later, our social editress tells me she saw Sir Redmond entertaining the Governor with a few verses of Homer. It all begins to fit into place ...

This extract, never before reported, contradicts several newspaper reports — including Pickett's own — of the trial, as well as the official transcript, which finishes before the new evidence was submitted and rejected by Barry. "My grandfather, possibly to avoid contempt charges, obviously stuck to the official story," says Ross Pickett.

Already, there is keen interest in the Pickett Diaries. Tom Cruise has optioned them for a film version, possibly starring himself as Ebenezer and Russell Crowe as Kelly. Penguin Books is looking at a pre-Christmas print run of 300,000 copies.

● *The 10 Things to Do column has been held over on account of April Fools' Day.*

Figure 12.2. The legend of Ned Kelly, the iconic Australian outlaw who was captured at Glenrowan in 1880, resonates still. His memory, supported by putative archives, makes this April Fools' Day item so believable.

---

[50] See Elena Lappin, 'The Man with Two Heads', *Granta*, 66, Summer 1999, pp. 8-65; for a fuller, more personal, equally decisive unmasking, see Blake Eskin, *A Life in Pieces*, W.W. Norton, 2002.

The exposure of a dishonest memoirist appears insignificant against the consequences of Australian courts according greater weight to written historical documents over oral testimony in native title cases. The most recent noteworthy case was the rejection in late 2002 of an appeal by the High Court of Australia by representatives of the indigenous Yorta Yorta community seeking possession, occupation and use of their tribal lands: public land and water, largely state forests and reserves, in northern Victoria and southern New South Wales. The High Court upheld earlier Federal Court rulings rejecting the claim. The majority in each appeal was not sufficiently impressed by the community's reliance on traditional knowledge, doubting they have had a continuous connection with their lands and had continued to acknowledge and observe traditional laws and customs inherited and adapted from their ancestors. Both courts took great note of an 1840s pastoralist's diary and an 1881 petition which contradicted Yorta Yorta claims.[51] Shauna McRanor's conclusion, made against the background of similar struggles by Canada's First Nation's people, is apt:

> Much of the disenfranchisement of aboriginal people that has occurred is due, in part, to the Eurocentric idea of the superiority of static objectified records over dynamic oral testimony as proof for establishing 'fact' or attaining absolute notions of 'truth'.[52]

---

[51] For the High Court 'reasons for judgement' see [2002] HCA 58 at www.austlii.edu.au/au/cases. Commentaries on this and related rulings from a range of perspectives include Peter Seidel, 'Tides of History: the New Terra Nullius', *Eureka Street*, March 2003, pp. 12-14 and 'Yorta Yorta High Court Appeal', *Hot Spots,* 3, available at: http://www.nntt.gov.au/newsletter/hotspots/issues/3.html (viewed 1 October 2004), and David Ritter, 'The Judgement of the World: the Yorta Yorta Case and the "Tide of History"', *Australian Historical Studies,* 123, 2004, pp. 106-121. The broader issue of the document and historian expert was at the heart of Iain McCalman & Ann McGrath, eds, *Proof & Truth,* Canberra, ACT, Australian Academy of the Humanities, 2003.

[52] Shauna McRanor, 'Maintaining the Reliability of Aboriginal Oral Records and Their Material Manifestations: Implications for Archival Practice', *Archivaria*, 43, 1997, p. 81.

Figure 12.3. Leunig's cartoon of the Yorta Yorta decision.

There is one last dimension to the point made when previously introducing Bernice Morris's story. It can tell us just how mistaken it is to see the corporate memory captured in an organization's archives as complete in itself. These alone do not represent an organization's corporate memory, and they do not, however partially, represent just the creating organization's memory. Returning to ASIO for a moment, within its own four walls, its corporate memory would have to embrace as well its internal culture, its oral history, the reminiscences and autobiographies of its retired operatives and so on. But in addition, 'its' files captured part of the Morris family's memory too. Similarly, Danish and US archival records of their colonial rule in the Virgin Islands capture a joint heritage and provenance.[53] Similarly, Bill Russell, in his study of the Canadian Department of Indian Affairs has observed its officials documented indigenous memory citing the 'registrar-cum-archivist' A. E. St Louis as someone who was clearly aware of this role, noting that while 'none of our papers can be classified as Indian myths or legends, ... all of them bear characteristics of historical monuments'. Colonial administrative structures from Australia and the Pacific provide many further instances. Representations of indigenous memories and practices are inevitably, if indirectly, captured in the journals of labour-recruiting agents, files of plantation companies, correspondence of officials and files of native welfare administrators and reports of missionaries back to London.[54]

---

[53] Bastian, op. cit., chapter 5.

[54] Bill Russell, 'The White Man's Burden: Aspects of Record Keeping in the Department of Indian Affairs, 1860-1914', *Archivaria*, 19, 1984/85, p. 52. Relevant local references covering this large topic include articles by Fran Jury, David Hanlon and Monica Wehner and Ewan Maidment in *Archives and Manuscripts*, May 1999. The 'stolen generations' report is also a key illustration of individual memory inadvertently recorded via so called 'dossier rule'. See Australia, Human Rights and Equal Opportunity Commission, *Bringing Them Home,* Canberra, HREOC, 1997, available at: http://www.austlii.edu.au/au/special/rsjproject/rsjlibrary/hreoc/stolen/ (viewed 1 October 2004).

Forgetting and the absence of archives

What then of archives and remembering's opposite, forgetting? To start, it is worth noting that here too a popular, yet mistaken, belief exists. This orthodox view asserts that memory is undermined by the absence of records. However, this absence arises from many factors, the most prevalent being benign neglect. The French-African saying, 'each old man who dies signifies the burning of one library', has its documentary – and alternative gender! – equivalents, and most of us expire from natural causes.[55] Business efficiency and inherent vice also take their toll. One aspect of the latter, technological obsolescence, is especially feared as an agent of social amnesia, as we noted earlier. The most popular reason remains, however, the deliberate targeting of cultural heritage collections and institutions during violent conflict.

Well, perhaps. Let us briefly recall the circumstances of Jenkinson's definition. Remembering by making a record actually means it is then safe to forget. Socrates saw the similarly ironic relationship in writing, which caused memory skills to lapse through lack of use. And Derrida thought deeply around this inner contradiction, famously naming it archive fever.

Nor should forgetting via archival destruction necessarily be seen in a negative light. This paradoxical fact is most readily understandable at the personal level, but it also has social and political dimensions. Often in conflict resolution, familiar injunctions to 'put the whole thing behind you', to 'forgive and forget', to 'wipe the slate clean', lead to symbolic, yet actual, destruction of documentation. Wanting 'to forget the whole sorry business', a jilted lover will burn personal photographs and letters. An unsuccessful job applicant will expiate disappointment by tearing up the application and notes for the interview. A different example of therapeutic forgetting is provided by Janine di Giovanni, a reporter who burnt all her early 1990s Bosnian notebooks, letters and documents because 'they represented war and misery' and she 'wanted to move on'.[56]

Utilitarian records destruction supporting memory can also have broader dimensions. The case for socially and nationally useful forgetting was put long ago by philosophers and political thinkers such as Plato, Nietzsche, Carlyle, Hobbes and Renan, although none extended their recommendations to actual book and document burning. But archivists who represent their role as preserving memory need to be able to explain their deliberate destruction of records in pro-memory terms. It is simpler when considering particular record categories. For example, some jurisdictions help those guilty of minor offences or

---

[55] On the French-African saying, see Brian Doyle, 'Respect for Fonts: Linguistic Documentation and Lesser-Used Orthographies', *Comma*, 2004.1, p. 77; on an individual's documentary existence, see Nils Nilsson's classic reflection on the journeyman carpenter John Kovacs, 'The Memory of a Person', *Comma*, 2004.1, pp. 179-182.

[56] Janine di Giovanni, 'Goodbye to All That', *The Weekend Australian Magazine*, 7-8 February 2004, p. 29. The destruction was regretted because her eyewitness records were sought by the International Criminal Tribunal for the Former Yugoslavia in The Hague. Di Giovanni still could not get Bosnia out of her mind – that took the book, *Madness Visible*, New York, Knopf, 2003.

granted pardons to make a fresh start by the destruction of criminal records. So too with multiple offenders: in return for full disclosure and remorse, a truth and reconciliation commission will destroy indictments against some categories of members of a former regime.[57]

Records destruction can also be intended to positively shape remembering. The example of Nobel Prize winning novelist Patrick White neatly combines several aspects of the subject. His need to keep records, convenient forms of artificial memory though they may be, was minimal given his prodigious memory. In his fiction too, White focused on the destruction of records intended to influence memory. In *The Tree of Man*, Stan Parker tells his wife of his wartime letters to her: 'It doesn't do to keep old letters ... It's morbid. You start reading back, and forget that you have moved on'. And in *The Solid Mandala*, Waldo Brown's use of the fire pit 'was both a sowing and a scattering of seed'. When Waldo was finished 'he felt lighter'. Papers gone, one need not remember the past. In other words, when you can't read them back, you can safely forget the past; you can remember you've moved on.[58]

Towards the end of his life White cooperated with National Library of Australia collecting and a biography, but for most of his creative years he shunned the accumulation of literary archives. Why? As he explained:

> My MSS are destroyed as soon as the books are printed. I put very little into notebooks, don't keep my friends' letters as I urge them not to keep mine, and anything unfinished when I die is to be burnt. The final versions of my books are what I want people to see ...[59]

Through destruction, White wanted to shape how he would be remembered – by just his publications, as he, in turn, preferred to remember Katherine Mansfield by her stories unsullied by outpourings in her letters. It is an attitude he shared with a sizeable minority of other writers, although not all take the extreme measure of emasculating their own papers.[60]

---

[57] On the general subject of positive destruction, see Brien Brothman, op. cit., p 73 and Lowenthal, op. cit., pp. 156-162. For a discussion on recordkeeping destruction and spent convictions, see Australian Law Reform Commission, *Criminal Records*, Discussion Paper No. 25, December 1985. For historical examples from Ferrara in late fifteenth-century Italy of pardons and amnesties plus attendant records destruction offered to people who owed money for minor civil infractions, see Richard Brown, 'Death of a Renaissance Record-Keeper: the Murder of Tomasso de Tortona in Ferrara, 1385', *Archivaria*, 44, 1997, pp. 1-43.

[58] Sue McKemmish was the first to bring this to archival notice. See 'Evidence of Me...', *Archives and Manuscripts*, 24, no. 1, May 1996, pp. 28-45. See also Patrick White, *The Tree of Man*, London, Eyre & Spottiswoode, 1956, p. 213, and *The Solid Mandala*, London, Eyre & Spottiswoode, 1966, p. 213.

[59] Quoted in McKemmish, 'Evidence of Me...', op. cit., p 34.

[60] For examples of the large literature on this subject, see Sandra Kemp, 'The Archive on which the Sun Never Sets: Rudyard Kipling', in *History of the Human Sciences*, 11, no. 4, 1998, pp. 33-48, and that by Janet Frame's biographer Michael King, 'The Compassionate Truth', *Meanjin*, 61, no. 1, 2002. Some writers just want to restrict access to their papers for reasons of privacy, J. D. Salinger

An even starker instance of destruction undertaken to support remembering comes from the Stalinist era of the Soviet Union. Anticipating his execution for treason during Stalin's purges of the late 1930s, the Communist leader Nikolai Bukharin composed a short letter of defence. He then read it over and over to his young wife and, once assured it had been committed to memory, destroyed it to guarantee Stalin's police could not find it. Another fifty years would pass before Bukharin's rehabilitation and his testament, faithfully preserved in his wife's memory, was published in *Pravda*.[61]

No survey of positive destruction would be complete without reference to the deliberate decision not to make records at all in order to underpin indisputably memorable and 'historic' acts. Among the most common examples have been agreements which echo still, though they required great secrecy to execute; agreements cemented as binding on the parties by the presence of remembrancers or made only when advisers and note-takers had been dismissed. Political leaders speaking 'off the record' or 'not for attribution' are equally familiar cases. None of this guarantees memories will survive beyond the moment of need or that alternative recordings will not be made and retained. One such instance from the First World War, cited by Paul Fussell, related to Gunner W. R. Price who, up to the carnage at Passchendaele, pursued his hobby as an amateur photographer. The casualities there made it seem indecent to continue. Ironically we know this because he set down why. 'Things like this ... did not need photographing by me', he wrote, in words subsequently preserved in the Imperial War Museum, and quoted in a publication that became a multi-edition classic![62]

In turning to forgetting through the deliberate targeting of records for destruction, it is traditional to cite the words of George Orwell or Milan Kundera. We face not only an abundance of depressing illustrations,[63] but also the challenge of discerning a secondary target of memory, and the need to disentangle issues of intent and consequence.

If one wants to talk at all of forgetting enforced via records destruction, the setting is almost always war and repressive acts of dictatorial regimes. Among the earliest cited instances involves China's first Qin emperor, who ordered the destruction of all writings predating 213 BCE. Recorded history, and – so the hope went – collective memory would begin with him. Virtually every century since provides examples of attempts to combine the destruction of a person or social group with a matching cultural destruction, though none

---

perhaps being the best-known example, but their actions impact no less on how they can be remembered and represented.

[61] Judith Miller, *One, by One, by One: Facing the Holocaust*, New York, Simon and Schuster, 1990, p. 204.

[62] Fussell, op. cit., pp. 88-89.

[63] For case studies of questionable and unauthorized destruction in the US and Canada, see Richard Cox and David Wallace, eds, *Archives and the Public Good*, Westport, Conn., Quorum Books, 2002. For a culturally broader canvas covering a range of library and archival materials, see Rebecca Knuth, *Libricide: the Regime-Sponsored Destruction of Books and Libraries in the Twentieth Century*, Westport, Conn., Praeger, 2003. I thank Professor Eric Ketelaar for bringing this title to my notice.

presents more horrifying examples than the various genocides practised in the twentieth century.

Within that number, the Nazi destruction of the Jews stands in a category of its own. On the German side, recordkeeping was an indispensable enabler of the Holocaust, as scholarship pioneered by Raul Hilberg has shown. On the Jewish side, their cultural property including organizational and personal records was threatened by dislocation, looting, attacks on property and places of worship, and the innumerable indirect effects of their persecution. But whether, within this deliberate targeting of a people, there was also the intent to target Jewish memory through archives is unlikely, though difficult to determine with certainty. There is even evidence to suggest the Nazis planned to celebrate the Final Solution through museums, the Jews to be 'not annihilated and then forgotten, but annihilated and then remembered forever'.[64]

In occupied countries there were many reprisals for partisan attacks and the like which focused on particular local populations and, on several infamous occasions, wiping their towns 'off the map' seemed the intention. Lidice in the Czech Republic ranks as the site of one of the worst, the SS being determined to obliterate the Catholic town because circumstantial evidence linked it to the assassins of Reinhard Heydrich. Its inhabitants were killed or deported, and for over two months the entire town was systematically destroyed: trees uprooted, ruins bulldozed and several feet of soil spread where buildings once stood.[65] In the process, personal and corporate records undoubtedly were destroyed, but the object was not them but a broader one and, with hindsight, totally counter-productive. In the case of 'martyred' villages, as with innumerable other massacre sites, the physical landscape itself becomes the focus, buttressed by oral histories, documentation strategies, web sites, histories and commemorative activities.

It was the conflicts of the 1990s in the republics of former Yugoslavia, however, that presented perhaps the clearest link between archives and memory. In places such as Kosovo, Mostar and Sarajevo, deliberate shelling and burning of churches, mosques, monasteries, architecturally and culturally significant sites, museums and libraries resulted in the coining of new terms such as 'cultural cleansing', 'cultural genocide' and 'memoricide'.[66]

---

[64] David Lowenthal, op. cit., p. 162. See also Knuth, op. cit., p. 85, and on similar practices by the Chinese in Tibet, pp. 221-222. Chris Healy has noted a similar process in Australia of dispossession (and some have argued, genocide) of indigenous Australians accompanied by possession through objects, and later image and text. See his 'Histories and Collecting: Museums, Objects and Memories', in Kate Darian-Smith and Paula Hamilton, op. cit., p. 44.

[65] Callum MacDonald, *The Killing of Obergruppenfuhrer Reinhard Heydrich 27 May 1942*, London, Macmillian, 1989, pp. 186-187. A similar though not so complete physical erasure was perpetrated at Oradour-sur-Glane in the Limousin region of west central France on 10 June 1944. See Sarah Farmer, *Martyred Village,* Berkeley, Calif., University of California Press, 1999.

[66] There is an extensive literature covering 'cultural cleansing' in Croatian, Bosnian and Herzegovinan cities, much of it available on the Internet. For a sampling, see Colin Kaiser, 'Crimes against culture', *UNESCO Courier*, September 2000, available at:

Manuscripts and archival materials were included in much of the cultural heritage destroyed, although not (so far as can be discerned) explicitly singled out as a documentary category because archives happen to be especially memory-laden. But there is no doubt commentators have seen the shelling as an attack on memory. Take for instance Michael Ignatieff's response to the destruction in 1991 of the Jasenovac museum and memorial centre, at Novska, seventy kilometres east of Zagreb, Croatia. It had been established by Tito in the 1960s to perpetuate the memory of a labour and death camp operated by Croatian nationalists between 1941 and 1945 resulting in the deaths of between 250,000 and 700,000 Jews, Serbs and Croatian communists. In 1991 the museum was systematically destroyed:

> Every book in the library has been ripped up … Every glass exhibit case has been smashed. Every photograph has been defaced. Every file has been pulled out of every drawer … all the walls have been daubed with excrement and slogans. An intense hatred, an overwhelming hatred from the past, has taken hold of the people who did this. *As if* by destroying the museum, they hoped to destroy the memory of what was done here.[67]

As if … they hoped … In fact, deliberate destruction of cultural heritage aimed at erasing memory (by denying the means to remember) practically guarantees such atrocities will be remembered. Of course *what* is able to be remembered, and *how*, inevitably changes, and almost always for the worst. There are also occasions, from the Roman use of *damnatio memoriae* onwards, when the intent actually is to leave evidence of the destruction. But if the intention is to target memory by targetting archives or any other cultural material (and rarely are just archives singled out), it is usually doomed to fail. More often the message is 'mind the gap', the gap being Paul Valéry's 'active presence of absent things'. More likely the intention is to desecrate, and demoralize; to strike symbolically as much as physically.[68]

This paradox should not blind us to the fact that, historically, deliberate attempts to enforce forgetting have indeed resulted in the destruction of records, of ephemeral and continuing value alike. Remembering, which depends on and occurs through the use of evidentially authoritative archives, such as genealogy and much history writing, is inevitably undermined. Bosnian history provides a case in point, where it was 'necessary to destroy documents demonstrating the validity of Muslim historical claims … because they directly

---

http://www.unesco.org/courier/2000_09/uk/signe2.htm (viewed 1 October 2004); Knuth, op cit., chapter 5, and; Janine di Giovanni, op. cit., esp. pp. 87, 221.

[67] Michael Ignatieff, 'The Highway of Brotherhood and Unity', *Granta*, 45, Autumn 1993, p. 230. Emphasis added.

[68] For a detailed case study of *damnatio memoriae*, specifically the purge and rehabilitation of the memory of Flavianus the Elder during the later Roman Empire, see Charles Hedrick, *History and Silence,* Austin, Tex., University of Texas Press, 2000. On symbolic archival destruction, see James M. O'Toole, 'The Symbolic Significance of Archives', *American Archivist*, 56, no. 2, 1993, p. 253-254. On the other hand, in the fictional world of Big Brother, Oceania and its retrospective alteration of records, brainwashing and use of the 'memory hole', erasures truly are forgotten. See George Orwell, *Nineteen Eighty-four,* London, Penguin Classics, 2000.

contradicted the Serbian expansionist claim that Bosnia had no legitimacy as a separate nation or civilization'. The European past of the Australian state of Tasmania, settled in 1803 as a destination for transported convicts, provides another. From 1810 until well into the twentieth century there was deliberate destruction of convict records such as indent lists. Civic leaders and the free-born were intent on obliterating the 'stain' of penal origins and the emancipists to hide their convict origins. Now the motivations are reversed, and the memory work of genealogists and historians are frustrated through lack of archives.[69]

Conclusion

The direct attack on archives because of their power to remind us of unpalatable truths brings us almost full circle. Our departure point was the background to inflated claims which implied 'archives equals memory' was the *summa* of the human past. What followed was a series of discussions exploring the reasons justifying more qualified claims. We should acknowledge however that there *are* times and circumstances when archives indeed are regarded as central to collective memory.

The first concerns social identity. Endeavouring to preserve one's place in the world through collecting archives is a very well-known phenomenon within modern society. It is practised by families, historical societies, schools, businesses, clubs, community groups and a vast array of non-government not-for-profit bodies. Typically, it is anniversaries that stimulate awareness, or a heightened sense, of the group's contribution to society, as can crises, threats, departures of very long-serving personnel and occasionally external encouragement. Collecting, followed by digitization and web site development now increasingly the focus of so-called 'memory projects',[70] will typically embrace all forms of recorded information and is usually directed to supplying a commissioned history with source material. Oral history interviews, sets of newsletters and publications, and objects and other memorabilia are among the most popular, but the pursuit of archival records will always be included. In addition, no group emphasizing a strong self-image to the wider society will exclude minute books, diaries, photographs, petitions and correspondence, especially of important early leaders. The expression of national identity through foundation documents of various kinds and through the collecting by institutions focused on broad societal themes or historical events such as war, is also well documented. Here the

---

[69] On Bosnia, see Knuth, *op. cit.*, pp 125-6. On Tasmania, see Henry Reynolds, '"That Hated Stain": The Aftermath of Transportation in Tasmania', *Historical Studies*, 14, no. 53, 1969, pp. 19-31, and discussion of destruction of convict written and/or physical evidence in Joanna Sassoon, 'Phantoms of Remembrance: Libraries and Archives as "The Collective Memory"', *Public History Review*, 10, 2003, pp. 49-50, Kay Daniels, *Convict Women*, Crows Nest, NSW, Allen & Unwin, 1998, p. 241, and Tom Griffiths, *Hunters and Collectors,* Cambridge, Cambridge University Press, 1996, esp. Chapter 5.

[70] See for example sites for memory projects for Greater Cincinnati and Ohio, see http://www.cincinnatimemory.org/about.html and http://www.ohiomemory.org/om/background.html (viewed 1 October 2004).

results of collecting were seen not primarily as resources for historical research, but as what Tanja Luckins calls objects of memory – part of the general transmission of memory.[71]

Just as for identity, so for remembering recordkeeping. There *are* occasions when archives can sustain a claim as ambitious as Bolotenko's. When captured and kept self-consciously, when deliberately executed as if anticipating conflicting oral accounts, the intent of recordkeeping (if not always the result) is to tell the future: 'remember *this*'. Constitutions, charters of freedom, parliamentary proceedings, certified copies of treaties, official registrations of births and land sales and many other records documenting the function of recording take on this character. They are agreed statements, from the present to the future, which say that this is what we collectively and officially agreed to say happened, was done and was said.[72] Of course, such records do not guarantee that subsequently there will not be repudiations or disagreements, as New Zealand has discovered in relation to the Treaty of Waitangi.[73] Other archives too can become invested with enormous memorializing power. Some take on deep symbolic significance, while others evolve to become classic conduits of collective memory. They take up meaningful representativeness by answering the needs of a family, group, class, social strata or even a whole nation. One of the best-researched and still evolving examples of such documents from the twentieth century is Anne Frank's diary,[74] but every country and age produces such documents.

Such documents are exceptional. More typically, the memory role of archives is collaborative, as we have tried to demonstrate. It also mostly works indirectly. When the mere existence of archives supports symbolic or other institutional or social purposes, or when archival institutions exploit them (guides, sponsored research, digitization, exhibitions), it is more direct. More generally, the users of archives – be they the creators and custodians, or genealogists, documentary film producers, historians or any number of

---

[71] Case studies and discussion on how archives have been collected, recovered and reinterpreted to underpin group identity in the archival literature is surprisingly thin, but includes Graham Carbery, 'Australian Lesbian and Gay Archives', *Archives and Manuscripts*, 23, no. 1, May 1995, pp. 30-37 and Elisabeth Kaplan, 'We Are What We Collect, We Collect What We Are: Archives and the Construction of Identity', *American Archivist*, 63, Spring/Summer 2000, pp. 125-151. See also the many relevant chapters in Carolyn Hamilton, et al., eds, *Refiguring the Archive*, Kluwer, 2002. Two new insightful Australian studies of war collecting at the broad societal level are Anne-Marie Condé, 'Capturing the Records of War: Collecting at the Mitchell Library and the Australian War Memorial', *Australian Historical Studies* (forthcoming) and Tanja Luckins, op. cit., esp. pp. 223-224.

[72] On this point, particularly in relation to photographs, see Susan Sontag, *Regarding the Pain of Others*, New York, Picador, 2003, pp. 85-88.

[73] For a survey of recent treaty and tribunal histories, see Andrew Sharp and Paul McHugh, eds, *Histories, Power and Loss; Uses of the Past – A New Zealand Commentary*, Wellington, Bridget Williams Books, 2001.

[74] According to Melissa Muller, the diary made Anne Frank 'one of the best-known figures of the twentieth century'. See her *Anne Frank, the Biography*, New York, Metropolitan Books, 1998, p. ix. The Anne Frank phenomenon can be readily tracked in the diary's publishing history, the films, plays and debates it has triggered, and through Internet searches on her name which run to over a million; see also Robert Sackett, 'Memory by Way of Anne Frank; Enlightenment and Denial Among West Germans, Circa 1960', *Holocaust and Genocide Studies*, 16, no. 2, 2002, pp. 243-265. Of course, for Holocaust deniers, the diary supports a completely different collective memory!

other categories – make their contribution to perpetuating and reinventing individual and collective memory. They do this by drawing on the archives, which are as a result reused again and again; archives which have resulted from active co-creation by records professionals and innumerable others alike; which have been flagged for destruction but used in the meantime; or which may have been once sentimental mementos but otherwise actively shaped by no-one and are now homeless chance survivals.

And so, finally, we might note the work of Gillian Tindall. In the 1980s Tindall transformed a cache of letters she found in a deserted house kept by an obscure innkeeper's daughter, Célestine Chaumette, who lived in central France from 1844 to 1933. Tindall explained the project thus:

> Now, when Célestine herself, all her correspondents, every single person they knew and most of those they were ever going to know, had vanished as if they had never been, I would bring them to life again.[75]

When the results of that use are known and shared, in this case through publication, it turns individual memory into collective memory. It also happens, though, when 'people decide that some thing that was personal and theirs should become communal and ours'.[76] The response of the people of Chassignolles to Tindall's researches was ambivalent. Sitting in the town hall archives, surrounded by minute books, she was accused by one of the local citizens of taking over their past. She was momentarily stricken with guilt, then protested:

> "But you didn't want it! *You* could have done this research. But you haven't." He relents. "Quite true. I haven't … Maybe we need you. Maybe you are giving our past back to us."[77]

Long after archival records have served their aide-mémoire role and individuals and their memories have gone and forgotten, the Halbwachian group collectively remembers through use – of 'their' archives: archives of and about them. Thus today's descendants of the original Australians and their supporters remember past injustices through archival research. Thus today's African-American descendants of slaves take advantage of legislation requiring insurance companies to publish lists of pre-Civil War slaves' names. Thus in generations to come the descendants of the Iraqis in SIEV 4, of the ministerial staffers and of the sailors on HMAS *Adelaide* will relive and re-remember the Children Overboard saga through archival research, just as others do so today for more immediate political, ethical, accountability and educational reasons.

---

[75] Gillian Tindall, *Célestine: Voices from a French Village*, New York, Minerva, 1996, p. 6.
[76] Tom Griffiths, 'Collecting Culture', *National Library of Australia News*, July 1997, p. 9-17. Griffiths called this 'de-privatisation'; others would see it as an example of pluralization.
[77] Tindall, op. cit., p. 270.

Readings

- Barbara L. Craig, 'Selected Themes on the Literature on Memory and Their Pertinence to Archives', *American Archivist*, 65, Fall/Winter 2002, pp. 276-289.

  An excellent starting point for archivists wanting to survey relevant memory studies literature. Craig summarizes the history of memory and collective memory as concepts and explains archives' relevance in remembrance via use, selection and context and, in doing so, also highlights a dozen or so key memory study titles and articles from our own professional literature which appeared during the past decade.

- *History of the Human Sciences*, 11, no. 4, 1998 and 12, no. 2, 1999.

  This double theme issue, 'The Archive', allows archivists to sample some of the scholarly and theoretical perspectives on archives in society by academics specializing across the social science and humanities disciplines, including cultural historians, linguists and sociologists. Their notion of 'archives' moves constantly between them as historical sources shaping histories and memories, as real institutions and documents, and a set of rules about 'what can be expressed at all'. The fifteen or so articles will especially challenge those who take a one-dimensional view of what archives and records work is all about.

- Mark McKenna, *Looking for Blackfellas' Point: an Australian History of Place*, Sydney, University of New South Wales Press, 2002.

  This is a beautifully written and illustrated account of the indigenous-settler contact in one corner of the extreme south coast of New South Wales. McKenna interweaves his own 'researcher narrative' about discovering what can be known, stimulated after purchasing land near Blackfellas' Point in 1993. He reflects on the historiography of black and white Aboriginal history, the preservation and transmission of memory and local history materials and oral histories, and how these link to an evolving reconciliation at the community level.

- Matt K. Matsuda, *The Memory of the Modern*, New York, Oxford University Press, 1996.

  Another text engagingly written and illustrated. Its value in this context is twofold. First it demonstrates that memory as a construct itself has a history, and secondly, that the way remembering happens depends on many agents in addition to records. Each chapter can stand alone, Chapter 6 entitled 'Identities: Doctor, Judge, Vagabond' being a superb case study of the state's 'memory' at work.

About the next book

We began this book with a discursive introduction to its contents and structure, and about our intentions and hopes for it. We mentioned the things we had asked the authors to bear in mind; we declared our own theoretical predispositions; and we admitted our wish for audiences beyond our profession and discipline. And once or twice, we named names (Horsman, Giddens, Foucault) as marker buoys for readers interested to make sense of our mental maps. Even so, we acknowledged that our readers may not read sequentially, starting at the start with its 'about' tag trying to say 'read me first'.

One of this book's many Australian contexts is *Keeping Archives*, which was commissioned by the Australian Society of Archivists and appeared in 1987 with a new edition in 1993. It attempted to describe, in a single volume, the how and why of basic analogue archiving. Directly or indirectly, all the editors were involved in that innocent, understandable and, in some ways, doomed effort. Two other relevant Australian titles, *Archival Documents* (1993) and *The Records Continuum* (1994), also represent broad scope efforts from our number.

Everything has changed since 'KA One', as it was called. Everything. Even in the late 1980s and early 1990s, thinking just about the history of the Internet, it was beginning to foreshadow profound changes for us. Yet the convenience and idea of, and need for, a new overarching project remain. This time, however, we and our authors have deliberately not looked back at those texts, but attempted to understand the breadth and depth of the what, why and multiple meanings and social institutional professional and cultural settings of archiving *and* recordkeeping. We knew of the classic and tiresome objections to single volume 'textbook' treatments. We knew from the beginning that such ambition could not have, nor would bring, one or any neat conclusion. For readers to have seen that from the preceding pages means we have already succeeded and doubly so if this book has set in train debates, discussions, rejoinders and proposals for other book-length treatments – as it has with us and our chapter authors.

This prospective 'afterword', which developed as the book took shape, serves a double purpose. Initially it became the editors' shorthand for, and way of managing, all of our intellectual off-cuts and out-takes. Secondly, to be frank, it compensated for our failure to produce the planned final chapter 'Recordkeeping and the global information society'. We should have known it would be an impossible challenge. Expecting it would somehow tie off the book, it became clear that it, more than any of our chapters, needed its own couple of hundred pages – although all chapters revealed aspects which needing further discussion.

We started talking about this book in 1999. As we developed the conceptual framework for the chapters and began thinking about authors, the world – and especially all that is implied by the phrases new world order, post-colonialism and the global information society and their myriad recordkeeping and archiving implications, seemed to be changing before our eyes. Indeed no single factor pushed our chapter themes closer to their tipping point, than globalism. Beyond that point, of course, is the need for the next book.

How it should address globalism, trans-national and cross-jurisdictional organizations is unknown for the present. To resort again to catch-phrases, however, it will need to cover our special aspects of 'Jihad vs McWorld', of the ideas behind Baudrillard's 'The gulf war did not take place', virtual communities, and of the ever-evolving increasingly ubiquitous Internet. It will need to follow Ann Stoler and look along, rather than against, the 'archival grain' of colonialism's paper empires and discern in their supreme technologies prefigured post modern states and corporations dominating globally through information. It will also need to account for the many new/old recordkeeping and archiving issues associated with straight information and communication technology developments, including robotics, personal communication devices, medicine, blogging and the response to global terrorism, to note just a few. They are indeed all-pervasive, and will continue to be, even as rumours circulate of the redundancy of Moore's law. Thus, as a final instance, the radio barcode: it promises a world 'where everything that *moves* can talk to everyone, everywhere all the time … cartons of milk, bottles of wine, clothes, wallets, tyres, cars, pets and people'.

Technology aside, as our book developed in the new century, archival and recordkeeping studies worldwide seemed evident. The best of our discourse has become richer, more interdisciplinary, and more mature about theoretical and conceptual ways of thinking. Fresh ideas found voice in new or revitalized journals (*Archival Science, Comma*) and in new monograph series (Kluwer's *The Archivist's Library*); old ideas were placed in or tested against new cultural political and post-colonial settings and challenges (the SAA classics' series; University of British Columbia's diplomatics perspective; South Africa's *Refiguring the Archive* and Jeannette Bastian's *Owning Memory*); and the first of a planned series of international conferences on the history of the record was held. Similarly, there has been recognition of and action addressing the need for international collaborative research on recordkeeping solutions (e.g. InterPARES) and standards (e.g. ISAD(G), ISAAR(CPF), ISO 15489).

The next book must take in all this as essential background, and similarly build from and on the continuum framework which underpins so many of the assumptions of this book. Those most directly responsible for its Australian development and articulation have always stressed the need for exegesis and discourse, as others such as Verne Harris and Terry Cook always recognized. Indeed this book itself elaborates on continuum concepts, be it 'trace' or 'collective memory', and demonstrates their value in contextualizing records in action such as the various dimensions of the 'children overboard' story. The continuum framework has provided a setting for developing ideas such as 'communities of records' and 'parallel provenance', and been applied to other concepts and functions related to records including information and publishing. Regardless of the specific themes of the next book, however, there is little doubt that the continuum's many concurrent applications in space-time will be needed and extended.

Indigenous inscribing practices and oral ways of recording and remembering must also be addressed directly in the next book. It hardly needs conceding here that we and our authors struggled to think outside our western mindsets, although that admission having been made, perhaps it is an illogical and presumptuous conceit to try. The necessity to be inclusive remains; it is underlined by the recordkeeping and archiving aspects of the stolen generations, reconciliation, documenting native title, and the preservation and transmission of indigenous community memory. There have also been issues surrounding the role of recorded and other evidence of the settler-indigenous interaction in the European settlement of Australia, as well as the larger historiographical and 'politics of memory' canvasses of the recent 'History Wars'. The recent special issue of *Comma* (2003.1: Archives and Indigenous Peoples) and the results of the Monash University led research project 'Trust and technology: building archival systems for indigenous oral memory' will help show the way.

In some ways this book is an artefact, an analogue container of content. It began with a formal agreement with our publisher ratified by hand written signatures; it incorporates two ancient inventions (paper and the hinge) and a relatively recent one (printing), and was distributed in very familiar and traditional ways. It is structured to be read from front to back, from left to right, and down the page. Yet helping us coordinate the writing was email, phone-conferencing, laptops, PDAs, mobile phones and an extranet, while behind them whirled the never-actual, ever-changing record. In a strange turn of events, the book's 'children overboard' leitmotif, a story of biblical values and modern recordkeeping technologies, returned to make headlines as we sent this book to the copy editor. What the next book looks like, how it is distributed, and where it locates *Archives: Recordkeeping in Society* remains to be seen.

Notes on contributors

Adrian Cunningham holds the position of Director, Recordkeeping Standards and Policy at the National Archives of Australia. In this capacity he has policy and research and development oversight of the NAA's work on current recordkeeping and metadata standards and appraisal policy. Adrian is Secretary of the International Council on Archives Committee on Descriptive Standards and Convenor of the Australian Society of Archivists Descriptive Standards Committee.

Robert Hartland was a Lecturer in the School of Information Management and Systems, Monash University from 1996 until 2004, following a career as a secondary school teacher. He contributed to the design of the Bachelor of Information Management degree, introduced in 1997, and was an innovative, popular and successful teacher of undergraduate and postgraduate students. He coordinated a number of projects to review and enhance both course content and delivery methods, including a project to develop materials for recordkeeping education suitable for international students. His professional interests particularly concerned the role of information in society and documentary form.

Hans Hofman is co-director of ERPANET and senior adviser at the Nationaal Archief (National Archives) of the Netherlands. The European funded ERPANET project aims to enhance the preservation of digital objects (www.erpanet.org) throughout Europe. In his position at the Nationaal Archief, he is involved in egovernment projects and initiatives throughout Dutch government with respect to access and management of digital records and information in general. On the international scene, he is co-investigator and representative of the Nationaal Archief in the InterPARES2 research project, and representative of the Netherlands in the ISO TC46/SC11 on Records Management. Within this committee he is chair of the Working Group on Records Management Metadata. Finally, he is a researcher in the Delos 2 project on digital libraries with respect to digital preservation. He has given numerous presentations and written many articles on topics like digital preservation, recordkeeping metadata and electronic records management.

Chris Hurley has worked for over thirty years in national and state archives programs in Australia and New Zealand. He headed the Public Record Office of Victoria from 1981 to 1990 and was Acting Chief Archivist of New Zealand for two and a half years from 1998 to 2000. He has served on the boards and committees of professional bodies in Australia and internationally and has authored many articles and conference papers. Chris has written on documentation issues and on archives legislation. Reluctantly, following what he regards as the inadequate professional response in Australia to the 'Heiner Affair', he now also writes and speaks on accountability issues.

Livia Iacovino's principal research and teaching interests centre on the ethical-legal context of recordkeeping. She is a Lecturer in the School of Information Management and Systems, Monash University, a Principal Researcher in the School's Records Continuum Research Group, a Co-Chair of the Policy Research Cross Domain Group, International Research on Permanent Authentic Records in Electronic Systems 2, and a Chief Investigator for the Electronic Health Records: Achieving an Effective and Ethical Legal and Recordkeeping Framework, Australian Research Council Discovery Grant. Livia is also a professional archivist and her previous appointments include the National Archives of Australia (Victoria) and the Public Record Office of Victoria. Her awards include the Australian Society of Archivists Mander Jones Award 1999, for the *Archives and Manuscripts* theme issue, 'Recordkeeping and the Law'. Her PhD, awarded in 2003, is titled 'Ethical-Legal Frameworks for Recordkeeping: Regulatory Models, Participants and their Rights and Obligations'.

Eric Ketelaar is Professor of Archivistics in the Department of Media Studies of the Faculty of Humanities of the University of Amsterdam (since 1997). His current teaching and research are concerned mainly with the social and cultural contexts of records creation and use. In 2000/2001 he was The Netherlands Visiting Professor at the University of Michigan (School of Information). He was General State Archivist (National Archivist) of The Netherlands from 1989-1997. From 1992-2002 he held the chair of archivistics in the Department of History of the University of Leiden. Over twenty years he served the International Council on Archives (ICA) in different capacities.

Sue McKemmish is foundation Chair of Archival Systems at Monash University and Head of the School of Information Management and Systems. She is engaged in major research projects and standards initiatives relating to clever recordkeeping metdata, archival description, and resource discovery, including the Breast Cancer Knowledge Online Project,and the Clever Recordkeeping Metadata Project. She leads the Australian team in the InterPARES Project, and is Co-Director of the Description Research Team. Professor McKemmish also directs the postgraduate teaching program in records and archives at Monash. She has published extensively in relation to the role of recordkeeping in society, records continuum theory and practice, recordkeeping metadata, and archival systems. She has a PhD in archival systems and is a Laureate of the Australian Society of Archivists.

Ann Pederson retired from her position as Senior Lecturer in Recordkeeping Studies at the University of New South Wales in 2000, after nineteen years. Ann is best known for her co-authorship of the SAA manual *Archives and Manuscripts: Public Programs* (1982), the first edition of *Keeping Archives* (1987) and the CD-ROM *Documenting Society* (1998-2000). Most recently she devised an award-winning web site, *Understanding Society through Its Records,* for John Curtin Prime Ministerial Library in Perth (http://john.curtin.edu.au/society). Ann is a Fellow of the Society of American Archivists (SAA), a Laureate of the Australian Society of Archivists (ASA) and was a member of the Steering Committee on Archival Education of the International Council on Archives (ICA/SAE) from 1996 to 2002.

Michael Piggott has been University Archivist and Head, Archives Special Collections and Grainger Museum, at the University of Melbourne since 1998. He was formerly with the National Archives of Australia, Australian War Memorial and National Library of Australia. He has postgraduate qualifications in librarianship, history and archives administration. His professional interests include appraisal, archival education and the history of archives. He has long-established links with the Australian Society of Archivists, including editorship of its journal, *Archives and Manuscripts*, and was made a Laureate of the Society in 1997. He is on its editorial board and on that of Kluwer Academic Publishers' series, The Archivist's Library. In 2003 he was made an Honorary Research Fellow of Monash University's School of Information Management and Systems.

Barbara Reed is a Director and Principal Consultant of Recordkeeping Innovation Pty Ltd. She has consulted in the records, archives and information industries for over fifteen years, particularly in the areas of recordkeeping metadata, standards-compliant recordkeeping frameworks and policies, managing web-enabled transactions and the functional requirements for recordkeeping systems. Barbara is the Head of the Australian Delegation to TC46/SC11 responsible for the development of the ISO 15489 in records management and a member of IT21, Standards Australia's Committee on Records Management. She is an expert adviser to the AGLS Working Party on Metadata Standards for Resource Discovery. She is also involved in delivering recordkeeping education and training through The Recordkeeping Institute. She is a member of the Archiving Metadata Forum, an international group associated with recordkeeping metadata initiatives. From 1994 to 1998 Barbara was a Senior Lecturer at Monash University's School of Information Management and Systems.

Frank Upward worked as an archivist, data manager, information manager and recordkeeping systems analyst in government positions and as a consultant between 1975 and 1988. Since then he has lectured within archives, records, information management, and knowledge management specializations at Monash University. As an academic, he is best-known for his work with Sue McKemmish on accountability and recordkeeping in the early 1990s and as a records continuum theorist whose model of the records continuum is widely referred to and used by teachers and practitioners. He has postgraduate qualifications in history and education from Melbourne University.

Index